THE MEGA MONSTER BOOK

100 ENCOUNTER STORIES

VOLUME 2

ETHAN HAYES

FREE REIGN

CONTENTS

INTRODUCTION

Welcome to *The Mega Monster Book* series, a captivating collection of encounter stories with some of the most mysterious and often terrifying cryptids that roam our world. Authored by bestselling author Ethan Hayes, this book series delves into firsthand accounts and chilling narratives that bring these elusive creatures to life. From the dense forests to the darkened skies, each tale explores the enigmatic beings that have fascinated and frightened us for generations.

In this comprehensive compendium, you'll discover a myriad of stories that detail encounters with both famous and lesser-known cryptids from around the globe all taken from Ethan's other book series.

Here's a glimpse of the cryptids you'll meet within these pages: Dogman, Mothman, Grassman, Chupacabra, Jersey Devil, Thunderbird, Wendigo, Flatwoods Monster, Dover Demon, Beast of Bray Road, and others.

This book is not just a catalog of creatures; it's an exploration of the human fascination with the unknown and the unexplained through vivid storytelling. Each chapter is a firsthand encounter as told by the experiencer. Whether you're a seasoned cryptozoologist or a curious newcomer, *The Mega Monster Book* series by Ethan Hayes is your gateway to the world of mysterious creatures that continue to elude discovery and provoke wonder.

Prepare to embark on a journey into the unknown, where legends come to life, and the line between myth and reality blurs. Welcome to the world of cryptids.

CHAPTER ONE

WHEN I WAS a little girl I loved nothing more than to go outside into the woods behind my house and get lost for the whole day. I had been doing that since I was very young and no one ever batted an eye because it wasn't abnormal for a nine year old to be out all day and not be in contact with their parents or guardians. I was heartbroken when I was eleven years old and I had to move in with my grandmother because I knew I would also have to leave the woods behind. I had gotten to know every single square inch of them by that age and knew I would miss hiding out in all of my secret places. However, my grandmother was a very kind woman and when she asked why I was so sad and I told her, she gave me a whole new way to look at the situation. She reminded me that the woods behind and surrounding her house were uncharted territory for me and that I would get to go on a whole new set of adventures as I got to learn them just as well. I had been to my grandmother's house before, many times but she lived a few states away from the one I grew up in and so when I did go to visit she always filled our days up with so many things to do there was never any time leftover to play outside by myself, in the woods. It was the beginning of summer and within a week of getting settled in, I decided it would be a good time to go out and start getting to know the woods behind her house. I had a little backpack with me and grandma packed me drinks and snacks. I took my favorite book and left. I didn't have to be back until dinner time and that gave me about five hours to really take my time and wander around.

The first thing I noticed was how different the foliage was at my grandma's. She lived in the midwestern United States, in the heart of the country and I had lived in the Pacific Northwest my entire life. It was like a whole new world and I was thrilled. I had no way of knowing that on that day, something would be opened out in those woods by me that I would never be able to close. I believe it was some sort of vortex but I'll get to that in just a few minutes. I wandered around and eventually I wanted to take a break, drink some water and have a snack. I found a circle made of huge stones and decided to sit there and take my break. I was so comfortable there and felt such a sense of peace and belonging, I decided to stay and read my book there too. I was one of those kids who everyone always called an "old soul." I didn't know what it meant at the time, I just remember having heard it most of my life and from a very young age. I loved to read and you'd be hard pressed to find me without my nose in a book. I'm still like that today and it's one of the things that just makes me, me, I suppose. So, I sat and read my book for hours and by the time I was finished, I noticed I had lost track of time. I had read the entire book but for the first time in my life, I couldn't remember a single word. I couldn't tell you anything about the book I was sure I just read from cover to cover while sitting inside of that stone circle. I knew there were people in the world who would read one sentence and forget what they had just read but not me. I retained information from reading very well but I couldn't recall anything past the first few pages. I was upset and knew I would have to read it again. I packed my stuff up and made my way back home. It was getting dark and I didn't want to be late for dinner.

I made it home with two minutes to spare and my grandmother gave me an odd look when I walked in the front door. I didn't recognize it for what it was at the time but I know it now to be what we would refer to as a look of "knowing." I ate dinner, washed up and went to bed. I was so excited about the stone circle and having already found my own little spot of sanctuary in the woods but for some reason, which was also very unlike me, when asked where I had been or if I had found anything interesting, I just shrugged and responded vaguely. That was unusual because normally I would love to share my secret worlds with my grandmother. She always seemed to be the only one who ever really understood me. My parents had me young and they were incredibly irresponsible and into some pretty bad things so I would call my grandmother often and we would imagine together all sorts of worlds come to life out in the woods, pulled right from my overactive imagination and the pages of my many books. Grandma didn't seem upset though and I finally said goodnight and went to bed. I had horrible nightmares that night. Well, at least at the time I thought that's what they were.

I dreamt of being in the stone circle and as I read my book something approached me that had come from the surrounding woods. It was tiny, only around two feet tall and at first it looked like a human child, albeit a very short one. It was a boy, or seemed to be, and he asked me telepathically if I would go with him somewhere, to his secret spot. I immediately felt fear, even at just the sight of him but once he spoke to me using only his mind, absolute terror kicked in. I recoiled from him as he reached his hand out to me and I backed up so that my back was leaning up against one of the stones. His face morphed from the friendly and smiling face of an innocent child to some sort of monstrosity that we know today as an "alien gray." I saw it change right before my eyes and the way its features stretched and moved around so unnaturally was horrifying to me, especially as an eleven year old child. It also grew several feet until it stood at around seven feet tall and was standing inside of the circle with me. I screamed and told it to get away. It didn't listen. I also screamed and asked it what it wanted and it responded by telling me that I was one of its kin and that it needed to do some painless experiments on me. I screamed and then I jumped up and was in my bed again. I must have screamed out loud because my grandmother was hurrying into my bedroom and had flipped on the light the minute I realized it had all only been a nightmare. I had tears pouring out of my eyes and my face was soaking wet. I was shaking uncontrollably and even recoiled from my grandmother as she sat at the foot of my bed and reached for me.

She was only trying to hug me but the image of the creature from my nightmare flashed into my head and I quickly pulled away. My grandmother waited until I calmed down and then invited me to go and have a cup of tea with her in the kitchen. It was the middle of the night and I was still only a kid after all, and so being invited to have a grown up drink at night with my grandmother was a big deal. I felt very special and that calmed me down a lot.

As we sat at the table and drank our tea, my grandmother asked me about the nightmare I had just had. I recounted it for her, in all of its horrifically detailed glory, and she looked very concerned. She asked me where the stone circle was and I explained to her it was right next to a narrow stream that ran through the woods and into her backyard. She told me to stay away from it but never explained why. I thought she was just being overprotective and though I agreed, I had no intentions of not going back there. In fact, I felt almost compelled to go back there. I thought she was foolish to be getting so worked up over a nightmare but I agreed not to go back there and after a few minutes she sent me back up to my bed. I became very ill the next few days and none of the doctors could figure out what was wrong with me. I didn't feel one hundred percent better until about three weeks later and I couldn't wait to get back out into the woods. I hadn't had any more nightmares and my mind was starting to forget the terror of the one I did have. Our minds have a way of trying to protect us like that, in the same way we forget how pain feels, we also forget terror and eventually, heartache. When I asked my grandmother if I could go and read in the woods I could tell she was reluctant to allow me to but I don't think she was ready to explain herself just yet. I was still so young. She agreed but first she reminded me of my promise to not go anywhere near the stone circle. I agreed but crossed my fingers behind my back.

I made my way right to the stones as if I had been there a hundred times before and in fact I felt so comfortable there it was almost like I had been there that much already. It was only my second time there and I had already started to forget the nightmare, like I said, and so I was once again at peace with the silence and sanctuary that was that little circle. I once again read a book there but I fell asleep that second time and I once again made it home just in time for dinner. I also remembered everything I read up until falling asleep. I was relieved by that. My grandmother asked me where I had been and I told her I had fallen asleep in a clearing and I apologized to her. She didn't make a big deal about it and we had dinner, watched a little television and went to bed. That night I had similar nightmares to the one I had a few weeks earlier right before I had gotten sick. My grandmother came running into my room in a panic but it seemed like she had run right into my nightmare itself. Either that, I very quickly realized, or I was wide awake and everything was really happening. The seven foot tall gray being was back but there were six of them and they were coming towards me from all around my bedroom. Then a creature that looked like a praying mantis insect came out from a glowing light in the middle of them and I somehow knew she was the only female and that she was in charge. She telepathically told me not to be scared and to stop screaming. I screamed anyway and that's when my grandmother had come running into the room. She managed two steps into the door before the mantis pointed her weird fingers at my grandmother and she fell to the ground. The being immediately assured me she was only asleep and only for a little while. I tried to scream again but one of the gray beings touched me on my nose and I passed out again.

I woke up the next day in a panic and immediately looked to where I had last seen my grandmother. She wasn't there and I smelled breakfast cooking so I went downstairs. It must have just been a very vivid nightmare I thought. However, when I saw the look on my grandmother's face I knew somehow, deep down inside, that it had all actually happened. She told me to sit and then she told me she needed to talk to me and for me to just listen. My grandmother explained that she too had found the stone circle when she was a little girl and she believes that she had been the first person in a long time to have stepped inside of it because of how overgrown it had been when she first came upon it. She spruced it up and decided to make it her own little sanctuary, just as I had thought to do. It wasn't long before she had been visited by the same creatures that had been in my bedroom and she had been being visited ever since. It happened constantly and she didn't know much about what they wanted with her. They explained a little bit about how she had activated a vortex from their world to ours and she was going to be their conduit until they replaced her with someone down her bloodline. I guessed that someone was going to be me. She told me they had visited her once a month from that point on and that she had been around thirteen years old when she had first found the stone circle. It was ancient and had been built on this planet, by those same creatures, in that spot, in order for someone to eventually come along and activate it again. It had been centuries since someone had. There is a lot more to what they told her but I wanted to tell of the encounters. They're all very similar and I am still having them. My grandmother stopped having them the moment I started to.

My grandmother was almost never sick throughout her whole life except for, she told me, once right after the first visit. It's like they were protecting her from illness. I know a lot of this is very hard to believe, or will be for some people, and that's why I didn't start telling my story until very recently, aside from at conferences and conventions held for others who have had the same types of experiences. There are things I'm not at liberty to talk about, not yet anyway, but I do travel the world and tell people the messages the beings allow me to. They feed me information to then relay to the collective. They no longer frighten or terrify me and I think of them as some sort of distant relatives. I wasn't ever able to have children but I do own the old farmhouse my grandmother lived in until the day she died at the ripe old age of one hundred and two. I maintain the vortex circle but don't ever allow anyone to get too close. I've lived a very solitary life because of my interactions with the extraterrestrial messengers but I think that I was always destined for that anyway. There's more to come but I warn you, a lot of the experiences are much more terrifying than this one. I merely started with it because it was the first.

CHAPTER TWO

I WOULDN'T EXACTLY SAY that I was the most popular kid in high school and in fact I would say that I was a complete and total outcast. I had four friends that I hung out with and back in the eighties everything was so cliquey that it was impossible to move up on the social food chain, so to speak. Needless to say, me and my four best friends didn't have dates for prom and this was before the age of embracement and there was no way we would ever be able to show our faces at school again if we had chosen to go by ourselves or all together with each other. So, we decided not to go at all. Luckily for us I had the coolest and sweetest mother in the entire world and she felt so terrible we weren't going to our own proms, she decided she was going to surprise us with something she thought that we would enjoy even better. She told us not to ask any questions, to pack enough clothes for three days and then she told my friends she would handle their parents. Our parents had all grown up together too and where I'm from in Georgia, especially back then, that wasn't anything unusual. We were excited and we did as we were told. Prom was on a Friday night and the moment it would have been just getting started, my mother loaded us and all of our things into her trusty old station wagon and we hit the road to... somewhere. I had no idea where we

1

were going and about an hour into the drive I started getting agitated. My mother pulled off the highway and eventually we were on a very narrow and extremely isolated dirt backroad. We drove for about another half hour or so and the entire way we saw nothing but wilderness. There were no houses and no people, there was literally nothing but a wide open space filled with trees and everything that lived within. Eventually we pulled onto another, even smaller dirt road and fifteen minutes later she parked the car. We had finally reached our destination.

I should preface this with the fact that my friends and I weren't very popular because we didn't like to drink or do drugs and we obeyed our parents and respected our elders. We were "good kids." My friends and I all exclaimed and jumped out of the car with excitement at the same time. My mother explained that she thought we would like to spend the weekend at a cabin in the woods. The cabin belonged to her father but we had never been there because she wasn't really close with him after she got married and moved out of the family home. I knew that my grandfather had just passed but I didn't go to the funeral or anything and neither did my mother. Apparently she had inherited the old cabin and had been fixing the place up ever since she came to own it. It was pretty big as far as log cabins go and my friends and I spent most of the time when we were at home camping and hiking in the woods surrounding our houses anyway so this was absolute heaven to us. I ran over and hugged my mom and she invited us in and gave us the grand tour. The place had a television and surround sound stereo as well as a VHS player. It was hooked up, I'll just say that so I can move into the actual encounter. Well, I'll move into the first one, at least. My mother left shortly after we arrived and told us to just have some fun and enjoy the privacy. She knew we wouldn't be throwing any parties or anything so I guess she felt comfortable leaving us there. Plus, back in those days being seventeen and a half meant you had already been considered an adult for a while, even though legally you were still a minor. Anyway, she told us there was a lake about a half a mile into the woods that she thought we would enjoy and she had even brought a ton of food and some of our favorite VHS tapes. I really did have the best mom in the world.

My friends and I didn't know where to begin but it was still early in the night and we hadn't eaten yet so we decided to grill some steaks. None of us really knew how but we figured it couldn't be that hard, and it wasn't. We knew we didn't have to worry about disturbing the neighbors, because there weren't any, and so we blasted our favorite rock music throughout the house using the surround sound. It was incredible, at first. While we were eating our food on the deck, we each had a chair and there was a long glass table there. We all smoked cigarettes even though that's one thing our parents didn't know about. At one point or another, right before we were going to go in and throw on one of the horror movies my mother had provided, we were all standing in a row on the deck, smoking and facing out into the woods. One of my friends said he thought he had seen a pair of eyes staring at us through the thick trees. There was only about fifty feet between us and the tree line where the entrance to the "real" woods started but none of us otherwise saw it. However, the one friend wouldn't let it go and he decided he wanted to take a flashlight and walk to the treeline to investigate. We thought that he was seeing things and he thought there was a human intruder who was trespassing on my mom's land. Either way I was the one who decided to go with him.

As we walked toward the tree line I saw something moving right where he had claimed he had seen two glowing yellow eyes staring at us. As we got closer we started to hear what sounded like strained breathing and the huffing of breath, kind of like a large human being who had run for too long and then couldn't catch his breath afterwards. There was a stench so horrible it's impossible to explain it to you here. It came on suddenly and it was strong. We were trying not to gag on it. Suddenly everything went silent and my friend and I were more scared of that than anything else. I forgot to say we first turned the music off so there was nothing but the sounds we were making and the sounds whatever it was that was out there in the woods were making. Then, suddenly, deafening silence. When we stopped, one of our other friends screamed across the yard at us, very loudly, and asked us what we were doing. That's when we heard something moving right in front of us and I shone my flashlight in that direction. It landed on the hairy and muscular abs and chest of some creature I had never seen before. Almost by instinct I raised the flashlight to its face so I could see what we were dealing with and it had a face that looked like a cross between a human being and a wolf. The face was all canine and so were the ears but the eyes were all human. It looked at first like it was in shock from the light, then a look of pain crossed its face for just a second and then, it looked angry. I yelled to my stunned friend next to me that he needed to run and to do it immediately. Then the beast let out a loud howl and I turned to run but my friend was just standing there, seemingly stuck staring at the creature. I could see he was crying cause his face was soaked with tears but he seemed to be almost literally paralyzed with fear. I called his name several times and then I heard a sickening cracking noise coming from the creature. I might add that by that time I was so focused on helping my friend I had made the mistake of taking my eyes off the thing in the woods.

I looked over to see what the horrible noise was and I saw that it had gotten down on all fours and took an aggressive stance. It was about to pounce on one or both of us. I slapped my friend as hard as I could across the face and he screamed. We both then turned and started running while the creature followed right on our tails. We could feel it behind us and if one of us had stopped for even a second it would have ripped us to shreds. Our friends on the porch were now seeing what was happening and they were screaming for us to get back inside too. We made it to the porch and ran inside to lock the doors. We turned all the lights off and sat perfectly still in the living room. As we sat there, catching our breaths, we all realized at once that we had no idea where the animal or whatever it was had gone. We all knew that it was a werewolf simply based on how many horror movies we had seen and how many comic books we had read. We must have sat there, with nobody wanting to go and look out the sliding glass doors to the deck, for an hour or more. Finally I decided to go and see if it was still out there. I mean, it could have still been in the woods and I would never have known but at least we would know whether or not it was lying in wait or something. Not that any of us planned on stepping foot back out there at night ever again, mind you.

I tiptoed to the deck's sliding glass door and peeked out. I didn't see or hear anything and I thought that I heard an owl hooting and took that as a good sign. Normally when there are predators around the woods go completely silent and I figured that meant owls too. We were all worn out from the extreme adrenaline rush and decided we had enough for one night. We got ready for bed and none of us wanted to turn on any lights at all and so we didn't. My mother had told us when she would be picking us up and there was no landline phone or anything. When I said we were stranded, I meant it in the most literal sense of the word. Of course, I was the one who had already agreed to sleep on the couch and my one friend took one of the bedrooms to himself and the other two shared the other bedroom. I felt completely exposed with that glass door practically staring me in the face all night. After a little while I started drifting off to sleep but I kept jumping up and thinking the creature was at the door. I couldn't take it anymore and got up and covered at least most of it with an extra sheet. Then, I fell asleep. I woke up at around three in the morning to what sounded like something clawing at the door. I was immediately too terrified to do anything but sit up and stare at the door in fear and terror. The scratching and scraping seemed to go on forever but there was no way in hell I was getting up to investigate. I don't know if it stopped first or if I fell asleep first but eventually it was morning time. I was up first and started to make coffee.

My friends must have smelled it and within a few minutes we were all standing in the kitchen with our cups in our hands. We all needed a cigarette and couldn't smoke in the cabin. We figured we were safe in the daylight and so we dared to go back out onto the deck. We immediately noticed the scratches in the wood and all the way through the door almost. It looked like whatever had been out there, the thing that woke me up, had scratched almost completely through the glass. We were stunned and that's when I told my friends what had happened after they all went to sleep. We agreed it was a werewolf but none of us knew any further what to do with that information. As we were going inside to let the information settle a little bit and watch some television, we noticed a nail sticking out of the side of the house, right next to the glass door on the deck. My friend grabbed it, curious as to what it was and then immediately dropped it, disgusted. He exclaimed it was a fingernail that looked like it came from something huge. It came from the werewolf. It didn't even need to be said. We all decided to just stay indoors until the following night when my mother was coming to get us. We would take turns sleeping on the couch. I silently thanked God that my turn was already over. Then we kind of just went about our day. Nothing else happened the whole time we were there but every time we looked out a window or even walked by one, we felt like we were being watched.

Other than the werewolf attack I daresay we had fun. I have a lot more stories about that cabin and do believe the surrounding woods and even the lake are haunted and supernatural. I still go there to this day with my family as I now own that cabin in the woods. There are a few neighbors now and there was one other thing I should mention here and I usually don't because it just sounds too good to be true. I swear it happened though and it always made me wonder. When my mom picked us up a man drove up and kind of blocked her car in. She told me he was the caretaker and she had told him to leave for the two nights and go and stay in his camper, which he parked out of sight on the property somewhere. Just in case there were any emergencies she said. As she introduced him to us I got a really weird vibe off of him and he went to shake my one friend's hand first and my friend recoiled in terror. I thought that was extremely rude and apparently so did the guy and my mother because she chastised my friend and apologized profusely to the caretaker. He looked annoyed and mean in general. I looked down at his hand and noticed he was missing an entire finger-nail. It wasn't even covered up or anything, it was just there with the dried blood caked on it and everything. My mother exclaimed and asked him what happened to him and he said the night before he had closed his finger in the door of his camper. Yeah, a likely story indeed. I'll send the rest of my stories. This was only the first one.

CHAPTER THREE

MY ENCOUNTER HAPPENED in the early nineties when I was on my way to a party at a random barn in the middle of the woods. We didn't have a lot to do back then to keep us occupied as teenagers and before the internet and social media it was pretty normal for kids to find things to do outside of the house and to be out of the house for as long as possible. I was visiting one of my favorite cousins over the summer. She and I had been close our whole lives because we were very close in age. She was only a couple of months older than me and so we usually went through all of our phases together. My aunt and uncle recently had to move to another state halfway across the country for one reason or another and my cousin and I were experiencing some sort of separation anxiety. Neither of us had any siblings and so we were closer than sisters. Anyway, the state where she and her parents had moved to was a place we would often make fun of. We were from a very populated city in northern New Jersey and she was basically stuck in the Bible Belt for her last year of high school. She wasn't handling it well and according to my mother she was rebelling a little bit. I decided to go and tough the summer out with her and try to give her some perspective and make her feel better. She had moved to the new house during the last semester of our junior year and she had made quite a few friends. She said that one of the things the teenagers liked to do was get together and have bonfires in the woods and just hang out. There was some drinking going on and drugs could be found but that wasn't really our scene and we normally went to socialize. We had done similar things where we were from but I had no idea that when she said "the woods" she really meant it. Normally for those of us in New Jersey "the woods" meant a patch of unoccupied land somewhere off the side of a main road somewhere. My cousin had to attend summer school and had gotten involved in one summer extracurricular program that would help bring her grade point average up more than just attending summer classes would and so that night she was going to be getting a ride from one of her friends who was in the same program. I had met most of her friends by the time I had my encounter and felt comfortable with them all so far. Students weren't allowed to drive themselves to summer school as part of the penalty for failing so badly and having to attend in the first place and so I was taking her car to this bonfire party.

We didn't have cellular phones and certainly no GPS so my cousin had told me, over a conversation we had on a landline phone, the directions on how to get to the party. I wrote them down and they seemed simple enough. She used obvious landmarks so I would know I was going in the right direction. Normally I would have just made sure I had some quarters on me to pull over and use a payphone if I had gotten lost or I would've just pulled over somewhere and asked for directions but she said it was out literally in the middle of nowhere, and if I got lost it could end up being really bad. I made sure I paid attention and was confident enough by the time I had gotten ready and left to head to the party. I said goodbye to my aunt and uncle and left. I had been driving for about fifteen minutes of what was supposed to be an almost hour long drive when I pulled off of the main road. I drove for what seemed like an eternity without seeing any signs of life and nothing but dense woods all around me and as far as my eyes could see. I remember her telling me that would happen but eventually I had passed all the landmarks and made all the turns I was supposed to and

I got to what was supposed to be the turn off that led up the road to the barn where the party was being held. It really was out there! When I pulled up to the barn I thought there had to have been some sort of mistake or that I had to have missed a turn somewhere because the place was completely deserted. There was literally nothing but a barn just standing there in the middle of an open field that was surrounded by more of those dark and very thick woods. I was immediately scared.

I thought I should get out of the car and see if I could hear anything because I was trying to rationalize the situation by telling myself that maybe there was another gigantic barn somewhere near to that one. I had basically run out of road and so there was no choice but for me to get out and start looking around on foot. I was wearing short heels and a dress and I didn't have a flashlight. I didn't expect to need one for this. I was terrified to get out of the vehicle but I started to become more scared of sitting in the car. I took a deep breath and got out. I walked over to the barn. It was about fifty yards from me and while I was walking out to it, it dawned on me that my cousin and some of her friends were most likely trying to prank me. I started to get really pissed off at the thought of it as I played out an entire scenario of them jumping out and laughing at how scared I was in my head. I stormed to the barn and swung open the door. It took two hands and was pitch black inside. I couldn't see an inch in front of me. The moon was full and there were plenty of stars so it wasn't as hard to see when I was outside but on the inside, there was nothing. I thought I had heard something scurry around as soon as the door opened and I was immediately disgusted and thinking that it had either been rodents of some kind or my cousin and her new friends. I called out and asked if anyone was there. Suddenly and all at once there was an extremely loud humming noise that pierced my ears and made my brain feel like it was vibrating. I covered my ears and looked around outside of the barn to see where it was coming from. I didn't see anything but the sound made me feel like my head was going to explode. I started to get dizzy and walked away from the barn, trying to make my way back to the car. The ground was shaking so badly all around me, vibrating with the sound of the humming, that I lost my footing and fell. I felt like I had sprained my ankle but couldn't take my hands off of my ears in order to touch it and see. Suddenly the sound stopped and I saw what looked like the beam of a flashlight coming out of one of the barn's windows. It looked like it was upstairs, like in the loft area. I was super pissed by that point and despite the pain in my ankle I was absolutely determined to storm back into that barn and give them all a piece of my mind. I also planned on not speaking to my lousy cousin for the rest of the time I was visiting.

I limped in pain all the way back to the barn and once again used both hands and all of my strength to get the door open. I could see what looked like legs standing up on top in the loft right where the bright blue beam of light was coming from. The light swung down and was shining directly in my eyes. I yelled for them to cut it out and started cursing at them. The light went out and I walked right into the darkness of that barn without a second thought because I was so stark raving mad I wasn't in my right mind. I yelled for them to stop being cowardly and to come down. The light blinked on again and I could see a little bit. When I finally made it up the stairs, that's when I expected them to all jump out at me, pointing and laughing about how dumb I had been to fall for their sick joke. That didn't happen though and I came face to face with a set of glowing yellow eyes. The illumination from the moonlight was shining through the window perfectly enough to show me an animal. It was crouched in the corner but not on all fours like you would imagine an animal would be. This one was crouched down like a human being would be and looked like it would have been at least eight feet tall if it were to stand up. It had the face and ears of a canine and the body of a really hairy man. The fur looked black with gray in some places and the animal let out a pathetic bark. It sounded like a wounded but scared dog.

I screamed and it made a move like it was going to lunge at me but before it could it let out a howl and a whine all at once. It was definitely a werewolf and it was definitely injured. I apologized and turned to leave as fast as I could and make my way back to the car. I thought I was going crazy, I was in a ton of pain due to my sprained ankle and I was scared beyond anything I had ever felt before. I no longer cared about the party and just wanted to get back to my aunt and uncle's house so I could try and wrap my head around what I was experiencing, but from the safety of anywhere but the actual place where I was having the experience. The moment I turned around and went to leave the extremely loud humming sound blasted through the air again and I heard the animal whimper. It was scared of something but it wasn't me. I was terrified too now that it dawned on me that a werewolf had become the least of my worries. This all happened so fast that I didn't have much time to even try and process it. I knew without a doubt there was no way I was going to make it down those steps not only with how much pain I was in because of my ankle but because of how violently that infernal noise had everything around me shaking. The beast continued to whimper and I stood perfectly still with my hands once again covering my ears. I started to cry and yell to absolutely no one that I was sorry I had intruded and I just wanted to go home and forget all of it. With that the sound stopped again and I heard something move behind me. I thought the wolf was going to attack me and so I quickly turned to face it. Instead I saw a little being standing next to the wounded cryptid and it had its pointer finger pointed right at me. The words "we'll be back" sounded through my head in what I now recognize as telepathic communication. The being was about three feet tall and looked so much like what we know nowadays as a gray alien. It gave off a friendly, almost peaceful vibe to it. It said "we are sorry, but this" and then it motioned to the injured wolf man to its left. I nodded and turned to get back into the car and get as far away from there as humanly possible. In fact, I decided right then and there I was going back to New Jersey on the next possible flight.

I slowly took a step, knowing my ankle was going to be searing in pain but the last thing I heard while I was in the barn was the word "healed." My ankle didn't hurt at all and seemed perfectly normal again like I hadn't sprained it less than five minutes earlier. The voice sounded relaxed, peaceful and somewhat childish. The being seemed like it was almost embarrassed and like I had caught it doing something it wasn't supposed to. That was my very first experience with those beings and the only one I ever had with something that's supposed to only be found in fairy tales. I ran as fast as I could out of the barn and back into the car. As I did I didn't look back but heard what sounded like an animal, a canine, howling in pain. Then, there was silence. As I drove away I stole a glance in the direction of the barn and saw that the door was completely closed again and there were no lights on inside. I also saw an extremely tall and hairy figure running from the barn and into the woods. I didn't know or care what was going on there but I was extremely happy to be escaping it all with my life. I got back to my aunt and uncle's house and told them I hadn't been able to find the barn. My cousin tried calling several times to see where I was but I pretended to be asleep so finally my aunt stopped calling for me every time the phone rang. The next day my cousin was mad at me but I didn't care. She insisted there was no way I could have gotten lost so I planned on pulling out the directions she had given me to show her because I was still convinced she had sent me to that barn on purpose so I would get lost and be scared. Maybe she wanted to do drugs or something and knew I wouldn't approve. I didn't have a real reason for why she would do such a thing but it didn't matter anyway.

The directions, which I specifically remember taking out of my purse and putting them in the glove box of her car in order to prove she had purposely given me the wrong ones, were missing. She hadn't been in her car since she had gotten home because I locked it and the keys were in my purse with me in the guest room where I was sleeping. She went over the directions with me again and I knew right away they weren't the same ones as the ones I had written down and then followed the previous night. I couldn't prove it though and eventually I just gave up arguing with her. We apologized to one another and I did end up staying the rest of the summer with her. I started receiving visits from the so-called gray aliens regularly after that and they started at my cousin's house, during that visit, and have continued for my entire life. It doesn't matter where I live, they will always know and find me. The thing that throws me off all the time is the werewolf but I think that was just an unexpected thing that happened when the creatures lured me to that barn for whatever purposes that night. Maybe they simply came upon it and it was injured or it came upon them, like I said I don't know. I wanted to keep this first encounter short but I have a lifetime's worth of experiences with being abducted by the gray aliens. Most of the time it's not scary but sometimes there are experiments and those are the times I wish I hadn't ever gone to that barn at all. Not like it would have mattered at all because I believe I channeled the directions there from one of those creatures, but still. It helps to think I might have had a choice about it.

CHAPTER FOUR

MORE AND MORE LATELY I have been coming across encounters on the internet written by people who are claiming to have had the most terrifying and insane encounters while out in the woods. The more I read through them the more I start to realize that it's finally time I tell my story. I haven't seen anything exactly like it, which I think is really saying something with all of the bizarre and frightening things people are coming across and/or witnessing while innocently exploring the great outdoors. Just like so many others, after my encounter I had nightmares and I truly feel like I was victimized by something I could never talk about because no one would ever understand unless they've been through something similar and that's if they even believed me at all. My encounter happened while I was camping near a lake in Florida that was near my family's home when I was growing up. It was super close to our house and all we had to do was walk through the woods that started in our backyard to get there. Back in the early eighties when this happened to me, that particular area of Florida was not only very underpopulated but also sort of run down as well. We had to drive for miles just to go and buy groceries and while we were bussed to school, my siblings and I didn't have that luxury when it came to visiting any friends we may have had. It was a lower income part of the town, where we lived, and our family only had one vehicle. My father took that vehicle to work every day and so we were left at the mercy of friends to help us get anywhere we needed to go. I bring that up because on the very rare occasion my best friend and I were able to work something out where one of us could visit the other one's house, it was a very big deal. I am the eldest of three girls and couldn't stand hanging out with my younger sisters. I was thirteen years old and going on forty, as they say. My friend Justine and I were more like sisters than anything else and on the night I had my encounter she was there with me.

It was a Friday night and school had just started again. Justine managed to convince her older brother to drop her off at my house and my parents said that as long as she went to church with us on Sunday, we would be able to drop her off back home again afterwards. I was so excited and knew exactly what I wanted to do. I shared a room with my one sister and she purposely went out of her way to be annoying and too involved in what Justine and I were not only doing but saying as well. I asked my mother if Justine and I could camp out in the woods the first night and then spend the night in the house on Saturday night. This wasn't anything unusual on the rare occasions Justine came over and in fact we had done that several times throughout our lifelong friendship. We had plenty of camping equipment at my house because my family normally couldn't afford real vacations and we always just went to some woods somewhere and roughed it for a week. Back then I hated it but now I look on those times fondly and as some of my best memories with my family. Justine arrived at around six o'clock and we immediately started packing our things for our night in the woods. We headed out and found a nice spot near the lake where we decided to spend the night. We were super pumped about it, until the sun went down. Yes, we had everything we needed but we had just gotten into watching horror movies and couldn't help but notice that a lot of them focused on teenagers alone in the woods. We were determined to make the best of it though and we knew if anything really crazy or scary happened we could just run back to my house. If we were walking at a normal pace it would have taken about thirty to forty five minutes, just to give you an idea of how far we were from my house. There was nothing else around for miles and miles except dense and very dark woods. We knew what to do about the animals and how to take care of ourselves. We had both been hunting since we could hold a gun and we weren't afraid to shoot if necessary.

Our night started out perfectly normal. We talked about boys we liked and girls we didn't and just hung out. We had a nice fire going and my mom packed us some food so that we wouldn't go hungry while we were out there. I don't remember which one of us came up with the idea to tell ghost stories around the fire but that's what we ended up doing. One of the stories Justine told was about the legend of an old witch that was said to have lived in those woods centuries ago. The legend said that she had been burned at the stake and cursed the land to never be fruitful and also the town and that it would never prosper. We eventually got to talking about who the witch could have been and how badly it must have sucked to be treated that way, things like that. We went to bed at around midnight. We slept in the same tent but it was large enough to comfortably fit the two of us. I woke up at around two in the morning to go to the bathroom. I grabbed the toilet paper and walked to the edge of the woods. The minute I was done and stood up I heard a strange noise coming from all around me. It sounded like whispering. It was weird because I remember immediately thinking that it didn't sound like human whispering. The voice was extremely deep and I had no idea what it was saying. I was absolutely terrified and I ran back to the tent as fast as I possibly could. I woke Justine up and told her to listen but by that time it had stopped. She was annoyed with me at first because she thought that I was just trying to scare her but once she saw the look on my face and the fear in my eyes, she knew I wasn't joking. She sat up and listened but that time we heard something different. It sounded like someone was walking around our campsite. We were both too terrified to scream or to look out and see who or what it was. It's hard to explain but again we could just tell by the sound that it was human and not animal. There was definitely someone out there.

After about five minutes Justine yelled out and asked who was out there but neither one of us had actually looked yet. There was no answer but the pacing immediately stopped as soon as she said something. We felt like now whoever it was knew for sure that we were there and they were probably retreating to go lie in wait somewhere for us to go to sleep. We couldn't possibly get out and run back to the house because we didn't know where whoever it was had gone. We both just looked at one another and although we were terrified for sure, eventually our exhaustion overtook the fear and we both ended up going to sleep. Justine woke me up by shaking me about an hour later. She didn't say anything but her eyes were wide with fear and there were tears streaming down her face. She heard the footsteps again and the sound of the leaves and branches crackling under someone's foot. I decided to peek out of the tent, not really expecting to see anything. Boy was I wrong. I very carefully looked out of the tent after I unzipped the flap just enough for one eye to be able to see out of it. At first I was really confused because all I saw was a weird green fog surrounding the campsite and going just a little further back and up into the woods. I kept looking and that's when I saw something hideous and not of this world making its way, very slowly, down the hill that led out of the woods and straight towards our tent.

The creature was on all fours but walking backwards in a sort of crab walk. It moved in jerky movements and motions and it sounded like its bones were cracking and breaking with every single movement. Once it reached the bottom of the hill and right at the edge of our camp, it moved a lot slower and I could see a lot more of it. I started screaming which automatically made Justine start screaming as well. We were crying and shaking and we didn't know what to do. The creature looked like the epitome of an old hag but like it said it was bent all the way over and backwards. Long, greasy gray and black hair hung over the face and the arms and legs were so skinny they almost looked like skeletons. The skin was gray and the elbows and knees looked like they were on backwards. We sat there for a moment screaming bloody murder when all of the sudden we didn't hear anything anymore and decided we should be quiet so we could listen and figure out where it had gone. The weird green fog had been providing luminescence to an otherwise pitch black night and it was then gone too. Our tent started shaking. We knew right away that this was being done simply to scare us because it was a very simple tent that had been set up by two teenage girls and could have easily been pulled up and tossed to the side.

We screamed and screamed as we kept seeing what looked like the shape of a human hand imprinted into the tent. It's like someone was trying to reach through the tent and grab us. Suddenly the tent started to be ripped to shreds by what looked like talons and all we could hear was deep and heavy breathing. It sounded almost like a primate but was just human enough that we could tell the difference. We were still screaming when all of a sudden, as soon as the hand came at us again Justine pushed as hard as she could, exited the tent and started running for her life through the woods and back to my house. I followed her lead but of course I fell and there was no way in hell she was coming back to get me. In fact, she didn't even look back to see where I was. I turned around while I was still on the ground and sure enough I saw the fog again and the creature coming towards me. This time it looked like a zombie but also like an old hag and it was crawling on all fours. Its face looked like it was half rotted off and it stopped for a moment to look me in my eyes and smile. The teeth were broken and yellow and it licked its pale, dry, chapped lips at me. The eyes were very wide open and the darkest shade of black you could ever imagine. I cannot even begin to describe to you the terror I felt in that moment. The entity kept coming towards me on all fours and was suddenly moving with lightning speed. It caught up to me before I could even get up off the ground and as it reached out to grab my ankle I kicked as hard as I could. Her head did a complete one eighty degree turn and I could hear the bones crack. She turned back to look at me and now I could see the damage because it looked like her neck was almost completely hanging off of her bony and disgusting shoulders. The stench was unbearable and I did the only thing I could think to do and I prayed out loud.

The entity immediately recoiled and hissed at me. It started backing up but I knew it still wanted to lunge at me and drag me with it though I had no idea and didn't even want to think about what it had planned for me should it have actually gotten a hold of me. I got up and kept praying out loud as I ran and once I was to the edge of my property, I dared to look back. There was no entity and no fog. Before I even made it to the back door my father came running out of the house in his pajamas holding a shotgun and my mother was on the phone with the authorities. Justine was so hysterical she couldn't properly explain what had happened to us and my parents thought some human woman had attacked us while we were inside of our tents sleeping. The police showed up about an hour later after we all calmed down and Justine and I decided to just lie and go along with what my parents had initially understood her to have been saying. We described a "normal looking" old woman and just said she had been smacking our tent and wandering around it the whole night. They went out to look and saw how our tent was slashed but we pleaded ignorance. We collected our stuff and they said to call them if we ever saw her again. I saw that entity again plenty of times when I lived in that house after that, but I never told anyone until now. Justine and I talked about it amongst ourselves but she was never allowed to spend the night again after that because her parents thought we had almost been abducted. I guess mine did too.

I believe that entity that I saw was some sort of undead creature. It was possibly the inspiration behind the legend of the old witch in the woods and the more I think about that the more I think it's more than likely true. Others had seen her and probably have been for a long time but whether or not the backstory is true I couldn't tell you. She/it was demonic and I know for a fact that I would have died a slow and painful death had she been able to drag me with her that night. The other times I've seen her she was just watching me from the woods while I was in my yard or while my family and I were out at the lake. Needless to say none of us ever spent the night out there again and that's that. It's amazing what we can allow ourselves to become used to when we feel like we have no other option. Once I moved out of that house I never looked back and I also never saw the entity again. I call her the demon witch but I have absolutely zero clue whether or not she was either one of those things.

CHAPTER FIVE

WHEN I WAS twelve years old I attended a summer camp near my home in New Mexico in the United States. New Mexico is known to be a place of mystery and so many strange things happen here all the time. I've had my fair share of experiences with almost all of them, including with some things I thought my whole life were merely legends. One of those things was an alien race that is said to make their home in the wooded parts of the state. There isn't a specific place where they're said to live except that they live in the woods and sometimes wander the deserts at night. I grew up hearing about this race of extraterrestrials and I'm sure that anyone from New Mexico will know exactly what I'm talking about the minute they start reading this encounter. I don't want to say the name because it's said that just mentioning them can draw them to you and I've already made that mistake once, back at the summer camp I attended in the late eighties. It was the most terrifying thing that has ever happened to me and they didn't stop coming to visit and scared the crap out of me for years after that. Even when I've left New Mexico and gone to other countries for vacations or for work, it never failed that the bastards followed me. I haven't seen them in about ten years now and I first saw them at that camp when I was twelve. I saw them at least twice a year, every year, until I just didn't see them anymore.

The year I'd like to talk about now was the third year I was attending the same camp. It wasn't any type of specialty camp like for sports or losing weight or anything like that. It was just like you see in the old horror movies from back in that time period too. The place was beat up and run down and the counselors were barely old enough to take care of themselves let alone be responsible for kids. I loved it though and had a core group of about four friends that I would always spend time with when I was there. Those kids didn't live near enough to me for me to be able to visit with them much outside of the summer camp but we did maintain our friendships over the phone for the rest of the year. I was so excited and couldn't wait to get there. The camp always let you choose three other people you wanted to bunk with in a cabin. It wasn't that you would always get to stay with any of those people but in a case like with me and my buddies, when all four kids put down all the same people, it was highly likely we would have been bunking together. There were eight kids in a cabin and the cabins were very isolated. There was a lot of space between the cabins and all the kids knew, the farther away you were from the counselor's cabin, the better off you were. That was my lucky year, or so I thought. Not only would me and all three of my friends be staying in the same cabin, we were in the most isolated cabin out of all of them in the entire camp. It's not like no one would hear us scream or anything but it was a lot easier to sneak out at night and go and do random stuff in the woods like smoke cigarettes or share a couple of beers we managed to steal from the counselors.

My friends and I settled in and noticed there wasn't anyone but us in the cabin once night fell. When the counselor assigned to that cabin came in to do a bed check for when it was lights out, we asked him about it. He told us that the camp wasn't at full capacity for the first time in dozens of years and that if we were lucky, we would get to have to cabin to ourselves for the rest of the time we were there. My friends and I were all going to be there for four weeks. We were excited and though I know it sounds more like something young girls would do, we couldn't contain that excitement and stayed up very late talking. I'm sure we discussed the most random things and I don't remember most of it. What I do remember is my friend Mike bringing up the alien race. The other two guys hadn't heard about them before and that was shocking to us because it was such a well known legend. They begged us to tell them about it but I was reluctant due to the fact that I had always been told that if you discuss them for too long out loud, you would bring them to you. I said that too and should have listened to my instinct. However, it was three against one and Mike and I started comparing what we had heard about the race of aliens so well known in New Mexico. They're said to don human clothing and cloak themselves so that they could just walk normally amongst the human race without anyone noticing. The only way someone would ever be able to see through their disguise was if they somehow knew or sensed that the "person" before them was actually an alien. I know it sounds so ridiculous but I'm telling you it's real and I'm also very sure that the so-called legend of this extraterrestrial race still exists and endures to this very day.

At first the other kids, I'll call them Kent and Bob, thought that me and Mike were pulling their legs. Once we told them everything we knew, they were scared and knew we weren't kidding. They knew that at the very least he and I believed what we were saying. I was so paranoid that we were going to be visited by these creatures because we had just spent over an hour talking about them. We didn't have a lot of nice or flattering things to say about them either. I didn't dare say that out loud though to the other guys because they would have made fun of me and never let me live it down. That's just how boys are. Eventually we made our way to our bunks and went to sleep. It was around two in the morning when a bright blue light came shining in through one of the cabin windows. The beds were bunk beds and the four of us were sleeping in the two closest to the window. The light was so bright it almost burned my eyes and all four of us popped up from sleep at the exact same time. I asked what the hell the light was and they all responded that they didn't know. Then, just as suddenly as it seemed to have come on, it was gone. It was almost like someone out in the woods had flipped a switch and shut it off. It was Bob who said what we had all been thinking when he blurted out that the aliens had come for us. None of the other three of us wanted to admit that we were thinking the same thing and we called him an idiot. None of us wanted to deal with what we had just experienced and chalked it up to the counselors messing with us like they always did. The counselors, at least most of them, were bullies.

Within minutes of the four of us laying back down to try and go back to sleep there was a tapping on that same window where the light had just been shining through. We were all terrified at that point and finally I went to go and look and see what it was. I didn't see anything that could have accounted for or explained the tapping but I did see a bright blue beam of light shining down into the middle of the woods about a hundred feet away from our cabin. I don't know why we chose to do what we did next and I honestly can't tell you whose idea it was but the next thing I remember was putting on my boots and jacket and following my friends out the cabin's door. We were sneaking out and we had brought nothing with us except flashlights. The counselors were all either sleeping or getting drunk anyway and when we left the cabin we could hear some of them making a ton of noise and blasting music throughout the place. Bob was worried we were walking towards a light that they were using for a party in the woods but we all knew that wasn't going to be the case. We finally got close enough to the beam of light that we didn't need our flashlights anymore. None of us wanted to walk any closer once we were about ten feet from it. There seemed to be no source for where the light was coming from but I'm pretty sure now that was just typical extraterrestrial cloaking. There had to have been some sort of ship there but we didn't know what to think at the time. We all just stood there, stunned and in silence, wondering what the hell we were doing out in the woods. It was like it suddenly dawned on all of us that we were standing in the middle of the deepest part of the woods and none of us knew why or how we had gotten there. I vaguely remembered the walk but it's like our minds were purposefully confused the whole walk there.

Suddenly there was the sound of branches cracking underneath someone's feet all around us. We looked in every direction every time we heard the noises but at first we didn't see anything. The light blinked off again and we were thrust into pitch black darkness. None of our flashlights would work and we were all in a complete panic. Then, I looked over and tried to stifle a scream as I nudged Mike and pointed to what I was seeing. There were at least six sets of glowing, yellow eyes staring back at us from behind some trees that were all around us. "It's them!" I exclaimed and my friends and I turned to run. We ran as fast as we could back to our cabin and once there we all jumped back into bed. We weren't planning on sleeping and we stayed up talking for another couple of hours before passing out. I'm sure we were exhausted just from all of the adrenaline, let alone the fact that it was five o'clock in the morning by the time we made it back. None of us knew where the time went and none of us wanted to discuss it any further past that night. We were just kids and we were terrified. I still have almost no memory of walking to the light that night or of what we discussed after we had gotten back to the cabin. I've remained friends with the guys and they're missing the same memories as I am. I was never able to remember and neither were any of us, so it wasn't the aging and years gone by that took the memories from us either. The next day we were woken up from the counselor coming into our cabin and ringing the bell for breakfast. We ate all of our food in a big cafeteria type building and it was loud and filled with kids and the adult counselors. My three cabin mates/friends and I all had serious headaches but we tried our best to eat anyway. Despite our best efforts and our plan never to mention it again, we couldn't stop discussing the creatures and what we had seen in the woods and at our window the night before. We were trying to keep it a secret and be as quiet as we could about all of it so when someone would walk by us too closely, we would stop talking altogether and just pay attention to getting our food. There were other adults who prepared and handed out the food and I swear something happened that I will never forget.

We were standing in a single file line holding our trays and talking about the extraterrestrials and what they could have possibly done to us the night before. We knew there were things we couldn't remember, even at that point in time and at that young age. We all noticed a counselor who was all the way on the other side of the room staring at us and she had been the entire time we had been in the chow hall. We kept trying to avoid her gaze. Finally we sat down and tried to eat so that we would feel better and be able to participate in some of the activities that were planned for the day. The woman just kept staring at us and Mike finally said, "what if she's one of them?" We all stopped eating and looked up and over at her. The woman started to come towards our table. She stopped and asked us if we were okay and we all silently nodded and tried to keep our heads down. She asked if we were sure and when we all silently nodded again she demanded we look at her. Her tone completely changed and she sounded almost demonic. We all immediately looked up at the woman and that's when she smiled at us, a mouth of sharp, pointy teeth and winked. When she winked it's like we could see underneath to her real, true self. Her big brown eyes were bright yellow for just a split second. Then she walked away.

We all looked around to see if anyone else noticed and no one had. We were terrified and when we saw her again just a few moments later she was laughing and talking with the counselor assigned to our cabin. She gave us one last look and then left the food area. The rest of the time we were there we were completely on edge and we started to notice that everywhere we were, that same woman was there. We finally asked our counselor who she was and he told us that she had arrived late, the first morning we woke up there. Which, by the way, is the same morning after we had our experiences with the aliens. She didn't ever do anything to bother or hurt us but she was just always there. Ever since that day we have been able to see through to the real beings underneath the humans when the aliens are out and in disguise. There's been recurring nightmares for all of us and one of my friends died very young because he drowned it all in drugs and alcohol. He just couldn't handle it anymore. There's so much more to all of this and if you look up the legendary extraterrestrial race in New Mexico, you will more than likely find more information. What scares me the most is how many people walk around each and every day who aren't people at all but that are these creatures. I have no idea what they want or what their end game is and I'm not sure I want to know. I've made a career out of investigating UFO phenomena though and have done pretty well for myself, at least as far as I'm concerned. That's it for now but I can't wait to tell you about some of the other ones I've seen. They stay in their real form when they're in the woods except when they come across people. I don't know how it all works or much about it at all but I know that much is true at least. Thanks for letting me get this out there and I just want the people who read this to know, if you think there's something weird about someone standing in front of you at the grocery store or if that park ranger seems a little off somehow, especially in this part of the country, take a closer look and then tell me what you see beneath the person.

CHAPTER SIX

I WAS BORN and raised in Alaska and that's where I still reside to this day. I have traveled throughout most of the rest of the country but there's something about Alaska that really is magical. There's so much untouched wilderness there and sometimes it can be dangerous if you don't know how to handle yourself out there. Where I'm from in Alaska there's a fair that takes place every single year and lasts the entire summer season and once fall rolls around the land where the fair was set up is simply empty land and not used for anything until the next year. Of course there are a ton of rumors about it being haunted but there's a lot of mystery in Alaska and so a lot of places are allegedly haunted or evil etc. I had my first experience with something supernatural and evil when I worked for the fair for the first time in the summer of 93. I was so excited because unless your parents work for them too, you have to be a certain age in order to get even the smallest job there. My mom and dad did the security detail and my older brothers would help them out from time to time. I turned thirteen that summer and the first thing I wanted to do besides have some cake and hang out with friends was go to work with my parents at the fair. I planned on heading to the fair with my two best friends and then, once they left and it closed down for the night, helping my parents and siblings with the security detail. I know when some people think of hometown fairs they think of those little traveling, sort of rinky-dink rides, food and games, but let me assure you now that this place is nothing like that. The area is gigantic and every single square inch is taken up with one thing or another that provides entertainment or refreshment. It would normally take my parents an hour, each with their own half of the grounds, to get all of the work done. The grounds were surrounded by very dense woods and it got very dark at night. Once the fair closed for the night the overhead spotlights and the lights from the rides and games all shut down on a timer, at midnight, and then my parents had to use nothing but their flashlights and memory of how everything was set up in order to get around and get their jobs done. That's everything you need to know about the night I had my brush with something incredibly evil at those fairgrounds.

I thought that if I ever were to experience anything then it would definitely be some sort of ghost or spirit. My parents loved the paranormal and enjoyed horror movies and creepy stories by the campfire and they had always talked very openly in front of everyone, including us kids, about their paranormal experiences both involving the job at the fairgrounds and otherwise. I hung out with my friends until around eleven and then went to help my parents start walking the booth owners and ride operators to bring their money to their cars or trailers, wherever it was going after cashing out for the night and at midnight sharp the lights went out all at once. The place was completely and totally deserted except for me, my parents and one of my older brothers. The place seemed very eerie without all of the noise and it was within seconds that we started to hear what sounded like dogs barking but it was coming from the woods surrounding the place which we all thought was kind of weird. Alaska isn't really known for stray animals and we first thought that someone had lost their pet dog or something but my mom and dad would have been the first ones to be told to be on the lookout for something like that. The dogs sounded vicious and were incessantly barking and growling at either each other or at something else, we couldn't be sure because we could only hear them. They were somewhere not too far into the woods but far enough that even when we shone our flashlights in the direction the noises were coming from, we didn't see anything unusual and we certainly didn't see any dogs. It was just creepy and I don't really know why I felt that way but I did, immediately. I went with my mother and my brother went with my dad and we were supposed to meet back at the front gates in an hour. Mom and I were about halfway through when we heard a strange noise coming from the fun house. It sounded like heavy breathing but also like low growling or groaning. I don't know what she thought it was but it worried her enough that she told me to stay outside and wait for her. I was only thirteen years old, remember, and though I did my best not to wander off, I heard a noise of my own that had me wandering away from the entrance to the fun house and out towards the woods more.

I heard what sounded like something big running around in the woods, on the outskirts, towards my right and back towards the tree-line that separated the fairgrounds and the surrounding woods. The dogs were no longer barking but there was loud howling coming from that area. I wasn't too worried about it though because I honestly thought, regardless of what my parents said, that someone had lost their dogs somehow. Whatever was moving sounded a lot bigger than a dog though and I instantly thought it was going to end up being my father and/or my older brother trying to play a prank on me and my mom. My parents did stuff like that all the time to us and to one another so it wasn't that far of a reach to think it was happening right then too. I boldly and confidently walked over to where I thought I had heard movement in the tree line but I didn't expect what I saw staring back at me. In the bushes and behind the trees there were several sets of bright red eyes looking right at me, seemingly unblink-ing. There were some that were coming from behind the bushes and shrubs that seemed to be about even with my knees or a little higher but the ones that were peeking out from behind the trees were much taller than me. I started backing up and heard howling in the distance. Then, one of the creatures stepped out of the shadows behind one of the trees and revealed itself to me. It was no more than ten feet away and between me and whatever it was there were at least two or three of the smaller or shorter ones. It stood at around nine feet tall, it was thin and muscular and had the chest, legs and arms of a man- albeit very hairy. Even its hands, though huge, looked like a very large and hairy version of a regular man's hands. It had the face, nose, snout and ears of a wolf but the eyes, despite being blazing red to the point that they were almost glowing, were somewhat human looking. I was too scared to scream and paralyzed with fear. I had my flashlight aimed at the creature but the whole time my mind kept going back to all of the other ones. Had I really come across a pack of bipedal wolves? The word werewolf didn't even come to my mind immediately. I was literally frozen and couldn't think straight.

I somehow knew instinctively that they wanted my flesh and blood and that they were going to devour me and then probably my family as well. Suddenly the rest of them stepped from the shadows and out from behind the bushes and trees and I couldn't believe what I was seeing. One right after the other I saw three of the same exact creatures except they were on all fours and two more of the bipedal ones. They were all staring right at me without blinking. They were snarling and disgusting drool and who knows what else was coming out of their mouths. They bared their fanged teeth at me and they really did look like a pack of rabid dogs or wolves, except for the fact that they were obviously some sort of human/wolf hybrid. That's the moment when the word werewolf finally occurred to me. I thought about running but knew if I did that then one or all of them would simply take one leap and be on top of me within a second. I stuttered and sputtered out some words, asking them what they wanted but they just growled and snarled in return. Suddenly I heard a gunshot ring through the air and echo across the woods and in the air around me. Every single one of them turned and took off back into the wilderness where they had originally seemed to come from. I was so relieved not to have been ripped apart I immediately fell to the ground and started crying. There was no time for that though as the minute I did my brother was next to me, with his gun in one hand and helping me up with the other, telling me it was time to go. The authority in his normally playful voice unnerved me and I immediately stood back up and walked away with him, back to the funhouse where my mom and dad were both waiting.

My mother was visibly shaken and so was my father but my mother was also furious that I had disobeyed her and walked off the way that I had. I tried to apologize but she seemed distracted somehow and I asked her if everything had been okay in the fun house. She and my father exchanged a look and she told me everything was fine but that my brother was taking me home and that I wasn't able to accompany them to work the security for the fair anymore, at least not for the rest of that summer. I had already forgotten my own ordeal, somehow, and went into complaining about how unfair that was. They didn't want to hear it and my brother drove me home. On the way there the encounter with the werewolves came flooding back to my mind and I started crying and shaking again. My brother told me that he understood and that he had seen them too, on more than a few occasions. He believed he even knew who they were and then proceeded to tell me he thought they were a family of all boys who lived at the edge of our town with their father and his brother, their uncle. They had no sisters and no one knew what happened to their mama except that she hadn't been seen in almost four years. I remembered how she had gone missing because it had been in all of the local papers. The police suspected foul play and that her husband and at least some of her kids knew what had happened or were directly responsible for it but they were never able to prove it. I don't know about all of that but I do know what I saw that night and also, I know what type of person that man and his boys were, deep down on the inside. It made sense but like with the disappearance, there was no proof. I asked him if he had ever told our parents what he had seen and he said he told our dad, or tried to tell him anyway, once but our dad thought it was ridiculous and brushed it off as his imagination.

I would ask my father about that later on in life and he said he did that because he knew werewolves were real but he felt like believing in them would make it even more likely you would come across one and so he did his best to make my brother feel like maybe he had been imagining all of it so that he didn't bring them back to him. That's something else I know nothing about. As far as what my mother experienced in the fun house that night, that was paranormal activity and I'll need a whole separate encounter story to go through that one. I remember right around the time I encountered the pack of werewolves the first time, that night at the fairgrounds, I saw them several more times right after that but never before. I would look out into the woods surrounding our house and see the glowing red eyes and hear the howling. I don't believe the full moon is the only time werewolves transform from their human forms but I do believe that on the night of the full moon they are the least in touch with their humanity than on any other night of the month. I've been on somewhat of a lifelong quest for answers and living in Alaska have come across some terrifying things while out exploring the woods and trying to find answers. I'm even pretty sure I met a group of actual vampires once, in the deepest part of the woods behind my house, but that's also for another time and place. I don't know what makes a werewolf become one but I sure hope I never come across one again. Throughout my life and since that first night I saw one so long ago, I have enough of my own proof to be sure that they're out there and they aren't alone. Shapeshifters, skinwalkers, vampires, bigfoot, extraterrestrials, fairies, you name it and it's real. I hardly think it's a coincidence that legends of all of those things so many others span generations and cultures and have been believed in and talked about for millennia. They are probably older than humanity, at least most of them, and therefore much better at hiding from us than we could ever realize. Also, I believe because of how old they are, especially in areas like where I'm from in Alaska and places just like it all over the world, we have encroached on their societies and on their land, which some of them consider to be very sacred, and that's probably why they relish in sneaking up on us they way they always seem to. They count on the fact that we will be too cocky, reasonable and self absorbed as a species to ever believe they could possibly exist. I'm going to get to work writing about some more fairground experiences and maybe also some more about what I've come across and learned in my almost lifelong quest to uncover answers about what I saw that night. On a final note, one other thing about the dad and his boys who my brother was so convinced were the human beings behind the werewolf pack, I don't know if this means anything but as soon as they were no longer in town. I never saw the werewolves again after that.

CHAPTER SEVEN

FOR OUR TEN year wedding anniversary in the early 2000s, my husband booked us a room at a local bed and breakfast that used to be a real plantation back in the days of slavery. It was a charming place and I was very excited because I have always been interested in history and this particular place was known to have a really rich one. It was built in the seventeen hundreds and most of it was made up of the original buildings. My husband and I had done a lot of traveling throughout our lives together but it was the first time we were really getting to know the area where we lived back then. We had just moved to Louisiana because he inherited a house and a lot of property attached to it so we were pretty excited to see what our town and the state in general had to offer. The history is incredible and you can literally feel it when you walk through the streets. So, he surprised me with a weekend stay at this bed and breakfast/old plantation home and I couldn't have been more pleased. The place seemed very busy for the time of year and the fact that we both thought, despite its size, that it was an out of the way place that not too many people knew about. We got there on Friday afternoon and planned on staying until Sunday afternoon and then maybe doing some sightseeing in the area after we checked out. We asked at the front desk when we checked in if they were always that busy and were informed that most of the people who were there at that time were waiting for the ghost tour to start. I was immediately worried. I am not one of those people who watches horror movies for fun and I've had more than my fair share of my own experiences when I was growing up with the paranormal and wanted no part of it. My husband tried to reassure me but all of his efforts went out the window once we got our room. We were told it was the "most active" room in the whole place. Apparently he had booked us a room at a haunted bed and breakfast. I was furious. He told me not to worry and that we weren't there for the haunted tours or ghosts and that we were only there for the incredible history of the place and all of the buildings. We weren't required to take any of the ghost tours and they also offered regular tours where they only discussed the other historical facts about the building and people who were known to have lived there. I knew he hadn't meant to upset me and so I put on a brave face and we got the most out of the weekend, despite the crowds of people traipsing through the place at night.

Though they didn't come anywhere near our rooms or anything the parking lot was a bit loud but we were celebrating ten years together and were determined not to let anything spoil our time together. I have to say too, for being in the "most active" room in the whole place, allegedly, we didn't really have many experiences that couldn't be explained. The only issue we both had were night terrors and we would both wake up screaming in terror at something that was right at the tip of our memories but that wouldn't break all the way through no matter how hard we tried to remember. That is to say, we also didn't try very hard. I am also a person who loves my photos and I took tons of pictures throughout the weekend. It was fairly uneventful and we had a great time. We did some sightseeing and then made our way home. We only lived an hour and a half away from the place and so we left early enough that we made it home at around ten at night with plenty of time to relax and get ready for bed. All in all we considered the weekend and our tenth anniversary celebration a great success. Our anniversary was the following week, on a Wednesday, that was the actual date and we were having friends and family come from all over to stay with us or nearby in order to formally celebrate together.

My sister Judy watched our two year old daughter while we were away and offered to come by early and help me get the house ready for all of the guests and the party. I agreed and when she dropped our daughter off that Monday morning she put herself up in the guest room and everything seemed perfectly normal. Digital cameras and cellular phones weren't a common thing that everyone had back then and smart phones didn't exist yet so all of the pictures I took were taken on several of those old disposable cameras. Judy was excited to see the photos but mainly because she loved being scared and anything having to do with the paranormal was right up her alley.

She convinced me to get the photos developed the day after she arrived and we had to wait overnight for them so by the time they were developed and ready to be picked up it was Wednesday and three days after we had come home from our trip to the plantation. My daughter was in daycare because I normally worked from home but had taken two weeks off to prepare for the festivities being held at my somewhat new house that most of my friends and family from out of state had never been to before. Once we got back from running errands and picking up the photos, she couldn't wait to look at them. Most of them were normal photos but there were two of them that really stood out to me. They were of our room and I had just been taking pictures of it to show everyone what it looked like. In the mirror there was the unmistakable image of a strange man. He was tall and pale and had long, black, greasy hair hanging down over his face. He looked like he was glancing upwards in a sort of evil stare and he seemed to be looking directly at me as I snapped the photos. I immediately started to panic as the night terrors my husband and I had experienced while staying in the room but that we couldn't remember came flooding back to the forefront of my memory. The guy in the photos was the man who was terrorizing me in those nightmares. I couldn't look at them anymore but Judy thought that they were interesting and wanted to keep them. I told her no way and that we were going out back to burn them right away. She thought I was overreacting and was disap-pointed but having grown up with me she knew how I felt about and what I had been through with the paranormal up until that point and so she agreed. I had a burn bin in the backyard that was close to the tree line but not too close to the woods that surrounded my property that anything would catch fire. The bin was to burn our own garbage and leaves when we needed to. I grabbed the lighter fluid and after looking over the photos again to make sure we got all of the ones with the strange man or anything else that didn't belong in them, we went out back. It ended up only being the initial two photos that we had seen originally and all of the other pictures were just regular shots of normal things. We went in the back, started a fire and burned them while praying the whole time. I put the fire out and that was that. One thing that I noticed that was strange to me was that while we were burning the photos, it looked like the smoke coming off of the bin was taking the shape of a person and it looked like it then walked off into the woods surrounding my house. Judy said she didn't see it that way and that I needed to stop being so paranoid or I would make myself sick. I agreed with her and we moved on with the rest of our day.

After dinner my daughter wanted to go and play on her swing set out in the yard and since my sister was sitting on the deck enjoying a book and her after dinner coffee, I didn't see an issue with it. Judy said she would keep an eye on her for me but I could see her myself from where I would be standing doing the dishes too. My daughter went out to play but within five minutes I looked up and saw the evil looking man from the photos standing behind her as she swung on her swings. She was giggling and yelling for him to push her harder and faster and that's when he looked directly at me and smirked. Suddenly my daughter went flying off of the swing and through the air. She screamed and landed hard on her back. Luckily she was okay but I knew I had made a terrible mistake in burning those pictures and actually in staying at that haunted bed and breakfast to begin with. I tried telling Judy what I saw but she once again dismissed me and when I asked my daughter who she had been talking to and who had been pushing her on the swing, she said "the man from the woods." Judy went completely pale and I was shaking so badly I couldn't even stand up. I thought I was having a heart attack. When my husband finally got home we told him what happened but he didn't want to talk about it and said if we give it attention it would feed it our energy. He also thought that ignoring it would make it go away. I didn't know what else to do and so I tried my best. My daughter had terrible nightmares that whole night and when I asked my husband if he remembered what his nightmares had been about when we were staying at the bed and breakfast, he said no but I knew he was lying and I knew he remembered the man.

My daughter started sleeping with us and we only had a few more days until more family started to arrive. I was a nervous wreck. The night before friends and relatives started showing up for the party, after everyone was already in bed, I got up in the middle of the night to go to the bathroom and on my way back I stopped in the kitchen to get myself a drink of water. From that window I could see the back-yard and the surrounding woods and I saw "the man" walking into the woods and he looked like he was not only coming from my house but he looked like he was holding someone's hand. It was a child and it didn't take me long to realize it was my daughter's hand. He turned and looked at me over his shoulder with that evil grin on his face and the wind was knocked out of me. I didn't even bother to check and see if my daughter was okay and I just ran out the back door, off of the deck and started chasing him into the woods. He and the little girl I was convinced was my daughter started running and I could hear her giggling. It was only a moment before I could no longer see them at all. I didn't care about anything and ran right behind them into the woods. I saw a very dense fog that looked almost like thick smoke and it seemed to have settled right near the brook that ran through the woods and into my backyard. I took a deep breath and then yelled for him to show himself. A shadow person that looked to be about his height and that was so black it stood out against the darkness of the night, stepped out from behind a tree at the top of the cliff area where the brook sat below it. I asked him what he wanted and that's when I saw the red eyes. He started to come towards me and I backed up. Of course, I fell and was completely at his mercy. I don't know what he planned on doing to me but I managed to get my bearings and I stood up and ran back to my house as fast as I could and without stopping before he made it to me. Right as I reached my back door I heard a maniacal laughing and when I turned I saw a bipedal smoke figure standing there. It was completely in the shape of a male human being and I knew it was the man from the photos.

I ran inside and directly to my bedroom where my daughter was sleeping soundly in bed with my husband. I didn't know what else to do so I curled up next to her and cried myself to sleep. I hadn't liked the feeling of the woods that surrounded the house from the very beginning and now I knew that I had either awakened something supernatural and purely evil or it had been there all along and was just playing on my fears about the plantation and the photos. I woke up the next morning thinking it must have all been a dream until I stood up and saw the dirt in my bed. It had come off my nightgown from when I fell. The house was so active from that day on and my daughter not only couldn't sleep in her own room but she also was terrified of playing in the backyard because of "the bad man in the woods." The party was a success but that was the only reprieve we got. We were forced after just a few more months and after trying, several different times and repeatedly unsuccessfully, to get rid of whatever was in the home and on the property. We had one medium come in that told me I was also a medium and that it was the woods. She claimed it had nothing to do with the plantation or the photos and that the evil in the woods was ancient, unconquerable and playing off of my fears about the place. Apparently, at least according to her, it was inevitable that we would have some terrifying experiences while we lived there.

She taught me how to protect myself and my family but was adamant that we couldn't stay there because the evil would not only get worse but would almost definitely end in loss of one or all of our lives if we didn't get out right away. We were very honest with the people who bought the house from us but apparently telling people a house is haunted sometimes makes them want to buy it even more. That house has changed hands at least ten times since my family and I moved out almost twenty years ago and I believe it's because the land is simply cursed and rotten to the core of the earth. There's no getting rid of evil like that. I work with my abilities now and try to help others and have since been back to the plantation in order to take the haunted tour. The man in the photos and who the evil portrayed in the woods of my home and in my family's nightmares was merely a heartbroken old man who lost his wife and child at childbirth and took his own life. He only looked negative because he was confused about his death and still very sad, missing his wife and child. I know that if it weren't for what was lurking in those woods my family and I could have been happy in that gorgeous old house but it just wasn't meant to be. Those woods are evil and I hope one day someone burns them to the ground.

CHAPTER EIGHT

I GREW up in the wilds of northeastern Pennsylvania. Seriously, there are woods everywhere and because my family didn't own a vehicle and lived so far off the beaten path we had to walk basically everywhere we wanted or needed to go. Most of the time we could get from one place to another by just cutting through the woods. The woods were all over the place in the town and at the time, in the late 1960s, the population was less than two hundred. So, most of the town was woods and they were all connected. There was a big natural lake somewhere inside of those woods too and everyone from the town would go there to cool off in the summertime. We would ice skate on it as kids in the winter and looking back now thats' crazy to me because I can't tell you how many people died or almost died from falling through the ice while walking across the lake or ice skating. My encounter happened in the middle of the winter while a friend and I were walking home from seeing a movie. It was really cold outside but neither one of us had enough money for the bus or a cab ride and so we decided to do what we always did and cut through the woods. Now, we were prepared to do that before we got to the theater because cutting through the woods is how we made it there in the first place. It had been snowing which made it a lot easier to see but we had flashlights in our bags anyway. I know nowadays it may be hard to understand why anyone would walk through dense and creepy woods at night, in the dark, just to get to a kind of crappy movie but we didn't have much to do back then, especially not in an old farming town. The movie theater had only been built the previous summer and it was really the only thing to do at all if you wanted to leave your house in the winter. The movie ended at eight pm and so she and I headed to the back of the theater and entered the woods there. We both lived fairly close to one another and would be walking the same distance and exiting the woods at the same time.

The snow on the ground wasn't too deep and it had stopped snowing altogether the day before. It was pretty cold out but not as cold as it had been and so the walk was as comfortable as it was going to get. My friend and I had been in those woods a thousand times before but never in that particular spot and right away we both felt weird about it. There was a sense of dread that washed over us and it seemed like it was too quiet. Even in the wintertime there still should have been some activity with smaller animals and nocturnal birds and creatures of all kinds but there were no other sounds besides the sounds of our boots crunching on the snow as we walked. She and I tried to brush the strange feelings off and started gossiping about other girls at our school and talking about boys we liked. I remember it so clearly we were both laughing and giggling about one thing or another when suddenly it almost sounded like something hushed us, really loudly. We both stopped in our tracks and when we just happened to look down we saw weird little footprints that didn't look like they belonged to any animals that we were familiar with that lurked in those woods. There were four prints at once, like an animal that walked on all fours, and they looked like they belonged to the same animal just with the way they were spaced apart. The prints looked tiny and when we bent to get a closer look, they kind of looked like large lizard prints. So, while they were very small prints, for a lizard they would have been almost gigantic. There was also a line that followed right through the middle of the prints and we quickly realized that whatever it was had a tail. We asked each other what it could have been that left those prints but neither one of us could figure it out.

We decided to keep walking but both of us were curious to see where the footprints led to so we kept our eyes on the ground. Eventually, when we were about halfway to where we would need to exit the woods, we saw the footprints just come to a stop at a large tree. We looked at the tree and saw those same prints, but climbing up the side of the tree. Now, please understand, the only way we were able to see the prints on the side of the tree is because whatever it was had snow on its feet, or whatever it was we were looking at, and we saw the same marks going all the way up the side of the tree. They were little tracks in the snow. It dawned on me that the prints wouldn't have just stuck there and should have quickly melted except it was more than likely that whatever the animal was it was only right in front of us. It had to have been, in order to have left snow on the tree that hadn't yet melted or blown away. I hope this is making sense, I am getting a bit shaky just writing about it here. I shined my flashlight up into the tree and saw the most hideous face you could ever imagine. I screamed and my friend did the same. She said she had only done so though because I did and that my scream had startled her. I told her to look in the tree and when she did, she also started screaming. We turned to run but I made the mistake of looking back and I saw the creature from the tree chasing us. It was leaving behind the same prints as whatever we had been following and I will describe it to you now as best as I can.

It was about two feet tall or a little less and it was very overweight for its height. It was round and grotesque looking, almost like a basketball with legs, only a little bigger. It looked slimy or greasy or something and it waddled as it ran on its tiny little legs and tiny arms. The hands and feet looked like they were webbed, like those on a lizard. It was dark green in color and its eyes were a weird orangey yellowish color and the pupils looked like those of some sort of reptile. They looked like they were vertical and oblong. Very much unlike any animals we had ever seen, with the exception of certain reptiles. If I had to compare it to anything it would be a gargoyle because it also had very small wings that puffed out as it ran after us but that didn't even look like they could hold its weight up in order for it to be able to fly. It made a strange squealing noise as it chased us and eventually my friend pulled me behind a tree. We thought we had been ahead of it enough that it wouldn't be able to find us. We peeked around the tree, both of us crying at that point, and saw that it had stopped. It was looking all around and the way it was walking was almost funny because it was being very careful in its tiptoeing so as not to make any noise. If it had been a stuffed animal or an actual cartoon it would have been cute as hell. However, it wasn't either of those things and instead it was a creature that was chasing us through the forest. After only two or three minutes of looking for us it seemed to have given up and flapped its wings until it slowly reached a low branch on a nearby tree. It was now in the tree and seemed to have closed its eyes.

My friend and I took off running and we immediately heard the strange squealing noises only this time they were much more urgent. We ran for our lives and when we were finally right where we needed to get out of the woods in order to get to the main roads that led to our houses, I dared a look back. I shouldn't have done that because I swear there were at least twenty of those same little round creatures and they were all chasing after us. My friend turned around too and she took off running out of the woods and up the street towards our houses. She had to walk further than me because my house was first and I knew she was thinking about that in those moments. She later told me I was right. The creatures followed us right out of the woods but they stopped chasing us once they saw the road and they all flew upwards and perched themselves on the street lamps. It was eerie and I remember thinking, how many times have those things been there and no one has even noticed because we don't pay attention to those types of things? Most of the time when we are walking or even driving in a car, we aren't looking upwards at all but in front of us or at the ground, depending on the situation and in normal circumstances.

The creatures watched us intensely but didn't follow us anymore and once we got to my house we just asked if my friend could stay over. We didn't tell my parents what happened but I knew my friend wasn't going to want to walk all the way to her house alone, not with those things out there, and I certainly wasn't going to volunteer to walk with her. Both of our parents agreed and so we went to my room and eventually we fell asleep. The next morning I wanted to know if what we saw was real. I knew that it was and so did my friend but the fact of the matter was I needed to go back into the woods during the light of day, in order to try and convince myself none of it ever happened. My friend didn't want anything to do with it and so after we had breakfast I left to go back the way we had come from in those woods and she continued on to her house. I looked up and all around at first but didn't see anything. When I got into the woods I saw some of the footprints from the night before and my heart almost stopped. I looked up into those trees but didn't see anything there either. I knew the exact path my friend and I had taken because like I said we had taken it so many times before it was like I knew it like the back of my hand or something. I walked a little further into the woods, following what was left of our footprints from the previous night and that's also when I noticed something that definitely hadn't been there the night before. There were miniature snow angels all over the ground. I'm not sure if everyone knows what a snow angel is or not but it's easy if you just look it up so you can understand better what I'm talking about. I don't know how to explain it but it just looked like some very small thing had left the angels in the snow. How ironic is it that creatures that looked like miniature demons had made angels in the snow? There's no other explanation as I know they weren't there the night before and I also know that I was in the right spot because the snow had been hard in most areas and so you could still see not only our footprints but the prints of the creatures as well and those little snow angels were all in between and around those prints. I never saw the creatures again and never spoke of them either and neither did my friend that was with me.

I originally thought that the creatures were evil or even demonic but the next day when I saw the snow angels I wondered if that was their way of telling us that they were friendly and that we didn't need to be afraid of them. If that was the case though then why hadn't we ever seen them again? I have a million questions and absolutely no answers and that's why I am only speculating here. I didn't know what to make of it that first night and all these years later I still have no clue what to think about any of it.

CHAPTER NINE

IT WAS late January and I was working late, I know it was maybe 1am or so. I was sitting at my desk, which happened to be positioned just a foot away from my front door. Engrossed in an online game, I decided to take a short break and use the bathroom. As I got up from my desk and turned towards the hallway leading to the bathroom, something inexplicable caught my attention. It was as if a mysterious force drew my gaze towards the front door. Intrigued, I turned to look out the window on the door, a habit I had developed over time, and that's when I saw it.

Let me clarify that all the lights in the house were turned off, with only the glow of the computer monitor and the television illuminating the room. The window on my front door was rather small, measuring about 4 inches in width and roughly two and a half feet in height. Nevertheless, I peered out that window and laid my eyes upon the creature. I hesitate to give it a definitive name because I am still grappling with the uncertainty of what exactly I witnessed. However, based on my recollection, I can confidently say it resembled something between Captain Caveman and an oversized cousin of Cousin It from the Addams Family. The creature was covered in dark brown to black hair, which obscured any discernible facial features. It possessed long arms and a seemingly absent neck, as the hair on its body and arms melded together seamlessly, resembling the exaggerated hairiness of Cousin It.

I must emphasize that my front yard was well-illuminated due to the presence of several streetlights nearby, and even with clouds in the sky, the moonlight provided decent visibility. So, it couldn't have been a mere shadow, as the figure I saw was far too solid. Nor was it an accumulation of haze from the cold outside, for I had not yet opened the door. Returning to the creature, I should mention that I stand around 5 feet 8 inches tall, and the bottom of my door is approximately 3 feet from the ground. Judging by its height relative to mine, I estimated that the creature stood at least 8 feet tall, reaching up to my chin or the top of its head.

Additionally, the creature's width matched the span of my steps, which are about 4 feet wide from handrail to handrail. It appeared to be hunched over, as if peering through the door, although it stood at the base of the steps on the ground, leaving me uncertain of its true intentions. While my desk was positioned on the right side of the door, about a foot away, my monitor, keyboard, and other items were located on the far side of the desk, roughly 4 feet from the door. Between the monitor and the door, I had my printer and various objects, including my camera.

In a rush to capture evidence of this inexplicable encounter, I turned my head to locate my camera and swiftly retrieved it, hoping to take a photograph. However, by the time I located the camera, grasped it firmly, and looked back towards the door, the creature had vanished into thin air. I scrutinized the yard intently, even switching on the porch light, but there was no sign of its presence. It was as if the creature had dissolved into the night. Perplexed, I closed the front door and proceeded to the bathroom, contemplating the strangeness of the situation.

Upon my return to the desk, a peculiar sound filled the air—an auditory experience akin to thunder, but considerably less deafening and of shorter duration, lasting only a couple of seconds at a time. Given that I was the sole person awake at this early hour, I was certain that no one else had witnessed or heard anything.

I have encountered numerous peculiar and wondrous sights during my travels to diverse locations, each with a logical explanation behind their existence. However, this encounter surpassed anything I had ever witnessed before—a wholly unprecedented phenomenon. Despite my apprehension of being labeled as delusional, I can only attest to the authenticity of what I saw and heard that night.

Thank you for allowing me to share my story.

CHAPTER TEN

I AM AN AVID ADVENTURER, deeply passionate about hiking, fishing, and camping. I often embark on solo camping trips, seeking solitude and connection with nature. One memorable excursion took me to the breathtaking wilderness west of the town of Bragg Creek, Alberta.

It was a warm summer evening in July of 2010 when I set up camp amidst the peaceful forest. As the night unfolded, an air of mystery seemed to envelop the surroundings. At around 10:30 PM, I became aware of subtle movements rustling through the trees. Curiosity piqued, I focused my attention on the forest, trying to discern the source of the commotion.

To my surprise, I began to hear distinct sounds, resembling the rhythmic banging of logs against each other. Intrigued, I decided to respond in kind, mimicking the pattern with my own actions. Yet, to my bewilderment, silence prevailed, as if my echoes had vanished into thin air.

The tranquility was short-lived, for around 1:30 AM, nature's fury descended upon the campsite. Thunder boomed, rain poured relentlessly, and lightning streaked across the sky. Amidst the storm, a peculiar occurrence startled me from my slumber—a loud cracking sound resonating perilously close to my camp.

Wide-eyed and alert, I lay in my tent, a concoction of fear and amazement swirling within me. Suddenly, the air turned heavy with the unmistakable sound of forceful breathing. My heart raced as thoughts of a bear's presence loomed in my mind. Anxiety gripped me, intensifying as the next few hours unfolded.

The sound of branches breaking pierced through the night, a constant reminder of the enigmatic presence lurking in the darkness. Outside my tent, I had set up a tarp as a makeshift cooking area. To my astonishment, I heard the animal approach, brushing against the tarp as if passing beneath it—a hair-raising moment that sent shivers down my spine.

Summoning my courage, I unzipped the tent flap ever so slightly, desperate to catch a glimpse of the source of this otherworldly encounter. And there, in the dim moonlight, I saw a creature walking upright, descending the hill toward the creek below, its form both fascinating and unnerving. Although I longed to investigate further, prudence anchored me to my current position.

As the night wore on, the mysterious entity continued to unleash its might. A deep grunt reverberated through the air, as if the creature exerted immense effort. It then proceeded to hoist a substantial boulder, hurling it with astonishing strength. As if that display of power wasn't enough, it proceeded to uproot a towering fir tree, toppling it to the ground, amplifying my terror.

With the approaching dawn, around 4:45 to 5:00 AM, the rain subsided, and the first rays of light began to permeate the forest. However, this newfound illumination only seemed to awaken a whole new symphony of bizarre calls. A deafening, bird-like cry pierced the air, unlike anything I had ever heard before. To my astonishment, this call was met with responses echoing from the north, west, east, and south, creating an eerie chorus that seemed to encircle me. I felt enveloped by an unseen presence, surrounded by an enigma that defied comprehension.

This orchestration of enigmatic calls repeated every morning during my three-night, four-day stay in the wilderness. When it was time to depart, a mixture of curiosity and concern compelled me to contact the local conservation officers. Inquisitive, I inquired if they were aware of any human presence in the area during those specific times. They responded with uncertainty, indicating they had no knowledge of such activity, leaving me with an unsettling sense of wonder and intrigue.

To this day, the memory of that extraordinary camping trip lingers in my mind, reminding me of the vast mysteries nature conceals and the profound experiences that await those who dare to venture into the unknown.

CHAPTER ELEVEN

THE EVENTS I'm about to recount occurred on a fateful night in late summer 2002 just outside of Springfield, Missouri. My 16-year-old son and I sought refuge from the bustling city lights, driving into the serene countryside to witness the spectacular Perseid meteor shower. Our journey led us miles outside of town until we found a perfect spot. It was a large hill with lush grass.

Eager to immerse ourselves in the celestial display, we turned west onto a gravel road and parked at the hill's summit. The absence of nearby trees or structures ensured an unobstructed view of the night sky. It was a remarkably clear night, devoid of any intrusive moonlight.

As minutes passed in the enveloping darkness, our eyes acclimated to the absence of light, allowing us to perceive our surroundings with increasing clarity. To the east, south, and north, open fields stretched before us, bathed in an ethereal glow. Looking west, we could discern the faint outlines of the light-colored road snaking its way down the hill, vanishing into the distance.

Engrossed in observing the celestial spectacle above, I caught a glimpse of something substantial in my peripheral vision, originating from the field south of us. Initially uncertain if my eyes played tricks on me, I shifted my gaze directly towards it, only to find it inexplicably vanish. However, by directing my sight slightly off-center, I could still perceive its presence in my peripheral vision. It seemed to move erratically, alternately darting west and east, as if zigzagging across the field. Intrigued, I inquired if my son had noticed anything, but he hadn't. Assuming it must have been a cow or a deer, I redirected my attention to the celestial wonders unfolding above, as a flurry of shooting stars captivated our focus.

Minutes later, while both my son and I faced northeast, an unearthly growl erupted from behind us, reverberating with a depth that sent shivers down our spines. In unison, we turned to each other, a shared sense of disbelief etched upon our faces as we exclaimed, "Did you hear that?" Swiveling around, our eyes fixated upon an imposing figure obstructing the road. Against the light-colored backdrop, we couldn't discern intricate details, but its sheer size was enough to inspire trepidation.

The colossal figure possessed a roughly humanoid shape, albeit with a peculiar cone-like head and extraordinarily broad shoulders. It swayed back and forth, positioned halfway down the hill. As I continued observing, I realized its swaying motion was a consequence of ascending the hill toward us. With another bone-chilling growl, a deep, rumbling sound that seemed to defy the laws of nature, the area fell eerily silent. Strangely, I noted the absence of any discernible sound from its gravel footsteps—a bizarre contradiction. By this point, it had drawn significantly closer, perhaps a mere three to four car lengths away.

Then, in a burst of primal fear, my son cried out, "Let's get the hell out of here!" Without hesitation, we leaped into our car, my foot pressing the accelerator pedal with unwavering resolve. We careened down the road, only relenting once we reached the safety of the town. The sense of urgency and lingering dread lingered long after the incident had passed.

The following day, under the comforting embrace of daylight, I mustered the courage to return to the exact spot where the enigmatic encounter took place. My gaze scanned the surroundings, searching for any traces left behind—an enigmatic clue that might provide solace or answers. Yet, I found no tracks or evidence of its presence. However, an intriguing revelation awaited my curious eyes: a four-foot-high barbed wire fence demarcated the boundary between the southern field and the road. If the creature I witnessed in the field was indeed the same entity, its massive size would have necessitated either leaping or stepping over the fence, as it lacked the strength for someone to climb it—especially someone as colossal as the figure we encountered.

Though the true identity of the entity remains shrouded in mystery, one thing became abundantly clear—it harbored a palpable hostility towards our presence that night, making no effort to conceal its animosity. I can't help but wonder if anyone else in the area has experienced anything similar recently, as the encounter has left an indelible mark on my psyche. It stood taller than any human, a sight obscured by the veil of darkness, save for its distinct outline. Its most striking feature, or lack thereof, was the absence of a discernible neck, with the head seemingly resting directly upon its broad shoulders. Having devoted countless hours to watching the YouTube and other stuff, I can attest that the unearthly growl we heard that night defied any known explanation. Its resonance, deep and crystal-clear, continues to send chills down my spine to this day.

CHAPTER TWELVE

IN THE SUMMER OF 1994, I had a memorable experience during a camping trip with my high school friends on a private preserve. We had obtained permission from the private owner at the time, and after setting up camp near the entrance, we spent the day exploring the caves and enjoying the natural beauty of the area.

As evening fell, we gathered around the campfire, cooking dinner and sharing a few beers. Suddenly, we heard clear footsteps approaching from the steep hillside to the east of our camp. We turned to see who it might be, expecting someone to appear at the top of the hill. However, the footsteps abruptly stopped, and no one emerged. We called out in a friendly manner, but received no response. Growing nervous, we realized we were defenseless if the situation turned hostile. Then, we heard the unseen person or creature sprinting away through the brush, quickly disappearing into the forest to the north.

Curiosity got the better of two of us, and we decided to investigate further. One of my friends went west and circled north on the dirt road, while I headed directly towards the area where we had heard the running sounds. After taking only a few steps, a deafening scream erupted from the darkness. The sound was unlike anything I had heard before—powerful, deep, and ear-splitting. It physically affected me, causing me to step back in shock. The scream had a bizarre owl-like quality, but much louder and more intense. My friend, startled by the scream, ran back to camp, and I stood still, listening as the unseen presence retreated further into the forest.

We spent the rest of the night sleeping in the safety of a van rather than in our tents. Though everyone was clearly unsettled, we made light of the situation, attributing the strange occurrences to alcohol-induced paranoia. However, around 3 AM, one of our friends woke up in a panic, claiming to have seen a hairy arm reach through the van's open window and grab the leftover food before retreating into the woods. We dismissed it as a raccoon sighting and went back to sleep. The following morning, we searched for tracks but found none, leaving us puzzled yet dismissive of the events.

In the subsequent summer, three of us returned to the valley for another camping trip. We spent the day exploring the log cabin, caves, and trails, and had a great time rock climbing. However, when we returned to our cars, we discovered that one of them had been spun around and moved a significant distance from its original parking spot. Scuff marks were scattered on the ground, but there were no foot-prints or other evidence to explain the incident. We brushed it off as local mischief, despite not encountering anyone in the area.

Later that night, as we settled into our tent, my friends soon fell asleep and started snoring. I, however, heard distinct footfalls above us at the top of the valley, followed by the sound of something sliding down the valley wall. The sliding occurred in intervals, taking around 30 minutes for the creature to reach the valley floor. I then heard two splashes in the nearby creek, indicating that whatever it was had entered our camp. I listened to rustling sounds and occasional periods of silence, punctuated by the sound of a cooler being knocked over. Strangely, I realized that apart from the creature's noises and the babbling of the creek, there was complete silence in the surroundings.

The footfalls eventually circled our tent, and they stopped right behind my head. Filled with fear, I mustered the courage to open my eyes and looked up through the rain fly. I saw a massive head looming above me, but I couldn't discern any details or features. It was simply an imposing presence. As soon as I made eye contact, the head moved back and out of sight. I never heard it leave the camp, but I did hear the sound of it climbing back up the valley wall. Once it departed, the normal sounds of the night returned, and my fear subsided. I stayed awake until one of my friends stirred, and I shared my experience with him. As expected, he dismissed it as a dream or misunderstanding.

The next day, we searched for footprints or signs of the creature's presence but found only the marks left by its descent down the valley wall. There were no missing belongings, and we couldn't find any further evidence. I attempted to peer through the rain fly again, mimicking the head's position from the previous night, and realized that the person responsible would have to be at least 6'5" to look directly down at me. We continued our camping trip for a couple more days without any further incidents before returning home, leaving us with lingering questions and a memorable, albeit unsettling, experience.

CHAPTER THIRTEEN

FOR SEVERAL YEARS, my family and I have endured a horrifying ordeal in our own home. We experienced a range of disturbing incidents, including forceful pounding on windows, loud thumping on walls, tampering with our doors, and even the unsettling sight of someone growling outside our windows. Adding to our distress, our daughter began approaching us in the middle of the night, filled with fear, recounting encounters with shadowy figures trying to communicate with her through her bedroom window. We dismissed these occurrences as mere nightmares, assuming she had been exposed to something on TV that she shouldn't have been watching—she had a habit of sneaking in television time when we were occupied elsewhere.

Being an avid hunter since the age of ten, I believed I had encountered every inhabitant of the Kentucky mountains where I reside. My home sits on the border of the Daniel Boone National Forest, and I hunt on private land that connects to it. One evening in the fall, I set out for a bow hunt on this land. After settling into my stand and allowing the woods to settle down, I began preparing myself for the hunt.

As I organized my gear, I noticed a series of banging and knocking noises nearby. I dismissed it as the sound of construction work, assuming someone was building something in the vicinity. Shortly after, I decided to try some rattling and grunting, followed by a snort-wheeze call, hoping to attract a buck during the peak of the rut. Within a few minutes, I heard the sound of movement approaching my location. Filled with excitement, I positioned myself, convinced that a buck was coming to investigate. However, I couldn't help but feel concerned about the amount of noise this animal was making. Regardless, I chalked it up to the buck preparing for a fight. As it drew nearer, I readied myself to draw my bow, eagerly anticipating the sight of the approaching animal. To my bewilderment, it emerged from a small creek bottom, making its way up the hill, and eventually stepping onto an old logging road. It halted abruptly, locking eyes with me as though it knew exactly where to look. I sat there, perplexed, trying to identify this creature. It was black and appeared to have initially walked on all fours, but as our eyes met, it raised itself up, standing somewhat erect. My initial thought was that it might be a bear, but I couldn't see any ears.

Confusion filled my mind as I considered the possibility that it was an enormous black coyote, but then I noticed its prominent shoulders and the continued absence of ears. We engaged in a silent stare-down for approximately 5 to 7 seconds until I uttered, "What the…" At that moment, it darted back in the direction it came from, moving with incredible speed on all fours, or at least that's what it seemed like until it neared the creek. However, instead of following its original path, it abruptly changed course, circling behind me and disappearing into a dense thicket. This sudden turn of events sent a chill down my spine. As someone familiar with local wildlife, I knew that animals rarely double back and approach closer, which left me feeling increasingly uneasy. I strained my ears, listening intently as the creature made its way through the thicket. I expected it to emerge at any moment, but it stopped just out of my line of sight, concealed by the dense vegetation.

For the next twenty to twenty-five minutes, I anxiously remained in my stand, my bow poised and ready to draw, in case the creature decided to charge at me. Throughout this tense standoff, it would take a few steps, reposition itself, and remain hidden from view. With darkness descending, and without a flashlight, I realized I needed to exit the woods while I still had some daylight left. I hastily packed my belongings into my backpack and stood up. The instant I rose to my feet, the creature emitted an indescribably eerie sound—a combination of a deep, deep sigh or exhale, fused with a guttural rumble. As soon as this noise subsided, it was as if someone had released a raging bull within that thicket.

Startled and alarmed, I swiftly descended from my stand and began walking backward along the trail, ensuring I had some light to be able to discern any movement from the creature, should it decide to make a move. As I made my way approximately 30 yards, the creature let out another piercing scream, closer to my position than the previous one. In a state of heightened fear, I ran back to my house, where I heard yet another vocalization in close proximity to me. After this encounter, my perspective on everything changed. We had never fathomed the existence of such creatures, and upon reflection, we realized that this was not the first time we had been in their presence. However, we were too ignorant to comprehend the true nature of what we were dealing with.

Prior to this encounter, my wife had seen what she believed to be a person on three separate occasions. I witnessed the third sighting myself and even pursued the figure through the woods with my pistol, infuriated by its intrusion near my garage. When I realized that this elusive entity was effortlessly outpacing me, I fired several rounds in its general direction, expressing my frustration. After that incident, things quieted down for a while, but a few months later, I had my own encounter. From then on, we viewed everything around us through a different lens. Although we still own the house, we have chosen to temporarily reside elsewhere, prioritizing the safety of our three children. The last confrontation with these creatures made me profoundly reconsider the security of my family.

CHAPTER FOURTEEN

IN THE HEART of the majestic sequoia forests, my brother, our friend Joe, and I embarked on an unforgettable camping trip. Our chosen location was a secluded spot off an old logging road, far away from the hustle and bustle of civilization. As evening approached and the moon hid behind a thick blanket of clouds, darkness descended upon the forest with an eerie swiftness.

Seeking a brief adventure, we decided to take a walk, equipped with modest flashlights purchased from a local Walmart. The three of us ventured a couple of minutes down the road before a sense of unease washed over us. A chilling cry broke the silence, startling us and sending shivers down our spines. It was my brother who had spotted a pair of eyes fixed upon us from the darkness.

Rushing back to his side, I directed my flashlight towards the source of his fear. As the light pierced the blackness, a surreal image materialized before us—a towering figure, approximately seven feet tall, lurking behind a massive tree trunk. The first thing that struck me were its eyes, widely spaced apart and gleaming in the beam of my flashlight. The creature's unnaturally fluid movements, reminiscent of an owl's head swiveling, captivated our attention. It observed us intently, its gaze filled with an uncanny curiosity, as if it were studying us as much as we were studying it. For a brief but haunting moment, time seemed to stand still.

Suddenly, our friend Joe hurriedly approached, shining his flashlight in the same direction. The creature, now aware of our collective presence, shifted its focus to Joe, using its left hand to push away from the tree and vanish into the darkness with a mere four strides. The outline of the creature remained etched in our minds—it was undoubtedly a formidable and imposing beast. Walking upright on two legs, its footsteps reverberated like the sound of breaking lumber with each powerful stride.

Stunned by the encounter, we stood frozen, unable to comprehend the reality of what we had just witnessed. We were acutely aware that the creature remained nearby, its eyes seemingly fixated upon us. After what felt like an eternity of contemplation, we made the unanimous decision to retreat to the safety of our car. Our minds raced as we considered the GoPros and camera we had left behind at the campsite, rendered useless in the cloak of darkness.

As we retraced our steps, our hearts pounding, we couldn't shake the feeling that the creature was shadowing us, stalking our every move from the safety of the trees that lined the road. The sounds of its approach grew closer, until a single step brought us to a halt. The creature had veered just five feet off the road, seemingly indifferent to whether its presence was detected. The tension in the air was palpable, our hearts lodged in our throats as we awaited the creature's next move.

Suddenly, propelled by a surge of adrenaline, my brother broke the silence with a resolute exclamation of "f**k it!" Without a moment's hesitation, he charged off the road, running full speed towards the enigmatic being. Joe and I followed suit, our actions propelled by an insatiable curiosity that temporarily overshadowed our fear. We sprinted towards the creature, propelled by an inexplicable fascination, with no concrete plan in mind for what awaited us.

Within seconds, we found ourselves within mere feet of the creature, its presence almost tangible. As if in unspoken agreement, we halted our advance, falling into a breathless silence. We knew the creature was beside us, lurking just beyond the veil of darkness. And then, it began to walk again, its footsteps resonating through the night. Without exchanging a single word, we resumed our chase, matching our steps to its rhythmic gait. This strange dance repeated itself four times, each time we stopped, the creature resumed its watchful proximity, as if playing an unsettling game of cat and mouse.

During our final pause, as we caught our breath, we realized with a sinking feeling that we had inadvertently raced deep into the heart of the forest. We were now disoriented, surrounded by an unfamiliar landscape, and with the creature still in our midst, its presence an unshakeable certainty. We cautiously treaded onward for what felt like an eternity, fearing getting lost in the labyrinthine woods.

Eventually, our intuition guided us, and we emerged from the dense foliage behind our trusty jeep. Overwhelmed with relief, we decided not to leave the area for the remainder of the night. The creature had proven itself to be a master of concealment, shadowing our every move with a level of expertise that defied explanation. It possessed an uncanny ability to elude us, returning to the same location with uncanny precision. The experience left an indelible mark on our souls, fueling a deep-seated desire to return to the very spot as soon as winter relinquished its hold on the land.

There, in the heart of the sequoias, we will venture forth again, armed with the hope of encountering the enigma that had captivated our imaginations. The lure of that mysterious creature, shrouded in darkness and secrecy, beckons us with an irresistible allure. We yearn to unlock its secrets, to unravel the truth behind its existence. For we know that within those towering trees and hidden depths lies a world brimming with wonder and untold stories—stories that deserve to be discovered and shared.

CHAPTER FIFTEEN

AS A DEDICATED LAW ENFORCEMENT OFFICER, I hold integrity in the highest regard. I have no ulterior motives for recounting what I witnessed, nor do I concern myself with whether others believe me or not. Throughout my career, I had heard whispers of such phenomena here and there, but I never paid them much attention or dismissed them with a chuckle. It wasn't that I doubted their existence, but rather I maintained a stance of reserving judgment until I experienced something firsthand.

The evening in question occurred during a sweltering late summer period, either just after or before Labor Day, in the year 2007. It was dark, approximately 8:30 or 9:00 PM, although the western sky retained a faint glow characteristic of that time of year. Engaged in patrol duties, I was driving westbound on Highway 17, en route to respond to an alarm call at a ranch property. Such calls were a common occurrence in my line of work.

As a law enforcement officer, one develops an acute sense for detecting anomalies. A car conspicuously parked in an unfamiliar spot, an individual walking along a desolate stretch of road, lights emanating from a closed business—these were the details that caught my trained eye, often unnoticed by others. So, as I continued along my route, heading westward, something caught my attention. Movement within the thicket adjacent to the road indicated the presence of a person emerging from the ravine. I couldn't provide a detailed description at that moment, but the motion among the brush confirmed the presence of an individual. People often try to evade law enforcement, and my initial thought was that I might have startled someone engaged in illegal activities, such as cultivating marijuana in the surrounding woods. It was an occurrence frequently encountered in our area.

Expecting to encounter someone attempting to avoid detection, I abruptly applied the brakes and swiftly reversed my vehicle. And there, illuminated by my headlights, I beheld an astonishing sight. Standing approximately 6 to 7 feet tall, covered in thick, matted brown fur, it walked upright. Regrettably, I did not catch a glimpse of its face, as it was walking away from me at a leisurely pace. Like countless others who have shared similar encounters, I couldn't fathom the reality of what lay before my eyes. It was an experience that I couldn't bring myself to relay over the radio to my colleagues. The dense tangle of branches and foliage obstructed my view, but there was no mistaking what I had seen.

Two distinct details remain etched in my memory. Firstly, the creature's fur was adorned with small leaves and grass, tightly entwined along its back. I observed this feature as it gradually moved away from me. The image remains vivid in my mind. Secondly, its movements were deliberate and unhurried. As it retreated, I watched as it employed its arm to sweep away small branches and twigs obstructing its path. I had the opportunity to observe its backside for a considerable 4 to 5 seconds before it vanished into the thick undergrowth. Paralyzed by astonishment, I emerged from my vehicle and stood there in silence for 2 to 3 minutes, engine off. I strained my ears, attuned to the same measured movements and the telltale sound of leaves and sticks crunching underfoot. The sounds persisted, emanating from the depths of the ravine, most likely where the creature had retreated—perhaps to the nearby creek.

Needless to say, I chose to keep this extraordinary encounter to myself. It was not a topic suitable for briefing sessions or inclusion in the patrol blotter. To divulge such an account would undoubtedly cast a long and uncomfortable shadow over one's career.

For a fleeting moment, I contemplated contacting one of our local Fish and Game Officers. However, familiarity among our small community dissuaded me from doing so, as he happened to be acquainted with many of my friends. Consequently, I opted to maintain absolute silence. Reading the testimonials of others on various platforms reassured me that I was not alone. While I have never witnessed ghosts, UFOs, or anything of that nature, this encounter has left me pondering the vast realm of possibilities that we often dismiss or laugh off without giving them serious consideration.

CHAPTER SIXTEEN

I WAS on a road trip driving from my home in Washington State to Upstate New York to visit my sister who had recently moved all the way across the country for her job. I was extremely excited for her. She was twenty-seven years old, and I was only eighteen. She's my half-sister but we share the same mother and grew up in the same home, so I don't refer to or think of her as a half-sister but it's just for clarity on the age difference. She and I were best friends our whole lives and we still are today. This was in the early nineties and after graduating high school I wasn't sure if college was for me or what I wanted to do with my life. I was somewhat aimless and so my sister invited me to go and stay with her for the summer and if I liked it and if I wanted to, she offered me to stay with her indefinitely and move permanently to the east coast to see if maybe I could figure it all out easier while I was there. I was looking forward to the open road and I wasn't in a rush to get there. I hadn't ever been further than Arizona at that point and so this was a real adventure for me. I had always loved the woods and I would consider myself an avid outdoorswoman. I was determined to visit every state possible, without going too far out of the way, and to stay one night in each state. I told everyone I was staying in hotels but what I was really doing was camping out wherever I could. I would look at maps and stop at information and welcome centers to find places where I could set up camp along the way. What can I say? I was a free spirit and thought at the time that I was invincible. I realized once I tried to camp out and spend the night in Mississippi how wrong I was about that.

I was having a great time and had met a lot of great people along the way. Once I got to Mississippi, I realized it was going to be a lot harder than it had been up until that point to find a free place to camp. It was late, and I didn't have the money to stay at a hotel, well not enough that I wanted to spare the money for that anyway, and I was exhausted. I had planned on driving through there earlier in the afternoon and hanging out but that didn't work out due to some traffic I hit. I don't want to bore anyone with details so let me get to where I ended up camping out. I saw some vehicles, two of them, that looked like they were hidden inside of some trees and where I come from that means people are camping somewhere in the surrounding woods. It was perfect because I knew other people were doing it and I also knew that I wasn't going to be out there alone. Well, these were my thoughts at the time. I parked my car and hid it as best as I could and grabbed my minimal camping supplies. I roamed the woods looking for signs of a fire and listening for others talking somewhere but all I heard was eerie silence. Like, the woods were dead quiet in an unusual way, with there being nothing peaceful about it, not even remotely. I was exhausted and it was late so I just sort of plopped my tent down right where I was standing, after walking about fifteen minutes into the woods. I figured someone would either come along and tell me to leave or I would once again and as usual meet some cool people. I didn't build a fire and I went right to sleep as soon as the tent was set up.

I remember the moon was full and I was scared by the silence that still seemed to be overtaking the forest when I woke up in the middle of the night to what sounded like some sort of loud growling or groaning. It was very creepy and with that surreal backdrop of silence, I was absolutely terrified the second I opened my eyes. Of course, I realized immediately after that I had to go pee. I cautiously crawled out of my tent and looked around. I didn't see anything, and the moon looked beautiful in the dark night sky. I went pee but immediately upon me standing back up and getting myself together something swooped down near my face. I didn't know what it was and immediately I thought it might be a bat. I screamed, ducked, and crawled back into my tent. Suddenly there were at least a dozen of them, and I could see them attacking my tent. They made odd groaning noises, and an overall feeling of terror and dread came over me. I didn't know what the hell was going on and I didn't know that bats attacked like that. I slowly unzipped the sky light thing in my tent to maybe see what was attacking the tent. Luckily whatever they were, they were small and not doing much damage. I saw that they were white but couldn't see anything else. From the angle I was looking at them in the tent, they looked like white bats.

I prayed they would go away but that didn't work so I started to cry helplessly. Suddenly and all at once the activity stopped and the forest was once again too quiet. I was scared and helpless because I knew it was the middle of the night and I had no chance of making it out of the forest at that time, especially with those things flapping around, whatever they were, and for how terrified I was. I had to think it through and decided to pack all my stuff up and run as fast as I could out of the woods and to my car. I was planning on spending the night in my vehicle because at that point that felt safer than staying in that tent and possibly having one of those vicious albino bat things get into the tent to kill or seriously harm me. I got out of the tent and immediately heard a very strange noise. It sounded like wings flapping but a million times louder than anything else I had ever heard come from something that flies. What I mean is, it sounded like whatever it was, it was gigantic. I looked over and couldn't believe my own eyes at what I was looking at. It looked like a giant white bat at first glance but then I blinked and looked a little bit closer. It was standing on the ground and not hovering in the air like I had first thought it was. It had the body of a man! It was humanoid and stood at around nine feet tall and six feet wide. It looked completely and totally human other than the enormous wings that were connected to and flapping behind its back. It looked at me. It was the palest white I had ever seen, and its eyes were huge and black. It had a human nose and ears, but it seemed like it was hairless all over otherwise. The arms were so puny and skinny, it's like there was only bone and skin and no muscles or anything else. It growled at me.

I put my arms out and told it that I was sorry and just wanted to leave and then I made the mistake of looking up. I saw about ten more of those things, tiny ones but the same otherwise, standing on branches in the trees. They were all glaring at me, growling, and flapping those Godforsaken wings. I know no one ever believes me but I recently saw another encounter of someone in the woods seeing something similar as the larger one while camping with their dad. They scared it off with a gunshot. However, I haven't yet read that encounter because the internet wasn't yet a thing and, I didn't have a gun with me or any weapon at all for that matter. I was crying and shaking and this thing, this man with giant wings and pale white skin sneered at me. It then smiled as it noticed my fear and confusion and it had a mouth full of perfectly straight, white, razor-sharp teeth. It licked its teeth with its tongue as the others stood very still on top of the tree branches. It dawned on me immediately what I sensed in the beginning about something being wrong in the forest because of the intense and unreal silence that had blanketed it the whole night from the second I had walked into it. I trembled in fear and then I heard a gunshot. The entity, whatever it was, glared harder at me and then it looked up.

All the smaller ones who had attacked me and my tent earlier flew down and they sort of disappeared into the larger ones' wings. I know it sounds weird but they didn't actually disappear but they were engulfed in the sheer size of the larger one's wings and they looked to be all but gone. I saw each one takes its place inside of those wings and then close their eyes until I saw them no more. Then, another gunshot and the giant humanoid bat took off. I heard voices and someone excitedly yelling that they thought they got it. I don't know what that was all about because I didn't stick around to find out. I grabbed my wallet and another essential or two and I left everything else there, including my tent. I was no longer keen on meeting cool new people, or anyone for that matter, and I just wanted to get back on the road and to my sister's house. I ran to my vehicle, got in and drove to the nearest motel. I stayed the night but had a restless sleep thinking that the bat things were going to somehow know where I was and come for me.

I spent the rest of my road trip taking the most direct route to my sister's house in upstate New York and never looked back. I didn't tell anyone about anything that happened to me that night and I never mentioned it. However, very recently, as I already said, I came across two more encounters someone on the internet wrote about claiming to have with the exact same entity. I knew I wasn't crazy but now my sanity and memories have been validated by these other strangers who have had the same exact experiences as me. They were in the woods and were attacked by a giant man, a pale man who had gigantic white wings. I have tried to wrap my mind around all this ever since it happened, and nothing makes sense except they were demons OR that they were extraterrestrials. I believe in both, and I believe that both of those explanations make a lot of sense. It didn't seem like it wanted to eat me or anything because it had at least three or four minutes where we were in a standoff and it could have easily killed me had it wanted to. Was it an energy vampire of some sort and would it have drained me? Who were those strangers? How did they know about that thing, and did they ever catch it? I believe in synchronicity so maybe they will read this story and know that it was them by the fact that I left my whole tent there, along with two pillows and a Barbie sleeping bag. I am still scared to this day that those things are going to come for me. I don't go into the woods ever, not under any circumstances and I am reluctant to go on long trips alone. I ended up staying in New York and building a great life here. Everything is wonderful except that I am haunted by that night so long ago in Mississippi.

CHAPTER SEVENTEEN

IT WAS 2009 and I went camping with my boyfriend somewhere along the Appalachian Trail. I am still convinced that what we saw was absolute evil, in its purest form and I don't want to say exactly where we were because I don't want anyone to get any ideas about going there in search of this entity. I have always enjoyed being in the woods and that's one of the reasons my boyfriend and I meshed so well together. We met when we were both at the same two week long spiritual retreat and realized we had so much in common. The retreat went well and after six months of being together, I moved to the Midwest to be closer to him. I was born and raised in Maine but because I can work from anywhere and he can't, I decided to make the sacrifice of moving. It ended up working out and once I moved there he showed me a whole other part of the country and a whole different type of wilderness than anything that I was used to. We are also both very interested in the paranormal and love to take ghost tours all over the place. On this particular trip though we were just trying to unwind from a long week of work, from the stress of my move and just from everyday life as twenty-somethings just starting to make and find our own way in the world. The campsite he chose was spectacular and I knew right away it was going to be a great time.

We had one very large tent that we were sharing and he knew more about the outdoors than I did and that's saying something because I was basically raised in the wilderness. Family vacations were always spent camping, hiking or doing some other amazing activity outdoors and as a family. We built a fire, had some dinner and, after stargazing for about an hour, we decided to go into the tent and call it a night at around midnight. Aside from the fact that we saw what looked like several shooting stars, only they were bright, glowing green, there was nothing creepy or off putting about the forest up until that point. It was almost like the second we got into our tents and got settled in, we both felt like the energy of the whole place had just shifted somehow. We couldn't put our fingers on it at first but eventually we decided that, although we couldn't hear anything and there wasn't anything there that we could see, we felt like we were being watched by something right outside of our tent. It was terrifying because we had both been looking into encounters in the woods right before we left for this trip. We were planning on camping for a week but after that first night we decided to move and find somewhere else to set up our camp. We hardly got any sleep and it wasn't only because of the eerie feelings we both had when we finally laid down either. The entire night we kept being woken up by a child yelling and pleading for help. Of course, we grabbed our flashlights and went out into the woods to look for the little girl we were hearing but we never found anyone. It just gave us a bad feeling. I mean, why would there be a little girl yelling for help in the middle of the woods, out in the middle of nowhere in the middle of the night? It didn't make any sense. After the fourth time we didn't even bother to go and look anymore and honestly we both felt like something was trying to lure us deeper into the woods. I always look back on that night and on that trip and thank heavens that he and I both were very aware of not only the fact that paranormal entities oftentimes stalk wooded areas and especially forests, but that they will lure you to your death sometimes as well. Who knows what would have happened to us if we hadn't given up for the night? It depends on what you're dealing with and, honestly, whether or not you believe in it.

There weren't any other people camping in the area where we

were, or at least we didn't see anyone and there shouldn't have been. The woods were very isolated and out of the way and so we didn't expect to see anyone. When we heard a little girl we knew something just wasn't right. We hardly slept and first thing the next morning we had some breakfast and then hiked two miles further into the woods in the hopes that we wouldn't have to deal with whatever was happening at the initial campsite. We weren't freaked out enough to give up on the trip and since the paranormal was kind of our thing, we were sort of exhilarated by the experience. Not enough to investigate, but enough that we thought it was gonna be a cool and creepy story to tell our friends. We hung out and hiked a bit and eventually it was time to go to bed again. All had been quiet up until that point and we hadn't seen or heard anyone else anywhere near us.

Sure enough though, as soon as we got into the tent that eerie and creepy feeling came over the both of us again and we somehow just knew that we hadn't heard the last of the little girl. We felt whatever it was, it was extremely negative, therefore we didn't try to record or photograph anything in any way. We hadn't seen it, yet, but I wish we had set up our cameras. We were equipped to have gotten the activity on video but we just felt like that would've caused us more trouble. We kissed goodnight and went to sleep hoping for the best but expecting to be woken up all night long again. We weren't wrong in having that expectation. Sure enough, right around two in the morning we heard a little girl crying. She wasn't yelling or screaming for help that time but she was moaning and crying like she was really sad. Of course this tugged at our heartstrings despite knowing what we were both feeling intuitively and also what we had obviously gone through the night before. We were considering leaving and calling the police. There was no cell service in that area anyway, even if we had cell phones, which we didn't at the time. After about fifteen minutes of incessant crying and moaning we had finally had enough and gave in. We grabbed our flashlights and went to look for the little girl. Neither of us expected to find a little girl but we had to look just in case there was one who needed help. It was highly unlikely I know but it's hard to explain how you react to something like this when you're in the moment.

We tried to follow the sound of where the cries seemed to be coming from. After about twenty minutes of randomly wandering the woods we were about to give up and go back to our tent. We had made the decision that the next day we were going to go into town and report it to the local authorities. Turns out we would have no reason to do any such thing. Suddenly the forest went silent and grew very still. The cries stopped as we stood directly in front of a really tall and wide tree. It was much taller than any of the others around it and the front of it looked like it had some sort of strange carvings or symbols on it. We hadn't remembered seeing it earlier in the night, despite it seeming like it would be really hard to miss, and we had circled back around to that area at least twice. There was grayish white fog starting to form around the tree and all over the place in the area where we were standing. It engulfed everything and it was suddenly very hard to see. He and I were both really scared right away because we knew this was not normal and the fog wasn't a natural phenomenon. I couldn't see my boyfriend but I could hear him and he told me to just stay still so we could think of how to get out of there without losing one another. I reached for his hand and he grabbed it, or so I thought. I heard him ask where I was and I told him I was "right here", meaning I was holding his hand. He asked me "right where" and that's when I told him I was holding his hand. He said I wasn't doing any such thing and that's when it hit me how far away he had sounded. I immediately tried to let go of who or whatever's hand I was holding but it clenched its hand around mine and squeezed. I screamed in pain and terror.

I looked over in that direction and I saw a creature next to me. I could somehow see it through the dense and very intense fog. It was about ten feet tall, white like the color of a crayon labeled as white, not caucasian or even just pale, and it had extremely large, black eyes. The eyes reminded me of a cat. They stared into mine and I felt myself start to get dizzy. I wanted to take in more of the creature before it led me to whatever fate it had in store for me. It had what looked like antennae on top of its head and there was a green light emanating from its whole body, all around it. Its fingers were long and spindly but they were circular at the end. Instead of having fingernails there seemed to only be circular little nubs at the tips. I kept trying to pull my hand away but its grip was too tight. I also noticed it had a nose and the shape of where the eyebrows went and formed the nose that also reminded me of a cat. Its mouth looked perfectly normal. I screamed and that must have been when I passed out. However, I didn't hit the ground because the entity wouldn't let go of my hand. It simply jerked my arm back up and I was once again standing normally and it had my full attention. I yelled for my boyfriend but got no response. The fog had lifted. I tried to look around to see if I could locate him but I also didn't want to take my eyes off of the being that had me by my hand and didn't seem to have any intentions on letting it go anytime soon. A bright blue light blasted out of the sky right in front of us. It almost blinded me and I used my other hand to shield my eyes. I looked over at the being and its mouth opened unusually wide and it reminded me of a snake who dislocates its jaw when about to or in the middle of devouring its prey. I screamed again but it just mimicked me and screamed my voice back at me. I was shaking and I stopped walking and stubbornly stood there. I was overwhelmed with and overcome by fear and complete and total panic. I didn't know what to do.

Suddenly and seemingly out of nowhere I was being pulled backwards by two strong arms around my waist. It was my boyfriend and he looked like he had been swimming or something because he was soaking wet. His brave attempt at freeing me had caught the creature off guard and it lost its grip on my hand. The light from the sky vanished, the remaining fog went with it and the creature turned to us and angrily howled. Then, as we watched, it floated right into the tree and disappeared. Within minutes we could hear the sounds of a little girl crying and calling out for help. We ran as fast as we could but we had no idea where our camp was. We were lured out there and didn't remember how far we had gone or which way we had come from. We ran and ran regardless and eventually we did make it back to our camp. We couldn't leave right then because it was the middle of the night and there were other, known predators out there that could attack and kill us. We had to wait it out. We got back in our tent and honestly, we didn't even talk about it. We were both so incredibly exhausted, probably from the extreme rushes of adrenaline, that we both just cuddled up and passed out. We woke up at ten the next morning. We got out of our tent intent on packing everything up immediately and hiking back out of there. However, we got out of the tent and realized we were right under that gigantic, strange tree where the entity had disappeared into. Our entire camp; our tent, all of our belongings, everything, had somehow been transported, while we slept, to that spot. We knew right then that something otherworldly had happened to us but we had no idea what. We just wanted to get the hell out of there and so we did.

We talked about it a little bit but my boyfriend, who is now my husband, wouldn't ever open up to me about where he had gone that night or why he came back soaking wet. It's too traumatic I guess and I hope that someday he will feel like he can tell me. We both believe wholeheartedly that we had been abducted and that it more than likely wasn't the first or the last time. We also are pretty sure we aren't the only ones. We are both considering hypnotic regression therapy but we aren't quite ready yet. Either together or individually, we are both still very fearful of what we might uncover. I put this out there in the hopes that other people who have experienced something similar, whether out in the woods, in that same area or otherwise, won't feel so alone and afraid. My boyfriend and I never discussed what happened to us with anyone other than each other. It just seems safer that way. I think my writing it all down is the first step to finding out more and being able to share our story with more people, all over the world. These things really do happen to regular people and we don't know why we were chosen, why at that time, in that place; we don't know anything at all except for our experiences. He doesn't know I'm sharing this but with all of the research he does he will more than likely come across it one day. I'm not sure how he will react but for me it's been very thera-peutic and I thank you for letting me get it off my chest.

CHAPTER EIGHTEEN

I INHERITED a cabin that belonged to my grandparents when I was twenty eight years old. It was a shock as they both died tragically, suddenly and together but also because no one knew they even owned a cabin. We are from the northeastern part of the United States and that's where most of my family was born and raised and where most of them still reside to this day. So, it was shocking when the will was read and I was told I had inherited a large chunk of money and a rustic, old cabin in the middle of the woods in Colorado. I was excited and couldn't have been more pleased. I could certainly use the money at the time even though I was unmarried and didn't have any kids yet. It afforded me the opportunity to be able to do some things I had always wanted to do but that I had been putting off in the rat race that is the corporate world where I worked. I broke the lease on my tiny apartment in the city, bought myself an old and used camper-van, stuffed it full of my belongings and headed out to Colorado within a week of inheriting the cabin. I had a job where I mainly worked from home but I took a few weeks off anyway because I wanted to be able to settle in and have some peace and quiet to myself. I was always very close with my grandparents, being the only grandchild, and though I was devastated at the loss, I felt so grateful to them for looking out for me the way that they had. My parents weren't happy about my moving to Colorado on what they called "a whim" but I knew it was the right thing for me to do at that time. Personally I just think they were jealous I was left a lot more than they were but I never would have said that to their faces. I promised my mother that as soon as I got settled in I would let her know and then if they wanted to they could come and check out the cabin. She settled for that much and I left without ever planning on looking back.

I had no idea how far out into the sticks the cabin was. I figured it would be fairly isolated given how my grandparents always valued their privacy but I got quite a shock when I spent a half hour's time driving on three separate, country, back roads, each! It was literally in the middle of nowhere and in the middle of the woods. I was definitely not used to being out in the country and had never been camping, hunting, hiking or anything like that my entire life. I had always wanted to do those things and I figured there was no time like the present. What I hadn't been told was that the cabin they owned was a part of an old summer camp that shut down in the sixties and they sold off the cabins one by one to the highest bidders. To me that was crazy but it ended up being pretty cool. I had neighbors, somewhere around in between all the trees and other woods and there was a huge lake in the compound as well. I didn't see any other cabins on the drive into the place and I hadn't even seen a gas station in the last twenty miles or so but I knew there had to have been other people there, especially at that time of year. It was the end of fall and winter was just starting to rear its ugly head. I knew it snowed a lot in Colorado but that wasn't anything I was used to, or so I thought, having lived in a big city on the northeastern seaboard my whole life. I had no clue what I was in for, and not only with the weather either. It didn't take long for me to get my first dose of the terrifying and the supernatural things that came from those woods and had, somehow and at some point, become a part of that cabin and everything around it.

I had to bring in some professionals to do small jobs on various parts of the building and land but it was all very minor things and initial inspections, stuff like that. They were all local companies I had found in the yellow pages. It was odd though that when I would answer the door they would always take a step back and every single one of them refused my offer to come inside and warm up for a minute before or after doing what they needed to do. Finally one of them, a woman who had to come in to make sure all of my wires and things were up to date, flat out said, "There's no way I'm going in there so please be honest and answer the questions I'm about to ask you."

I thought it was kind of rude and she blatantly explained that my cabin was said to be haunted and all types of crazy things had been seen and heard coming from there, mainly at night throughout the course of all the years since the camp closed down. While she refused to get into any more detail she said that a few years back my grandparents had to be called out there because there were people performing rituals in there and someone had called the police and she also claimed that the tragedies there were unnatural and occurred way more than what would be considered a normal amount, starting all the way back when it was still a summer camp. She told me it was a literal portal to hell because it had been built on top of one. I was in shock and thought she was crazy. I answered her questions and couldn't have been more pleased when she was finally off my porch.

At first I noticed a lot of little, weird things happening in the cabin but nothing that alarmed me or made me feel unsafe or like I was living on top of a portal to hell. The one thing was the constant and almost obsessive banging that would happen every single night when I would lay down for bed. I would lay down and listen to my music fairly loudly on the radio because it helped me to unwind and fall asleep faster. I listened to classical music before bed but it seemed like every single time I would turn it on, there would be a strange banging sound like someone was stomping up and down on the floor right next to me but there was no one there. I heard it a lot when I was in my bedroom specifically but it was never as bad as when I was playing my music before bed. I'm gonna make a long story short here but one thing aside from the banging was a feeling like I was always being watched, not just inside of the house but outside as well. It felt like the woods had taken on a life of their own and something within them was always watching me. It was eerie and made spending time on the back deck and enjoying the beautiful view not even worth it anymore. I didn't go out there much after the first month.

Finally the time came when my parents were insisting they wanted to come and visit and so they did. It was right before the first major snowfall of the season and they got to my house just in time to end up snowed in with me. We had a good time but my mother came in one day and asked me if I had met the old woman who used to live here. I asked her what she was talking about and she said she had been on the back deck smoking a cigarette when a little old lady came up and asked her how she likes the place. My mother explained to her that she loved it and was thinking about buying one of them in the area herself. The old woman told her that she used to live in my cabin but now she lived somewhere else. The woman pointed in the direction to the back of the house and into the woods. That wasn't too worrisome or unbelievable because the other cabins were located all within the woods and throughout the area. It was very rugged and also very massive so I knew I hadn't seen all of the cabins yet despite having been there for a little over a month. The activity in the cabin was getting bad and my parents and I noticed shadow entities in the corners and they also seemed to be standing at the foot of the beds in the middle of the night but it was all chalked up to us possibly seeing things. When it came to the things that would be there one minute and gone the next like keys, the remote or even a hairbrush, we convinced ourselves that we had simply been mistaken about where we had left those items in the first place. Then one night, everything changed.

I was upstairs in my room, listening to my classical music and getting ready for bed when the banging started. There was an empty bedroom in the room below me where I had one bed and the rest of my boxes I still had to unpack. Across from that room, on the ground floor was the guest room where my parents were staying. The banging was so loud I went downstairs and asked my parents if they could hear it and they said they thought it was coming from the room across from theirs and they had been hearing it every night like I had. I think up until that point none of us wanted to accept that maybe the place was haunted. We all went into the spare room to look and see if we could figure it out but there was nothing there. As we all turned to leave something caught my eye in the mirror and I kid you not I screamed like a little girl. There, sitting on the bed directly across from the mirror was a little old lady with blazing red eyes. She had a broom in her hand and as she looked at me and smiled a terrifying and evil grin, she started slamming the broom handle into the ceiling above her. That was what the banging had been the whole time. Suddenly, as both my parents turned to look, the lady could be seen on the bed and she got up and angrily stormed towards us. She yelled in a demonic voice for us to get the hell out of her house. I didn't know what else to do so we ran from the room and I slammed the door in her face. We were in such a panic we ran out the back door and were on the deck. It was snowing like crazy.

There were footprints in the snow leading from my back deck, down the few stairs and into the woods. I thought someone had broken in and my rational mind said the old lady was in on it. When my mother told me it was the same old woman she had seen that had said she used to live there, I became furious and thought my hillbilly neighbors were trying to rob me. I grabbed my jacket and ran into the woods to follow the footprints. It was dark outside at that time but I had brought a flashlight, thank God for my mother who had thought ahead. I shined it everywhere but didn't see anything around me but I knew someone was watching me the whole time. I yelled for whoever it was to show themselves and called them a coward and some other choice and not so nice words. Suddenly, the footprints stopped at the lake. I looked up but there was no one there and other than my own there were no footprints anywhere. That's when I looked up and saw shadow beings with glowing red eyes all around me, coming out from behind the trees. They started walking towards me and in my terror I could do nothing but scream. They all looked startled for a minute and I thought for a second it was me who had somehow been able to intimidate them. They all turned their heads at the same time towards the lake, which was frozen over and snow covered. There, directly in the middle of the lake, there was a huge, black figure. It was blacker than the darkness of the night and looked like it was wearing a cloak or hood of some kind. It was at least thirteen feet tall and carried a scythe. It looked almost like the comic book and horror movie images of Death itself. And it was coming right towards me.

As the regular sized shadow beings closed in on me I took off running. I ran as fast as I could back to my house but on the way the old lady came out from behind a tree. She was almost snarling, her eyes blazing. She shook her broom at me and told me, again in the demonic voice, to get out of her house. I didn't stop and ran right into her, knocking her down into the snow in the process. She let out an ear piercing howl behind me and when I turned around she was gone. There was a huge mark in the snow though where she had fallen on the ground. I kept running but right before I got to my house, I saw that the giant shadow/Death being was standing on the stairs to the back porch. It was perfectly still and its cloak wasn't blowing in the breeze or anything. It also seemed to be completely unaffected by the snow as it remained pristine and untouched by the stuff. It pulled a pocket watch or something similar out of its pocket, looked at it, and then looked back at me. It started to walk towards me and all I could think to do was pray. I prayed fervently like I had never prayed before. When I opened my eyes it was gone but I could still feel a presence watching me from the woods. I ran inside and eventually I calmed down enough to tell my parents what happened. They believed me but there wasn't anywhere we could go. We were snowed in, in a cabin in the middle of nowhere and there was no way out. There was a state of emergency outside and in most of the state at the time so only emergency vehicles were allowed to be on the roads for any reason. We were stuck there, at least for a little while.

The activity got worse and worse as each day passed and I could write a book about everything terrifying that went on in that place. My parents and I all slept together in the living room and eventually we came to discuss why my grandparents had given me the cabin and none of us could understand it. Once the snow cleared my parents went home and begged me to go with them. I couldn't though because I loved the cabin itself and the land around it too much. I called in some specialists who deal with the paranormal and one of them was a medicine woman from a Native tribe in the area. She told me I had angered the Great Spirit in the woods and that he felt like he and I were at war. Therefore he was attacking me and sending in all of the resources available to him. She said that if I earnestly apologized and gave a peace offering, that he MIGHT allow me to stay and live there in peace. I thought it was all mumbo jumbo and thought that I was dealing with something definitely evil and from hell itself. However, I was willing to try anything at that point and so I did what she told me to do. I bought some tobacco and a small bottle of liquor and went out to the edge of the woods. I apologized with my arms out to what or whoever the Great Spirit was and suddenly, for the first time since I had been there I felt at peace. I even felt something touch my hand as though it were shaking it. The "war" was over, apparently.

I bring gifts to the Spirit at the start of every season and I still live in the cabin. I had to learn to live with the shadow beings but the huge one I thought was death hasn't shown up again since I made peace with the entity in the woods. They torment me sometimes but it's always in waves and then for a few months it'll all be quiet. I had to bring in a medium to get rid of the old lady and the rest is, as they say, history. I've contemplated just selling the place but it has a hold on me and I'm somewhat attached to it now. Also, I don't want anyone else to have to go through what I went through with the Spirit in the woods or that I still go through with the shadow beings. Since no one knows what they are or where they come from, there's really no getting rid of them. There are several documented cases where they're said to have killed people but I keep close to my faith and that's all I can do. Thanks for letting me share.

CHAPTER NINETEEN

WHEN I WAS a little girl my brother and I would play in the woods for hours on end without ever getting bored. We made up all sorts of wild stories and our own imaginary lands. It was the sixties and we didn't have the luxury of lots of toys and other things to keep us amused. We made our own fun. I look back on those days with so much fondness and while there have been a few times we came across something scary or unexplainable, for the most part my childhood from as far back as I can remember until I was ten years old, was just one peaceful blur of happy days and fun nights. We would go out in the morning after we ate breakfast and did our chores and we didn't have to be back or check in until dinner time. Our mother was always kind enough to send us out with snacks and sometimes she would make us a picnic lunch to take with us on our woodland adventures. When my encounter with the pale man happened I was ten and my brother was twelve. It started out like any other normal day for us and once we were done with everything else, we had our little picnic basket and were walking along our favorite trails through the forest behind and all around our home. We had no idea what was awaiting us in those woods that day, there's no way we could have but it's something I've never forgotten and that still haunts my dreams to this very day.

We had all of our favorite places and secret spots and knew those woods like the backs of our hands. One of our favorite things to do was play hide and seek. We would make a game of that stretch on for hours because we always found such amazing places to hide. The perimeter we set up for where we could hide was very large and there were all sorts of places we could squeeze into, being thin and small kids. My brother and I played princess and Ogre and knight and old hag, all of our usual games, before we sat down and had our picnic. I always laid out our little blanket and we would lay down and eat the treats and sandwiches mother had made us while we told each other which shapes we saw in the clouds. It was a perfectly ordinary day. We lived in Arizona and while it isn't really known for its woodland areas I assure you, at least back then, there were plenty. The forest we played in was near our home but it covered hundreds if not thousands of acres and we had the run of the place. We had never run into another human being in all the years we had been playing out there and we never really encountered any sort of dangerous animals either. I should mention there are many legends around that part of the country and there always have been. Where we lived we were always warned of the skinwalkers. We had plenty of friends whose families had taught them those legends from an early age and who believed in the legends very seriously. For me and my brother the skinwalker became just another fantasy monster to slay during our games. We never expected it was real and being raised as Catholics, we thought that if they did exist, it was probably some sort of hell demon just like everything else we had learned. I brought the skinwalker up because it's the only thing that makes sense when trying to figure out what I encountered that day but in all the years since it happened, I've gotten any closer to figuring it out. Whether it was a skinwalker, a hell demon or some-thing else, I surely don't know but I figure whatever it was very easily could have been any one of those three things. It could have also been something else altogether. The only thing I am absolutely sure of and was from the moment I had my encounter with it is that it was pure evil.

As we laid there on the blanket looking at the clouds in the sky we heard what sounded like a deer screaming. We had heard that sound before because these woods connected to the ones that were in our backyard, basically, and from time to time we would hear the sounds of a predator devouring and slaughtering a prey animal. The deer were the ones we heard the most often, screaming like that during the daytime. We tried our best to ignore it. We knew it was more than likely a hungry bear who left its home during the day because it was starving and honestly, it was better to be the deer than us. We made a note of where it sounded like it was coming from to make sure we remembered not to go over that way and we moved on with our day. We decided to play hide and go seek and it was my brother's turn to hide first. I much preferred seeking and was much better at it than hiding. I went over by a large rock to start counting. We put the word Mississippi between the numbers to make the count to fifty go much slower, in order to give the other person a better chance at being able to hide further away. It made the game more fun and it would last longer too. He ran off to hide and I started counting with my hands covering my eyes. Right when I got to number twenty five I heard something moving around me. I thought it was my brother so I told him he better get a move on because I wasn't giving him extra time to hide. He didn't respond and I thought that was weird. I counted to thirty and then heard movement again and at that point I thought he was going to try and do something to scare me. I removed my hands from my face and opened my eyes, looking around to try and see where he was. I thought for sure he was going to jump out at me but he didn't. I finished counting to fifty and yelled the infamous "ready or not, here I come" phrase that we used to let the other person know we were done counting and about to start looking for them. As soon as I looked up, I saw something that immediately scared me.

There was a really tall man leaning against a nearby tree. The tree was about twenty feet in front of me and the man was very odd looking. He was leaning up against the tree with one arm and the other one was at his mouth. His face was round but not like a normal person's head and I remember immediately thinking of the moon. The color of his face was off a little bit as well because, while he was white, he was really, really pale white. He wasn't a regular caucasian's color. His eyes were black orbs and there didn't seem to be any white or other color to them. He had to have been ten feet tall or more and he was extremely thin, almost like that skeleton everyone loves so much from that animated Halloween movie that's also about Christmas. I believe his name is Jack. Anyway the guy had on a black suit with a white, short sleeved shirt, a black skinny tie and a black fedora- style hat. He had on shiny black shoes and I remember thinking they looked awfully fancy, and also they looked awfully expensive, for someone to be traipsing around in the woods with. I could see his extremely long, bony fingers and the sharp, yellowed fingernails on the one hand that was leaning on the tree. He was terrifying yet somehow I couldn't take my eyes off of him. He stood straight up, tipped his hat, and winked at me. Then he gestured for me to come to him with his long, bony pointer finger. He made the "come here" motion but I didn't want to approach him. I didn't approach him but mainly because I was too scared to move. I started looking all around for my brother but as I went to call out for him the man started walking, very slowly, towards me. He gestured with that same gross finger for me to be quiet and he shook his head as if he knew I was trying to find my brother. I stood there, stone still, completely unable to run or scream, as he walked towards me.

It seemed like I was watching him approach me for an eternity and before I knew what was happening, the bright blue and sunny sky was disappearing behind a mass of dark clouds. The sound of thunder boomed in the distance but I didn't see or hear any lightning. In fact, I couldn't hear anything else and it seemed like the forest was completely abandoned except for me and this strange man. Well, I somehow knew, deep down inside even then, that it was some sort of creature posing as a man. He wasn't doing a very good job but still there was nothing I could do. I stared straight into his coal black, soul-less eyes as he made his way towards me. Before I knew what was happening I peed myself and I didn't even have my wits about me enough to notice or try to do anything about it. The surrounding woods got more and more blurry with each step that he took towards me. I was so frightened and everything inside of me was screaming at me to run and get as far away from this man- from this thing- as humanly possible. But still, all I could do was stand there, helpless. The man finally made it to where he was only an inch or two in front of me and since he was that close, he seemed even taller. It was like he was fourteen feet tall or something, as I stood there, my little ten year old self looking up at him. His mouth was a thin red line, almost and his nose looked like a normal human's. He towered over me and started to lean down and as he did that, his eyes glowed and turned the colors of a blazing fire. They weren't black anymore but orange and red, black and even some blue. He stared down at me as he leaned in and he never seemed to even blink. The more I looked into his eyes the dizzier I became. Then he reached out his arms as though he were going to scoop me up in them. The skin on his arms looked much different from his face and even much different than the way his hands had looked when he was still standing against the tree. Whereas before he looked a sickly pale color, now his skin, all but his face, looked like it was made out of ash. It was gray and sort of peeling off or blowing away every time the wind blew.

I had the presence of mind, somehow to take a couple of steps back. That made him mad, I could tell by his eyebrows and the way his eyes blazed when I did it. He smiled at me as his hand touched my cheek and his teeth were razor sharp fangs, and they were covered in blood. The second I noticed that about his teeth, the moment I saw the blood on them, I could tell his mouth wasn't red at all but black and only looked red because of all the blood, meat and fur that was hanging and dripping off of it. He put his other hand up like he was going to touch my other cheek with his other hand. Something inside of me told me he wasn't going to touch my cheeks and that he was about to grab me by my face. That same thing, maybe it was intuition- even at that very young and tender age, told me that if he did that, I would die. I started to feel like I was going to pass out though and couldn't keep myself standing much longer. That's when I was brought out of my stupor by my brother calling my name. I heard a loud yell and saw that the creature had screamed as he shot backwards into the ether and disappeared as he flew away. He wasn't actually flying, mind you. It was almost like a gigantic gust of wind hit him in his skinny body and blew him backwards through the air at his chest and stomach area. I slumped to the ground and could feel myself falling. I woke up with my brother kneeling over me looking worried but relieved I had woken up. The sky was bright blue again and the clouds were fluffy and white. Everything seemed to be as it was before I had my encounter with the man.

He asked me if I was okay and I immediately tried to jump up and I asked him out loud where the man had gone. He looked very confused and said that we were the only two out there, as we always were. Something struck me right at that moment when the first thought that entered my head as a response to what my brother had just said and it was, "you've never been alone out here." I knew all at once that the creature was always there and that those woods were its home. I told my brother I thought the heat had gotten to me and I wanted to go home. He didn't argue and we packed up our things and walked back to our house. When we got home and it was nowhere near dark outside my mother asked what happened. She knew we wouldn't have come home for no reason but I told her what I had told my brother already, and that's that the heat had gotten the better of me. She came and felt my head and neck, deemed me as not having a fever and "fine" and I went to lay down in my bed. I was sick for almost an entire month with all different symptoms to the point where every time the doctor would be called and think he had it figured out, the symptoms would change and he would do more tests and decide it was something else. I can't even count how many different things I had been diagnosed with over the course of that month. I have come to think two things about that and I know that either one or the other is the truth. Either I had all of them, one after the other or I never had any of them, and it was something supernatural that had been plaguing me. It didn't really matter and within that month my parents thought I was going to die several times but one day I woke up with no symptoms of anything and I was my usual self again. Much to everyone's relief there were no long term or permanent effects of whatever it was that had been plaguing me.

Something that most people I tell the story find very odd is that the moment I was better I wanted to go into the woods and play. My brother was so excited and he immediately obliged me and my parents were so grateful I was feeling better that they didn't think to keep us out of the woods either. I didn't tell my mother or anyone what had actually happened until much later. My mother thinks it was a skin-walker and that my brother and I had somehow called it to us. She thought it was either our elaborate games that we would play all day and the energy they created in the air or the fact that our friends, even the ones who should have known better, often discussed skinwalkers with us and therefore put us at risk for one to visit. I'm not sure what it was that drew it there that day and like I said earlier I'm not even sure if that's what it was. I know it was always there, even after I felt better and from our first day back in the woods. It didn't scare me though and that in and of itself does scare me very much. I felt a connection to the creature, somehow and I can't even explain that either. It meant to kill me. It meant to devour my body, blood and bones and then collect my immortal soul for its hellish purposes. Yet, I still wasn't fearful. I haven't seen the entity again except in nightmares where I'm never sure if I'm sleeping or awake because most of the time it's there, in my bedroom or my home with me. Maybe it's always with me or maybe it always has been. I truly have no idea.

CHAPTER TWENTY

MY ENCOUNTER TOOK place when I was seventeen in the mid to late seventies. There was absolutely nothing to do back then, especially not for kids my age, and we had to get creative when it came time to have some fun. School had just let out and my best friend Jack and I were bored. My older brother Will and his buddy were going camping for the week at a nearby spot that not too many people knew about. They had invited some other people and it sounded like a really good time. My brother was twenty one, so not too much older than me and so when I asked if me and Jack could tag along, he said okay. My brother had bought his camper from my grandparents and while it definitely wasn't anything fancy, it was big enough to hold the four of us and a few more people as far as hanging out. It didn't really matter because it only slept two people so me, Jack and whoever else showed up were bringing individual tents. It was going to be an awesome week and we were all super excited. My parents were reluctant at first to let me go because they knew there would be drinking but eventually they relented and we were on our way. We stopped at a few stores to grab some food and supplies and headed off to start the hour-long drive it was going to take for us to get to the site where we wanted to set up our camp.

We got to the campsite on a Wednesday and everyone else was joining us that weekend on either Friday or Saturday. There was a small water source in the woods near the area where we were setting up and I call it that because I don't know what the proper name for it was. It wasn't a lake but it wasn't really a pond either, we just called it the swimming hole so that's what I'll refer to it as from here on out, if it comes up again. We got to the spot and took the only trail that was big enough to drive the camper through. We were listening to loud music the whole way there and just being like regular young people having fun at that time. There was nothing at all out of the ordinary or even the slightest bit unusual that would have led any one of us to think that we were walking into any sort of dangerous situation or that we were about to be confronted with pure evil. We pulled up when the sun was just about to set and so Jack and I got out and set up our tents while my brother and his friend gathered some wood and stuff to make a fire. There was beer there but Jack and I hadn't had any money so we didn't plan on drinking that much of the beer my brother and his friend purchased, if we drank any of it at all. My brother wasn't big on sharing his booze and I really didn't like the taste of the stuff anyway, I never have. I bring that up so you will know I was not drunk or under the influence of any mind altering substances, and neither was Jack, at the time of our encounter. It didn't take long for us to get set up and we put the radio on inside of the camper and just hung out by the fire. We talked about everything under the sun and by the time one o'clock rolled around, we were all ready for bed. We were planning on hiking to the swimming hole the next morning and it was going to take about a half hour. We didn't want to be too tired so we all laid down at the same time.

My brother and his friend slept in the camper and they went inside and within seconds all of the lights turned off. Jack and I flipped off our flashlights and the fire had already been put out. I know in a lot of the encounter stories I read or when I've spoken to other people about their experiences out in the wilderness, that there's a weird and unnatural silence that falls over everything right before something bad or terrifying happens. That wasn't the case for us and the woods were alive and buzzing with the usual nighttime sounds. I fell asleep almost immediately but was jolted awake by Jack shaking me. He looked panicked but at first I didn't understand what was going on and was annoyed he had woken me up. He was whispering and telling me that I had to get up. I sat up and he told me to listen carefully and be quiet. I rolled my eyes but after only a few seconds I heard what he was talking about. There was something very big moving around through the trees directly above where we were sleeping. I started to ask him what it was but he shushed me and shook his head no. We listened like that for another minute or two and it was constant movement. There was something in the trees above us, possibly moving from tree to tree and then back again, all in one big circle and whatever it was- it sounded huge!

I grabbed my flashlight and was going to shine it up there into the trees because at that point I thought it was just an extra big owl or something but the minute I did that Jack snatched it out of my hands. He was in an extreme state of panic and while I was definitely nervous, I wasn't as bad as he was and didn't really understand what he was so incredibly scared of. I asked him if he knew what it was and he said no and I asked him why we can't shine the light and just see and he replied he just thought that was a bad idea. Within five minutes of him waking me up there was suddenly the sounds of very loud clicking, also coming from the trees above our tents. I stood up and Jack followed suit. I was trying to see what was in the trees but at first I couldn't see anything but darkness. Then, I suddenly spotted it. There were several sets of what looked like bright red eyes staring down at us and whatever belonged to those eyes were also what was making the clicking sounds. It was no more than a second after I saw the eyes that something came crashing down from the trees on top of the camper. The camper was within inches from where Jack and I had set up our camp so it was clearly visible to us. My brother and his friend immediately started yelling curses from inside and one of them swung the door open. It was my brother and I could tell he was pissed at first but when he saw both of us standing there a look of confusion crossed his face for a second. It was like he was wondering how we were standing there in front of him because he surely thought one or both of us were what made the noise on top of the camper in an attempt to play a prank on him and his buddy. That look only lasted for a second though.

Before he had time to do anything and before the confused look even had time to settle into his features, a huge talon came down from the top of the camper and grabbed at him. I'm not going to lie, I screamed like a little girl. The animal or entity, I wasn't sure what we were dealing with yet, turned its head towards me when I screamed and opened its mouth. An extremely loud and grating squawking noise came out and it shook the ground we were standing on. My brother slammed the door shut and I could hear the lock click into place. Jack was too scared to do anything but stand there, stunned. We didn't know what to do and I heard my brother waking up his friend in the van with him. They were yelling and the creature started slamming its giant, taloned hands onto the windows. It was so huge that all it had to do was spread its arms out and one hand was on each side of the van. It was just open palm slapping the two windows. I heard my brother screaming so I took Jack's flashlight from him and shined the light right on the thing. It immediately stopped slamming the windows, looked at me and squawked again. Then more clicking noises started coming from the trees above us and I remembered that we were literally surrounded and there were more of that thing up in the trees. I didn't know exactly how many but I thought there were at least four.

While the creature stood there squawking I got to see most of the rest of it. Its skin was black and looked sort of like it was dripping with tar. It wasn't dripping though, that's just how the skin looked. It had extremely long arms that went down to almost the feet, which by the way were about four times the size of your average human man's foot. The nails on the gigantic hands were like talons and the nails on the huge toes were the same. The eyes were glowing, bright red but there was something else about its appearance that struck me as kind of odd. Its head was the same shape as a normal human being's. It didn't have horns or anything and its nose and mouth were like a regular human's nose. Its ears were almost like a human being's but a bit more sharp and pointy at the tops. I hadn't even seen the full extent of it yet because although it seemed like I was standing there and staring at this thing, taking in every detail that I could about what it looked like in order to try and determine what we were dealing with and the best course of action, for a very long time, it couldn't have been more than a minute or two at most. There was one part of its body it hadn't yet revealed and it was right about to.

It was hulking and extremely muscular, standing at about ten or eleven feet tall. It looked from me and Jack up to the trees at the others it had brought with it and it leaned back and squawked very loudly into the air. It then stood straight up again, turned to me and Jack, smiled and sprouted giant wings. The wings were almost magnificent. I mean, I was blown away by the sheer size of them. They had to have gone about two feet above his head and started right at the shoulder blades. They were the exact same color as the rest of its body which is why I think I didn't notice them right away. They had bright red veins running all the way through them and they almost looked moth eaten. What I mean by that is, there were several odd shaped holes in them and I knew instinctively that it had been in some pretty serious fights. It had to have been in order to attain that much damage. Its body, the closer I looked at it, also had the red veins running through it but they were a darker red and blended in more than the ones on the wings. Its eyes looked like the eyes of an animal and they weren't the same as humans have. They had crescent pupils and I remember that sticking out to me. Its eyes reminded me of a fish's eyes and that sent a shiver of terror through my body. So, it took me less than two minutes to take all of this in and come to all of the realizations I just explained and now it had turned to face me. I heard whooshing sounds coming from all around us followed by loud thumps on the ground. We were being surrounded. I knew without even having to look or see it that the others had come down from the trees. Jack and I made a beeline for the door of the camper and started banging on it. My brother opened it right away and pulled us inside. He slammed the door on the thing's hand.

It howled in pain and the others all let out loud squawks at the same time. It moved its hand and we were able to shut and lock the door. The camper immediately started rocking and the beast on top of it was once again banging on the windows with one hand on each side. The good thing was that the creatures weren't smart enough to know, or at least they didn't seem to be, that if they all stood on one side and pushed together they could tip us over and we would be done for. They were pushing from both sides, front and back. Jack was just staring at the one in front of the van. I think he went into some sort of shock or something. I yelled for my brother to get the keys and get us out of there but of course he couldn't find them. I tried honking the horn but that was a big mistake because the one that was standing in front of the van then leapt onto the front and started head butting the windshield. My brother found the keys and he started the van. The squawking was so loud and they all started shrieking too. I could tell they were in a panic and knew we were about to leave. Just as the van started up the one that was on the roof and trying to smash in the side windows succeeded in his mission and at the same time both of the windows were smashed in. The creature howled in pain as it had just put its hands through glass and probably had some pretty sick cuts at that point. It could definitely feel pain and I remember thinking too that we should have brought a gun. My brother took off like a bat out of hell, no pun intended, and while the one on the roof seemed like it must have been knocked off, the one on the windshield wouldn't budge. It was holding onto the sides of the van with all of its might. However, eventually, once we were almost out of the woods, it let go and stood perfectly straight up on the windshield, even as my brother drove. I knew what it was about to do before it even did it. I just said, "Oh no! This isn't good!"

I was right because it immediately let out its wings and shot backwards, hovering in the air in front of the truck. It was smiling. It looked like it had human teeth, albeit extremely yellowed and stained, somewhat crooked, but human nonetheless. It came at us like it was going to crash into the windshield and as it did my brother swerved and momentarily lost control of the van, almost sending us right off the side of the road and into a ditch or something. The next thing we knew it was on the roof. It hung over the side and tried to stick its head in through the broken window its buddy had just smashed out a few minutes ago. We were speeding down some remote, desolate back-roads and there was no one else around. When it tried sticking its head through it was licking its lips and groaning. I don't know what that was all about but it was almost like it was messing with us, like it knew we were terrified and was enjoying the fact that it was the cause. My brother's friend took the large boombox we had and smashed it in the face with it. It must've not been expecting that because it had a momentary look of surprise on its face as the radio was going towards it and it went flying off to the side of the road. Actually, it probably landed in the middle of the road because it had stuck its head through the window behind the driver's side. We heard it land with a thump and as we sped away we heard a very loud squawking noise and then, out of nowhere, a loud howl. That was the end of that and we sped off into the night and made our way home.

The whole way there we were all panicked and asking one another what the hell those things were. Of course, none of us had any answers. We all just went back to the house and parked the camper in the backyard. Me and Jack went up to my room and my brother and his friend went to his. My parents were a little concerned, especially because it was still the middle of the night and we had woken them up. My dad came down asking what the problem was but we told them our camp had been attacked by bears. He didn't really believe that but he let it go. I don't know what we encountered that night. The closest thing I could find to even a similar description is the mothman but that thing didn't behave like the mothman is said to. Also, there's never been a mothman sighting, as far as i can find- and trust me I've looked everywhere- in my home state where this all went down. I'm just grateful we got away. I talk to people about it all the time and so does my brother and his friend. Jack is still traumatized I think because he won't even go camping anymore and hasn't since that day. He won't go anywhere near the woods if he can help it and I guess I kind of don't blame him. I think something happened to him that night that he hasn't come clean about yet. He woke me up which means he was up before me so who knows what it could have done to him or what he could have seen. I've asked him about it many times but he says he just heard something in the trees and shook me awake. I'm not buying it though because he was terrified from the very second he woke me up and before we had even seen anything weird. I'll keep searching for answers and though I've been hiking, hunting and camping hundreds of times since then, including in that exact same spot, I've never seen those creatures again and honestly have no idea what they were.

CHAPTER TWENTY-ONE

I DIDN'T REALLY KNOW what to call this encounter because I'm still not really sure what it was that I witnessed on a cool summer evening back in 2008. I was fifteen years old and visiting some family who lived in a much more rural part of our state than we lived in. My grandparents own a farm and were having all of their kids, grandkids and kids-in-law over for the weekend. I can't remember what the holiday or occasion was but I remember being excited because I would get to hang out with my cousins. My mom was one of six kids and all of her siblings had between three and six children themselves, with the exception of her. She only had me and I had been adopted at birth. We got to my grandparent's house and all of us kids went down into the huge basement to set up sleeping bags for ourselves. It was so peaceful out on that farm and some of the best memories of my childhood had been made there. It was early in the evening, around eight o'clock when the adults decided to light the fire pit outside and us kids couldn't have been more excited about that either. We loved the land and being on the farm, despite some of us being creeped out by the surrounding woods. I'm not talking about a farm where there are crops or many animals but it was just a huge swath of wide open space with a large barn and it was surrounded by woods. We hung out outside and some of us older kids decided we wanted to sleep outside and camp in the yard that night. The younger kids were too scared so it was only going to be me, my fourteen year old cousin Beth and her sixteen year old brother Matt. Our parents didn't think it was a good idea but our grandparents helped us talk them into it and we excitedly went into the barn to grab our grandparents camping equipment. We didn't need much, just a few small tents, some flashlights and things like that. We only planned on being out there for one night and though the woods creeped us out a little bit, we figured we could always just go inside if things got weird or too scary. We set everything up very close to the tree line that separated the backyard and the woods just to make it seem like we were really camping in the woods and not in our grandparents backyard. Eventually everyone else went inside. They put the fire out and within an hour all of the lights in the house were off. They left the light that was on the back deck on for us, just in case we needed to go inside and use the bathroom or grab something to eat.

My cousins and I sat up and talked about things going on in our lives. We all lived so far from one another that we didn't see each other unless the family was getting together for some sort of holiday or special occasion and normally it was at my grandparent's house that those events were held. Eventually we were tired and it was almost one in the morning. Our cell phones didn't work out there but we wanted to take pictures and so we left them on and used them to tell the time as well. We had taken a bunch of photos and couldn't wait to show them off once we were back at school the following week. We all laid down and within minutes I heard Matt snoring and assumed Beth had fallen asleep as well. I kept hearing what sounded like something moving right next to my tent but behind some of the bushes and trees that were there. I peeked out of my tent but didn't see anything at first, despite hearing it non stop. Whatever it was seemed to be getting closer and closer as the seconds ticked by and eventually I whispered loudly to Beth, asking if she was awake. She didn't answer. I was getting nervous because in that area of the country, at that time of year and considering it was the middle of the night, it could have been any number of predatory animals that had come upon our makeshift camp.

I kept peeking out of the tent but couldn't see anything. I didn't want to shine my flashlight on it at first but finally, after like twenty minutes of constantly hearing whatever it was moving, I shone my flashlight out of my tent and into the trees. As soon as I sat up and did that I smelled a terrible smell that was like a dead animal or as I would come to find out later in life, the smell of a rotting corpse.

Within seconds of the smell hitting my nostrils Matt and Beth both peeked their heads out and asked me what the smell was. I shrugged but told them that I kept hearing something moving around in the woods beyond our tents, specifically near the back of my tent. They thought I was kidding but then realized it was obvious something or another was there because of the smell. It was rancid and unlike anything any one of us had smelled up until that point. Beth was gagging and finally we all just decided to give up for the night and go inside.We crawled out of our tents and started walking the fifty feet or so to the back deck and the back door. As we did so we heard a crashing sound coming from the barn which was located about fifty feet away as well but to our left. We all jumped and Matt immediately wanted to go and see what it was. I was reluctant and Beth was having no part of it. Matt called me a few choice words and while Beth made her way to the house, Matt and I turned on our flashlights and walked towards the barn. The same smell, but much stronger, was coming from out of there too. We tried to be quiet but didn't want to turn our lights off. As we approached and got closer to the barn we heard something akin to a human being grunting but also what sounded like the snorting of a pig. It was like both sounds were happening at the same time and it was unlike anything we had ever heard before. Matt and I pushed the barn door open and shined our lights inside. We immediately saw some sort of figure standing there, rummaging through my grandfather's things. Matt started cursing at whoever it was and it dropped whatever it had in its hands and turned around. It was about eight feet tall and had very pale skin. It looked like it was covered in long hair but not fur. It looked like cousin It from the Addams Family almost, as far as the hair went. The figure took a couple of steps towards us and we backed up a bit and Matt shone his light right onto the things face. It shrieked an inhuman sound and stumbled backwards, but not before we got a look at its face.

It was the very tall, extremely hairy body of a human being but with the face of a bear. Its eyes looked somewhat human but black and the face and head were the only parts of it that weren't covered in long, black hair. It put its arm up across its face for a minute and then, looking extremely angry, started walking towards us very quickly. It seemed almost inhumanly fast and Matt and I turned and took off running. As we did we saw my uncle and my grandpa come running out the back door and through the yard towards us. We looked over and the thing was moving faster than anything we had ever seen before along the treeline and towards the front of the house. It ran on all fours and sort of hopped every few minutes. It was bouncing off the trees and just doing crazy, supernatural things. We were terrified and stunned. We just stood there. My uncle and grandpa followed it to the front and we followed behind them. The entity was very obviously hiding behind a tree and we could see its eyes reflecting back at us from the four flashlights that were now aimed at it. My uncle raised his shotgun and the thing came charging, on its legs and just like a human would, out from behind the tree and right at him. My uncle pulled the trigger but nothing happened and it was almost like whatever that thing was, it knew nothing was going to happen. My grandfather raised his shotgun and at that moment the thing's attention turned to him. His gun also didn't work. My uncle hit the thing directly in its face with the butt of his gun and told us all to run. We did as we were told and the thing retreated back into the woods on the other side of the street.

Matt and I were completely panicked and kept asking our uncle and grandfather what it was that we had just witnessed. They told us they didn't know and they were visibly shaken. They told us to be quiet and go up to the guest room and go to bed. We did as we were told and didn't ask anymore questions. Matt and I woke up at around ten in the morning with our grandpa and uncle, the one who was outside the night before and had hit the animal, coming into our room and telling us we were to tell everyone we saw a bear. They said they didn't want to scare anyone else or any of the other, smaller kids. They promised to let us know if they ever figured out what it was. The day progressed fairly normally after that but I noticed we didn't stay outside after the sun went down. Also, there were never any outsiders or people who weren't family ever invited to the family get togethers but that night at around eight in the evening, as all the younger kids and some of the adults were getting ready for bed, a man none of us had ever met showed up. My grandfather answered the door and introduced the guy by simply saying, "everyone this is Doug and he's staying the night in the second guest bedroom." The kids all thought it was weird but the adults didn't question it at all. Eventually Matt and I made our way to the other guest room, the one we had slept in the night before. There were two beds in there and we were still so freaked out we didn't want to be in the basement with everyone else. We fell asleep around one in the morning. We woke up to someone yelling in some language we never heard before and we ran to the window to look out front. We didn't know what was going on but once again we saw that same strange and horrific creature storming towards my one uncle and my grandfather who were both holding guns on it. It didn't seem to care at all about the guns and they didn't slow it down any. Well, not until one of them actually did go off and a bullet whizzed right past its face. Doug continuously yelled in some weird language without pausing the whole time and the creature retreated back behind the tree again. My grandfather shot again and it sounded like he landed his target on the creature. It howled in pain like an injured wolf or dog or something. It then limped out from behind the tree on all fours like it was going to go towards them. Doug either threw something at it or sprayed it with something and it flinched, howled again and took off, much slower than we had ever seen it move up to that point, back into the woods.

We had a very hard time sleeping that night and couldn't wait until the morning to ask our grandpa and uncle what was going on and what all of that had been about. We got up and had something to eat around eleven o'clock and Doug, my grandfather and my one uncle who had been involved in all of this were noticeably missing. I asked everyone where they were but everyone told me it wasn't my concern and Matt received the same responses. We stayed for the next few days without incident and my grandfather and uncle returned eventually. They never said where they had gone and when Matt and I asked them about what we had seen from the window the night before they left, they said we weren't supposed to have seen that and that we needed to stop asking questions. No one ever mentioned it again and as an adult I've tried to ask several members of my family, including asking my grandfather and that uncle again, but no one will talk about it. The thing was like something out of your worst nightmares and could only have come from the deepest bowels of hell itself. I've tried to research it on the internet but never could find a single thing that even came close, even when scouring stories of people's personal encounters. It's so odd and no one ever talks about it either. My grandparents still live on that same farm and we still have the same get togethers but Matt and I seem to be the only ones willing to mention it and every time we do we are immediately told to be quiet lest we scare the little kids and those in the family who didn't witness it. It's all very bizarre and my wife thinks Matt and I made it all up to try and scare her. She's been to the farm and we've brought it up but when she is there or when Matt's wife is present, everyone acts like they're foolish for believing in such nonsense as that story we tell all the time. It's very frustrating and I don't plan on stopping until I get to the bottom of it all. I have no clue how I'm gonna do that but I know one day, or so I hope anyway, one of the adults will talk and give Matt and I some answers and some closure. We never saw or heard anything about that guy Doug again either and though all of mine, Beth's and Matt's photos, taken with our cell phones that first night came out perfectly, none of them that were aimed at the barn took and ended up being black with blurs of gray throughout them.

CHAPTER TWENTY-TWO

MY FRIEND and I had just finished having dinner and were on our way back to her house. As I stepped out of the car, a strange moaning sound caught my attention. It seemed to be emanating from behind her home. The sound repeated every 10-20 seconds, growing louder with each occurrence. It had a peculiar quality, similar to a cow's moo but without the initial grunt, just a prolonged and amplified "ooo" sound. The mournful tone of the calls sent a chill down my spine.

Curiosity got the better of me, and I decided to investigate. I walked out onto the back porch, hoping to spot the source of the sound. However, I found no cows or other livestock in the vicinity, only vast soybean fields stretching into the distance. To my right, there was a stand of trees, accompanied by several houses. The trees seemed to form a triangular shape, following the angles of the properties, and extended until they reached the farm fields. As the moaning sound grew nearer, the dogs in the neighboring houses began barking fiercely, only to retreat and hide shortly after. The whole situation was extremely eerie and puzzling.

Eventually, the moaning sound reached the edge of the trees and abruptly ceased. Bewildered, I turned to my friend and asked what that could possibly be. Her response sent shivers down my spine. She casually mentioned, "Oh, that's the Troll." According to the locals, this creature was known to inhabit the area beyond the farm fields and occasionally ventured close to the homes. Just as she finished speaking, I caught a glimpse of a grayish blur darting from the stand of trees and disappearing behind a hill directly in front of us. The trees were approximately 300 feet away to the northwest, while the hill was roughly 200 feet away to the west. The blur moved swiftly, with its body low to the ground and arms pumping in parallel. I could only see its legs, as the head was either tucked down or held parallel to the ground, concealed from view. A sense of unease washed over me, and I felt an urgent need to retreat indoors. My friend mentioned that the "troll" had been known to peer into people's windows on occasion.

Refusing to tempt fate, I resisted the urge to look back outside. After about 15 minutes had passed, I began hearing a commotion from the outside. When I finally mustered the courage to take a look, I was greeted with a scene of chaos. The lawn furniture, situated roughly 150 feet from the back door, had been flung around in a haphazard manner. It appeared as though someone had thrown a massive temper tantrum. While nothing had been propelled a superhuman distance, it was evident that mere toppling over wouldn't account for the scattered and disarrayed state of the furniture. Sensing the danger, my friend warned me against going out, emphasizing that it wasn't safe. I decided to heed her advice.

I stayed indoors for another hour, but neither saw nor heard anything else out of the ordinary. Eventually, I made the decision to return home, eager to leave behind the unsettling encounters of that evening. The memory of the moaning sound, the enigmatic blur, and the tumultuous aftermath continued to haunt me, leaving me with an unshakable sense of intrigue and trepidation.

CHAPTER TWENTY-THREE

MY FRIENDS and I liked nothing more than to go archery at my father's property. It was a vast area that had everything to offer in terms of expansive meadows and dense forest. During the hunting season, we met there for several days to replenish our meat supplies and to talk about the past year. It had become a tradition. Something we all needed by the end of the summer.

We always camped in an abandoned barn that was close to the hunting hut my grandfather had built. It was a fantastic afternoon as we boys had decided to go out for a quick hike to enjoy the beautiful nature. Our route led us past an old railroad track before we left it and slowly walked into the dense woods. Gentle rolling hills and bottoms surrounded us, and we knew there was a small lake in the distance where we could stop for a quick break and a skinny dip. After we climbed a steep hill, we paused momentarily and enjoyed the view when something caught my eye. I noticed something black moving quickly through the woods, and it was out of sight in seconds. I was a bit irritated since bears and wolfs were not at home in these woods. Also, the next farm was many miles away. A fact that made the hunting grounds so much more compelling. On returning to camp, I asked my mates if they had seen anything strange or weird. I was not sure if I just had imagined the strange fleeing thing. Neither of them had seen anything but were curious why I had asked. I gave them a short explanation about what I had seen and changed the topic. I didn't want to provide them with grounds to tease me. Later that evening, back at the barn, we had dinner and laid down fast to sleep. We planned to get up early the next day to start our first attempt at hunting some deer. It was a chilly night, and we lay close to keep warm. We all had trouble falling asleep because we were more than excited about how the next day would go. So we started making animal noises. One of my friends tried an owl, then another a hare cry of fear. All three fell into the game. We had a lot of fun and tried to push each other to make new noises. We were sitting giggling like little boys in our mattresses when we suddenly heard something crack in front of the house that didn't sound like a fox.

We stopped and listened. Maybe I had seen a bear after all, which was now attracted by our noise. We quickly grabbed our bow and arrow and kept an eye on the gate, which was wide open for a good bit. in the distance, we could see hills and trees lit by the light from our campfire burning in the barn.

The woods had become dead silent. Then we heard it, a deep roar that almost sounded like a moan. We all looked at each other in shock, with one of my friends pulling out his smartphone and starting to record the audio. My other friend, who was particularly good with low notes, did the raven's cry again and we both stared and listened with bated breath. The throaty roar sounded again. It almost sounded like the creature was looking for the injured animal, but we couldn't assign the noise to any species.

I didn't believe what we just heard. Again, my friend made the look, and again, the deep, questioning roar sounded from afar. But this time, it sounded a little closer. The noise was so loud that it became scary and scary. We drew closer together, weapons at the ready, staring out the open gate into the darkness. The hair on the back of my neck and arms was standing straight up, and goosebumps had come up all over me.

We all trembled slightly as if we couldn't swallow what we had just heard. We lay close together, weapons at the ready. Sleep was out of the question now. Almost breathlessly, we stared out of our hut and hoped that we hadn't looked up at some animal that was looking for a new home in this region.

The next day we all got up. Nobody had slept, and nobody felt safe enough to go hunting. So we spent the day in our barn chatting and scanning the surrounding woods to see if a beast would pounce on us if we weren't careful.

It was only a short time before we decided to pack our things to get home quickly. We wanted to get this over with as soon as possible. Preferably after dark. Who knew what was lurking in the woods lately? We had hardly packed our things when we sat in the truck and raced up the path to the interstate like possessed. I kept staring into the woods, expecting an animal with a dark feel and large claws to pounce on us.

We were hardly at home when we told our wives and children the story. They thought we were all crazy and tore their mouths with theories about what it could have been. It only stopped when my friend pulled out his cell phone and played the audio recording from the night before. They just looked at us in shock and closed their mouths.

Since that day, we only go into the woods for small day trips, and we still have a shotgun with us. Better safe than sorry.

We had heard the call of the strange animal a few more times over the years. Yet far away, as the creature wanted to tell us, it deliberately stayed away from us.

We were very grateful for that because none of us had the need to discover a new species that might still be dangerous. These days I am used to the possibility of a strange animal squatter.

CHAPTER TWENTY-FOUR

I SAT in my living room in front of the TV, trying to beat the heat that had been suffocating me all day. The air conditioning was on full blast, but that didn't seem to be enough. I was about to fall asleep when I suddenly heard a strange noise coming from my garden. I went into my kitchen to peer into the back yard and see if raccoons were messing around my trash bins. But I saw nothing. Annoyed, I sat back on my couch and closed my eyes when I heard another rustling and bustling from the garden. Why couldn't animals stay in their woods? We had that issue every summer, and the mess the little creatures left behind was more than annoying at times. I remember now thinking the sounds were louder than the coons would make so I began to wonder if it was a larger animal, but what? Then it got even louder, I started to feel uncomfortable. I exited my couch, walked to my window, and entered the darkness. That's where I saw it.

In the middle of my garden stood a large, long-furred creature whose eyes shone in the darkness. I couldn't believe what I saw. Was that some kind of wild animal that had wandered into my yard?

I stood frozen, not sure what to do. The creature began moving closer to my window, and I could see it had long, sharp claws. My heart was pounding in my chest as I backed away from the window, trying to find something to defend myself with. I was unprepared for a stranger to come to my property to rummage through my belongings. But while I pressed myself against the wall next to the window, still trembling, I watched the oval back of the head of the thing, which slowly took each individual pot in its hand. What was that creature? I asked myself, trying to get my body to calm down. I had started shaking and sweating even more than I did already. The figure hadn't even spotted me. And when it did, it seemed to ignore me completely. It now growled quietly to itself as it looked around and glanced at the second box.

The creature wandered past my window, heading directly to the container where I kept my older flowerpots. The figure bent over the box and began rummaging around in it. It kept making growling noises and disapproving huffs.

It was a curious sight, with its wide blue eyes and deep brown fur, but its gigantic hands really caught my attention. I took more steps from the window as the chest was right under the window where the giant was digging. At first, I was curious to know if the figure was dangerous or friendly. But as it murmured and growled softly, I couldn't help but feel sorry for it. I slowly walked back towards the widow and watched the clawed fingers gently move my flowerpots from one end of the container to the other.

As I got closer, the creature seemed to sense my presence and turned to face me. His eyes widened in surprise and fear, but I calmed it down with a gentle smile. The creature slowly relaxed, and I could see its curiosity taking over. Stiff like a pole, I stood in front of it while it looked away and continued its hunt after whatever it was looking for.

With big round eyes and a curious expression, it continued to rummage around in my box before turning away with what seemed to me a frustrated huff and looking at the small cluster of pots and flower boxes that lay next to the chest. Again, it seemed interested in examining the pots and boxes as if searching for a particular item. I watched in fascination as the long fingers gently set the Kramnik to one side, and the vast feet silently ran across the floor as they took a look at my entire collection. I collected flowerpots in all colors, sizes, and shapes for many years.

The frustration could be seen and heard more and more because it started stamping its foot with a throaty growl. The big hands soon became fists, and the gaze that had been curious like a child's had now narrowed with anger and disapproval.

My heart started pounding again. Would it break in my house if it didn't find what it was looking for? Would it attack me? I wasn't sure if it saw me or not. The hairy creature was just snarling in rage when it suddenly stopped and put its head to the side in silence.

I watched as the creature waddled over to a little flowerpot I had placed on the ground. It looked at the pot with great interest, tilting its head to one side as it examined it closely. I couldn't help but smile at the adorable sight. This figure was so broadly built and obviously had so much strength in its tall body, but slowly it bent down and gingerly picked up the fine china to examine it more closely. It turned the pot back and forth, let the light fall on the colorful painting, and snorted contentedly before it sat up and looked around.

So, the figure hadn't discovered me. I carefully hid behind the curtain and peered motionlessly out of the window.

The creature started walking away with it. I was a bit scared initially, but I quickly realized it didn't harm my property. In fact, it took a liking to the little pot.

I stared after it for a very long time. Then I remembered what old Betty had said when I briefly saw her in the supermarket. She had told me at length that several flowerpots had been stolen from her. Although she hadn't seen anyone on her property, one or the other pot that she had prepared for planting flowers had gone away in the last few days.

Could this gigantic figure be the thief?

CHAPTER TWENTY-FIVE

I HAD BEEN WORKING as a psychologist in Chicago for years, and the stress of my job was starting to take its toll on me. I needed a break from the constant pressure and the long hours, so I decided to take a week off and go fishing. I packed up my gear and headed out to a remote lake. The drive was long, but it was worth it when I finally arrived at the cabin I had rented for the week. It was a small, rustic place, but it was exactly what I needed - a quiet place to relax and unwind.

The first few days were perfect. I spent my time fishing on the lake, reading books, and taking long walks in the woods. I felt like I was finally able to breathe again after months of stress and anxiety.

But on the fourth day, something changed. I woke up feeling restless and irritable. My mind was racing with thoughts of work and all of the problems that my patients were facing. I tried to shake it off and focus on the fishing, but it didn't work.

As the day went on, my mood grew darker. I found myself snapping at other fishermen who came too close to my spot on the lake. I even threw my fishing rod into the water in frustration when I couldn't catch anything. That night, I sat alone in my cabin, feeling more stressed out than ever before. It was then that I realized that I couldn't just run away from my problems. They would follow me wherever I went.

The next day, I thought about packing up my things and headed back to Chicago. I thought I would give myself one last chance to relax and stay a few more days. I felt a sense of calm wash over me. It was as if the act of leaving had given me the perspective that I needed.

I knew that when I returned to work, things would still be stressful, but I felt like I was better equipped to handle it if I just took one more day to take a break. I started taking more breaks throughout the day to clear my mind.

My clients ranged from hardened gangsters to housewives who were struggling to find happiness in their lives. Dealing with such heavy emotional burdens every day took a toll on me, and I knew I needed a break. Woodford County was the perfect place to fish and just forget about all one's trouble. It was a small, quiet town located a few hours away from Chicago, and I had heard that the fishing in the area was great. As I drove through the countryside, I felt my stress slowly begin to fade away. The quiet beauty of the fields and forests around me was mesmerizing. After a few hours, I finally arrived at the cabin I had rented.

I spent my last days exploring the surrounding area. The next morning, I woke up early and headed out to the lake. The water was calm, and the sun was beginning to shine. For the first time in a long time, I felt completely at peace. As I cast my line into the water, I began to realize how much I had been neglecting myself. I had always been the one to help others, but I had forgotten how to take care of myself. Being out in nature, alone with my thoughts, was exactly what I needed.

I spent the next few days fishing and exploring the area. I met some locals who showed me their favorite fishing spots and told me stories about the town's history. I even caught a few fish along the way. I felt rejuvenated and ready to face the challenges waiting for me back in the city. I knew I couldn't stay in Woodford County forever, but I promised myself that I would take more breaks like this in the future. Sometimes, the best way to help others is by taking care of yourself first.

As I sat by the lake, enjoying the peacefulness of the surroundings, I noticed something strange in the woods. At first, I thought it was just a deer or some other animal, but as it got closer, I realized that it was something else entirely. It was a figure that seemed to be walking on two legs, but it was covered in fur and had a long snout like a wolf. I had heard stories about skin walkers before, but I never thought I would actually see one.

I froze in fear as the creature approached me. It stopped just a few feet away and stared at me with its glowing yellow eyes. I could feel its breath on my face and the hairs on the back of my neck stood up. I didn't know what to do. Should I run? Should I try to fight it off? But before I could make a decision, the skin walker turned and ran back into the woods.

I sat there for a few minutes, trying to catch my breath and process what had just happened. Eventually, I gathered my things and headed back to my cabin. That night, I couldn't sleep. Every time I closed my eyes, I saw the glowing eyes of the skin walker staring back at me. I knew that this wasn't something that I could just ignore. The next day, I decided to do some research on skin walkers. I talked to some of the locals and read up on Native American folklore. What I discovered was both fascinating and terrifying.

Skin walkers were said to be witches or sorcerers who had the ability to transform into animals. They were believed to be evil and could bring harm to those who crossed their path. I knew that I had to be careful from now on. The woods were no longer a place of peace and relaxation for me. They were now a place of danger and uncertainty. Despite the fear that I felt after encountering the skin walker, I couldn't shake the feeling that I needed to investigate further. I knew that it was dangerous, but I felt like I had to know more about this creature.

The next day, I set out into the woods with my camera and a sense of trepidation. As I walked deeper into the forest, I felt like I was being watched. Every rustle of leaves or snap of a twig made me jump. But eventually, I came across a clearing where I saw something that made my blood run cold. There were several figures in the clearing, all of them covered in fur and with glowing eyes.

I realized that these were not just skin walkers, but a whole pack of them. And they were all staring at me. I tried to back away slowly, but one of the skin walkers started to approach me. It was then that I knew that I had made a mistake. I should have never come here alone. I turned and ran as fast as I could, my heart pounding in my chest. The skin walker chased after me, its snarls and growls echoing through the woods.

Finally, I reached my cabin and slammed the door shut behind me. For the rest of the night, I sat there in silence, listening for any sign of the skin walkers outside. The next day, I packed up my things and left Woodford County for good. It was clear to me now that some things were better left unknown.

As I drove back to Chicago, I couldn't help but wonder what would have happened if I had stayed in that clearing just a few moments longer. Would I have been able to escape? Or would the skin walkers have caught me? One thing was for sure - I would never forget my encounter with those terrifying creatures in the woods.

After returning to Chicago, my life was never the same. The memory of the skin walkers haunted me, and I found it hard to shake the feeling that I was being watched. I tried to go back to my normal routine, but I found it difficult to concentrate on anything. I would often find myself staring off into space, lost in thought about what I had seen in the woods. I tried to talk to people about my experience, but most of them just dismissed it as a figment of my imagination. They didn't understand how real and terrifying it had been for me.

Eventually, I decided that I needed to do something to help me move on. I started going to therapy and talking about my experience with a professional. It was a slow process, but eventually, I started to feel like myself again. I also started writing about my experience. At first, it was just for myself - a way to process what had happened. But as I continued to write, I realized that there might be others out there who had experienced something similar. I started sharing my story online, and to my surprise, I received an outpouring of support from people who had gone through similar experiences. It was comforting to know that I wasn't alone.

Over time, my life started to return to normal. The memory of the skin walkers still lingered in the back of my mind, but it no longer controlled me. Instead, it had become a part of who I was - a reminder that there are some things in this world that we may never fully understand.

CHAPTER TWENTY-SIX

GROWING UP IN RURAL APPALACHIA, I was immersed in a world of superstitions and eerie legends. These tales were mostly concocted by parents, aiming to instill fear in their children, ensuring they wouldn't wander off into the treacherous woods. Over time, these stories became woven into the fabric of our community, passed down from one generation to the next. While I now recognize their fictional nature, as an adult, I appreciate the underlying wisdom and cautionary advice they held.

For instance, we were always warned never to respond if something called our name in the woods. And if we ever heard whistling outside our homes at night, it was believed to be a foreboding sign that the devil himself was lurking nearby. Of course, these cautionary tales carried real-world implications. If a stranger were to call out to you in the woods or if eerie whistling permeated the nighttime air, it was only natural to feel fear, especially as a child. Although I never experienced such supernatural occurrences during my time in the mountains, the scariest incident of my life unfolded in the arid landscapes of New Mexico.

My early life was marked by loss. Losing my mother at a young age was a devastating blow, and when I was twenty, my father also passed away, leaving me with only my brother as immediate family. Though he didn't leave behind much, my father bequeathed his house to my brother, and I received just enough money to purchase two acres of land and a decent used camper. My boyfriend, now my husband, longed to return home and be closer to his mother, so we embarked on a plan to build our own house eventually. At the time, it felt like a thrilling adventure—an opportunity to immerse ourselves in the desert landscape. Our chosen plot was a dusty, off-the-grid location, nestled amidst other barren lots, devoid of electricity or water connections. Such remote land was still relatively affordable, as the inconvenience and cost of establishing a comfortable life in that area deterred most people. We had to rely on hauling water from my in-laws' house and powering our needs with a generator. Given that my husband worked night shifts as a security guard, I often found myself alone in that camper, night after night.

Initially, the isolation and quietude felt mundane and safe. After all, I had Zeus, my stalwart companion—a massive and protective Rottweiler—who would have defended us with unwavering loyalty. However, as events unfolded, I came to realize that my assumptions of safety were sorely misplaced. That fateful night started like any other. I had been outside, stargazing while indulging in a moment of relaxation, smoking a bowl. Eventually, I returned to the camper to prepare for bed. Just as I undressed and settled into bed, a haunting whistling sound pierced the air, accompanied by a sudden shift in the camper's structure, as if a gust of wind had forcefully slammed against it. Initially, I dismissed it, attributing the commotion to the harsh desert winds, which occasionally grew quite fierce. However, Zeus's reaction shattered any semblance of calm within me. The normally composed and gentle dog transformed into a growling, snarling beast, his gaze fixated on the doorway, ready to defend us at any cost. Fear gripped me, as the realization dawned that a flimsy aluminum door was the only barrier between myself and whatever ominous presence lurked in the darkness outside. Memories of my granddad's warnings flooded my mind—his stories of eerie whistling at night. Though I generally lacked religious inclinations, in that moment, the inexplicable unease was undeniably palpable.

The whistling itself possessed an unnatural, high-pitched quality, resembling the wind but distinctly different—a mournful melody that chilled me to the bone. What perplexed me was how the sound managed to penetrate through the relentless hum of the generator, engulfing the surroundings. I mustered the courage to consider peering outside, but my body refused to obey, paralyzed with fear. Zeus's behavior escalated into a frenzy of barks directed at the wall, as if he were possessed. Suddenly, everything ceased, as if the tension in the air had dissipated into thin air. Zeus, now equally shaken, couldn't settle down until I finally relented and let him outside—an hour that dragged on for what felt like an eternity. He cautiously sniffed the back of the camper, near the bedroom, before reluctantly turning away and returning indoors. However, I remained too petrified to venture outside myself.

To make matters worse, cell service was spotty in that remote location, and with only a flip phone in hand, I lacked a reliable means of escape or calling for help. The following morning, when I recounted the harrowing experience to my husband, he was convinced that it had been potential traffickers or worse attempting to breach our defenses. He theorized that Zeus's ferocity had scared them off. While his explanation held some plausibility, it didn't feel quite right. After all, no actual intrusion had occurred. It would have been a peculiar group of kidnappers indeed, content with standing outside, whistling into the night. That's when my husband mentioned rumors of a small cult residing in the area. Perhaps, he postulated, they were attempting to frighten us away. The thought sent shivers down my spine, for if the rumors held any truth, there was a lingering possibility of their return. Nevertheless, in the comforting embrace of daylight, alongside my husband, the notion seemed slightly absurd. Yet, the memory of Zeus's focused sniffing around the back of the camper compelled us to investigate further.

As we explored the sandy, soft dirt surrounding our abode, it became evident that numerous footprints, of varying sizes and shapes, had trampled the ground near the small window overlooking our bed. Strangely, there were no tracks leading away from the camper in any other direction—just those outside the window and a solitary set encircling the rear wall, coinciding precisely with the spot where Zeus had erupted into a frenzy of barks. Suddenly, the notion of an eccentric cult didn't seem far-fetched or trivial. And so, living in constant fear of harassment or worse, I found myself taking refuge with my mother-in-law for over a year. Although we still possess that plot of land, we eventually acquired a property in town, prioritizing our peace of mind and security. The desert's allure and beauty remain, enticing me to embark on hikes with fellow adventurers. However, I've come to recognize that the arid landscapes have an uncanny ability to attract individuals of unsound mindsets.

CHAPTER TWENTY-SEVEN

I NEVER THOUGHT I'd be a single mom. When my husband left me for a young woman who worked at a coffee shop, I was devastated. I felt like my whole world had fallen apart.

But then, I looked down at the tiny bundle in my arms - my newborn child - and I knew that I had to be strong for them. I moved back in with my mom for a while, but I knew that I couldn't stay there forever.

So, I started working two jobs - one during the day and one at night. It was exhausting, but it was the only way that I could save up enough money to move out on my own.

Finally, after months of hard work and sacrifice, I was able to rent a small apartment for me and my baby. It wasn't much, but it was ours.

My mom retired around the same time, and she offered to watch the baby for me while I worked. It was such a relief to know that my child was being taken care of by someone who loved them as much as I did.

Slowly but surely, my life started to come together. I found a better-paying job, and even started dating again. It wasn't always easy, but I knew that as long as I had my child and my family by my side, I could get through anything.

Looking back now, it's hard to believe how far we've come. From the depths of despair to a place of hope and happiness - it's been quite a journey. But through it all, one thing has remained constant: the love that I have for my child, and the strength that they give me every single day.

I was exhausted. Being a single mom was tough, and I had been working two jobs just to make ends meet. I had finally managed to get a few hours of sleep, and I was on my way to pick up my baby from my mom's house. But first, I needed to stop and get gas. It was quarter past 9:00 pm when I saw the very lone station sitting off Route 9. Its only purpose is a stop off between stations. Everything typically closes down here around eight and being such a small town there is no need for places to stay open any later.

I grew up in a small town, surrounded by rolling hills and fields of wildflowers. It was the kind of place where everyone knew everyone else, and you couldn't walk down the street without running into someone you knew. As a child, I spent my days exploring the woods behind my house, riding my bike down country roads, and swimming in the local creek. I went to the same school from kindergarten through high school, and my classmates became like family to me. Now that I have a newborn daughter of my own, I want her to experience the same kind of childhood that I did. I want her to grow up surrounded by nature, with the freedom to explore and play without fear.

I want her to know the joy of catching fireflies on a warm summer night, or picking apples from a tree in the fall. I want her to feel the rush of jumping into a cold creek on a hot day, or the thrill of sledding down a snowy hill in winter. But more than anything, I want her to feel the sense of community that comes from growing up in a small town. I want her to know that she is loved and supported by her neighbors and friends, just as I was. I knew that in a city there was more to do and more jobs but there was nothing quite like this. Although as I looked at my dwindling gage and the spooky gas station with blacker than black shadows, I weighed my options again. I felt childish for being afraid of the dark but right now I had no other choice.

I pulled into a self-serve gas station, feeling groggy and disoriented. As I got out of my car, I noticed two children standing nearby.

They were both around 10 years old, with pale skin and black eyes that seemed to stare right through me. They smelt like something old and rotting. I smelt so acidic I could taste it in the back of my throat. Their clothing looked older and a little dusty. But it was a weird dusty. Not like, 'I've been playing outside- don't judge me' dirty but 'I've been crawling in places you don't want to know about' dirty. I was a kid once and yes, there is a difference.

At first, I didn't think anything of it. Maybe they were just waiting for their parents or something. But then, as I started pumping gas, they approached me. "Excuse me," one of them said. "Can we come with you?" I felt a chill run down my spine. Something about their voices was off, almost robotic.

"No," I said firmly. "I'm sorry, but I can't take you with me." They didn't seem to take no for an answer and kept insisting that they needed to come with me. But then my baby started crying from inside the car. It was a loud and panicked cry that made my heart race. I quickly finished pumping gas and got back into my car. That's when they stepped in front of me, blocking my way.

"Please," one of them said again. "We need to come with you."

I didn't know what to do. My mind was racing as I tried to figure out how to get out of there without hurting them or myself. But then, something inside me snapped. I put the car in reverse and made a U-turn, driving away as fast as I could. As I looked back in the rearview mirror, I saw the children standing there, watching me go. The eyes somehow got blacker and more malicious. Their black eyes seemed to follow me, even as I drove further and further away. I saw their faces turn more skeletal and hallow out as I drove away. I deeply questioned my own sanity at this point.

I didn't stop until I was miles away from that gas station. My heart was pounding in my chest, and my hands were shaking on the steering wheel. I had never felt so scared in my life. When I finally got to my mom's house, I told her everything that had happened. She listened patiently, but I could tell she didn't believe me. "It was probably just some kids playing a prank," she said. "Don't worry about it." How could she explain the eyes and the smell and the thinning of their faces. I had no idea about what I had seen. My mom offered to take the baby overnight. She claimed that because I hadn't been resting that it could have been my eyes playing tricks on me.

But I couldn't shake the feeling that something was off about those children. Their black eyes had been so unsettling, and their insistence on coming with me had been so strange. For weeks after that incident, I couldn't sleep properly. Every time I closed my eyes, I saw those black eyes staring back at me. It wasn't until I started researching online that I discovered the legend of the black-eyed children.

According to the legend, these children are supernatural beings who appear to people in moments of weakness or vulnerability. They try to gain entry into people's homes or cars, and those who let them in often suffer terrible consequences. I shuddered at the thought of what could have happened if I had let those children come with me. But I was grateful that I had trusted my instincts and gotten out of there as fast as I could.

From that day on, I made sure to always be alert and aware of my surroundings. And whenever I saw a pair of black eyes staring back at me, I knew to stay far away. Over the years, I've heard many stories about encounters with black-eyed children. Some people claim to have let them into their homes, only to regret it later when strange things started happening. Others say that they've seen them lurking outside their windows or walking down deserted streets late at night.

Despite the many stories, there's still no concrete evidence that black-eyed children actually exist. Some people believe that they're just an urban legend, while others swear that they've had real-life encounters with them. For me, the experience was all too real. Even now, years later, I still get chills thinking about those black eyes staring back at me. And while I hope that I never encounter them again, I know that I'll always be on the lookout, just in case. And I will never go to that gas station again.

CHAPTER TWENTY-EIGHT

MY ENCOUNTER HAPPENED in 1997 in the middle of nowhere, Oklahoma. My family didn't have a lot of money so most of our vacations were spent camping in the woods. I was thirteen at the time and I didn't mind because I loved the woods. That year it was just going to be me and my parents because my older brother had gone off to college the year earlier. It was the end of August and the last fun thing I was going to get to do before school started up again. I had spent my life in the woods, basically, and I was familiar with all of the animals in the region. I knew all the normal sounds of nature and I had also gotten to know what wasn't normal. I was a bit of a nerd and loved facts and research so every time before we would go camping, I would bone up so to speak on my knowledge of the area we were going to. It wasn't always the same place though it was always in Oklahoma. That year we were going to some new spot my dad had heard about from a friend at work. It was much further off grid so to speak than any of the other places we had gone and I was happy about that. I was always expected to try and "make friends" with other kids who were camping or otherwise around the areas where we went and I was awkward. I was looking forward to it and we left on a Friday with nothing but ten whole days of being out in the middle of nowhere with no one else around but us. Even the hour-long car ride there flew by because of how excited we all were.

We had to park our car in some trees and hike out to the campsite. We hiked for about forty minutes before my dad found a spot he thought was acceptable and there was a large water source nearby for fishing and swimming. I should have been relaxed and feeling good by the time we got there. Despite how tired I was though it was like I couldn't let my guard down. From the time we entered those woods right after we had parked the car, I could not relax and enjoy myself. My beautiful and outgoing mother had the voice of an angel but instead of singing with her along the trails like I usually did, I kept feeling the need to look over my shoulder and keep watch on what was going on around us. It must have been evident in my lack of responses when my parents were talking to me because eventually, once we started setting up the tents, my dad asked if everything was okay. I smiled and told him I was fine but I felt anything but. There was a very eerie feeling in those woods but because my parents hadn't seemed to notice, I tried my best to shake it off as just my overactive and juvenile imagination. I couldn't shake it though and by the time night time rolled around and it was dark outside, I found myself sweating and my body shaking, and it had nothing to do with the chill in the air or the heat blazing off of the giant fire my dad had going. We roasted some s'mores and told our usual scary stories but no matter how hard I tried, I just couldn't relax. I kept not only feeling like we were being watched but I kept hearing little rustling noises coming from the surrounding woods. Now, normally those sounds wouldn't have been unusual but it sounded like it was something much bigger than your average animal that would be running around that close to human beings and their campfire. It sounded big, whatever it was and I felt a malevolence in the air that I couldn't possibly explain and there-fore didn't try to. Eventually and much to my relief my parents were tired and decided to call it a night. We were going to get up early and go fishing and swimming and I was hoping that by that time, and after a good night's sleep, I would feel refreshed and much better. I knew if I couldn't shake those feelings that it was going to be an extremely long trip for me.

That night I had a hard time falling asleep and kept feeling like there was something right outside of my tent. I didn't hear anything other than the rustling that I had been hearing all night. This sounded much closer and whatever it was sounded larger than I had initially thought. You know the sound a snake makes as its body slithers through some thick brush? That's what I kept hearing except it sounded like a human sized snake. I don't even know really if that's what I was hearing or if it's something I kept imagining in my head. I tossed and turned and eventually I looked at my watch and it was one in the morning, three hours after we had all initially laid down. I was in a small, single tent and my parents were in a double right opposite of me. They were mere feet away but I felt like I was all by myself all of a sudden. I started feeling claustrophobic in my tent and needed to get out and get some fresh air. I went to the bathroom in some nearby trees and as I turned to walk back to my tent I thought I felt something brush up against my bare ankles. I only had on my boxer shorts and a pair of slip on sandals. I jumped and looked down immediately but didn't see anything except some tall grass and laughed at myself for being such a scaredy cat. However, as soon as I took one step, something did reach out from that bush and overgrown grass and grab me. It wrapped around my ankle and yanked me down to the ground before I had even been able to register what was happening. I turned around while I was on the ground because I had fallen on my stomach. I was sitting up then, still with whatever that thing was wrapped around my one ankle and trying to drag me away with it. To where, I still don't know but I do know what I saw, it's burned into my memories and something I see in my nightmares still to this very day.

It was a hand, but not a human one. The fingers were at least twice the size of a human being's and it was a dark gray color. The fingers were gnarled and looked a little disjointed but the grip it had on my leg was strong and no matter how much I wiggled and squirmed, I couldn't get it to let me go. The knuckles were huge and all I could see that was connected to the hideous looking hand was a bit of an arm. The arm was extremely thin, again it looked too thin to belong to a human being, and it was the same color gray. The skin looked leathery and spotted, and like it was peeling off in clumps in some places. The rest of the arm and whatever was attached to it seemed to be hiding inside of the thick and overgrown brush underneath the tree. I took all of that information into my brain in a matter of mere seconds and then I started to scream for my mom and dad. I kicked and pulled but couldn't get it to release its grip on me. Finally I took my other foot and started smashing my heel down on top of the hand and arm and I heard a very loud, very angry sounding hissing noise as it released me and slowly disappeared back into the trees. I jumped up and ran back inside of my tent. Then it finally dawned on me that my parents hadn't come running when I was screaming for them and flashes of them having already been carried away were running through my mind. I got out of my tent and peeked into the sky pocket of theirs. They were sound asleep and somehow didn't hear me screaming at the top of my lungs and fighting that strange thing off, even though they were only about twenty feet away from where it had all just happened. I ran back into my tent and sat there with my knees up to my chest for I don't even know how long. I was shaking and crying and eventually I looked down to see where the thing had grabbed me. I couldn't believe what I was seeing.

It looked like I had been burned. There were finger marks there, and in fact it looked just as if someone had grabbed me and wrapped their fingers around my ankle but the skin was raw and bubbling as though I had gotten some sort of chemical burn or something. It didn't hurt and I even touched it with one of my fingers but it still didn't feel like anything was wrong at all. I felt like, at least if for nothing else, they would serve as proof I wasn't lying when I told my parents about it all at breakfast. I was still very scared but the adrenaline and fear must have been too much because I fell asleep rather quickly after that. I didn't get up to go to the bathroom or for any other reason again that night and in fact I slept right through until I smelled bacon cooking. I opened my eyes and the sun was brightly shining. I could hear my mom and dad giggling about something as they made breakfast and was reluctant immediately to tell them about what had happened to me the night before. They hadn't been getting along with each other for a really long time and it seemed like they were finally enjoying each other again. I somehow knew how important that was, even at that young age, and decided not to tell them. I took one more look at my ankle but of course, there was nothing there. I was so well rested at that point I had begun to think I had merely imagined the whole thing the night before and knew for sure at that point that I wouldn't be telling my parents about it. I might tell them once we were home, but I wasn't going to bring it up to them and ruin their good time together. I put on the biggest smile I could and got out of my tent to have some breakfast.

I said good morning to my parents in my most cheerful voice and we ate and laughed together. Eventually it was time to go to the stream but I still felt like we were being intently watched the whole time and no matter what I did or how hard I tried, I simply couldn't shake off that feeling. I tried not to let it show and neither one of my parents even seemed to notice. I tried to forget about it and just have fun and for the most part it worked. About an hour into our swim my father realized he had forgotten something we needed back at our camp and my mom wanted to walk back with him. There was no one else around and probably wasn't for miles and they asked me if I would be okay by myself for a little while because they were going to go, grab the item and come right back. I must've looked nervous because my mom offered to stay with me but before I could answer my father decided I would be fine and told me not to move and they'd be right back. I smiled and said okay and watched them disappear into the woods. The second they were out of my sight the entire forest went quiet and something happened that I don't understand to this day. There was no sound at all.

I couldn't even hear the sounds of the water splashing as I moved around in it and even tried jumping into the water to see if it would make a sound but it didn't. There was a slight humming in the air but it wasn't so distinctive as to be overwhelming. I froze in place as I watched some of the bushes surrounding the water part, the whole while thinking something was going to come walking out and grab me again. That didn't happen but I was far too nervous to stay in the water and had decided to just sit down on a rock and wait for my parents to get back. I started to swim towards the rocks so I could pull myself out and that's when something grabbed my ankle and started pulling me down into the water. I instantly panicked and every time I would get myself back up to the surface, I would barely be able to catch my breath. Remember there was no sound, including that of my own splashing so I knew that my screams weren't going to be heard by anyone. I could hear myself screaming but it felt far off, like someone screaming through a shield a mile away. Finally I was able to break free and got out of the water as fast as I could. I ran away from it and that's when I finally saw the whole creature that belonged to the arm and hand that had grabbed me the night before and that I was absolutely sure had just tried to pull me under the water and draw me right there too. It came slithering out of the water and it was looking right at me.

It looked almost like a human being but it was that dark gray color and looked like it had leather and beat up skin. It was peeling and chunks were falling off as it slithered slowly on its stomach and made its way towards me. I could do nothing but stand there and watch as I slowly kept backing away from it. It had two legs, two feet, two arms and two hands with those abnormally long fingers. The nails were long, yellowed and sharp which was something I hadn't noticed the night before. It had one long arm and hand reaching out to me. Its mouth was wide open and it had no teeth. In fact its mouth was extremely and unnaturally wide open and I just kept thinking of a snake the whole time. It had gigantic black eyes, similar to what we commonly attribute to the gray aliens nowadays but it was not an extraterrestrial, at least not fully, and it wasn't fully human either. It kept staring at me as it came towards me and my trance was only broken when from behind me I felt someone grab me and at the same time heard my mother scream in horror. My dad yelled that we needed to get out of there and we all turned and ran. We heard an inhuman scream coming from behind us and as we ran back to our camp I noticed the sounds were back and the woods were alive again. My mother kept asking my father what that was but my dad just kept repeating that we had to get out of there immediately. We didn't argue. We packed our things as fast as we possibly could and ran most of the way back to where the car was parked.

On the way home my mother and I kept trying to discuss what we had all seen but my father started getting mad and told us to cut it out and stop discussing it before we somehow called it to us and it ended up at our house. We were quiet but from that day on my mother and I often discussed it in private, never having actually found out what it was that we saw that day. I eventually told her about how it had grabbed me the night before and she was just horrified. I still don't know what it was but I've never been able to swim in anything where I can't see the bottom and still to this day won't even go near any other water. I've since been camping and hiking and have spent a lot of time in the woods. That's mainly due to the fact that my dad was so stubborn he refused to accept what we had seen and kept forcing us back into the woods. We never went back to that particular spot again and I've never seen the creature again except in my nightmares.

CHAPTER TWENTY-NINE

I DIDN'T KNOW what to call my encounter because what we experienced that night can be called by so many different names. So, I'll let you all decide what it was. I was eighteen years old and enjoying my first few months of not being under my parents guardianship anymore (even though I still lived in their house, but that's an eighteen year old's logic, right) and decided to go on an overnight camping trip with my girlfriend in an area near where we lived at the time in New Mexico that was a good and cheap place to be able to do so. I picked her up and we went to the place but immediately noticed it was really deserted. There were hardly any other cars there when we pulled in and when I asked the security guy at the gate about it he leaned in and whispered something about the skinwalkers. I was a little freaked out and thought it was weird that an employee of the camping site would be talking about skinwalkers, especially in an area like where we were, and thought it was no wonder no one was there. Everyone in New Mexico knows you don't talk about skinwalkers, you're not even supposed to think about them and most of the time it isn't just the natives who feel that way. It's sort of just ingrained in the culture. My girlfriend's family lived on a reservation though and she was really put off by it and even a bit angry. I tried to laugh it off because I wanted to make sure it didn't ruin our first overnight together. We hadn't been allowed to stay at one another's houses overnight because we were both minors. She turned eighteen six months before I did and my birthday was three months before we had this encounter. Neither of our parents would let us spend nights together at our houses, but at least we were able to go out for the night without them saying anything. I wanted the night to be special and I made sure to try and keep her mind off of the fact that the idiot at the gate had mentioned the unmentionable. I could tell she was scared but we did our best to distract ourselves.

After we ate and set up our little camp we sat by the fire and just talked about life. Normally we would have told scary stories but I could tell she was too freaked out. She believed that even someone just mentioning skinwalkers to or around you would make you susceptible to them either coming for you or overtaking you altogether. Instead, I put the fire out after a while and we just laid there and looked at the sky. The stars were bright all over the sky and the moon was round and full. It was like heaven, being there on that cool night in the middle of nowhere and all alone. I had been camping my whole life but my girlfriend had only been a few times and like I said this was our first time camping together. I had a large tent that would sleep two people and eventually we decided to call it a night. She seemed to be in better spirits and feeling better and for that I was really glad. There had been an area with actual public restrooms back by the main entrance but we had hiked out pretty far and weren't anywhere near them at that point. It would have taken at least ten minutes to get there and ten to get back and in the dark that could be really dangerous. We had been using the nearby woods and that's where she went in order to use it one last time before bed. I had to go too and so we each went on opposite sides of the camp in order to give each other privacy. As I was finishing up I heard what sounded like a whooshing noise coming from where my girlfriend was but when I called out and asked her if she was okay, I didn't get a response. It sounded to me like something being dragged through the trees. I didn't think much of it at the time and just went back to the tent to wait for her. I could hear her rustling around in the bushes and knew she would be right back. I didn't want to turn off the flashlight until she was done and had made it back safely.

I saw her flashlight go out by where she was standing and shined my light in that direction, figuring it would help her in case she needed to see. I thought her battery had died or something. She immediately whispered loudly for me to turn it off, I listened to her and flicked it off. My girlfriend walked slowly back to the camp and I noticed she was only wearing a t-shirt and her underwear. That was odd to me because we were both brought up in very religious households and we were both very strong in our faith. While we definitely struggled with temptation, we had the talk before and both decided we wanted to wait until marriage. I know that sounds insane nowadays but it was the seventies and it wasn't that unheard of back then, not really and not where we were from anyway. I asked her what she was doing and she just said she was hot. Her voice sounded a little deeper than normal and I asked her again if she was okay. She said she was, again in the deeper, more raspy sounding voice, and I just shrugged it off.

We laid down next to each other and cuddled and she asked me if I would rub her back. I said okay and started to rub it for her. The sounds she was making were animalistic and I didn't understand what was happening. I told her she was making me feel uneasy and asked her one more time if she was okay. She turned to look at me and her green eyes were almost blazing as she told me she was fine and that I needed to quit asking her. I was immediately taken aback because my girlfriend's eyes, though hazel, were normally bright blue. I was a little nervous but then just thought it had been my imagination and that my adrenaline was pumping extra because of the way she was dressed and how she had sounded. Then, she sat up and did something that scared the crap out of me. Well, it wasn't what she did, it was more what she said that scared me. She sat up and hugged her knees into her chest, covering both with the t-shirt, and started talking about how she couldn't believe the security guard had brought up the Yenaldooshi. Now, Yenaldooshi is not what the guy had said and that's a word specific to one of the local tribes, not the one her family was affiliated with, but it's another word for skinwalker. I knew there was no way in hell she was going to ever bring that up and even on the small chance that she did bring it up she would have used something else to describe it. She wouldn't have used the word skinwalker, let alone another, more specific name for it. I backed away as I sat there. Her blue eyes being bright green, the way she was (un)dressed, how she had asked me to touch her intimately by rubbing her bare back under her shirt and the way her voice changed; it made me start to think that something supernatural was happening but my hormones were making it so that i couldn't put my finger on what it was.

I asked her to pray with me. She hesitated and looked away but she tried to sound nonchalant when she said she would. I grabbed her hand and hung my head in prayer. I started praying out loud and she was suddenly shaking like a leaf. I looked over at her as she yanked her hand away from mine and she looked really pissed off. She looked almost feral. She asked me, again in that deep and strange voice, if we could just go to sleep. I said okay but knew there was something supernatural at play. I wasn't as familiar with the specific legends and lore like she was but I knew a lot about the devil and how he works. I can't lie, I was terrified and had a feeling something wasn't right with my girlfriend. With how suspicious I was though it never occurred to me the scope of what was actually happening until a little later on. My girlfriend once again cuddled up against me and I put my arm around her and started praying again. I was only praying in my head but she jumped up and told me, in a very low and almost inhuman voice, to cut it out. I asked her what she was talking about and then I heard someone calling my name from the nearby woods beyond the tent. My girlfriend seemed to perk up at this and a look of rage and hatred crossed her face. She did the most terrifying and insane thing next. She crawled out of the tent and, while still on all fours, proceeded to run into the woods. I jumped up and yelled after her but the response came from behind me. It was my girlfriend. I was instantly terrified and backed away from her.

I yelled for her to get away from me and started making the sign of the cross. She laughed but when she saw that I was serious she became immediately concerned. She was wearing pajama shorts and a t-shirt. She was no longer in her underwear. I told her to let me see her eyes and she did, they were blue, just like I had remembered them. Her voice sounded perfectly normal too and there wasn't a feral look about her anymore. I started sobbing. She immediately clung to me but I flinched and told her I didn't know if I could trust her. She told me to tell her what had happened and I did. She was scared then too. She explained she had gotten her monthlies and had no choice but to walk in the dark to the restrooms in order to get something to take care of it. I'm trying to keep this as decent as possible so I do apologize but it's a crucial part to the story. She had yelled to me that she was just going to run there fast and come right back and she did say that she wondered why I had only followed her halfway then had turned and left her there, wordlessly nonetheless. She thought she had done something to anger me. I was so confused and honestly, so was she. We both knew what had really happened but we were both too terrified to mention it. We laid there in the tent all night, both of us hardly sleeping, and once the sun rose we packed up our things and got out of there. So much for our romantic weekend together. On the way out the a-hole security guard was there and asked us why we were leaving so soon and it took all of my strength not to punch him in the face. I leaned in and whispered in his ear one word, "yenaldooshi." He pulled back from me, his eyes wide with fear, as I sped off back in the direction towards my house.

My girlfriend and I were both really upset and worried that somehow the creature would be able to get to us while we were at home too. We believed that the guard had somehow brought or led it to us, probably completely by accident, when he mentioned it to us when we first got there. We also believe that at first the entity, the skin-walker, was planning on attacking my girlfriend while she was in the bathroom area or at least on her way there but she said she saw other people both there at the place and also on her way to it. The scent of her blood probably didn't help. It must have noticed she wouldn't be alone and so it changed its mind and transformed or shifted into her image in order to try and seduce me. It wanted me to break my sacred vows and therefore give up my promise to and possibly my faith in my religion and everything she and I believed in. Of course we had no way of knowing and weren't even able to discuss it further because we were both so afraid of bringing it back to us again. I spoke to my mother about it and she convinced me, as my girlfriend's family did for her when it came to me, that our relationship was tainted because of the encounter and that we should stop seeing each other immediately. I know it's hard for a lot of people to understand unless you are as enmeshed in superstition and legends and even religion as she and I were back then. We remained friends and we even attended each other's weddings.

Aside from when I talked about it with my mother that one time, I never told anyone about this. I highly doubt my girlfriend did either because she was actually forced to go and see one of the healers on the reservation once she finally admitted to her family what had happened. I wonder if this is going to bring it back to me somehow. That girl and I are still friends and we are both still very reluctant to speak about it, either with one another or with anyone else. However, lately I've been having nightmares of that night and I see her being attacked and ripped apart and also, I see it in the tent with me. I see it under the guise of being my sweet girlfriend and ripping me apart as well. I don't know what it all means and maybe I'll bring it up the next time I see her. I've since gone through a lot with my religious beliefs but at the end of the day I think that only made the two of us and our chaste relationship more tempting. I don't for one minute believe that religion was the bottom line at all. That jerk at the guard station brought it up and then it smelled her blood. Who knows how many other people who were there that night, before or since, camping or otherwise in those same exact woods who have encountered that same type of evil. It takes many different forms and werewolves are actually the most common sight around those parts to this day. They always have been. Anyway, that's my story and it still baffles, amazes and terrifies me all at once. I'm not sure what to do with all of that. I have other encounters with other entities in the woods I'm going to write out now as well. Thanks for letting me get this out there and I hope it doesn't bring the evil to anyone reading this. Maybe it's best they don't read it while out in the woods anywhere, although, if you're reading this now, it's probably too late. Sorry.

CHAPTER THIRTY

I AM STILL TRYING to process what I saw back in 1973 when I was only twelve years old. It has haunted me my entire life and I never really talked about it until recently and I only did so then because someone else in my family, someone who grew up in the same house as me and who didn't want me to name them in this story, also admitted to having seen the same thing. He said he saw it right around the same time that I did, and he also claims to have seen it more than once. I can't even imagine having to go through all that terror more than one time. He tries to make a joke about it, but I can see it terrified him, just as it does me. I was twelve years old and would often hang out or go on walks through the woods next door to our house. There wasn't a lot to do, and I was often bored. I had several siblings, but I was the only one who seemed to have "caught the nature bug" as my mom called it. She would say that when referring to my love of being in the woods. I would go out there alone for hours on end and get lost in my own little, made-up worlds. I would hike, fish and camp and I never felt scared or threatened at all, by anything. I had come across several animals that would be considered predatory to humans, but I learned quickly that if I left them alone, they would hardly even notice I was there. It was a day that was perfectly normal in every other way.

I asked my mom to pack me lunch and I was going to go fishing at the creek for a few hours. I grabbed my food and shoved it into my backpack, along with other snacks and some waters and I set off onto the trail that led to my favorite fishing spot.

I walked for about forty minutes to get to where I wanted to be, and I took my time setting everything up. I noticed at about twenty minutes into my walk that the forest seemed much quieter than usual that day, but it didn't dawn on me that there was really anything wrong with that or that it was anything I should be concerned about. I whistled a little tune as I walked and eventually ended up right where I wanted to be. I had a snack and threw in my line. I heard what sounded like someone whimpering or crying and as unlikely as it was that there was someone else out there at all, let alone that they were out there crying and whimpering, I decided to stick my fishing pole in the ground and after securing it, I went off to investigate the strange noises. I was a precocious and curious kid and again, I didn't even consider that I might have a reason to be worried or fearful. I left the main trail I had walked in on, and I was then wandering through the tall weeds and grass in the denser parts of the forest. I didn't usually leave the trail except when I would come to one of the few clearings in those woods and where I was exploring at that point was somewhere I hadn't ever been and was very unfamiliar with. I heard the whimpering, but it sounded like whoever it was kept moving deeper and deeper into the woods because every time I would think I had caught up to it, it would start to sound further off. I was getting tired of looking around and turned to start making my way back. I originally thought it had been a person who was upset or in some sort of trouble, but I was only a kid and didn't care enough to continue walking through the dense woods to offer them help or otherwise see what was going on. I wanted to fish.

I made my way back to where I had left all my stuff but as soon as I sat down, I heard what sounded like someone walking up behind me. They sounded very close and almost like they were trying to sneak up on me. I turned around as quickly as I could but there was no one there. At the time I saw a deer take off running into the woods where I had just come from and so I thought that maybe my mind had been playing tricks on me and I thought the deer had been closer than it was and that's what I had been hearing. I still had the whimpering in the back of my mind, but I didn't really know what to do about it, if there even was anything that I could do, and I decided that once I went home, I would let my dad know what I thought that I had heard out there. I walked to a large rock and laid my lunch out on top of it. I had a couple of sandwiches, an iced tea and a bag of some chips or another. I was starving and happy to be eating. However, after only taking one bite of my food, I heard someone creeping up on me again. I turned quickly and didn't see anything but that's when I started to smell something awful.

It smelled like my sister's hair would smell when she left it in her curling iron for too long. It smelled exactly like burning hair but with something else too. It was horrible and I started to gag on the food I was still trying to chew at that point. I got up and walked around some of the nearby trees but didn't see anything. I heard the whimpering again and it sounded at that point like it was coming from behind me, which was where I had just left my food. It flashed through my mind for a minute that one of my brothers must have been playing some sort of prank on me and I turned around, prepared to be angry and ready for a fight. However, when I turned around, it wasn't my brother that was standing there. It looked like a person, a grown man by the height of him and the clothes he was wearing. He didn't look dressed for the weather, even though I could only see the back of him as he stood there, seemingly looking down at my lunch that was still spread out on that large rock. He looked about six feet tall even though he was a little hunched over and he had on a light brown, long trench coat. I yelled over and asked if I could help him with something and he froze for a minute. He looked like he was just about to reach down and grab my food. I yelled for him to get away from my stuff and that's when he turned around and I realized something was seriously wrong.

His face looked completely burned and it looked like it didn't have any skin left. It was like something out of a horror movie. I watched them all the time and what was happening to me looked like a scene right out of a cheesy and bad one. The "man" looked almost like a fake. It was like he was some sort of prop or puppet and he moved very jerkily too. He opened the burnt and skeletal mouth and started whimpering. There was smoke coming off his body, through his jacket and I realized instantly that's what I had been smelling. The man turned around, grabbed one of my sandwiches and slammed it on the ground in front of him. I don't know how I knew he was angry because his skeleton face was expressionless, but I knew that with absolute certainty. Before I could react or respond in any way to what he had just done to my lunch, he opened his mouth and started screaming at the top of his lungs. I didn't waste any time in getting the hell out of there. I ran as fast as I could back to my house. As I was running, I heard laughter that sounded almost maniacal and then I heard loud whimpering, which was exactly what I had been hearing the whole time I had been out there almost. It had been that man- that thing- all along. I often wonder if it was trying to lure me deeper into the woods for whatever evil and obviously nefarious purpose it had in mind. I tried to stop thinking about it and to just focus on getting home.

I was so terrified, and my heart was pounding. My chest and lungs burned from running and not being able to breath and I even tripped a few times but there never seemed to be anyone behind me. I never saw that thing again but like I said I recently found out I wasn't the only one who encountered it. The other person in my family had seen it in our backyard and wouldn't leave the house for the rest of the summer. I didn't know why he wasn't leaving the house at the time, but it never dawned on me that maybe he was scared or that he had seen that grotesque, burning, whimpering evil that I had encountered as well. I got home and, in a panic, told my mother what I had just seen. She was convinced I had fallen asleep out there in the heat and that I had been having a very vivid nightmare. I often wonder, if she would have believed me from the beginning, if I would have maybe talked about it with other people sooner. I really don't know because it wasn't cool to have these types of experiences back then and I already didn't have a lot of friends as it was. When my dad got home later that night, he was furious with me that I had left not only my fishing pole but all my gear out there and tried to make me go and retrieve it alone in the dark. I absolutely refused and though I was terrified of getting a whooping

THE MEGA MONSTER BOOK

from my dad and his trusty leather belt, I was more scared of that creature lurking in the woods. I was grounded for two weeks and not allowed to leave the house, but I was perfectly okay with that at that point in time. My dad and brother went to retrieve my stuff the next day. Mostly everything was there but all my food and water and all my bait were gone. My dad chalked it up to an animal having come across it, but I knew better.

I still don't really know what I saw that day except to say that it was downright evil. It could have been a demon or a spirit or even a man who had somehow been killed around those woods at some point in time. I've also come to learn that maybe he had been buried in those woods and was what people in the paranormal community call "an earthbound spirit" but I don't know enough about those things to be sure. I thought that maybe my getting this all out would help me to heal and I've since started investigating old deaths in that same area. My parents moved us away from that house and those woods when I was sixteen and I never went back there. However, in the interest of finding some peace or maybe just making some sense of it all, if that's possible, I might go back there soon and walk through those woods. I want to go and fish in the same spot and see if maybe that thing is still there and if maybe it'll approach me as an adult the way it did to terrify me as a little kid. Who knows? I'll keep you posted if I decide to eventually do that and if I have another encounter.

167

CHAPTER THIRTY-ONE

ABOUT TWENTY YEARS ago I went out for a hike in some nearby woods to my house with a co-worker and friend. I still don't know what we saw but I know that whatever it was, it was evil. I also don't think we were meant to see it. I believe wholeheartedly that things exist beyond our sight in this world and sometimes we end up catching a glimpse of some of it, for better or for worse. The encounter left me traumatized and desperately searching for answers ever since. I have woods all over where I live and there are even dense woods surrounding my house. It's not uncommon for me to go for hikes all along the trails in my backyard either but ever since this encounter I have been very scared when I am out there and have lost my sense of peace when in mother nature. My friend and I met at my house at around noon, and I drove a few miles to a popular and usually very busy hiking spot. The very first thing we noticed was that this normally very busy spot was completely deserted. It was odd right from the door, but we didn't think too much into it and honestly, we just thought that it was our lucky day. We both grabbed our backpacks, which each had some snacks and a couple bottles of water and set out on a trail that was easy to navigate. We were both very familiar with most of the trails in that area and in fact we had gone on hikes there before both together and separately.

We hiked for about twenty minutes or so before stopping to look out over an overlook which had a great view of the town, we lived in. We were just chatting about work and other things happening in our lives when we heard what sounded like someone running up behind us. We both stopped talking and turned but when we did, we didn't see anyone. There also didn't seem to be anyone around us at all and so we just continued talking until after five minutes we continued up the trail. We were going to hike all the way to the top, have a snack and then hike back down and go home. The whole thing normally took us about two hours due to frequent stops because we liked to take our time and take in the scenery and all the beautiful nature that surrounded us up there. The whole time we were walking, and we walked very slowly, we kept hearing what sounded like feet running on the trail right behind us but when we would turn and look there would be nothing and no one there every time. It started to get to the point where we felt like we were being watched, followed, and generally unsafe. Neither one of us had cell phone service anywhere in the area and we both left our phones in the car. We talked a little as we walked about how creeped out, we were despite the beauty of our surroundings and the fact that there seemed to be no obvious reason for it. We both felt watched and like we were being stalked or something. It was eerie. Eventually we were at the top of the trail but neither one of us was talking because by that point we were downright scared and didn't know how to explain it. We both just understood that's what the other was feeling at the time.

I heard running again and once again I turned around. My friend hadn't heard it I guess because she continued to just stare straight ahead, looking over not only our town but neighboring towns as well. The view was much vaster and more expansive from the very top than it was where we had previously stopped. There was a long, stone wall that was only about waist high that we were both sitting on at the time, but we had our backs to the trails and woods. There was a very steep drop off underneath where we were, but it never bothered us before and the noises we kept hearing were coming from behind us. Finally, I couldn't take it anymore and needed to go and investigate a little bit and see if maybe we were hearing some sort of animal or some other explanation that was perfectly normal for what we had been hearing the whole time. My friend didn't want to join me and urged me to hurry up because she just felt so scared and confused for seemingly no reason that she didn't even want to be out there anymore at that point. I didn't blame her, but I knew it would keep bothering me if I didn't at least try to get an explanation for what we were hearing. I wandered further into the woods and looked around. There were all the normal sounds and animals around and everything looked, sounded, and seemed very normal. Just another regular day; that's how it seemed at first anyway.

I heard something crunching some leaves to the side of me and when I turned and looked, I saw a beautiful buck with gigantic antlers. I gasped because I had never seen one so large before but also, I hadn't ever known them to get so close to human beings. I tried to stay as still as possible and was kicking myself for not bringing my cell phone with me to at least take some pictures. The buck seemed obviously unaware of my presence which I immediately thought was very strange. They are usually very alert, and I always thought they had excellent hearing. I stared at it and it eventually turned and stared right back at me. I got the chills all throughout my body the second it looked me in the eyes. Something inside of my head just kept repeating that it was all wrong. However, it seemed perfectly normal and even regular to me. That's when I looked a little closer and couldn't believe what I was seeing. The buck stared directly at me the whole time and now I think that's because it was enjoying my reaction to seeing what it really was underneath that disguise. It wasn't a buck at all, and it made perfect sense because a buck never would have just ambled out to stand five feet away from a human in broad daylight and it wouldn't have taken five minutes for it to notice me either. Its fur was the normal color but when I looked closer at the rest of it, I was scared. Its front legs didn't end with a hoof like a buck's should have and it looked more like a bird's claw, with three long and pointy "fingers" that bordered on being talons there instead. The moment I noticed the strange way its legs ended it turned and walked away from me. It walked very slowly as if taking its sweet time to enjoy either the peaceful serenity that surrounded us or my reaction to it.

I went and got my friend and had to almost force her to come with me and look. It was to the point I thought that maybe the heat had gotten to me, and I was hallucinating things. Not only the way the front "feet" looked but also, I felt like there was something more behind the eyes than a simple buck. It felt evil somehow and in a way I still can't explain. I really felt like it was enjoying itself and reveling in my terrified reaction to it. My friend begrudgingly followed me into the little clearing where I had seen the animal or whatever it was, and it was still facing away from us, but it was close enough that she could see what I was talking about with its hooves. She gasped and wanted to immediately run out of there, but I stopped her. She kept yelling, "Oh my God! What is that?! What is that?!" The buck didn't even flinch at the sound of her screaming in terror, and it simply stopped and looked like it had started to graze. Then, it lifted its head and turned to face us again. When I first saw it, it looked perfectly normal as far as the body and the face were concerned. Now its face was entirely flat and had no nose to speak of. It had a mouth, but it was a mouth that belonged on a flat face, and I swear when we both started to scream at the sight of it its face morphed and we saw the evil that was underneath for just a split second. The animal or whatever it was underneath the disguise, turned back to the ground, seemingly to graze again, and then it turned and ran right past us and into the woods beyond where we were then standing. We both jumped backwards because it came so close but that's when the oddest part of the whole thing, well almost the oddest, happened. As it ran past us it looked like a perfectly normal, albeit a very large, buck. Even the hooves were as they should have been.

I know a lot of people will question whether my friend and I were drinking or under the influence of other substances, but I assure you we were not. We don't even drink socially, and we are both still sure of what we saw even though five years have passed. Neither one of us ever told anyone about it but our husbands and they didn't believe us. They thought the heat had gotten to us and that we were just seeing things through a distorted and over tired lens. That wasn't the case, and it was so offensive, their implications, and left us feeling so horrible that even our own husbands didn't believe us, that we let the issue go. My husband went so far as to mock us and will often bring up the "secretly demonic, massive buck with eagle claws and a flat face" but I don't find it funny at all. I believe what we saw that day was some sort of forest or nature spirit either during transformation or something evil that was feeding off of our terror and shock. We had felt strangely all day and the place where we were on that hike was one we both loved and felt perfectly safe and comfortable in up until that point. There was no real reason we should have been feeling so scared from the very beginning. I haven't been able to put it all together yet but I also think that thing had something to do with why no one else was out there that day. I had never been there before when it was totally empty and had been going there my whole life and I have since been back and still haven't found it completely deserted a single time.

There was something very evil underneath and behind its eyes and of that I am certain. I always thought nature spirits were kind and helpful but ever since that day I have been almost incessantly researching them and I have come to find that, in most cases, they are the exact opposite. I decided to write about my encounter because I wonder if there are people out there who have seen either the exact same thing as we did that day or even something similar. I have found a handful of encounters people have had, while out in the woods, with strange looking animals that they felt were something else and while it terrifies me every single time, it also brings me and my friend comfort because we don't feel so alone in our experience. I'm going to keep searching for different types of encounters and don't plan on giving up until I find a decent explanation to what I saw. When I do, I will show my husband and let my friend show it to hers so we can get some vindication and stop being mocked for our terror. That's all I have for now though. Thanks for letting me get this out there and off my chest.

CHAPTER THIRTY-TWO

I GREW up west of Little Rock, Arkansas in a small town, I won't say specifically where. It was a hot summer day in August of 1989. I was bored and all my friends were off at either camps or on family trips. This left me alone and I really needed to get out of the house. I rode my bike down to the neighborhood basketball court.

Me and my friends had been playing there for years and never before had I ever felt off, but after about thirty minutes I got this sense I was being watched.

Now I should set the scene and area. The court is a part of a park and playground. It sits at the end of a road in a neighborhood. Behind the court are woods and they go on forever, at least that's what I remember.

So I'm there throwing the ball and having fun when I suddenly heard a scary sound that made me freeze in place. It was like something heavy had rattled the fence of the court. I looked but saw nothing. I went back to dribbling and just before I took a shot I heard the sound again. I was definitely the chain link fence being shook. I again looked around but saw nothing.

Now the woods literally come up to the fence which is about eight feet tall. I look left and right down the fence but see nothing. The woods themselves are dark and full of thick bushes. I'm imagining its some other kid, they're either messing with me or they just crawled up and over the fence. But what's odd is I didn't see anyone so it makes me think whoever shook the fence was in the woods.

I was seventeen at the time and already in talks with a recruiter to join the Marines, so my ego wasn't about to let some sound spook me, but I'd be lying now if I said I wasn't a bit disturbed. I brushed off the sound and set up to make a free throw shot. I raise the ball up to shoot and just, like a millisecond, before I release the rattling of the fence sounds and this time close. I flinch just as I release the ball and watch it miss the backboard and the balls goes over the stupid fence and into the woods.

I'm pissed now, not only because I missed but because I have to go into the woods to get the ball. Aggravated, I head towards the gate, I'm cursing loudly and just plain annoyed.

As I'm closing in on the wood line I see the ball fly from the woods and back into the court. Now I'm a combination of freaked and annoyed. I call out for whoever it is to just stop messing around or that I'd kick their ass.

I turn back to head off, I don't want to deal with this and I'm just sick of it. I get my ball, throw it in my backpack and head for my bike. I'm calling it a day. I hear the fence rattle again, I turn to yell at whoever is doing it and this time I see someone. I pause for a moment as I can't quite make out what I'm seeing is real.

Standing next to the fence, completely out of the woods is a chimpanzee looking thing. It was covered in black hair, stood about six feet tall and had long arms. Its head appeared smallish, and just sat on its shoulders. It lifted its left arm, grabbed the fence and shook it vigorously then let out a loud scream. It reminded me of what chimps do when they get excited.

I took off running for my bike.

Behind me I hear it scream out again. I look over my shoulder and see it come around the side of the fence and towards me. This thing is running on all fours, again, like a chimp, but I'm telling you, it wasn't.

I hop on my bike and pedal as hard as I can. I take a quick glance over my shoulder and see it has stopped near the gate. It reaches out and slams the chain link gate and screams.

I don't know what to make of this. I get home and I'm freaked out.

When my friends get back into town I tell them and they all make fun of me. Not a one believed me.

I played there not long after with some friends, but never saw that thing again.

CHAPTER THIRTY-THREE

I LOVE DRIVING my truck at night. There is hardly any traffic, and the number one concern anyone could have would be a wild animal perhaps running about the forest roads. Of course, there is a risk involved. But honestly, I've had precisely five nocturnal encounters in the last ten years, but one of them is still inexplicable to me to this day.

I was on my way with a load of corn to a farmer who used it as fodder for his animals when I saw something I didn't think was possible.

It was night, and I was relaxing with the music of my favorite radio station, driving through the frigid Nebraska countryside, when I heard a shout over the music. I was so confused by the noise that I turned the radio down and rolled the window down a little. But at first, I didn't hear anything except the hissing of the wind and the roar of my engine. And then, just as I was going around a junction, it came on again. A deep, booming call that sounded like a dying animal. I got so scared that my foot was too heavy on the gas for a moment, and my truck skidded slightly. I just managed to apply the handbrake so that I skidded to a halt with squeaking tires.

My heart was in my mouth, and for a moment, I felt like I was blinded by the snow illuminated by my headlights.

Steam was coming out from under my hood. So, I quickly left the driver's cab and opened it to use the damage.

While I examined my engine with the flashlight, I heard steps behind me. At first, I thought I had imagined this one. But then they sounded again, louder this time. The unmistakable crunch of ice and snow under heavy steps.

I paused for a moment and continued listening. The footsteps had stopped, and nothing but my heavy breathing could be heard.

The engine wasn't damaged, and the clutch looked fine. So, I didn't have to worry about how I got out of the parking bay I ended up in.

Then I walked around my truck. Examined the tires. A burst tire in these temperatures was more than wrong. I controlled the front and walked slowly along the truck, back to the bed, when I heard the heavy skids digging deep into the snow again. I paused again and looked around, shining my light between the surrounding trees, which looked like ghostly shapes in the dark.

But I saw nothing. I quickly walked around the truck bed, ensuring the cargo was secured, when they rang behind me again. Heavy footsteps that seemed to come closer.

I peeked around the side of my truck and eyed the other trees. But again, I couldn't see anything that could have caused the noise. I was sure I had imagined it. There just couldn't be anyone lurking around here in the freezing night. I checked the other tires and was about to climb back into the cab when I heard heavy breathing behind me. I frowned and turned, hand on the knob of my door. And then I saw it. A tall figure standing between two trees. The breath steamed in front of the narrow face that was covered with thick fur. The eyes almost glowed red while the hands twitched nervously. I wasn't sure what I was seeing. What was that? The long arms were muscular, and I was sure I was doomed if the creature attacked me.

With a throaty growl, it stepped toward me, but I couldn't move. I was too distracted by the dark fur covering the slim body. The face looked confused, then changed to blank before the brow furrowed, and the monster bared its teeth.

That was my sign. I quickly yanked open the door to the driver's cab and climbed in, letting the door slam shut behind me and staring out the window, shaking. The beast was still standing there, glaring at me like I had disturbed its peaceful night. And then the big mouth opened, and the roar sounded again. The one I just heard on the street. I shuddered as the gigantic hands clenched into fists. With trembling fingers, I started my truck and struggled with the gears before my car got rolling. I didn't dare look in the rearview mirror or side mirror. I didn't want to know if it was following me. Did it follow me? I didn't want to see the long legs sink into the snow. I was sure I would never come home if the creature reached me. It was so angry and so much stronger than me. One wrong move with its muscular arms and my head would roll off. I was sure of it. As fast as the road would allow, I accelerated the truck and sped away. I looked back again as I was about to round the next turn. But it hadn't followed me. Nothing could be seen in the red light of my tail lamp. Nothing but white snow.

I drove as fast as I could out of the snowy valley, praying to all the goods to not get into an accident. I never saw this figure again. Nothing like that either. When I got to my client, he just looked at me with concern. It was evident that something had happened on the way, but I couldn't tell anything. How could I explain to him what I had seen without him calling me crazy? So I kept quiet and hoped I was wrong. I hoped I would never see this creature again.

In fact, I never saw it again until this day. But others did. Another truck driver who frequented the road. They spoke about the encounter in pubs and at gas stations. One even went missing after telling his wife about it while being on a call.

CHAPTER THIRTY-FOUR

I'VE ALWAYS LOVED to ride a bike. Even as a small child, I would shoot over the hills in my neighborhood and challenge the other kids to a race. My mother just shook her head; I was that obsessed when it came to biking. I followed the Tour de France almost religiously, and instead of dealing with girls, I preferred to spend my time in a friend's classmate's bike shop. That lasted until my late teens. I had managed to qualify for a mountain bike tournament, which, if I won, would put me in the ranks of professional cyclists. With this as a potential I began to train harder.

It was late summer of 2019 and I was seventeen at the time. I was training in an area known as a 'lover's woods'. You know the types of spots. Not so secret locations for couples to meet. The weather was warm and dry, the wind wasn't too strong. I could see the last of the campfires as I went by and remnants of beer and the snacks, they had eaten the night before. When I reached the highest point, I could see the whole area. Out of the corner of my eye, I saw a bright spot that seemed to be moving slowly. At first, I thought it was just a paper bag left forgotten on the ground. I turned around slowly and braked sharply because I could now see it wasn't a bag, but something else.

What I was seeing was a pale creature. It was sitting crouched on the ground and running its long fingers through the grass. I don't know if it saw me or knowingly ignored me. I was shocked and couldn't understand what I was seeing. From my perspective, I would say the creature was white or gray, but it wasn't pristine, it had mud smeared on it.

It didn't really look human, but neither did it look like an exotic animal you might have seen at the zoo. The face was turned away from me, but I could see flat ears that seemed to be twitching slowly. From what I did see, the figure wasn't just squatting. It probably tended to walk bent over on its hands, as was known from chimpanzees or other primates. It didn't look like it was bigger than me. In fact, I estimate it to be under 6 feet. However, the physique was much more stable than a human. The muscles were more pronounced, even under the apparently thick white fur. It looked over its shoulder at me momentarily and seemed to regard me with indifference. It was not afraid and raised its long-fingered hand to shove a worm or bug into its mouth.

I took out my phone and took some pics, but the thing was too far away to make out what it was. In the pics it looks like a white blob.

I calmed myself than turned and sped down the mountain like a madman. I was still determining exactly what to do with what I had seen. Should I call the police? Warn the residents of the small town? Would they believe me? I returned to the site a few days later.

But no sooner had I arrived at the spot where I had seen the figure than I was shocked to find that nothing was to be seen. It hadn't rained the last few days, and even if teenagers had been hanging around at the spot, I couldn't imagine there hadn't been any trace of the figure. Neither footprints nor fingerprints in the dirt. I had seen that it had touched the earth. Why wasn't there any sign of it? It hadn't rained in the last few days. There was also no fur. No footprints. Nothing. For a short moment, I thought I was going crazy.

I was beyond amazed. There was absolutely no sign of the creature I had observed. I was just about to ride off without having achieved anything when I saw something out of the corner of my eye. I turned around quickly and froze. There it was. Its strange human like face peering out of the bushes. It wasn't huge. And it appeared to be crouching again. It simply stared at me with its large black eyes. I saw part of its chest. It was not completely covered. There were patches of whitish skin covered in dirty white fur or hair. The figure was clearly not human. But not a monkey, either. It was almost as if it was a mixture of both, but then something completely different. The damn thing cocked its head and opened it wide mouth to reveal several rows of razor-sharp teeth. The facial expression it had was terrifying. It was trying to look menacing, but there was something in its black eyes that I found utterly creepy.

I feared for my life. I didn't know how to deal with it. I hopped on my bike and rode home and found my mother in the garage, who looked at me with concern. I immediately told her everything. She just stared at me in confusion and told me to sit down, which I did. Then my father came along. And then I told him what had happened. Both of my parents just looked at each other helplessly before they eyed me thoughtfully.

My dad simply told me to calm down. That I had probably just seen a bear, maybe an albino one. I begged for them to come to the spot, they refused.

I've since heard about pale crawlers, but this thing doesn't match the exact description. It was white, but it also had fur or hair. From what I've found pale crawlers or rakes don't. Could it have been a hairy rake? Who knows.

I have been back to that spot with friends, not alone, never alone again; but nothing came out of the bushes. I did tell my friends and they all made fun of me.

I hope you can help identify what this thing was. Thanks.

CHAPTER THIRTY-FIVE

I HAVE ALWAYS ENJOYED CAMPING, hiking and fishing. I grew up in Maine and that's what my friends and I would do together and/ or with our families whenever we got the chance. I was no stranger to the woods and I knew several spots all over the state where I could go and camp and be left alone to be at one with nature. Don't get me wrong, as I got older and started a family of my own, there's nothing that I love more than taking them into the woods and spending time with them doing all of those aforementioned things as well. However, once I got to the age of twenty and all of my friends had moved away or I otherwise lost touch with them, I started to spend a lot of time in the woods alone. I was a schoolteacher most of my life and once the summer would come I would take every chance I got to get out into the woods and spend time in them doing several different things. In all the years before my encounter and since that I had been spending days and sometimes even weeks at a time in the woods, oftentimes alone and with no one else around for miles, that my encounter would have happened one of those times. However, it wasn't until there was a death in my family that I had my encounter and I was merely out for a walk late one afternoon. My encounter changed my life a lot but I would say it changed it for the better. Before it happened I wasn't religious or even spiritual but I did believe in ghosts and the supernatural. Things like that weren't discussed as much back then and it certainly wasn't cool to talk about it in a public setting or at the dinner table and in fact, in doing so you could earn yourself a bed at the local psych ward. I have kept my encounter to myself for all these years and finally I am ready to talk about what happened to me.

My grandmother died and when she did my family started to fall apart at the seams. She was a true matriarch and almost everyone in the family depended on her for one thing or another. She was old but she died suddenly and without warning and it left a lot of us distraught and confused. My siblings and I were her only grandchildren and our parents expected us to step in and help in any way we possibly could. It was the summer time and a twenty year old, unencumbered young man, I offered to go and stay with my grandpa until school started up in September. I would stay with him until the end of August and my parents and my grandfather thought that was a great idea. I packed everything up and the day of the funeral I went home with my grandpa after loading all of my stuff into his car. My grandparents lived only about twenty minutes away from where I lived with my parents so it wasn't really a big deal and wouldn't affect me in any sort of drastic way. My grandparents house sat on a huge plot of land that they had inherited from her mother. The property sat in front of a cemetery and the only thing separating the two were some dense woods. It wasn't a cemetery that was used anymore, at least I didn't think it was, and it looked more like it was from the eighteenth century or something like that. When we were kids we would go and hang out in the graveyard and try to scare the crap out of one another. By the time my grandmother died I was twenty years old and well past believing in any of the urban legends associated with the town and with the cemetery in particular. I had finally decided to take some classes at a local community college and was working a job in construction that paid fairly decent. Okay, so about the encounter. I went to my grandfather's house and made myself at home in the guest room where I would normally stay when we visited. Like I said they had a huge house and me and each of my two siblings all had our own rooms for when we were there. My grandparents shared the master bedroom and there was another bedroom that was down in the basement that was the guest bedroom where my parents and everyone else stayed when they visited. My grandfather was a wreck and immediately went to take a nap as soon as we got home from the funeral.

I told him not to worry about anything and that I would order us some dinner and I did but when it got there he didn't feel like getting up to eat right then. I decided to go for a little walk through the woods in the yard and then come back, just to have something to do besides sit idly by and watch how devastated my grandfather was. It was hard for me because we were super close. I left out the back door and told him that I would be back in one hour or less and that I was just going to walk the trails in the back, he knew what that meant. He told me, as he always did, to stay away from the cemetery but instead of arguing with him like I would have any other time, I told him that I would and I left. I was planning on walking to the cemetery and then walking through and around it, back to my grandpa's house. I'd done it so many times before it was like second nature and each and every time he and my grandmother would warn me about the cemetery being haunted and overrun with evil. I usually gave them a hard time because I didn't want to lie to them and always ended up there but I didn't have the heart to argue with him right then. It was a fairly cool night and I was wearing a light jacket that kept me mostly warm. I had a flashlight on me though it was dusk and I didn't plan on being out there in the dark for that long. It was beautiful out and the woods looked and felt perfectly normal. Once I got to the cemetery though everything changed. It felt creepy and I had never been afraid of that spot before so I noticed it right away.

I sat down on a large rock to have a cigarette and just listened to the sounds of the night despite the creeping feeling of dread that seemed to be rising up from my stomach and into my throat. The air suddenly felt a whole lot cooler as well and I shivered. I was planning on just finishing my cigarette and turning back anyway and those feelings made the urgency to leave all the more urgent. It had been late afternoon when I left and it was still seemingly dusk and light enough outside that I wouldn't need a flashlight or anything on the way back if

I left soon enough. I was just about to stand up and flick my cigarette when I heard what I thought was my grandmother calling my name. I jumped and of course I was really confused. I looked over to the corner of the tiny cemetery to where I had heard the voice come from and while I obviously didn't see my grandmother standing there or anything, I did notice something very odd. I wasn't sure if it had been that way the whole time that I had been sitting there or not but there was one spot that looked like it was almost shrouded in darkness. What I mean is, it was dusk but not dark enough where you couldn't see anything and that one spot looked like it was pitch black and fully nighttime. I blinked, thinking my eyes were playing tricks on me. It looked the same when I opened my eyes. Also, I couldn't see through the darkness and it looked like it was some sort of solid black wall. I heard my grandmother calling my name again and it sounded almost like it was blowing in on the wind, it was so faint. I knew what I was hearing though and so I started to walk over to that spot that seemed to be darker than the rest of the graveyard and the surrounding woods and also where I heard her voice coming from.

As I walked over there I swear it looked like a giant black shadow lifted from that spot and had moved to another spot in the cemetery, a bit deeper into the woods on the side opposite where I had originally come from. I know people will be thinking it had something to do with the sun but that wasn't what this was. The darkness had a density to it and though it wasn't in any particular shape and was massive, it seemed evil somehow and like it had a life of its own. I thought about following the large mass into the woods but I decided I didn't want any part of whatever was going on. I turned to go back the way I had come and just as I did I heard some pretty severe growling. I immediately turned around and was expecting there to be some sort of predatory animal there, I never expected what I actually saw.

It was a gigantic dog and I swear if I didn't know any better or if it were just a little bit darker I would have thought it was a large bear. The giant, dark shadow mass had disappeared and I could see everything now and it was clearly a huge dog. The dog's eyes glowed and burned bright red and it just stood there, staring at me. It let out another bark and I could see that its mouth was covered in large streams of thick drool that was tinged with red. It was disgusting. For reference I remember thinking it had to have been at least the size of a very large mastiff but honestly I would say it was twice that size. Maybe in my memory I'm exaggerating it a bit though but I often wonder if that's the case or not. I felt a strange sensation wash over me and it was almost like I knew the dog was just waiting for me to turn and run so it could chase me and kill me. I thought for sure that I could outrun a dog but something inside of me immediately sensed that the giant shadow mass wasn't just a dog and that I probably wouldn't be able to outrun it. It was a supernatural dog. I slowly backed away and the dog kept snarling, barking and growling at me. It was at least thirty feet away from me but aside from a few broken down and crumbling headstones there wasn't much standing in between us. It would have easily gotten to me. Once I heard my grandmother's voice coming from either that dog or something I couldn't see that had to have been standing right by its side though, I knew that it was time for me to get the hell out of there. I took a deep breath, turned and ran.

The dog immediately gave chase and I could literally feel its breath on my back. I was terrified to turn around and once I got almost to the edge of the woods that met my grandparent's property I heard a very loud growl and then an even louder yelp, followed by a whine. I stopped and turned and saw the dog almost flying backwards through the air. It landed with a thud and then vanished into a cloud of black mist. It was very shocking, disorienting and terrifying. I just stood there with my mouth open because even though I knew there was something supernatural about the dog, it didn't really register and remained something I could easily have talked myself out of up until that point. Just before I turned to quickly walk out of there I saw something step in front of where the dog had just landed on its side. It seemed to have walked right out of one of the trees. It was fully dark by that time but whatever this was, I recognize it nowadays as a shadow person, it was darker than the night and everything surrounding me. It also had glowing red eyes but no other features. It didn't have a hat or a cape and it just immediately struck fear into me and I was almost paralyzed by it. Suddenly I heard my grandmother's voice again, or what sounded like her sweet voice, and it seemed to have been coming from the shadow man. It told me that I needed to go to the man and walk with him. I turned and ran as fast as I could until I got inside of my grandparent's house. I didn't even bother to look back and once inside I locked all of the doors and refused to look out any of the windows for the rest of the night. When I first turned my back on that thing I heard the loudest, most terrifying and animalistic howling sounds I had ever heard in my life, before or since. I shuddered and I couldn't get back to the house fast enough.

I never told my grandfather what happened and stayed with him for the rest of the summer without ever going into those woods again. I eventually got over my fear and traveled back into them, even camping and fishing in them many times but I never went back to that cemetery. I knew that whatever evil was lurking there had been trying to mimic my grandmother and when I wouldn't budge and go to it, as it moved further and further back into the woods, it became angry and manifested itself as something it thought would either scare me into paralysis or terrify me into complying with it. Neither of those things happened and I never saw or heard it again. My grandfather was really superstitious but he got really overboard with all of it once she died and I somehow knew that something was attacking him in that same way as well, with it mimicking my grandmother's voice. He never said it to me though and I never told anyone about any of it until now.

CHAPTER THIRTY-SIX

I PUT the word crazy in the title of this because I already know how insane what I am about to tell you will sound. However, there have been several sightings all over the United States and almost always where there seems to be some sort of underground tunnel system of this creature. Now, I still have no idea as of this day what it was that I saw and from what I understand most people who see it don't have a clue. It was either not of this world or it is a leftover relic from a time long ago that has chosen to go underground, and come out sometimes, that possibly feeds off the terror it causes humans to feel at the mere inkling of it. I felt something was wrong and very off before I ever laid eyes on that thing, and I believe that was my own intuition alerting me to it. I had my encounter back in 1982 and I still remember it so vividly, it's like no time has passed from the second I saw it up until right now as I sit at my computer typing this. I was almost twenty years old, and I was a college student in one of the southern states at the time. I have since moved and I haven't been to that area in about two decades and no longer know anyone there, so I have no idea if it's still the case now but back then the university had a lot of deep and very dense woods surrounding it. I had an off-campus apartment and sometimes when I was running late, I would do what so many other students did and what my own roommates did as well and cut through the woods in order to get to class on time.

It wasn't unusual for me to be coming back from the library late at night and going through those same woods to get to my house. One night, right around when the sun was just about to set, I was leaving the college from attending one extracurricular activity or another and there was no one who was able to walk me home. I didn't prefer walking alone through the woods but like I said it wasn't uncommon and I did it all the time. That night though I had a strange feeling before I had even left the campus and I had asked several of my friends if they were able to either walk with me or give me a ride. I was asking people for so long that I lost track of time and realized I wasn't even going to be able to take the roundabout way back to my house because I had a very big first date that night and if I didn't take the shortcut through the woods then I was going to end up being very late. I didn't want to do that to my date, who is now my husband and whom I have been deeply in love with since that night, and so I just went for it. I talked myself into going into those woods alone, knowing fully well that it would be dark before I got out of them and reached the end of my street. The woods I am talking about weren't connected to the college in any way and were a little out of the way but not enough out of the way for them to make it take longer than it would have for me to walk the regular roads home. I was scared from the very beginning but thought it was just my mind playing tricks on me and all the horror stories my parents told me about what happens to young girls out by themselves at night. Surely, they meant human dangers, but my mind didn't have the capacity to understand the danger I was about to put myself into or the creature that would end up being the cause of it.

I walked only for a few minutes before I smelled something terrible. I didn't know what it could have been and just tried to take shallow breaths but eventually it was overwhelming. It smelled like sewers or something. I also felt like I was being watched. I ignored it as best as I could but started to walk a little bit faster so that I didn't get stuck out there in the middle of those woods once the sun fully went down. I heard a strange noise that sounded similar to someone, or something being strangled and then I heard a very strange sort of laughter. It was coming from right next to me but behind some heavier brush. I hesitated to leave the trail I was walking on and every inch of my body and ounce of my mind told me to just keep going and to mind my own business. However, I couldn't do that and wondered if maybe someone was being hurt. I crept as slowly and as quietly as I could and over to the brush, bent down so I was mostly hidden behind it and peeked through it to see if I could spot what the heck I had just heard. I couldn't see anything immediately and was about to turn around.

I heard a loud banging sound that didn't belong in the middle of the woods, and it sounded like a very heavy door had been just left to slam on its own. I jumped and fell backwards onto my behind but quickly got myself back up to a squatting position and saw something moving between the trees. It wasn't particularly fast or anything, but it looked very blurry at first. I was immediately horrified but I think that's only because my mind and my eyes weren't connecting to put together what I was looking at and all I was sure of was that whatever it was, it was "wrong" and something I didn't think that I should be seeing. I still smelled that horrible stench and started gagging. I couldn't help it and despite my best efforts to be quiet, I knew whatever that thing in front of me walking was, it had heard me. It stopped suddenly, sniffed the air deeply and turned to look right at me. I finally saw it face to face and it was about twenty feet away from me, through the trees. It was at least seven feet tall and had very pale skin. The skin wasn't normal though and later I would understand that was because it looked exactly like a decomposing body's skin would look. It was bloated and even looked like the pores were leaking some sort of water mixed with green or black sludge. It had two very large, completely black eyes but it also had something that looked like an additional eye in the middle of its forehead. The mouth on that thing was all bloated too and it was bright pink and even looked like it had red lipstick, or something smeared all around it. Its nose was almost nonexistent on the normal shaped head, and I couldn't see any ears. It looked like it was wearing silvery, metallic one-piece suit but it only covered up to the elbows on the arms and to the knees on the legs. It bared its teeth at me, and I noticed they were sharp and horribly discolored. I also noticed it couldn't see me very well because it kept looking in my general direction, despite my now standing straight up and unable to do anything but stand there, staring in horror at whatever monstrosity was before me. It was able to look directly at me and seemed like it was trying to do so but it never did. It never made eye contact.

It sniffed the air again, then it made that strange and somewhat strangled laughing sound I had heard earlier which had made me leave the trail I had been on in the first place. Then, it moved faster than anything I have ever seen move in my entire life and swooped something up off the ground. It turned its back to me and went into a squatting position. It looked like it was doing something bizarre with its arms, but I could no longer see the front of it. Then I heard a low shriek, a quiet squealing sound and the creature was suddenly growling. I also heard weird and seemingly out of place crunching sounds. That was enough for me, and I turned and ran back the way I had come and into the university. I was terrified the whole time that it had been chasing after me or that it had otherwise followed me, but it didn't. I used the payphone to call my roommates and asked if one of them could come and get me. I was hysterical and could barely verbalize what I had just seen. They sent my date for that night, and he asked me what had happened to me. I reluctantly told him, after much coaxing by him and reassurance that he would believe me no matter what. He insisted I show him where it happened. He grabbed a flashlight out of his car and walked with me to the spot where I had seen the monster. Now, I know people will ask why I went back there, and I did so because after twenty minutes or so of listening to him tell me it was probably some random homeless person trying to scare me, I started to believe that. I stayed behind him the whole time and as we walked, we both heard sounds like we were stepping on gravel.

I don't know if I just hadn't noticed it earlier when I was there or if it was new but there were carcasses of tiny forest animals all over the trail and off to the sides of it. Little skeletons of squirrels, birds and even mice. It was disgusting. We both heard that same loud banging noise and I started to back away, but he pushed forward and went to look while I just stood behind him, refusing to go any further but also

THE MEGA MONSTER BOOK

not wanting to be out there by myself as he went and investigated. He raised the flashlight and I swear his skin turned completely white. He was, as they say, as white as a ghost. He turned and grabbed my hand and told me we had to get out of there and we had to run. I knew he had seen what I saw earlier and that I wasn't crazy. Once we got back to the car, he asked me what it was, and I told him the truth. I told him that I had no idea but that it was terrifying and seemed to not be human or any animal I was familiar with either. We did some research and learned that there are a series of tunnels underneath those woods that led directly underground to the college back then. I don't know if it's still like that today, as I already said, but that isn't the only interesting thing that we found. Those were the days long before the internet and we had to do a lot of research but we came up with several encounters, at least one each decade from the early eighteen hundreds to our own modern time, where someone would report something that was exactly like what we had just stumbled upon there in those woods but sometimes it was seen going in and out of manholes and into the sewers as well as in the basements of some of the homes in the area to the woods themselves, where we had seen it.

We never went to investigate further and I'm glad we didn't. I recently, and I mean just in the last three years or so, saw an encounter online that happened in the same area where someone said they saw the exact same creature in those exact same woods near that exact same college. So, it brought it all back up for me. I told my husband about it, and we decided that I should write it out and put it out there. I kept the name of the college a secret because the last thing I want to be responsible for it a bunch of kids going out there on a ghost hunt or something and ending up getting hurt because of my encounter story.

197

CHAPTER THIRTY-SEVEN

IT WAS the fall of 2019 and my wife and I were on our annual trip to spend time with our twin daughters who lived in California. We made this trip each year to celebrate their birthdays. We were about an hour from arriving but I needed to stop for gas. It was late at night, close to midnight.

I had just stopped and gotten out to pump gas when my wife looked at me with wide eyes. At first, I didn't understand what made her react like that, but then I turned around and saw it too. It was a huge figure huddled behind the air and water station off to the side of the lot.

At first, I just thought it was a frightened homeless man trying to avoid us, but the more I looked, the more I saw that the creature was covered in hair. It attempted to crouch all the way down to avoid us seeing it.

It had its knees drawn to its chest and its arms pulled around its legs. At first, I considered moving closer to get a better look, but something told me what I was seeing wasn't right. My wife begged for us to drive off, but I'll admit now, I was mesmerized. What on earth was I seeing? I wondered if the ape-like figure was wounded and needed help. I wasn't sure if it was dangerous, but if it was hurt, the last thing I should do was approach a wild animal. I couldn't even tell what kind of thing it was.

My wife hollered at me. This got the creature moving. It slowly rose allowing me to see just how big this thing was. It towered over the air pump by at least six feet. It was completely covered in a brownish dark hair. Its frame was massive, like a linebacker. I could tell that if it wanted to, it could rip me apart. The face was shadowed and I couldn't really make it out.

My wife also saw it stand up and screamed in horror.

The thing took a step towards me then turned and limped off. It was definitely injured and must be why it was huddled where it was. Had it been hit by a car or something?

I didn't want to wait around just in case it looked at me as a threat. I jumped in the car and sped off.

We found another gas station, topped off and eventually made it to see the girls, but I could not forget the being we had seen on our way. My wife also seemed to think about it for a long time.

As we were on our way back home, I stopped again at the gas station we stopped at the first time, but during the day. After filling up I made my way to the spot I'd seen it, but there was nothing there. I then went inside the mini-mart. I asked the attendant if he'd ever seen a 'tall hairy person' hanging around.

The kid gave me the craziest look and then laughed.

Back at the car I told my wife and we both agreed to never tell anyone what we saw. I have since done some inquiring online and have even found numerous stories of sightings around these parts. By the way this all happened just west of Tahoe. Our girls live in Roseville, CA.

It's truly the strangest thing I've ever had happen.

CHAPTER THIRTY-EIGHT

AS A UTILITY PERSON it's not uncommon for me to come across strange things on the side of the road or when working at someone's house. I normally do my work outside of the house or in the streets but sometimes I will have to knock on someone's door or ring the doorbell to gain access to one thing or another that I need to fulfill my duties as a public service worker. I work and live in New Jersey, and I always have. I live in the more central part of the state, which most people who live either north or south of me say doesn't even exist but it's different because central is where most of the farmlands and more densely wooded areas are. It's not often I have to go out at night but when I do it's even more creepy. Another thing about my job is that I normally work alone. If there is a big job or some serious work to be done then you will see several of us out there, up on the poles and what not, just divvying up whatever needs to be done to be more efficient. However, on any normal given day, it's just me and I ride from place to place and do whatever needs to be done at each one. That's what I was doing on the day I had my encounter.

It was 2016 and I had just started working under a new supervisor. I didn't particularly care for him, but my job is my livelihood and I take great pride in it. The issue that I had with him, or the main one anyway, was that he wouldn't answer when I would call with a question, and he would end up holding me up with the job I happened to be doing. It was this bad and annoying habit of his that had me in the middle of the woods one day in June of that year. I went out on a normal call but the home I was sent to seemed to be far out in the middle of nowhere. I was nervous just driving out there and I couldn't explain why I was feeling that way. I am almost sixty years old and have worked the same job at the same place and with the same company since I was in my mid-twenties. There were times when I would go out to a job and would need access to the home, but I won't know that or expect it to go in and therefore I will have to call my supervisor if no one answers the door at the home. I've never been more scared before I even arrived at a job. Don't get me wrong and like I said, I've seen some crazy stuff before and have met some even crazier people, but this was something altogether different. I wanted to be done and out of there before I even pulled up. It was the summertime and so it was getting darker outside much later. I was grateful for that because I just had a feeling I was going to be held up and stuck at this place, wherever it was, for much longer than usual. I guess that's what some people would call my "intuition" but I don't know anything about that. I just knew what I knew at the time and ended up being right.

I drove for at least twenty minutes on a desolate and deserted road that looked like there was no life anywhere the whole time. I didn't see anything except the surrounding woods, and they were everywhere. Eventually I came to what was no bigger than a wide trail and followed the directions I was given to get to the house. Once I got there, I saw that there was a small house which was even more isolated and seemingly surrounded by even denser woods than the ones I had passed driving into the place. The job was an initial installment and would take me a little while. I knocked on the door and rang the doorbell, but no one answered. I phoned my supervisor, and it took him ten minutes to return the call. I told him to contact the homeowner and tell them I needed access, or I would have to go back the next day or whenever it was convenient for them to be home and let me inside for a couple of minutes. He seemed annoyed at the request, but it couldn't be avoided. I knew his annoyance meant that I would be waiting a while and while normally that wouldn't have been an issue, something inside of me was itching to get the hell out of there and never look back. I tried to do what any rational person would do in that situation and told myself I was being ridiculous.

I lit a cigarette as I leaned against my work vehicle and right when I took my first puff of it, I heard loud giggling coming from the woods somewhere nearby. I stopped and listened, and the giggling turned into screaming. It sounded like a little kid had been or was being hurt and I knew I couldn't just sit idly by and pretend I wasn't hearing what I was hearing. Somehow though, once again deep down inside somewhere, I knew I was being lured. The screaming turned into low moaning and groaning, as if someone were in a lot of pain, as I traversed the trail forward and to my right. Once I had walked only for about five minutes the house disappeared behind me. That's how deep and dense this forest was that surrounded it. I mean, I had no idea where I even was and couldn't see anything except for trees in front of and all around me. Finally, after I had walked for about seven or eight minutes and heard the moaning and low cries coming from my right-hand side. I looked over and saw a little girl, she wasn't facing me, but she looked to be on the ground and holding her knee. I saw two pigtails in her black hair and looked like she was wearing a black dress of some sort. Her arms and the back of her neck looked extremely pale, and she had her head in her lap, like any normal little kid would if they were hurt, on the ground and crying. I walked up to her and asked her what was wrong. She didn't answer and continued to just sit there and whimper with her head in her lap. I asked her again and the hairs on the back of my neck started standing up as I realized there was nowhere this little girl could have come from but the house, I was waiting for permission to enter or for someone to let me into. I didn't think at the time it was anything supernatural and honestly thought that I could kill two birds with one stone in that I could maybe help the little girl and she could in turn allow me access to the house. All I had to do inside was flip a switch or two. I asked her where she was from.

She didn't answer and continued to whimper. Suddenly, coming from only a short distance away, I heard what sounded like a group of children singing ring around the rosy, that song that's supposed to sound sweet but that's really said to have been written about the black plague? Yeah, that one and the sound was so monotone that it made it even creepier. I walked just a few paces ahead of me, leaving the injured little girl behind me. I wasn't leaving her. I was just curious as to why all these little kids would be in the woods playing or whatever they were doing. I wondered where their guardians or parents were. I saw about twelve kids, in a circle and holding hands in a clearing in the middle of those woods. They stopped singing and spinning the moment one of them saw me and they all turned to look at me. They had pitch black eyes but otherwise they looked perfectly normal for the most part. They were all dressed a bit oddly in that they looked like little morticians or something. They wore black, old fashioned and very fine attire. The eyes were enough for me though and my thought was to turn and run.

That didn't happen right then though because as soon as I did turn around, the little girl who previously seemed hurt that I had first tried talking to was laughing hysterically and looking up at me. She also had black eyes, no whites at all, and she looked like those pitch-black eyes were somehow bleeding. I asked her what was wrong, pretending not to see the eyes but before she could answer, if she was going to stop laughing like a maniac and respond to me, that is, I heard something behind me. I turned again and looked, and all the other kids were slowly walking towards me. They were lined up in a very straight line and walking in perfect tandem with one another. There was one boy who looked older than the others who was walking about two inches ahead of the rest of them. None of them were older than twelve or younger than eight. Of that, I was sure. I wasn't taking any chances and turned to run out of there.

I heard them all chanting something as they walked more quickly behind me. They weren't running and I was, but they were somehow keeping up with me. Whatever they were chanting I couldn't understand it and when I turned again, I saw the little girl that had been on the ground, and she was walking next to the one who seemed to be the oldest and the male leader. I kept running. They all looked terribly mean and evil, and I somehow knew, my intuition again I guess, that they would seriously injure or kill me if they caught up with me. I ran right into something solid. I screamed and the large man standing in front of me laughed and put his hand out. He introduced himself as the owner of the home and said he had only been in the barn and had gotten the call that I needed him to let me into the house. My heart was pounding as I tried to sputter out what I had just come upon in what was basically his backyard. Suddenly he asked me if I said I had seen a bunch of weird looking kids and since that had been what I had already told him, at least for the most part, I said yeah. He suddenly looked very mean himself and the reassuring smile that had been plastered on his face only a second earlier upon meeting me disappeared in an instant. He looked pissed and said, very sternly, "come with me. I'll show you to the basement." I turned to look and see where the kids were but only saw the back of the little pig tailed girl. She was facing a nearby tree. The man didn't acknowledge her, but I did see him look right at her and then saw his eyes scan the woods. I took off running back to my vehicle.

At that point I thought that if I went into that house that I wouldn't have come back out alive, and I absolutely cannot explain to you why I knew that with absolute certainty. I knew it with all my heart. The man yelled and asked where I was going but I was already in my truck and rolling up my windows. I locked my doors and as I struggled to get the key in the ignition, I saw several of the children, including the little pig tailed girl, all walking quickly towards my vehicle. The large man just stood behind them unmoving and with his arms across his chest. I was terrified and shaking and fumbled a bit with the keys. I managed to get them in and get the hell out of there and I never even bothered to look back. I thought that my boss would be furious with me, and I swear he had been looking for a reason to fire me since he started months before. He never even mentioned it and so neither did I. I didn't know anything about the black-eyed kids' phenomenon before my encounter but I've done a ton of research ever since.

I live my life terrified that I will encounter one again and I don't know what happened with that one house but the company I worked for never hooked him up. No one ever mentioned what happened to me that day or asked me why I ran off in terror and never reported it.

There has been nothing. The more I research into the black-eyed kids the more I come up with my own theories and one of them is that those kids have human handlers who are assigned by some supernatural, demonic, or extraterrestrial forces to take care of them and help them feed. Maybe they even are hired or appointed somehow to help them try to blend in more. Whatever the case may be, I am convinced that I was supposed to be their meal that day. I don't know if I would have been killed, injured, taken indefinitely or if I would have walked out of there none the wiser as to what was done to me. If I ever have another encounter or gain more information about this one, I'll surely let you know but for now that's all that I have. Thanks for letting me get this off my chest.

CHAPTER THIRTY-NINE

I NEVER LIKED WORKING the late shift at the little convenience store a couple miles from my house, but the fact of the matter is, I didn't have much of a choice. I was trying to save up to get my own apartment to break free from my overbearing and overly strict parents. Don't get me wrong I have nothing against rules, but I was twenty years old and if I wasn't at work I had a nine o'clock curfew on week-days, ten on the weekends and I wasn't allowed to have keys to the house. I also wasn't allowed to have friends over or leave the house when my parents weren't home. If I left while they were gone, I would have had no way of locking the doors and they couldn't have that. I love my parents, but our relationship has always been strained and I don't know if I'll ever be able to forgive the bullying, I suffered all throughout high school when I was always the only one who couldn't go out on dates, sleep over friend's houses or have friends over to my house for sleepovers. Alright, enough ragging on my parents but that was just to explain a little bit about why I would choose to work a shift that had me alone in a small store on the side of the road in the middle of nowhere from ten at night until four in the morning. My parents made an exception with work as far as my curfew because I think they wanted me out as badly as I wanted to get out. However, they still claim it was to teach me responsibility. Whatever the reason, I found myself alone in the woods in the middle of the night one night, and that's when I encountered something horrific and not of this world.

I took the test for my license and failed it three times. I grew up in a very rural area of Florida and there were woods everywhere and because I also wasn't allowed to ride in cars with people my parents didn't know and hadn't approved of, or members of the opposite sex that weren't blood related, I had to walk almost everywhere. My parents wanted to instill responsibility in me, but they weren't about to change their schedules around to accommodate me and help me out with a ride or two every now and then. Sometimes my mom or dad would drive me to work but they never picked me up and I wasn't allowed to accept rides from coworkers, even when I wasn't working alone, and someone would offer me one. I know most people think that I was twenty years old and should have just left but I was really sheltered and would have had nowhere to go. Plus, it was the nineteen seventies and things were just very different back then. I obeyed my parents' rules because I lived rent free under their roof. One night I worked my six-hour shift and had everything ready for the person coming in at four so that I could leave right away. There was a route that I could take that wouldn't have had me going through the woods that was a little bit shorter but I felt safer in the woods because there was never anyone else in them, at least not in the areas I needed to walk in order to make it home, and it was less likely I would run into someone offering me a ride and harassing me about not taking it. My friends stayed up all hours of the night because none of them had curfews at twenty like I did, and I would often run into them when I took the main roads. It was embarrassing. So, I walked two blocks from my job and into the dense woods that surrounded almost every-thing in that town at the time.

I used to like to sing while I walked because it kept me calm and I wouldn't have jumped at every little noise. Don't get me wrong, I wasn't completely unaware of the dangers that were lurking in the woods at any given time, especially at night. I was young and some-what naive though and thought that I would rather be mauled by some animal and make my parents feel guilty for the rest of their lives than be embarrassed when I once again had to tell a friend I wasn't allowed to accept a ride from them. If I said I just didn't want to take the ride, repeatedly, then I looked like a snob, and they would no longer be my friend. It felt like a catch twenty-two at the time, which I realize now is quite dumb. The night was mild, and I had my backpack with me and a flashlight. I was walking along, and everything seemed normal at first. I thought I saw something move really fast out of the corner of my eye but when I looked there was nothing there. I tried to ignore the feelings of dread and terror that started to well up inside of me from that point on. I also had to do what I could to ignore the fact that the forest was no longer making any noise at all. It was like someone had flipped a switch and turned off all the sounds I would normally hear. Not only was there nothing coming from anywhere in the forest, but I remember thinking that it was unusual I wasn't hearing any sounds coming from the road either. It wasn't abnormal for me to have heard a horn blaring or the sound of tires squealing, things like that. There was literally nothing to the point I thought that maybe something was wrong with my ears. However, I could hear myself singing so I knew that wasn't the case.

After a few minutes of the silence, I stopped singing because I once again saw something dark dart past me out of the corner of my eye. I could only see whatever it was in my peripheral vision but even then, it had been moving so incredibly fast that it couldn't have been another human or an animal. I loved horror movies and I wholeheartedly believed in ghosts and the supernatural. However, when I thought of things that go bump in the night or something lurking in the woods waiting to attack, I thought of places like camps or farms. I hadn't ever even considered that the forest I walked through in the middle of the night all the time could have been the home of hellish, demonic thing that creeped around waiting for the right time to strike. I couldn't have known how foolish that was. I kept walking but after the fifth time I saw that thing speeding across my peripheral vision, I stopped to wait for it to happen again. That was a big mistake that I regret to this very day, and I often wonder if I hadn't stopped if I still would have had the experience that I did. Someone was standing by one of the trees, about twenty feet to my right. He was quite tall but not abnormally so, and he stood at about six and a half feet. He looked slim and muscular. His clothes looked funny, almost as if he had come from some sort of costume party. Well, that's what I thought at the time. Once the mid nineteen eighties came about, I realized that his clothes weren't strange or outdated but they were futuristic. He was wearing a leather jacket, a white shirt underneath it and a pair of tight-fitting blue jeans. He had blonde hair and was gorgeous, but it was his eyes that had me mesmerized. They were bright green and somewhat unnatural looking. I was too transfixed to realize that I was in a very precarious and downright dangerous situation. He was dreamy, as my mother used to say. I said hello and playfully asked him why he was creeping around the woods and sneaking up on young women in the middle of the night.

He avoided the question, but he said hello back. He smiled and had the most intense gaze and cutest dimples. He looked to be about my age, but my town was so small that I knew I would have known him if he had gone to my school or if he was related to almost anyone that did. He said that he was new in town and couldn't sleep at night, so he enjoyed walking around in the woods to clear his mind. I asked him if that worked or helped, and he smiled again and said that it did. He asked if he could walk with me, and I said it was okay. I mean, he was gorgeous and honestly, I don't think I had full autonomy over my decisions, even that early on in the encounter with him. His name was Vincenzo, and he said his accent was one from a small village in Italy. He looked at me like he knew me and like he could see deep down into my soul. I shuddered when he looked me in my eyes, but it never occurred to me to fear him. After all, monsters looked horrific, and grotesque and this man looked like he was sculpted by the hands of the angels themselves. I tried to stare at the ground instead of making eye contact as we walked. I had very minimal experience with boys and had only ever kissed one once. It was regrettable.

Eventually we had walked in silence for about five whole minutes, but I could see out of the corner of my eyes that he was staring at me the entire time. I was blushing, I'm sure but didn't look back up at him. I had about ten minutes left until I would exit the woods and walk a few blocks to my house. He grabbed my arm suddenly and when I turned and looked at him, I couldn't conceive of what I was seeing. His face had become distorted with his eye's bright red, his skin super pale and his teeth jagged. His mouth was no longer luscious and perfect looking but black and opened wider than it should have been able to go. His skin almost looked like it was peeling off in places and his beautiful blonde hair was gone, replaced by a bald, white, scabbed up head. At first, he only grabbed my arm but before I knew what was happening, he had me by the back of my neck. Listen, I know many people think that I was merely the victim of an attempted assault and saw my attacker as a "monster" because of how he tried to hurt me, but I assure you that is not at all what happened. It was a monster and it posed as a gorgeous and beautiful, well-spoken young man. Suddenly black wings burst through his jacket, and I didn't stick around to see what would happen next. I kicked and fought with all my might, but he just laughed. I got loose somehow and ran for my life. As I ran as fast as I could out of the woods, I saw the same fast-moving shadow in my peripheral vision. I turned around once and though I didn't see him there, I knew he was still following me. I knew he was the fast shadow. I heard him yelling my name, which I hadn't given him, and he kept telling me that it was my destiny and that I shouldn't tempt or go against fate. I eventually got out of the woods, and I jumped directly in front of the first car I saw driving along. It was also someone I didn't know but they just looked like an average human being. They let me into the car and drove me home.

Of course, my parents didn't believe me and thought I was making it up for attention or lying as an excuse to not have to walk home. I wasn't surprised. That's what happens when you have emotionally immature and inept parents. I know what happened to me and I still have terrible nightmares about that guy. There have been times through the years and still to this very day that I thought I saw him in a crowd, just standing there, blending in but watching me intensely. I don't know if that's happening because every time I blink, he is then suddenly gone. He appears as the angelic and perfect man and not as the bat winged, pale and peeling beast he really was underneath that facade. I don't know what else to say except I believe vampires are very real and that's the best guess I can make as to what I encountered that night but of course I can't be sure. It's scary too because of all the talk about shadow people nowadays and that's exactly what I have come to believe was darting around in my periphery the whole time I was in those woods that night. I quit my job and eventually disobeyed my parents and their wishes and moved in with a friend. It was the best decision I ever made and aside from some nightmares and the thinking I see him everywhere all the time, I've led a fairly normal and beautiful life.

CHAPTER FORTY

WHEN I WAS AROUND 5 years old, I used to play near the woods behind my grandmother's house all the time. My grandma would keep an eye on me from the kitchen or living room, thanks to the large windows facing the woods. Occasionally, she would come out to see what I was up to. Back then, I had this fascination with digging in the dirt and collecting unique rocks and arrowheads scattered around my grandmother's property. We lived in Midwest Illinois, not too far from Cahokia Mounds, so finding arrowheads wasn't that uncommon.

One day, while I was engrossed in digging, I noticed something peculiar up in the tree next to me. It's hard to explain, but it looked like a sort of heatwave shimmering off the tree branch. It was autumn because I remember wearing my pink jacket and worrying that my mom would be mad at me for getting dirt on the arms from digging. There were plenty of leaves on the ground too. As I stared at this strange phenomenon, I realized it had a human-like shape. Imagine being a 5-year-old, trying to comprehend why there was an invisible person in the tree. I felt scared but unsure of what to do. Then, it started moving and emitting a faint clicking sound. At that moment, I decided I shouldn't be witnessing this, so I sprinted back to the house.

My grandmother could tell I was shaken, and I recall telling her I had seen an angel. As a 5-year-old, I couldn't think of anything else it could be since I hadn't heard of aliens, ghosts, or monsters.

Fast forward to when I was about 12 years old. By that time, the encounter was a distant memory. I loved watching action and sci-fi movies, and one day my dad rented a movie called Predator. As I watched it with him, the first appearance of the invisible/cloaked Predator scared me to the core. Memories of that day I was digging in the dirt came flooding back. I even asked my dad if Predators were real or if he knew of any animals or people with cloaking abilities. He assured me it was all fiction. Unlike today, where I could simply Google it, I had no internet access, so I brushed it off once again.

Now, let's fast forward to around 2004. I was all grown up, with three young children, going through a separation from my husband. I had moved to an apartment in the next town over, which consisted of one-level duplexes. Our building was the last one, located on the outskirts of town. Behind the buildings, there was a deep ditch separated by a chain-link fence. We had about 6-7 trees on our side of the fence, and if you followed the ditch, you'd reach a small forest that eventually led to the countryside with larger forests and farmland. As a smoker, I would step out onto the back porch for a smoke break, avoiding smoking inside due to the kids. One night, while doing laundry and other tasks late into the night, I decided to take a smoke break before heading to bed.

I went out to the back porch, and that's when I heard a faint clicking sound. My first instinct was to look towards the ditch, as I had seen a groundhog there a few days prior, and I thought maybe it had returned. The yard was dimly lit by an outside light near the playground to the right of my porch. Since it was just a quick smoke break, I didn't turn on my porch light. However, I couldn't spot any groundhog or movement in the ditch. So, I resumed smoking my cigarette, but the faint clicking sound persisted, and a slight movement caught my attention. I glanced up at the tree on the left side of my porch, and there it was—the same invisible entity I had seen when I was five. It appeared as a distortion, taking on a humanoid shape, crouched on a branch with one arm grasping the tree trunk. I couldn't believe my eyes. I thought, "Is this really happening? Has it come to harm me for seeing it all those years ago?" My mind raced, thinking about my sleeping children inside the apartment. I rushed inside, slamming and locking the door. I hurried to my kids' rooms, making sure all the windows were locked, and then I turned off the lights in the living room. I stood by the blinds, staring at the tree, hoping to catch another glimpse of it. I sat there for a good ten minutes, but I couldn't see anything. Eventually, I convinced myself that I must be tired, and my mind was playing tricks on me.

Just as I started calming down, my neighbor's dog came running across the yard, barking furiously at the same branch of the tree where I had seen this "predator" entity. This startled me even more because the dog rarely barked at anything. Not even at the groundhog that frequented the ditch. The barking continued for a few minutes until the neighbor called the dog back inside. Reluctantly, the dog turned and headed home, glancing back at the tree branch every few feet until it disappeared from my view. I didn't sleep that night, and I haven't seen anything like it since. I'm left wondering what to make of the experience. As a grown woman with kids and a successful career, I just want to know if anyone else has ever had a similar encounter. I know what I saw.

CHAPTER FORTY-ONE

IT'S BEEN MORE than a few years, but I can remember vividly the day I found myself sitting alone in the midst of the timber, surrounded by the tranquil beauty of nature. It was a calm afternoon, and the gentle rustling of leaves and the distant chirping of birds provided a soothing soundtrack to my thoughts. However, amidst this serenity, a peculiar sound pierced the air—an elongated, drawn-out yell that seemed to echo through the trees. It was reminiscent of someone urgently trying to capture attention from afar, with the pitch fluctuating throughout. In that moment, I instinctively believed it to be the voice of my father's friend, Mike, attempting to get my attention.

Driven by curiosity and the desire to reunite with Mike, I began traversing through the timber, making my way toward the source of the calls. As I ventured deeper into the woods, the enigmatic sounds persisted, growing louder and more unsettling. It was as if immense logs were being lifted and hurled with immense force, resonating through the forest. The sheer impact shook the very ground beneath me, jolting my senses with an eerie mixture of awe and apprehension.

Each step I took brought me closer to the supposed location of Mike's presence. However, as I drew near, the disquieting vocalizations gradually ceased, leaving behind a haunting silence. Not a single chirp from a bird or the scurrying of a squirrel could be heard—just an unnerving absence of all other sounds.

It was then, out of the corner of my eye, that I caught a glimpse of something enormous and black, leaping gracefully from one tree to another across a nearby creek. As it landed, I instinctively shifted my gaze, locking eyes with a figure standing facing away from me, seemingly engaged in the act of sniffing the air. Time seemed to stretch, as though the world had come to a standstill. In reality, only a few seconds passed, but it felt like an eternity. The figure took four deliberate steps, disappearing behind a dense cluster of evergreen trees.

Based on the awe-inspiring sight I beheld, I estimated its towering height to be between 6 and a half to 7 feet. Its arms were exceptionally elongated, extending almost down to its knees. The creature possessed a robust physique, devoid of a discernible neck, with bulging muscles that exuded immense power. Though not of colossal proportions, its arms exhibited considerable strength. It brought to mind the likeness of a seasoned athlete rather than a young Arnold Schwarzenegger. The creature's legs were notably sturdy, reminiscent of a skilled softball player—an imperfect analogy, perhaps, but one that best conveyed their muscular build. As for its hands, they were undeniably massive, capable of gripping an object with ease. In fact, it appeared as though it could effortlessly lift me by my head with a single hand. Unfortunately, I did not catch a glimpse of its face during our brief encounter.

Strangely, despite the awe-inspiring nature of the creature's presence, I never sensed any malevolence emanating from it. Rather, it seemed more an expression of its desire for solitude, a silent plea for me to respect its domain. I had no inclination that it intended to cause harm; instead, it conveyed a profound sense of territoriality.

That, my friend, is the crux of my encounter—an encapsulation of the sights, sounds, and emotions that permeated that unforgettable moment. I must admit, I'm uncertain if my story aligns with what you were seeking, but I felt compelled to share it with someone. Until now, my wife has been the sole confidant of this remarkable experience, yet even she harbors doubts about its veracity.

CHAPTER FORTY-TWO

MY ENCOUNTER STARTS off average in that I was on a hike in the middle of the woods, in the middle of nowhere. I live in Tennessee and that's where it happened as well. I took my dog everywhere with me. Her name was Minnie, and she was a pit bull and Labrador mix. It's a good mix and she was the sweetest dog I ever knew. She was also intensely loyal and protective. It felt safer having her with me. I wasn't on any sort of intensive hike or anything but there were some dense woods around my cousin's house, and I was merely out for a night-time walk to get some fresh air and explore a little bit. The woods have always comforted me, and this was the first time I had ever been to my cousin's house and in fact it was the first time I had seen him in about twenty years. It was 1984 and I was thirty years old. Our parents used to be close and at one time we were like brothers. Both of us are an only child and so we enjoyed our time together. However, when we were both about ten years old our parents had a major falling out and because of that we never really spoke again. My aunt, his mother, had recently passed and so I offered to drive the two hours from my house in Tennessee to his house in another part of the state, to help him go through some of his mom's stuff. It was too much to stay in her house, the home he grew up in, and plus he had a family. His father and my dad both died young and so I knew that as far as blood relations went, me and my mother were all he had left. My mom still hadn't come around, but I knew she would once she found out that I did. I had supper with his wife and two kids and then I asked if he minded if I took a little walk with my dog to clear my head. He said to go right on ahead and so there I was.

I planned on staying with him and his family for a week and during the day he and I would go to his mother's house and clear out and sort through her belongings. I had gone for a walk all three previous nights that I had been there and nothing about the woods seemed out of the ordinary to me. In fact, the day before I had gone on a short hike and little fishing trip inside those same woods with his son and I didn't have any issues. The boy was only two years old, but I was still excited to be able to spend some quality time with him. After all, as far as blood relation went, he and I were kind of in the same boat. I should mention now that I was never a very religious person, but I have become very spiritual. My spiritual awakening happened after this experience because it changed my life in so many ways and opened my eyes to what the world is really like outside of what we as human beings can see. I didn't mean to disturb anything out there, but it seems as though I did, and my poor dog Minnie is the one who suffered the most from it all.

I walked for about ten minutes at the time and knew that the trail eventually curved and gave me the option to circle back and walk the same way back to my cousin's house. His home was out in the middle of nowhere. He had done very well for himself and had had some of the forest cleared to have the house built from the ground up. He was really humbled about it all though and that made it easier to be genuinely happy for him. He and his family were devout Christians which was something I was having a hard time getting used to. Other than that, it was all good. I knew it would take me a little over an hour to walk the whole trail and end up back at his house, but I was okay with that. He didn't allow smoking in his home and so I took the opportunity of my after-dinner walks to get as much nicotine in as possible before I went back and went to bed and couldn't have another one until the morning. As we walked, I noticed my normally happy and somewhat dumb dog was acting strangely. She seemed anxious and reluctant to follow me when normally she would be off and running, bounding so far ahead of me that I had to constantly call her back to me. Even on our walks on the previous nights she had thoroughly seemed to enjoy it all and was excited. She seemed genuinely scared and at one point she just stopped in the middle of the trail, several feet behind me, and urinated all over her own legs. If you know anything about dogs, you know that's extremely bizarre behavior.

I don't know why I didn't just take a cue from her and turn around. I guess I just thought that it was all the excitement from traveling and being away from home for the first time for more than a night at a time. I didn't travel often, and I worked from home. I was divorced and my kids lived with their mother and so my dog wasn't used to a full house with very small kids. That's how I rationalized it anyway. By the time we were twenty minutes into our walk I regretted not putting her on a leash because she refused to move. I had to yell at her, which I hated, and eventually she reluctantly resumed slowly walking behind me. She would stop here and there to bark and growl at trees and at what otherwise seemed like thin air. I tried to ignore it. I tried my best anyway. Eventually we came to the circle where the trail rounded back to my cousin's house and Minnie seemed more scared and her behavior was more bizarre than ever. There was a little clearing at the end of the trail where the circle was and there was also the option to continue, either to the left or to the right. It was a gorgeous and very mild night with a nice, cool breeze blowing through the air. I didn't want to rush back and honestly at that point my dog was just getting on my nerves. The moon was full, and the dark sky was full of beautiful stars. I stopped to look for a moment before continuing.

When I stopped, my dog ran into the clearing a little bit and started barking incessantly at a bush. It was weird because it was only a lone bush and there wasn't anything else around it except for everything, the rest of the forest, behind it. I looked up at the sky and heard my dog yelp loud. It was a noise unlike anything I had ever heard before and I immediately was worried. She sounded like she was in pain, and it couldn't have been longer than a split second before I was staring at where she just was by that bush. I took a step to start running over there to get my dog, but she suddenly came bounding out from behind the bush. I knew right away something was wrong because her eyes were no longer dark brown, but they were glowing bright red. She came up to me and stared me in the eyes while snarling and barking at me. She had never done that before and obviously, between the aggressive behavior and the eyes, I was terrified. I didn't want to squat down to look at her and rub her head, which is something I normally did when she was angry or otherwise in distress, because I was afraid, she would attack me. She looked strange too and it wasn't just the eyes.

Her face looked distorted somehow, as though it were somewhat stretching and then snapping back again. Her whole body was vibrating, almost like she was having trouble staying in this reality or something. Like I said I wasn't very religious, but I did believe in the supernatural and I was a huge believer of UFO phenomenon which unlike today was very unusual at the time. Something was terribly wrong, and I didn't know what to do. Before I could even try and comprehend what was happening, the wind started to pick up and suddenly there were black, dark shadows all over the place. They were darting from one spot to another, faster than the blink of an eye. I tried to follow them with my eyes, and I think there were at least ten of them. My dog turned and ran, snarling and barking at the entities, until she got to one of the trees. One stood there, the only one wearing the hat, and he put his shadow hand on my dog. She suddenly whimpered and whined, and her face distorted in pain. She literally fell over. I wanted to run to her, but the shadows were still everywhere, and the red eyed hat man was still standing over her limp body.

It just stood there and stared at me, my lame dog now at its feet, for a good ten minutes or so. I had tears in my eyes but didn't even realize I was crying. I was terrified and if it weren't for Minnie, I would have taken off and run the second I saw the shadows. Eventually, within that ten-minute time frame, all the shadows that had previously been darting around had each disappeared, seemingly inside of the trees, and the hat man eventually slowly faded into the darkness around us as well. The minute he was gone I ran over to my dog. She was alive and only looked like she was sleeping. I cautiously bent down to pet her, and she immediately jumped up and started licking my hands and face as if she were so happy to see me and hadn't seen me in months or something. I told her let's go and whistled and she came along easily, leading the way back to my cousin's house. She would stop every two minutes or so and look back at me, as though she were confused about what just happened or where we were. I wish I had taken a few more minutes with my dog because she died very shortly after.

Minnie was only four years old which is only twenty-eight in dog years, I think and depending on who you ask. However, she was hit by a car a couple of days later before I even left my cousins to go home. It was devastating and I knew it had something to do with what happened to us in the woods though that's only my instinct and not something I can prove at all. I hadn't taken her with me ever again on my nightly walks, but I continued them for the entirety of our trip because my mind wouldn't allow me to rest or let it go. I needed answers and sometimes I wonder if maybe I was being punished for being so curious with the death of my dog. I never mentioned my encounter to anyone, and I never saw anything like that again. I never saw it near my house, in any other woods I've been in while hiking, hunting, camping or just walking along somewhere, and I honestly don't know what the hell I accidentally walked up on that night, but I do know that it was supremely evil and it's probably for the best. That's my encounter and I wonder if anyone else has ever had any experiences with shadow beings or entities, specifically the hat man, influencing their dogs or other pets. As far as I can find in my research they aren't normally harbingers of death or catastrophe like the mothman but who can really be sure. I needed to get this out as it's been tormenting me all these years and I still can't explain it, but I also can't bring myself to talk about it either. Thanks for letting me get this out there and off my chest.

CHAPTER FORTY-THREE

WHEN I WAS sixteen I was camping in the woods with some friends for the weekend. We were all having a really good time as camping was one of our most favorite things to do and something we did all the time. Where we grew up there really wasn't much else for young kids or teenagers to do in the town and life got pretty boring. So, more often than not, especially in the summertime, we would all get together and drive out to a local spot that used to be a summer camp way back in the nineteen fifties. This all happened in the eighties so that seemed like a lifetime ago, even then. It was private property and illegal to be there without permission but we weren't loud or rowdy and didn't cause any trouble. We didn't drink or do drugs and so even on the few and very rare occasions that we would get caught out there, normally a security person would come and tell us we shouldn't be there and needed to be gone by morning. Our parents didn't know that that's where we were and because we were all females and all best friends, we would just tell our parents that we were at one of the other one's houses and that was that. It always worked and we hadn't ever been caught by our parents being out there. We had been going to that old, abandoned camp for a little over a year at that point and we were just starting to become familiar with everything there and all of the land and stuff. It was a place to be alone and to feel like we were grown up. We always camped outside and didn't really go in the cabins. There was no electricity and the plumbing didn't work inside of the ten or twelve cabins but they were in almost pristine condition, despite having been completely abandoned for about thirty years. There was wildlife in most of them though and we didn't even want to think about what else. We got our kicks off of horror movies too and it would sometimes get really scary at night.

Not only was the old camp located in the middle of some really dense and desolate woods but it was also way out in the middle of nowhere. Our friend Ronnie's sister would drive us out there sometimes, when we had enough money between the four of us to chip in for either her booze or her cigarettes and then we would just hitch a ride home. So, it was just another summer night and we were laying in the middle of the lake on one of the docks and looking at the stars. There weren't as many out that night as there usually were at that time of year and the moon was barely a sliver in the sky. There was enough light though, somehow, and we were having a good time when all of a sudden we started hearing really loud clicking noises, sort of like someone incessantly clucking their tongue at us, but it sounded like it was coming from all over the place. We all immediately stopped laughing and giggling and got quiet. We had no idea what it could have been but we were immediately scared. The symphony of clicks and clucks lasted for about fifteen minutes but while it was happening we were all too afraid to move let alone get back in the water and swim back to shore to investigate. Eventually though it died down and then there was nothing but silence. Looking back on it now it was as if everything was way too silent and quiet but back then we just laughed at how scary the noises had left us and went right back to looking at the stars and gossiping like the normal teenage girls that we were.

Suddenly something red that looked like it was on fire blazed across the sky, and then one right behind that. It was in no way, shape or form a shooting star and I say that because I remember seeing shooting stars all the time back then because the sky was always so clear around those parts and these things looked nothing like them.

My friends and I jumped up again as we watched the blazing balls of fire shoot through the sky and disappear. They looked like they were falling fast from the sky and as we turned around to see which direction they were going in, it seemed to us like they were falling into the woods. One right after the other they fell and we counted eight altogether. Our suspicion that they were landing in the woods was confirmed when we saw over our shoulders that they seemed to be falling through the trees about a hundred feet from where we were on the docks. We were all really scared but knew that we had to get out of the water and back on to the relative safety of dry land again. We all jumped in and made our way back to shore and back to our little camp as fast as we possibly could.

We didn't dare start a fire lest we risk someone telling us we had to leave and we used flashlights for most of our illumination along the trails and also as we sat there around our tents talking some more. We hadn't seen or heard anything strange the whole time we were making our way, cautiously, back to our tents but we were all terrified and wondering what in the hell had been falling from the sky. We thought that whatever the objects were that they were on fire but once they seemed to drop into the woods there weren't any actual fires that had sprung up anywhere though. We finally called it a night at around one in the morning. We had discussed going to investigate but decided to wait until the morning before we did so. It was around two thirty when I woke up to go pee and walked to the edge of the woods that were surrounding our little makeshift campsite and I was startled by the sight of my one friend, Josie, already awake and standing there, facing the woods. She didn't seem to be doing anything like going to the bathroom or anything so I went up to her and asked her if she was okay and what she was doing. She didn't respond and was staring straight ahead into the woods, her mouth was moving but she wasn't actually saying anything. She didn't turn to look at me and she wasn't blinking either. It was the creepiest thing I had ever seen, up to that point in my life anyway. I shook her and when she still didn't respond I slapped her, hard, across her face. That did the trick and she immediately put her hand up to her cheek, turned and looked at me wide eyed and asked me what I had done that for. I told her she was being weird and not answering me and she swore she had only been out there going pee. She was angry and stormed off, going back into her tent. I didn't know what was going on but I was exhausted so I went and did my business and turned to go back to my own tent to go back to sleep. I heard rustling in the bushes.

I turned back towards the woods and saw something standing there, between two trees and when I shined my flashlight on it I almost screamed. It was hideous and terrifying and I didn't know what in the world it was. It was at least ten feet tall, had a gigantic and bulbous head that was sort of in the shape of a light bulb, and the biggest, darkest black eyes I had ever seen. I stood there and my mouth was still open because of sheer terror and the inability for my mind to grasp what it was I had come face to face with. Its arms were extremely long and thin as were its legs. It just stood there, staring at me. Its skin was a bluish gray color and it didn't even flinch at the light I was shining into its face. cIt lifted one long and gnarled looking finger and pointed at me. I immediately lowered my light without even thinking about it. It had forced me to do that, of that I was sure and that scared me too. Suddenly there were others, all stepping out of random places behind trees and bushes, all walking up to stand with the one I had initially seen. They were all different shapes and sizes but they all had the same giant, bulbous head and humongous black eyes. They all had the same color skin too. They started walking towards me. For at least a minute I was too scared to move but eventually my adrenaline kicked in and I turned to run. The clicking and clucking noises my friends and I had heard earlier while we were lying on the dock started again and once again it was like it was coming from everywhere all at once. I was crying by the time I got back to my tent. I got fully back into my tent before I realized I should have woken up my friends and none of them seemed to be awake because none of them were making any noise at all. I looked out of my tent to see where the creatures were but didn't see anything. I got under my blanket, closed my eyes really tight and started to pray.

It seemed like as soon as I did that the noise stopped all at once and just as suddenly as it had started. I slowly opened my eyes and peered out from under my blanket and once I didn't see or hear anything after a minute or two, I decided to look out of my tent again and see if the creatures were there or if my friends were awake. I slowly crawled to the front of my tent and looked out. There, surrounding my friend Josie's tent, were five creatures. It didn't seem like she was awake because she wasn't moving around inside or screaming. I was sure if she had seen what I was seeing she would be screaming non stop and waking up the whole town. Not that I would blame her. They were at least ten feet away from me or more and I was about to lose my mind and just start bellowing out for help. The creatures had no mouths, I forgot to mention that but yet they seemed to be communicating with one another. What made me think that was they were all looking at one another and they would all pause for a moment and then one would nod its head in the negative or in the affirmative and then they would look into her tent. I was just about to crawl back underneath my covers and cry myself to sleep until sunrise when something told me to look up. I did and the last thing that I remember was seeing a gigantic set of dark, black eyes staring back at me. I opened my mouth to scream but I don't think that anything came out.

The next day all four of us woke up at the exact same time and we were all outside of our tents. Josie didn't remember anything from the night before, not even my smacking her and in fact, she was also the only one who hadn't remembered what we had seen and heard while out on the docks either. My other friends did and so did I but we were all just very confused by why we were outside of our tents and how we had gotten to be that way. We couldn't figure it out. There was no one who knew we were out there who could have been messing with us and all three of my friends were suspicious of one another, and me. I wasn't because I had full recall of the middle of the night and what I had seen. I remembered it all but was still too afraid to say anything. We had planned on staying another night but we all felt very strange, like we had been drugged and though none of us outright said it, we all felt like something terrible happened and was still going on in the woods all around us. Josie seemed to be the least concerned and asked if we wanted to go for a quick swim before we left but we all said we didn't want to. That seemed to upset her but she didn't push the issue. No one asked if we were going to explore and see where those fireball looking things had landed the night before either. Josie didn't remember it but the rest of us did. Just as we were about to leave Josie mentioned that the back of her neck was stinging and when we looked she had what looked like an old surgical scar back there. Whatever it was looked healed already and the skin was puffy and raised. We asked her how she had gotten the scar but she said she didn't have a scar there. The rest of us checked the backs of the others' necks but no one else had anything there and no one else felt any pain there either. As we made our way out to the main road, Josie talked about the strange nightmare she had the night before about strange creatures and even mentioned how I had slapped her in the dream because she was staring out into the woods. I laughed along with her but our other two friends didn't laugh. It was like something unspoken hung between us but we weren't able to put our fingers on what it was.

It would take about twenty years before we would all realize we each had a different piece of the memory from that night. We met for our usual annual lunch back in early 2007 and that's when one of us brought up that night in the woods. It turns out my other two friends had seen the beings surrounding Josie's tent as well but they didn't remember it all until years later. They also noticed they had the same type of healed wound she had suddenly woken up with as well. One of them on her right ankle and the other behind her left ear. Mine is behind my right knee. We had all noticed them the day we got home while showering but we just never thought to mention it. We haven't been hypnotically regressed yet though it's definitely on the table and we all have a feeling it somehow started with and revolves around Josie. Maybe it's just the camp and we happened to be in the wrong place at the wrong time but I doubt it. We keep in almost constant contact now and have been incessantly researching. You see, after it happened all the way until that dinner we had together in 2007, it's like we simply forgot about it. Every time I would remember, and this turned out to be true for the other three girls as well, we immediately would forget and it would be fuzzy and like it was only a dream anyway. It's very hard to explain but the more we learn, the more we hear others' encounter and abduction stories, the more we believe that's what happened to us. We believe we were abducted. We had even gone back to the camp just as regularly as we always had gone right up until we graduated high school and moved on with our lives but none of us ever gave any of it a second thought because we couldn't remember even our own conversations about it or other connections we had already made about all of it. It's still very confusing but I am sure that something happened to us that night, probably other times since then and possibly even times before that but we simply can't remember. I am terrified of learning the truth and so are my friends. Josie is the only one who doesn't seem to be as scared and she will more than likely be the first one to be regressed. I'll write about how that goes when the time comes. I have no memory of ever seeing the beings again; not in dreams, nightmares or otherwise. But I know somewhere deep down in the recesses of my mind that the memories are there because I just instinctively know that I have seen them other times. I just know it. We are planning on going back and seeing what's left of the summer camp nowadays and if we can legally camp out there for the weekend. I'll write about how that goes too, provided I leave there with my memory intact. Thanks for letting me get this all down and out there, before I forget it again. Maybe someone with a missing link or piece will come across it, who knows? After all, stranger things have happened.

CHAPTER FORTY-FOUR

I WAS in my late twenties when I had my encounter with something I have never been able to explain but that nowadays many more people are also encountering and I don't feel so crazy about it anymore so I finally decided to write it all down. I was camping near my house in Tennessee, just me, and I had already been out there for three days when I came across something terrifying and still very unexplainable. I had chosen a spot way out in the middle of nowhere and there were so many trees and so much brush, there almost wasn't any space even for my small tent. I cleared a space though and I was having a great time. I was out there just because I had some free time and I loved hiking and being in the wilderness in general. There were no other people out there and normally there weren't any because I always went to one spot that's private property. However, my boss at the time owned it and had planned on clearing it all out and building on it but for whatever reason the permits and all the legal stuff was holding the project up. So, not only was I able to hike to my heart's content and be left alone while I was doing it, it was a win-win because in exchange for letting me camp there he expected me to keep an eye on the place and make sure there were no trespassers or vandals, things like that. I kept a shotgun on me at all times but I didn't hunt and otherwise never had to use it before. I was trained on how to use guns properly, I just never felt the need to use one before. I had just gotten back to my camp, made a fire and had something to eat. I went to bed at around eleven at night but all night long I kept hearing the sound of something large moving around in the woods directly surrounding my tent. At one point the sounds got so close it was like someone was standing right outside of my tent. I kept looking out but didn't see anything and eventually I convinced myself that it was probably a smaller animal than what it sounded like and that more than likely it was more scared of me than I was of it. I went to sleep.

The next morning I woke before sunrise and had some coffee and breakfast then went to go and explore one of my favorite trails. I didn't know the whole area yet but I was quickly becoming acquainted with most of it. It was the nineteen eighties and I had my walkman with me, complete with an array of cassette tapes for my listening pleasure and I normally had them on full blast when I would go out on my hikes. That entire day though I felt like I was being watched and normally I would have brushed that feeling off too but because of the noises the night before, I was starting to think that I wasn't alone out there after all. The day was uneventful despite the strange feelings of creepiness and terror that would wash over me seemingly randomly and for no apparent reason. It wouldn't be long before something proved my instincts to be correct but it's somewhat of a long story in getting to that. Once night fell I built a fire again and as I was sitting in my chair and eating dinner, I had the headphones off. It was just me and the sounds of nature and perfectly normal, at first. I was looking up in the sky and saw a giant flash of light like lightning but it was in the shape of an oval and it was bright orange. It almost looked like a giant ball of fire that just flashed into existence in the sky. I almost dropped my food when I saw it and stood up in order to try and get a better look. The giant ball of flame got smaller and larger several times and it seemed like it was pulsating or something. Then, just as quickly as it had appeared, it was gone and though I was a bit rattled, I considered myself a practical man and tried to forget about it. That night passed the same way as the night before, with me hearing someone or something lurking around my camp all night but once again I didn't see anything. The next day my whole life would change.

I woke up and once again just went about my usual business. There was no sign that anyone or anything had been anywhere near my camp and once again I rationalized it all. I was planning on exploring a new area of the land that day but had run out of batteries for my walkman. I couldn't find the extras I had bought and so I just went on my hike in the silence of mother nature. I noticed right away there didn't seem to be as much activity as there normally was for that time of day and once I reached a certain spot, where I believed was dead center in the middle of the forest, or at least the part of it that my boss owned, there was no noise at all. It wasn't like a slow fading of noise or anything but it was like someone had flipped a switch and not only did the whole forest fall silent all at once, but the sky was very suddenly overcast as well. There was no rain in the forecast for the whole week I had planned on being out there and I still had three more nights and four days left before I planned on or wanted to go back home. I said a silent prayer that it wouldn't rain because I hated being out camping when everything was wet and slippery. Just as I picked my bag back up and started walking towards where I thought the lake was, I heard a strange clicking sound. It was coming from two different places and seemed almost like communication of some sort. It wasn't any animal or insect that I knew of and it immediately and seemingly for no reason at all struck a terror into my soul unlike anything I had ever felt or experienced before. It sounded like it was coming from somewhere above me and as soon as I looked up, it started to rain heavily. I decided to put my backpack over my head and continue on to the water. Despite the rain being unusually heavy, especially for something that hadn't been picked up in the forecast at all, I figured it was a sun shower and would quickly pass. The clicking sounds continued the whole way to the lake. I was getting agitated. There was something about the noises that made me absolutely terrified and it blew my mind because there seemed to be no rational explanation or reason for why I was feeling that way. I kept going.

I eventually made it to the clearing where the water was and went to go and sit down near where the water met the woods, so to speak. I was determined to wait out the rain and after a while I was bored and started looking all around for the source of the now incessant clicking sounds. I didn't see anything right away. Then, I saw something I will never forget. I looked over to where the sounds were coming from as they had moved from seemingly above me to somewhere over to my right, right on the shore near where I was sitting. I saw something that was walking on two legs, just like a human being, and that looked like a human being from the feet to the neck area, but had the head of some sort of creature. It seemed to be looking straight ahead and not at me, just from judging how the legs were moving and the swinging of the arms. At least that's what made the most sense at the time. I couldn't take my eyes off of it because it wasn't there, not really, and I was only seeing it because it was raining. It was some sort of entity that was very obviously cloaked and a movie I had recently seen in the theaters immediately came into my head. It was the predator, from the movie with the same name. I was shocked and had somehow forgotten to be terrified for a few minutes. The entity was clicking but then I heard a loud squawking noise come from behind me which not only snapped me out of my complacent daze but that also seemed to have alerted the creature to my presence. Its head quickly whipped over to look right at me. It didn't have any colors to it and was visible only because it was wet but the shape of the head was very odd. The skull seemed to be elongated and, as crazy as it sounds I know, it looked like it had dread-locks for hair, on the elongated head. It looked at me and I immediately jumped up, ready to run. Then I remembered I had my gun on me and grabbed it.

The entity or whatever it was started walking towards me very quickly. I aimed the gun at it and it squawked again, this time much louder. It seemed angry and its walk showed me it was feeling aggressive towards me. I kept hearing the other one, despite not being able to see it, and that one sounded like it was also getting closer and approaching me as well, but from behind me somewhere. I took a shot at the one in front of me and it seemed to be more stunned by the noise than anything else. Here's the thing, I KNOW I hit it. The bullet seemed to go right through it though but instead of making it more angry it turned and took off at a superhuman speed into the woods. I don't know if I was in some sort of induced daze or something but I actually took off after it. It was moving so quickly though I didn't stand a chance at catching up to it and something told me it was actually going slowly to keep me able to see it. As soon as we got to the edge of the trees it scrambled up to the top of one, again at lightning fast speed. I just stood there, looking up at it. I watched as it ran incredibly fast across the tops of the trees until it was so far away I only knew it was still there because I could see the effect its weight had on the treetops. Understand though that it was in the actual tops of the tree and those branches couldn't hold a little kid's weight without snapping let alone a full grown man's or whatever this thing was. Yet, I watched it with my own eyes. I was suddenly aware of the one behind me that I had forgotten about when I started chasing the one I had taken a shot at. I turned around and saw more of them, about three or four, come walking nonchalantly and like it was nothing, right out of the water. I took off running and left everything but the gun at the water's edge.

I could hear it behind me for a little while and I didn't dare turn around. By the time I got back to my camp I was out of breath and fairly sure that it was no longer following me. However, there were at least six of them out there and those are only the ones that I had seen. It stopped raining just as suddenly as it had started and I was aware immediately that unless the sun hit them just right, I would no longer be able to see them or even know they were there if they had decided to quietly sneak up on me. I was petrified and wasn't going to stick around another second. I packed up as much of my gear as I could in a hurry and as I did so, suddenly, all of the trees started bending down towards me at the tops. They were there and they were standing on top of the trees, surrounding me. I yelled out that I didn't want any trouble and that I was sorry for encroaching on their land. The tree tops bounced up and went back to normal once I said that and I bolted out of there as fast as I could. I left a lot of my belongings behind but it didn't matter and I never went back there again to retrieve them either. I never went back there again, period! I tried to tell my boss about it but he just laughed. I eventually stopped mentioning it. I wonder if the light in the sky had anything to do with the creatures or if they came from under the water. Maybe the light in the sky landed in the water and those things had gotten out somehow. I don't know what their intentions were except that somewhere deep down they seemed extremely evil and despite my not really being able to see them they were downright terrifying. In the past ten years or so I see more and more stories about these same cloaked or translucent entities and for the most part people think they're extraterrestrial. I would like to know how the people who made the Predator movie got it so right though. I mean, how is that even possible? I don't know what I saw but I never stopped searching for answers. Even if an entity were cloaked it stands to reason to me that they could still be shot but my bullet went right through the thing, of that I'm sure. I wonder if there really are secret extraterrestrial bases not only underground but underneath water sources all over the planet as well, not just in oceans like a lot of people seem to think. I've never seen them again and my boss ended up building a huge house on the land but I never went to visit and ended up quitting after not too long after my experience on his property anyway. I do wonder though if he or anyone else in his family has ever seen anything out of the ordinary or not. I might look him up and ask him if he's still alive. This wasn't my last experience with extraterrestrials either, though it was my first and it was my last with that particular entity. I am still too terrified to write about the other experiences though, but this is a good first step I think.

CHAPTER FORTY-FIVE

MY BEST FRIEND and I went camping with my family in 1995 and we did something so incredibly stupid that has changed our lives forever and we had an experience we will never forget because of it. My parents had a very large and state of the art, for the time, camper van that they had just bought and they wanted to take it into the woods to camp for one of our vacations that year. I was eleven years old and didn't want to go without my best friend Gina. Gina lived next door and our moms had been pregnant with us at the same time and were also best friends. Of course our parents were okay with her coming with us and off we went for our end of summer vacation in the woods. There was an area near our home, about an hour's drive away, where you could bring your camper into the woods and park it for your stay. There was also a place for people who wanted to camp out the old fashioned way in tents and stuff but the areas were just a little bit separate from one another. While we had our own spot where the van was parked and where we could barbecue and build our own fire, there were other people around and it wasn't like we were all alone out there in the deep dark woods. It was a National Park, I don't want to say the name of it and somewhere we had gone so many times before. We knew we would have fun and this was Gina's first time ever camping which made me even more excited about the whole thing. I was like a kid on the night before Christmas and Gina was really excited too. We made it to the park and found our spot. We went to work making food and building a campfire.

Though the camper was very modern and a little fancy, it wasn't brand new. While my parents went to work outside of the van, me and Gina hung out inside and started planning all of the things we wanted to do while we were there. We were hungry and waiting for my parents to get dinner ready. We were looking through the cabinets for something to snack on to hold us over when we found a Ouija board. We both loved horror movies and had been watching them for years at that point and though we hadn't ever seen or handled one in real life, we had seen the board in movies and thought we knew what it was and what it did. Needless to say we had no idea and I wish we hadn't ever found that board. But, we did find it and we were excited about it. My parents were religious but they weren't fanatics or anything. However, I knew my mother would blow a gasket if she knew there had been a Ouija board in the van when they bought it and not only that but that me and my friend planned on using it. We hid the board and decided we would wait until we were able to go into the woods and do something by ourselves to use it so my parents didn't see it. If we had to, we figured we would just leave it there in the woods and forget about it. We were dying to try it though and were excited by the alleged danger using it brought with it. Finally dinner was ready and we went outside to hang out with my parents. We knew there was a place to go swimming and so we asked my parents if we could go there the next day. They said that they had wanted to do some hiking to the other side of the park but that if we promised to stay together and if we agreed to take the map, that we could go swimming without them the following morning. After all, it stood to reason that we wouldn't be alone and even that there would be other kids there too because the place had looked very busy when we pulled in and paid for some park extras at the welcome station. It was the nineties and things were very different back then than they are nowadays.

The first night there was really fun and my parents even joined in when we told spooky and creepy stories by the campfire. The van slept four people which was perfect because me and Gina always shared a bed at sleepovers anyway. We stayed in the back of the van and my parents pulled their bed out of a wall in the front of it, right behind the driver and passenger seats. The next morning we woke up bright and early and my dad already had breakfast almost done. Gina and I put on our swimsuits, we put our clothes on over them and then we packed our backpacks with snacks, drinks and other things we wanted to bring swimming with us. I put the Ouija board and planchette in my bag and we left after a very long and boring lecture from my parents about staying together in the woods, the areas where we could get help, reading and following the map and what we would call today "stranger danger." We hiked through the woods and though we passed maybe one or two elderly couples, we didn't see as many people as we expected along the way. We didn't think anything of that and kept going. Finally, we made it to the swimming spot but we were surprised that there were only about ten other people there and no other kids. There were no little kids and no kids our age. There were no older teenagers either and in fact we noticed that there were only old people, which to our eleven year old selves consisted of anyone over the age of thirty.

We thought it was weird but it didn't concern us or anything. We knew we had to be back to the van for dinner, which was going to be at seven o'clock and we brought our lunches with us. We swam and played for a while and after we ate our lunch and a few hours had passed, we decided to try out the Ouija board. I didn't notice it at the time but looking back on it it's like as soon as we made that decision, for one reason or another every single person vacated the swimming area and Gina and I were all by ourselves. It was a bright and sunny day, despite it being almost fall, and we dried off fairly quickly in the sun. We remembered seeing people use one of the boards in a movie we had seen a few times and we just decided to do it like we remembered. We went to one of the tables in the little picnic and park area near where we had just gone swimming and placed our hands on the planchette. We giggled nervously and asked if anyone was there. In an instant the planchette moved to yes. We both had agreed beforehand that no matter what we weren't going to move it and we trusted each other so we were both shocked with how easy it had been to get an answer. Gina asked who was there with us and the word demon was spelled back to us. We both took our hands off the board immediately because, despite it being broad daylight and the fact that we were in a safe place, it scared us. We were little kids and it scared us enough that we quit right there on the spot, both of us pretending that we didn't want to stop except to please the other one and we both promised one another we would try again later on. We didn't say goodbye or thank the board or anything. We simply put it back in my book bag and went on with our day.

We had originally decided to swim some more but the day turned overcast rather quickly and we both had the distinct feeling that we were being watched. Because there was no one else around us anymore it was a scary feeling and we both knew that whatever was watching us had to have been doing so from somewhere in the woods. We played a few games of cards but eventually the feeling became too much and we decided to go back to our camp earlier than we were going to at first. We made our way through the woods but it seemed like all at once everything was different. We didn't see any of the signs we had noticed coming in and couldn't find where we were on the map my parents had given us. We both knew how to read maps fairly well and yet, somehow, we got lost anyway. We weren't too concerned at first because we figured we would eventually come across someone who would be able to help us but after what seemed like forever but was really about an hour of walking and not seeing anyone, we became not only very worried but we were also pretty exhausted as well. We sat on a large tree stump waiting for someone to walk by but no one did and to take our minds off what was going on we once again decided to pull the Ouija board out. We placed it on the ground and knelt in front of it. After saying hello we once again asked who was there and we got the response "death." That was it and we were so frazzled by that point that I took the board and tossed it into the woods along with the planchette. Gina and I knew it would be dark soon and we were definitely not equipped to be out there in the middle of the wilderness, alone, at night time. We just kept right on walking in the direction of where we believed our camp was, hoping we would just run into it somehow, eventually.

It was dark out and we were still lost. We were both crying by that time and still hadn't seen a single sign or other living soul the whole time. It was eerie because we knew that we should have seen several of both of those things. Finally we stopped to rest again and that's when an old man seemed to come out of nowhere, and asked us if we were lost. We were crying but so thankful to see him we both jumped and told him that yes we were lost and we needed help. He smiled but when he did it was terrifying. His smile didn't reach his eyes and his teeth were broken and stained by what looked like tobacco. We were good kids and didn't want to be rude so we suppressed our initial fear and gut instincts and told the man where we needed to go. He was really thin and looked like your average old man. He was a bit hunched in the back, had very thin, white hair and his skin was very pale and full of liver spots. He told us he knew right where that was, where we told him our camper was, and he told us to follow him. He whistled a tune as he walked and it was creepy. I don't know how else to describe it. The man had a flashlight he handed to me and though he was leading the way and the forest was pitch black, he didn't seem to need one. He was also dressed very oddly for where we were because he was wearing what looked like a tailor made three piece suit and very shiny shoes. His cane looked like a big snake and was perfectly carved by hand. Gina and I just looked at each other and after fifteen minutes of walking we realized we didn't know this old man and that we could be putting ourselves in even more harm's way than we were before we met him. He could be a psycho for all we knew. We didn't say anything though in case he was helping us we didn't want to be rude to him. We both were still crying and we were both extremely scared.

Eventually he turned to us and I will never forget the look on his face. It was evil and his whole appearance had somehow been trans-formed. He wasn't a kindly old man anymore but a grotesque thing that neither me nor Gina knew how to classify. The old man was still there, we could still see him, but we also knew there was something else underneath. We both screamed. He told us to shut up and knew both of our names despite us knowing for sure we hadn't given it to him. He told us to stay put and we did as we were told and sat on a log there in the middle of the forest. There still hadn't been anyone around and within a minute the old man returned. He looked even more devilish at that point and it was almost like the facade of the old man was slowly fading away and the evil underneath was seeping through more and more. He pulled the Ouija board out from behind his back and said we had been bad girls for throwing it the way we had. He pointed to me. "You!" he said, and his voice was almost a growl at that point, "come here." I didn't move and started screaming. His eyes were flames in his head and weren't kind and bright blue anymore. By that time Gina was screaming with me and he told us both to shut up. Suddenly he was standing straight up and had to have been about nine feet tall. His body contorted and turned into a half man, half goat looking thing as we looked on in terror. "Use the board" he demanded. We both shook our heads no and started screaming again. Then, coming from out of the darkness I heard my father's voice calling mine and Gina's names. I must have passed out and I guess Gina did too.

I woke up lying next to Gina on our bed in the camper. I immediately called for my dad and Gina grabbed my hand. We were both too weak to do anything other than lay there but we were also both absolutely terrified of what we had been through. My dad came running into the van while my mom spoke to the park rangers outside. I looked up at my dad and he smiled and told me it would all be okay. However, standing right behind him but too blurry almost for me to be able to see, was the old man. He wasn't in the old man form but the top of his body was that of a very physically fit god and the bottom that of a goat. He still held his snake cane but then he pointed it at me and Gina and started to laugh the most evil laugh I had ever heard. I started crying and sobbing and Gina must've seen him too because she was also shaking like crazy and sobbing. My dad tried to comfort us but the devil stood behind him the whole time, mocking him. We went back to sleep and didn't wake up until breakfast the next morning. My parents looked at us, concerned but asked us anyway what happened the day before. We told them everything except for the part where we played with the Ouija board and the part where the old man transformed into a devil. We knew they wouldn't believe us anyway. They told us the rangers said no one fitting that description, as far as they knew, had been in the park at that time. They also asked us why we had ignored all the people we passed along the way while we were lost who had asked if we were okay and offered to help us. That really confused us because we hadn't seen another living soul the whole time we were wandering around out there. Gina and I just looked at each other and my parents must've seen how it was upsetting us, though they couldn't have possibly guessed how much or why, and thankfully, they dropped the subject.

We weren't allowed to go off on our own anymore for the rest of the trip but that was okay with us because we really didn't want to. We never saw that Ouija board again but that old man/devil beast haunted our dreams and even visited us sometimes while we were wide awake, usually in the middle of the night and when we were together, many times after that. Finally when we were sixteen we came across some information that said if we got a Ouija board and properly closed it, by saying goodbye, it would be the end of the whole ordeal. We did it and it was but I still wonder what it was we were really dealing with that day and if it/he is ever going to come back for us. I know it's a lot and somewhat hard to believe but I implore you, please don't ever mess with something like an Ouija board or other divining tools unless you know what you're doing. As an adult I've searched for answers and have come to the conclusion based on my research that we hadn't encountered a devil that day but some sort of forest demon that feeds off of fear, especially the fear of children. I think we woke whatever it was up with the board and though I haven't gone back there since then to see for sure, I think it's probably still roaming around out there preying on people. It makes sense because that particular national park is known for bizarre events and people mysteriously dying and disappearing and while that's always been the case with that place in particular but also for places like it all over the world, there seemed to have been a huge uptick in cases since the mid nineties when me and Gina used the board. We must've opened a portal or something. I am going back there next summer and I am going to bring my own Ouija board, now that I know how to use it, and see if I can somehow close whatever portal or vortex we opened. While I know we aren't responsible for most of what happens there, I can't help but feel a little guilty because I do believe we played a role at least in some part of it. Thanks for letting me share this.

CHAPTER FORTY-SIX

WHEN I WAS twenty-six years old back in 2012 I had an encounter that terrified me and that also changed my life. I still have nightmares about it and despite having done as much research as I possibly could to figure out what it was and why it happened to me, I still really don't have any answers. I decided to use my vacation time to go and visit my parent's cabin in Colorado. They bought it when I was a little girl and I have so many fond memories of going there as a family and with all of our family, ever since. It was the middle of winter and I was going through a lot in my life and needed to get away. I hadn't ever asked to go by myself before but my parents weren't concerned at all with giving me the key and they handed it right over. We live in Pennsylvania but my older sister lived in Colorado at the time with her family and she still does. She said she would stop by and spend a night with me while I was there. I was planning on staying for a whole week.

There was a ton of snow on the ground by the time I got to the cabin. It was one of those places like you always see in horror movies. It was desolate, way out in the middle of nowhere and there were no neighbors. I should mention that I had always had nightmares when we stayed there but that wasn't anything completely new and I was always very sensitive to things around us at all times that other people can't see and aren't aware of. I thought about that on the drive to the place from the airport. I had always had bad dreams and visions, sometimes even when I was wide awake and it was dark in my bedroom, of a strange looking, tall man who would either come from under the bed or out of the closet and just stand at the foot of the bed watching me while I laid there. I got the chills but decided that it was all little kid's stuff and I wasn't going to allow it to ruin my sanctuary for the week. I really needed to get away and just go off grid for a while and that's exactly what I intended to do. I was even initially reluctant to have to visit with my sister, despite not having seen her for almost five years. We didn't have a falling out or anything. It's just she was busy with work and her family and I had a full time job where it felt like I never got any time to myself to do anything other than work. As far as the cabin, my uncle- my mother's brother- had a run of bad luck and had been staying there for the last ten years and so other than to visit him we didn't go there. We stopped being able to vacation there once he moved in because he was a weirdo and a drunk and though she helped him the moment he came to her and expressed he needed somewhere to live, he and my mother weren't that close because of his erratic and sometimes violent, drunken behavior. I knew my uncle wouldn't be there though because he had died six months earlier and my sister had just gotten done cleaning out all of his possessions and having the place professionally cleaned. So, that's the back story, now let's get into my encounter.

I pulled off the access road and almost didn't make it to where I had to put my car because of all of the snow. It didn't matter to me because I had hiked in the snow before, admittedly never while there was this much still falling and on the ground, but I wasn't worried. The cabin wasn't like a house where you pull up and into a driveway or anything. It was in the middle of the woods and it was going to be quite a hike to get there. Once I saw what the weather was like I knew that my sister wasn't going to be coming to visit until possibly the end of the week or at the very least for a couple of days. I was going to end up snowed in and in the middle of the woods. I relished the thought. It was hard living, being in the cabin. The bathroom was in the woods and the electricity came from a little generator. It was almost like camping in a camper van but it was bigger. I finally made it to the cabin with almost no time to spare before night fell. I was lucky because I don't know how I would have made it through the snow and the woods to continue on or to turn back in the dark. I didn't plan the hike out there very well. My sister had stocked the place with food but all I wanted was a hot shower and some sleep. I took a shower and settled in my bedroom. Before I was able to go to sleep though I realized I had forgotten to turn off the generator for the night. I reluctantly put on my jacket and sneakers, grabbed my flashlight and went to head out the front door. I stopped short before I got to it though because as I walked up to it it was turning. Someone was trying to get in. Now, my rational mind knew that it was impossible because nobody lived out there and my parents owned miles of land as far as the eye could see so even if someone were dumb enough to have been camping out there at the time, they would have seen the private property signs. Still, I thought that maybe it was someone who was out there and hadn't known it was going to snow and was now seeking shelter. I'm sorry but I wasn't their girl. I never had a good deed done for a stranger go unpunished and plus I was all alone out there. Unless it was a young woman or a child, there was no chance anyone was obtaining shelter through me, that was for sure. I asked who was there but there was no answer. I walked over to the door and stared out the peephole but there was no one there. As soon as I looked through it, the knob stopped jiggling and turning. I took a deep breath and opened the door. All I needed to do was walk to the back of the cabin, turn off the generator and run back through the front door and into my room. I stopped immediately in my tracks though because mine weren't the only ones out there.

The other tracks weren't human though, and they looked like hooves instead of any sort of known animal in the area or another human being's. I was terrified but knew that I would never get any sleep and had to at the very least go and turn the generator off. I didn't have too much extra fuel and didn't know when the roads would be accessible again. I followed the hoof prints all the way around the cabin and to the back but they didn't lead to the generator, they led into the woods. The cabin was placed in a spot where hikers would have set up tents if the cabin hadn't been there. It was in the middle of some very deep and very dense woods. I took a deep breath and decided I needed to find out what sort of animal had been trying to get in. I reluctantly followed the tracks into the woods. I knew it was dangerous but I was going through a lot at the time and was tired of feeling like everyone's victim. I was going to face and confront the fear of the entity that had always tormented me in the bedroom of that cabin for once and for all. I walked for about five minutes before suddenly the forest went silent. The moon and stars that had just been in the sky were covered by dark gray clouds and everything got that much darker. I had a flashlight with me but it wasn't much help if I'm being honest. I stopped when the hoof prints stopped, after I had been walking in the freezing snow and cold, deeper into the woods, for about ten minutes. I shined my flashlight all around but didn't see or hear anything at first. Then, I heard someone whispering my name from behind a nearby tree. I yelled out and asked who was there. That's when the tall man stepped out from behind the tree and smiled at me.

He looked exactly like I had remembered him. He was at least ten feet tall, had large ears and an equally large, crooked nose. His skin was a pale green color, it could almost be mistaken for white if you didn't know better. Almost like something that glows in the dark looks in the light. His teeth were brown and jagged and he wore a long black duster jacket that went down to his ankles. He had on an all black suit, shiny black shoes and his eyes were blacker than anything I had ever seen before. His hair was gray and hung down to his shoulders and he wore an old, beat up looking black cowboy hat on top of his head. He said my name again but before I could respond he opened his duster. Four little creatures seemed to come right out of the lining of his jacket and the only way that I can describe them is that they looked like miniature hell demons. I started to slowly back away. His eyes flashed and suddenly they were burning red and hot like the flames of a fire. The little minions danced around him and excitedly jabbered away in some gibberish language I couldn't understand. I asked him what he wanted but he just laughed and laughed. Then, he started to come towards me. I turned and ran as fast as I could back to the cabin.

I knew he was following behind me despite my not being able to hear anything. I ran inside and locked the door and heard the little demons jabbering away in their unknown language while the door-knob jiggled and someone, I'm pretty sure I knew who it was even though I didn't dare look through the peephole again, was banging on the door. He screamed for me to let him in and his voice was more of a growl than anything else. In the past, when he had approached my bed, his voice had been even and smooth but he sounded enraged just then. I was terrified he would kick the door down at any minute. I had shut off the generator so I only had my flashlight. I started barricading the door with furniture and once I was satisfied he wouldn't get in, I went and locked myself in my bedroom. I hid under my covers like a terrified little kid and eventually the banging stopped. I looked out my bedroom window in the middle of the night because I couldn't sleep and saw that the hoof prints were no longer there and had been covered up by a fresh blanket of snow. I was starting to think that maybe I had lost my mind. I began to pray. Just as I did so it sounded like someone was stomping on the roof. It sounded like what you imagine reindeer on the roof sound like when listening for Santa at Christmas time or something and then there were four lighter sets of footprints that also seemed to be jumping up and down, stomping and stamping. I continued to pray and after two minutes or so I heard what sounded like an animal howling. I looked up and saw an incredibly bright flash of light in the sky and everything was suddenly quiet again. I must have passed out because I didn't open my eyes again until it was morning.

I immediately got up and looked out the window but there was nothing there. I went and moved everything away from the front door, opened it and looked outside to see if any footprints were left. There were hoof prints all over the porch. The tall man had taken his animal form when he was trying to get into the cabin. It hadn't all been some sort of terrible nightmare and despite the fact that I had known that all along, it terrified me even more nonetheless. The snow had let up and so I figured I had one more night before I was able to hike back out of there and go to where I had service to call my sister and see when she was coming. I no longer felt safe there all alone and my peace of mind had been shattered once again. I was a nervous wreck and constantly looking over my shoulder at every little noise that whole day but once nothing happened and it was nighttime again I began to relax, just a little bit. I decided to leave the generator on and let it run out in the middle of the night because there was no way I was going back outside or anywhere near those woods at night time. Not ever again. I went and read by the light coming in from the full moon and my flashlight, tucked up nice and comfortable in my bed. My comfort didn't last long.

That whole night I was woken up over and over again to sounds on the roof alternating with someone tapping on the bedroom window. No words were ever spoken except the whispering of my name and it was so low as to make it so it almost seemed like it was nothing but the wind blowing. I knew better though. The next morning I woke up to my sister knocking on the door but at first I thought it was the tall demon man and didn't answer her. I went and stared at the door and it wasn't until I saw her in the peephole that I finally opened the door. She came in and had brought breakfast. I immediately began to tell her what I was experiencing and she reluctantly told me that not only had she experienced that same entity, every time we had visited here when we were growing up, but also that towards the end of his life my uncle had been ranting and raving about miniature demons under his bed and a devil man in his closet. No one believed him, his track record for insanity was too long and distinguished by that time. We both sat in silence for a few minutes trying to comprehend that what we had each individually experienced, the entity and his minions who had so thoroughly terrified us and whom we both were starting to begin we had simply imagined, was a real being. We decided I would spend the rest of my vacation week at her house with her family. I didn't want to be alone anymore anyway. I never went back to that cabin and neither did my sister. My family sold it in 2018 and lately, mainly because I had been having nightmares about the tall demon and the little devils again, I was wondering if I should go there and see if the new owners had experienced anything like what my sister, my uncle and I all had.

I don't know what it all means but I do know that the tall man was the devil or at least a devil and that he had come for my soul. He didn't get it that time but that doesn't mean he won't keep trying. I've since gone back to church and have become stronger in my faith so maybe that's why he has been visiting me again. I don't know if it would have been anyone who was staying in that cabin or if it was just our family and I don't know what the reason was. Maybe he and the little ones feed on human being's fear. Maybe I will never know. I know a lot of people will think I'm a lunatic but I'm not looking for validation and not trying to force people to believe. I wrote this all down in case someone else has experienced that man or his minions and to let them know that they aren't alone and they have to remain strong. Otherwise, they could lose something even more precious than their minds, in that, the devil is normally only interested in your immortal soul. Thanks for letting me share and though the story isn't over yet because I haven't really learned anything new or gained any answers to my many questions, I feel like someone needed to read this anyway.

CHAPTER FORTY-SEVEN

IN THE AUTUMN OF 2008, my friends and I embarked on an exhilarating adventure along a remote game trail, hoping to catch sight of majestic deer and elk. After trekking through the wilderness for over an hour, a mysterious noise emanated from the undergrowth, capturing our attention from both the right side and up ahead. It was a distinctive snort/huff, reminiscent of a horse's exhale.

Drawing from our knowledge of animal behavior, we recognized that deer and elk often produced similar sounds before punctuating their displays with a rhythmic stomp of their legs. Sensing an opportunity, I whispered to my companion that he could seize the chance for a shot. In an instant, our bodies froze in unison, my friend firmly raising his rifle, poised for action. Miraculously, the enigmatic presence ceased its movements, leaving an eerie stillness to permeate the air. Intrigued, I attempted to replicate the snort/huff, hoping to establish some form of communication. Unexpectedly, a loud, sharp whistle pierced the silence, originating from the exact opposite direction. Perplexed, my friend cautiously lowered his firearm, turning his gaze towards me, an expression of bewilderment etched across his face.

Refusing to dismiss the possibility of encountering a fellow hunter,

I bravely whistled back, longing for a response that never materialized. Unfazed, I called out, under the assumption that our mysterious companion might reveal themselves. Little did we know that our actions would trigger an unforeseen chain of events, plunging us into a realm of chaos. In a breathless moment, a massive, obsidian figure emerged from the dense foliage, looming tall above the bushes. Swiftly, it pivoted with a single fluid motion and propelled itself forward, dashing toward the protective embrace of the distant tree line. Astonishingly, its agility mirrored that of a human, defying conventional expectations of what one might associate with a creature of such stature. The sheer speed at which it traversed the landscape left us awe-stricken. In the midst of the commotion, my friend, overwhelmed by the spectacle, involuntarily released his prized rifle, allowing it to fall to the ground.

Though the encounter lasted but a few fleeting seconds, the memory of that remarkable sight remained etched in our minds. While the whirlwind nature of the encounter made it impossible to discern specific facial features, I can vividly recall its distinct black appearance and the fur that adorned its body, more akin to hair than anything else. In particular, its forearms bore an abundance of long, untamed strands, while its running posture revealed a slight inclination, its robust thighs and calves pulsating with raw power. The intensity of our observation lasted no longer than six seconds, during which the entity exhibited an unwavering determination, effortlessly obliterating anything obstructing its path, shattering branches with ease before vanishing into the abyss. As quickly as it appeared, tranquility was restored, enveloping the surroundings in an enigmatic silence. Taking a moment to compose ourselves, we cautiously approached the spot where the creature had emerged, discovering subtle traces of its presence, evidence of its concealed vigilance along the game trail. Had it not emitted that curious noise, our obliviousness would have led us to walk past without a second glance. Needless to say, our encounter left an indelible mark, compelling us to retreat, allowing the mysteries of the wilderness to retain their enigmatic allure.

Upon sharing our extraordinary tale with friends, the predictable responses fixated on the notion of encountering a bear. However, I implore you to trust in the veracity of my account. Having encountered numerous bears throughout my lifetime, I can confidently affirm that this was no ordinary bear. Rather, it embodied the characteristics of a profoundly hairy gorilla, its movements mirroring those of a human in its agile stride.

CHAPTER FORTY-EIGHT

I WANT to share a harrowing experience that occurred to me and my friend. Before I dive into the details, let me provide some context. At the time of this incident, I was enlisted in the Marines, and as part of my preparation, I frequently ventured to high-elevation mountainous areas to condition myself physically. My friend often accompanied me on these excursions. In anticipation of our trips, I had him purchase gear from a surplus store, while I was the only one armed with a .45 ACP Springfield 1911 pistol.

On this particular day, our destination was a mountain peak that required a strenuous two-mile hike. Laden with our equipment, we pushed ourselves to reach the summit, eager to savor the breathtaking view. However, our tranquil moment was shattered when my friend scrambled atop a cluster of boulders and his face turned ashen, aghast at something he had encountered. Without delay, he darted away, his panic prompting me to shout, "Hey, what's going on?"

Coming to a halt, my friend informed me that there was a massive black bear on the other side of the boulder. Intrigued, albeit cautious, I decided to verify his claim. Retrieving my pistol, I proceeded cautiously around the boulder. And there it was, a bear of immense stature, easily matching my own height of 5'10" and weighing an estimated 300 to 350 pounds. Aware of the potential danger, I signaled to my friend that we should make our exit discreetly, so as not to attract the bear's attention. Unfortunately, our efforts proved futile as the bear, undeterred, began closing in on me at an unsettling pace. In a desperate bid to fend it off, I yelled and discharged a round into the ground, which promptly prompted the bear to retreat.

However, merely moments later, an overwhelming sense of dread engulfed me. The hairs on my neck stood erect, and an uneasiness settled within me. Sensing imminent danger, I urged my friend to start descending from our lofty position. We found ourselves a considerable distance up a steep and treacherous slope, with daylight fading rapidly. The initial descent was incredibly steep, but I grasped my friend's backpack and guided him down cautiously. In that instant, a sound akin to a colossal baseball hurtling through the air narrowly missed his head, colliding with a pine tree with such force that it nearly stripped it of all its needles.

Never before had I experienced such primal fear, not even during the times I faced live gunfire. What followed was an auditory assault that resembled a cacophony of thundering footsteps, reminiscent of a dinosaur, echoing from the cliff directly above us. A bone-chilling scream, akin to that of a 500-pound demon-possessed woman on her period, reverberated through the air. In the chaos, I felt a gust of wind brush against my temple, as if something had grazed me. In that moment, I snapped out of my paralyzed state, overwhelmed by a primal instinct to fight or flee.

With trembling hands, I withdrew my pistol, urging my friend to run, and emptied the entire clip in the direction of the noise. We descended the mountain in a fashion reminiscent of the film "Lone Survivor," glancing back only once to catch a glimpse of what seemed like a face lurking among the trees, approximately 200 yards away. The terrain was unforgiving, and our mad dash left us battered and bruised, with me sustaining a torn ankle. Throughout our hasty retreat, our conversations were punctuated only by expletives, our tears betraying the depth of our terror.

When we finally reached the base of the mountain, exhaustion and relief washed over us, leaving us emotionally shattered. The two-mile descent, traversing treacherous terrain, had taken us a mere 20 minutes, a testament to the sheer urgency and fear that gripped us. When seeking medical attention, I refrained from divulging the true cause of my injuries, simply accepting pain medication and retreating to the comfort of my home. As of now, only my friend's mother and my wife are privy to the details of our traumatic ordeal. It is my belief that bears do not throw rocks or emit blood-curdling screams. This incident has forced me to reevaluate what we think we know, igniting a newfound curiosity about the mysteries that may lie beyond our conventional understanding.

Thank you for letting me share my story.

CHAPTER FORTY-NINE

I GREW up in rural Illinois and my brother and I spent all of our free time camping and hanging out in the woods. It was something we were able to do together and our encounter happened while we were out there one day, in the same woods we had been in thousands of times since we were little kids, that were connected to our parent's house and the surrounding property that they owned. I was twenty years old at the time and Jim, my brother, was twenty five. We had grown up in those woods and whenever he would visit our parents, who I still lived with at the time, we would go and camp for a night or two. Sometimes there would be other people who owned property that connected to all different parts of the woods and when we were younger we used to love meeting people out there but this time we decided we didn't want to hang out with anyone or meet anyone new. Plus, with the way the world was, we thought it was so bad in the early nineties, we were suddenly worried about getting robbed or killed or something. We made our way as far out as we could and didn't pass a single person along the way. Once we thought that we were safe and that we wouldn't be near anyone else who had also decided to venture out into that particular forest, we set up our camp. We each set up our own tent and went to work building a fire.

My brother had recently become engaged to someone none of the rest of the family had met yet. When he graduated college he moved to California for his job and we didn't see much of him. He was planning on bringing his fiancé with him on the next trip but had just broken the news to me and our parents. I was very happy for him but our parents were narcissists and of course they had to try and take the joy out of the situation. That's another reason why we spent so much time by ourselves and in the woods. Jim told me that once I meet the woman of his dreams, as he called her, that I would more than likely be able to move out to California with them and start fresh for myself. I was never that good at school and had skipped college altogether. I was excited about that fact and listened to him talk about it and about his life there and his woman, for a few hours. Eventually, after we had done some fishing and some hiking, it was time to go to sleep. We put out the fire and decided to call it a night. The only thing I had in my tent with me aside for some fresh clothes, was my flashlight and a very small pocket knife. I knew that's all my brother had in his tent with him as well. We didn't like guns and so we never brought them with us. We hadn't ever seen any of the large, predatory animals that supposedly roamed around in those woods anyway and so we weren't really that scared of them. We thought if anything we would see a bear and just leave it alone, as we had done when they would pass through our backyard from time to time. It was no big deal. We hadn't even considered that there were unknown creatures and things lurking around in those woods that we needed to fear more than mother nature and all of her wonderful and natural predators. We went to sleep.

Please keep in mind that we were about three hours into the woods and couldn't easily just run out of there. Also, we had chosen a spot near several watering holes so we could swim and fish. We loved the water almost as much as we loved the woods and always made sure there was some sort of water source near to us, at least so we could fish if nothing else. We found a spot for the first time with the best of both worlds and were looking forward to going fishing, hiking and swimming again the next day right after breakfast. The next morning we woke up and did just that. I can honestly say that everything was fairly

THE MEGA MONSTER BOOK

normal up until that night. We hadn't seen any people at all the entire time so far and that was a little weird but once we considered it we figured we were further and deeper into the forest than we had ever been and therefore we should've expected not to see anyone. That was kind of the point. We also noticed that, while they weren't completely silent or anything, the woods were a lot quieter than they should've been or than they usually were. We also both felt like we were being watched the whole next day. We explained those things away though and brushed them off as our overactive imaginations getting the best of us. I really wish we had paid attention to our guts, but you know what they say about hindsight, right? Nevertheless and despite the feelings we both had that something was a bit "off" we persisted and made it through the day without any incidents.

That night we ate and sat by the fire talking again. We were really close, me and Jim, and we were honestly just enjoying each other's company and the conversation. It was a cool night and as soon as the sun went down the chill in the air was instant and very noticeable. It was a little later in the year than we had ever gone out into the woods to camp before but it was the only time he could get off work to come and visit. If I wasn't still living there he probably never would have visited. No sooner had we decided to put out the fire that we both noticed things started getting really creepy. The light of the fire doesn't illuminate much further than a few feet around it in any given direction and our flashlights were in our tents at the time. We started to hear what sounded like someone sneaking around, sort of like they were weaving in and out of the trees. It seemed and felt, instinctively, that someone was out there just beyond our line of sight, and stalking us. It didn't sound like an animal or something that walked on four legs because we could hear the stride of it and something on four legs has a much smaller stride, and a much lighter step, than something with two legs does. We always played jokes on each other, especially when we were kids and out in the woods doing whatever we were doing at the time, and those noises sounded like someone trying to creep up on us but then it also sounded at the same time like someone trying to remain out of sight. It was definitely a human, or so we thought. We knew whatever it was walked on two legs.

When Jim asked me if I was hearing what he was I only nodded yes. I was trying to keep listening intently so I didn't lose track of where I thought it was. It didn't feel like my brother was as scared as I was because he kept talking and I kept on trying to shush him. I felt a primal sense of fear and somewhere deep down inside of me I knew we were in a lot of trouble. I kept thinking, over and over again, that whatever it was that was around our camp not only wasn't human, but that it was downright evil and had us both in its sights. Suddenly, there was the sound of whistling. It sounded just like a human being would sound when it whistled but it was accompanied by what sounded like someone running around really fast in a circle all around our campsite. The wind picked up and again Jim didn't seem as freaked out as me and said he was going into his tent to grab his flash-light and jacket. He suggested that I do the same but I was so scared I couldn't move and I begged him not to move either. He was trying to play it cool, that I could tell, and he fake laughed like I was being ridiculous but I felt and finally heard his fear nonetheless. I snapped out of my terror induced trance, got up and went inside of my tent. The fire was still burning at that point because we hadn't gotten the chance to put it out. The whistling was getting louder and louder and something was still running, at a superhuman speed, around and around our campsite. I heard Jim yell for me to stay in my tent. I immediately went for my blade and had no intentions of leaving my tent. I was, however, going to keep my eyes on the surrounding woods. They seemed to look like a blur every second or so when what-ever it was would pass through my line of vision.

I grabbed my knife, turned around and a pair of eyes was staring right back at me. The whistling had stopped as well as the incredibly fast running, and there were no other sounds except the sound of my heavy breathing. I knew my brother had his knife in his hand and was watching the woods too but I was too terrified of the eyes in front of me to be able to yell out to him. I opened my mouth to scream after what seemed like an eternity of being face to face with nothing but a set of glowing yellow eyes but as soon as I did that the whistling started again. I don't know how to explain what happened next, not really, but the eyes suddenly moved upwards, as if whatever they were attached to had been scooped into the air some how. I quickly grabbed my flashlight and shone it up in the direction they had just gone, which was up into the trees that were surrounding us. It was about eight feet up in the tree. I didn't only see the eyes and once again I was shocked and terrified into silence. I just kept my light on it. I could hear the whistling and it was definitely coming from whatever was in the tree. It had jumped, seemingly in one leap but it was so fast that I couldn't be sure, eight feet up into one of the trees directly above us. I saw it in its entirety now. It had long, skinny arms and legs and they were almost translucent looking. I often wondered if it hadn't been for the campfire if I would have been able to see anything but the eyes. Maybe my flashlight helped with that but I honestly don't know. My brother yelled at me again and asked if I was okay. I could only respond by saying, "up there, in the trees." I saw his flashlight shining all over the place until it finally landed on the creature or whatever it was up there. The thing was super agile and impossibly fast because the second my brother's light was also on it, and I mean that very second, it jumped. We heard it land somewhere in the surrounding woods. It landed with a very loud thump and the rustling of some trees.

My brother asked me what it was but I was scared speechless. My flashlight was still shining up in the tree even though I knew the entity, whatever it was, was gone. I crawled out of my tent as fast as I could and crawled over to my brother's tent. He let me inside and we were both still listening to see where it had gone. We heard the whistling again but it was once again connected to movement and the thing was blasting through the trees and thickets all around it. Then, we heard a very loud splash. We both jumped and that seemed to be the thing that knocked us out of our trance. There was nothing but unnatural silence in the air and we both looked at each other but we didn't say anything. After a few minutes, my brother said that we would be leaving as soon as the sun came up and I didn't argue with him at all. We both wanted to leave right then but knew we wouldn't make it through the woods that late at night. Just because we didn't see any bears or other natural predators, that didn't mean they weren't there. It wasn't just that though and we both knew it. We somehow knew, deep down inside, maybe you would call it instinctually, that the thing we had just seen was hunting, and it wasn't alone. There were more of them, they were still out there, and they would kill us if we tried to make it out of there just then. It was unspoken knowledge and there was nothing left to do but try to go to sleep. Jim took the first shift, or at least he was supposed to. I felt safe enough with him keeping watch that I was able to fall asleep rather quickly, especially given everything we had just been through. He never woke me up, not until sunrise, and he had already packed most of our belongings. We had a very long hike out of there and neither of us could move fast enough. We were so desperate to just be out of those woods. We were almost to the last twenty minutes of our hike back to our car when we heard the whistling again.

It was coming from everywhere but it seemed like it was also coming from nowhere and that's the only way that I can explain it. Jim and I stopped and looked at each other and then we both just took off running. We could hear the leaves rustling and the wind whooshing all around everything, right behind us, but we never stopped and looked back. We made it back to the car in what felt like just in the nick of time. We drove back to my parents house but we never discussed it with them or anyone else. We tried our best to forget it and ever since we have made sure that we camp in places where there are definitely going to be other people. We also arm ourselves with guns and we don't take any chances. I have no idea what we encountered that night or why but Jim and I have always felt like whatever it was had been pure evil and not of this world. We've gone back to those woods many times since that night but we've never gone anywhere near as deep as we went in that one time and like I said, we always make sure there are other people around if it's just the two of us.

CHAPTER FIFTY

I HAD A REALLY strange and bizarre encounter with what I am still convinced to this very day was something unnatural and downright evil.

I'm not a religious person but I do very much believe in the paranormal and supernatural and I love anything having to do with true crime and horror movies. It all fascinates me. I also think that had it not been for how many of those scary films I had watched up to that point in my life, I could have possibly fallen victim to the entity and probably wouldn't be sitting here right now writing all of this down. I've had more than my share of encounters with things from the other side, both good and bad, light and dark and most things in between but there was something about the entity I encountered back in 1975 when I was twenty years old that I'll never forget for as long as I live. You'll understand that better after you hear the whole story. I still have no idea what it all means but have come across a few encounters lately with women who have had very similar experiences and who think they've gone mad. They haven't, at least not if they're anything like me.

I lived in what most people refer to as Appalachia and the trails and forests all along the part of the trail in my state were very familiar to me. I used to love to go hiking and went every chance I got in college. I went to a local community college in my home state and spent a lot of time not only exploring the woods there but also partying in them. On the day when my encounter began I hadn't been drinking or doing any drugs and it was broad daylight. I was planning on camping out for the night near an area where I knew someone else was going to be having a party. The party was on a Saturday and would probably go right on into sunrise Sunday morning but I went out there on Friday morning in order to just have some time to myself. I lived in a sorority house and it was otherwise impossible to get even a minute to myself unless I was either out there in the woods or locked in my bedroom. Even with being locked in the bedroom there was always a lot of noise and someone knocking on the door every ten minutes or so for one drama or another and I just wasn't in the mood for it that night. I was even considering blowing off the party but that's why I was camping a few miles away, so that if I decided not to go no one would know where I was anyway. I told my sorority sisters and my family back home that I was simply "going camping" and gave no additional details. I hiked about two hours into the woods and set up my camp. It wasn't unusual to see other people hiking or camping as well and I had passed a few people on my way in. It had been about an hour by the time I got to where I was setting up my camp that I had seen anyone though. I was further in the forest than I probably had ever been but it was only because I was super stressed out and needed to clear my head and make sure no one could find me out there and bother me.

I had just found out that I was pregnant and didn't know what I was going to do. I needed some space. I set up my camp and decided to hike to a lake that was a little further up the trail I had come in on. I grabbed a few things I knew I would need and headed out. On the way there I came across a woman sitting on a large boulder. She looked like she was about my age but she was very overdressed for mid June in Tennessee. She had on a long sleeved black shirt and black jeans. She was wearing boots and a black vest over the long sleeved shirt and her hair was dark black and went down past her bottom. I knew that even though she was sitting because she was actually sitting on her hair and

I thought that was weird too. She was staring straight ahead and didn't even seem to blink as I jogged past her. I initially did go right past her but when I looked back, she hadn't even turned her head to look at me and was still staring straight ahead just as she had been when I had initially approached her and said hello. Of course she didn't respond and so I kept going. However, once I turned around and saw she was still sitting stone still and unblinking, I thought that maybe she needed some help and my curiosity got the better of me.

I turned and jogged back over to her. I asked her if she was okay and she didn't answer. I offered her a bottle of water from my backpack but she still didn't move or respond in any way. If she hadn't been sitting upright then I might have thought she was dead and in fact it didn't even look from where I was standing like she was breathing. She had to have been though, I reasoned, because she was sitting there like that. I once again asked her if she needed any help and told her my name. She looked up at me and that's when I saw that her eyes were completely black. There were no whites and they were darker than the darkest brown eyes I had ever seen. It was like the creatures we know today as the black eyed kids. I backed away in fear and terror and she proceeded to laugh like a maniac. Her teeth were yellow and looked sharp. She put her hands out to me but I didn't touch them and backed away even more. She then proceeded to start scratching at her face and eyes and blood was dripping everywhere. Her skin was pale white and her fingernails were yellow and very sharp as well. She was still laughing and I screamed and ran back to my camp. I looked behind me several times but she wasn't following me. I didn't know what to think or what to do. I thought that surely she had been some drug addled homeless person who was maybe hopped up on one thing or another and that she only looked creepy. I thought about calling the police but would have had to have packed up all of my stuff, hiked two hours back out of the woods and then gotten in my car to drive to a phone somewhere. I decided it was her own fault for being high in the woods alone and figured that she would sober up, hate what she had done to her face and make her way back to wherever it was she had come from. It was terrifying, don't get me wrong but our mind has a way of making us question what we see with our own eyes and within minutes of being back at my camp I was feeling very foolish for not having continued on to the swimming spot because of that crazy lady.

I hung around at my campsite for the rest of the night and built myself a fire once the sun went down. I kept getting the chills and felt like someone was watching me from the woods all night long. I immediately thought of the weird lady I had seen and made sure that my little pocket knife was within my reach just in case it was her and she wanted to hurt me or something. I had never been scared of the woods before but that night something was different. The energy was just off and I was terrified for seemingly no reason. The forest was much quieter than usual but not totally mute. There was just something inside of me that felt like I was in danger and I really couldn't put my finger on it at the time. I decided to call it a night and go to sleep. I crawled into my tent after putting out the fire and I laid down to go to sleep. I was woken up at around three in the morning to the sounds of someone screaming in the woods. I jumped up and got out of my tent. I shined my flashlight all around me but didn't see anything. I thought that someone was being hurt or worse because it sounded like a woman screaming bloody murder and for dear life. I tried to follow the sound with my flashlight but I wasn't about to walk into the woods. Just then I realized that if there was someone being hurt or something there was nothing I could do about it and that my flashlight was definitely going to alert whoever was doing the hurting or murdering to my presence and I could have possibly been next. I was a coward, I know, but I had watched enough horror movies to know that it wouldn't end well for me if someone caught me out there and they had evil or bad intentions. I turned off my light and crawled back into my tent. I prayed that it was someone playing some sort of dumb joke on other people who may have been camping around that same area where I was.

That was a comforting thought and I fell back asleep. An hour later at around four in the morning I woke up to a horrific and disgusting stench that seemed to have completely invaded my tent. I had to choke back the urge to vomit. I held my breath for a second and as I did I heard what sounded like footsteps, very light ones, creeping around my campsite. I tried not to breathe too loudly and it was hard too because of the rancid stench that still hadn't gone away or even diminished any. I decided that I couldn't just sit there and wait for who or whatever it was to attack me, thinking I was asleep and so I grabbed my little pocket knife and sat quietly for a minute. The soft steps seemed to be getting closer and closer to my tent. I was terrified but knew I had to do something and so I decided to peek out the tent to get a better look. I did just that and saw someone standing right next to where I had made my campfire. It was a very dark figure, tall and lean. It looked like it had very long hair and though at first it looked like nothing more than a shadow, it suddenly dawned on me that it was a person who was simply dressed all in black. I didn't know how I didn't see her extremely pale, almost glowing white skin from the second I looked out of my tent. I couldn't move and the stench at that point had become unbearable. I asked out loud what she wanted but didn't get a response. I stayed inside of my tent and had no plans of getting out, now that I thought I knew what I was dealing with. Still thinking it was the crazy, drug addled woman I had encountered earlier, and thinking she was human, I was still scared but a little relieved too that it wasn't a serial killer or something else straight out of one of the horror movies I loved watching so much. I thought the knife would help me defend myself and announced, again out loud, that I had a knife and wasn't afraid to use it. She laughed at that and then suddenly, she was in my head.

She was telepathically communicating with me. She told me I didn't need a knife and that she was a friend. She said she knew of my "little problem" (I assumed she meant my baby) and that she had the perfect solution. "What's that?" I thought in my head. She responded by telling me that I should give the child to her. I told her I wasn't sure if I planned on giving birth and she told me she knew that and it wasn't what she meant. I was scared and asked her what she was and what she was really doing there. Suddenly she was right up in my face again. We were eye level to one another and I was still sitting in my tent and only peeking out. The stench was overwhelming and I puked in my lap. She was two inches from my face and her eyes were glowing red. It looked like she was made of fire and her eyes were only like the little window inside of ovens that let you see inside and look at the food you're cooking. The warmth coming off of her was making me sweat. For as terrifying and horrific as all of that was, I couldn't look away and kept waiting for the moment when I would wake up. She must have heard that thought and laughed at it. She told me once again that she was there because of my baby, that she wanted it and that there was nothing I could do to stop her .I asked her what she planned on doing and she laughed. She said she was going to eat me and take the baby to raise as her own. My human logic, and the fact that I still thought that I was having some sort of really vivid night-mare, made me almost giggle. I had only just found out I was preg-nant. Before I could say anything else the atmosphere shifted again and she moved.

She moved so quickly I didn't know where she was until I once again saw her glowing red eyes standing next to where I had made the fire earlier in the night. Between the fear and terror, the vomit in my lap and the stench from this… whatever it was, I knew I had to get out of the tent for fear I might suffocate. I stepped out and the wind imme-diately picked up. The forest had changed and no longer looked like anything that was familiar to me. What I could see of it, anyway. It was pitch black except for her burning red eyes and I couldn't see anything else at all. She kept moving and I was getting very dizzy. I tried with all of my might not to pass out but it seemed almost impossible. There was no more moon and there hadn't been any stars out that night to begin with. I suddenly could smell what I thought was something like when people burn wood or logs in their fireplaces in the winter time. That wonderful smell that I had always thought was so lovely and reminded me of my favorite holiday, Halloween. I was so lost, I don't even know what I was thinking in those moments or why. I passed out.

When I woke up inside of my tent and the sun was already out. I jumped up with a start and put one hand to my head and one to my stomach. I giggled at how real the nightmare had seemed. It had already started to leave me but something didn't feel right and I decided to just leave right then and there. I wasn't going to attend the party and I was planning on having a conversation with my boyfriend at the time, the one who fathered the child I had just found out I was having, and telling him he didn't have to be involved but that I was going to keep the baby. I would deal with whatever came next as it did so. I packed everything up and made my way out of the woods. I passed by a deer on the way out and I remember its eyes, the darkness of them and inky blackness. It immediately brought back the memory of the nightmare and the witch" that had been in it. I had been thinking that I really had seen the drug addled woman earlier in the day and it had made me so uneasy that she was a real witch after my first born child in the nightmare. I suddenly smelled that nasty and rotten stench though and the deer wasn't moving as I got closer to it. I started to gag and when I hung my head down to try and stop myself from puking, only then did I notice the dried vomit already in my lap. It all came rushing back to me and I looked up at the deer as it seemed to be moving closer to me and everything started to spin. Its eyes blinked and suddenly were like the flames of a very hot, very old oven. I leaned against a tree for support as the deer's eyes went back to being black and it ran off into the woods.

I got out of there as fast as I could and never looked back. I left school that same week and also never went back there. I have had a really great life despite that part of it being so hard. I went to the doctor a week after that encounter in the woods and they told me that while I had been pregnant, I no longer was. That made no sense to me but it made no sense to them either because only the fetus was missing and everything else that goes along with pregnancy, everything that should have been "lost" with the baby, was still there and right where it was supposed to be. I didn't want to talk about it and moved on as quickly as I could with my life. I moved to Washington State and started my life over again. I never could have kids after that and I never told anyone about that pregnancy or what happened to me in the woods that night. I never even told my boyfriend at the time because we broke up within two weeks of that night in the woods. I've recently come across some information that a lot of women who are abducted by aliens lose their babies or pregnancies the same way I did but I know deep down inside something much more terrifying happened to me. Not to downplay those women's experiences but I believe a demon took my child. I don't know what for or why, but I know that to be the truth. I have had a tremendously amazing and very long run of good luck ever since about a month after that encounter in the woods. "The witch, as I have come to know and call her, visited me a few times a year in my nightmares and she always had an equally as hideous and grotesque, younger woman with her who at first was a child and then grew as the years went by. I know that was my daughter.

I don't know what it all means but I haven't gotten a visitation in about ten years now. I don't know why I was chosen or if maybe I wasn't chosen but just happened to be in the wrong place at the wrong time. It terrifies me and I wonder so often what could have or what would have been had it not been for my need to go camping that weekend. Why did I have to go alone? I don't know but I know what happened to me was real and I still have the doctor's paperwork to prove it. Please be careful out there because there are far too many things we don't know about and can't even, as human beings, conceive of. The particular area where I was camping is one that's almost known for a spot where a lot of small children go missing "in the blink of an eye", literally. Thanks for letting me get this off my chest. I've never told another human being about it until now and don't ever plan on telling it to anyone or mentioning it ever again. Some things are better taken to the grave with us.

CHAPTER FIFTY-ONE

MY ENCOUNTER HAPPENED LONG before I had ever heard the words black eyed kids. It was 1971 and I was hiking in some woods out by where I used to live in Colorado. It was an area I knew well and that I had been hiking and camping in hundreds of times before. I believed in the supernatural and paranormal and even knew that extraterrestrials existed, which was also unusual for that time. I hadn't ever had an experience with any of it before though and never expected to either. I had driven my beat up old pick up truck out to the hiking spot and parked it on the side of the road near where the trail I was hiking began. My truck was red and I mention that because it will come into play later on. It was around four in the afternoon and would have been getting dark in about three hours. I had to decide if I was going to camp there for the night or not because it would take me almost an hour to hike back to my truck and then almost as much time to get back to where I was currently hiking, which was a great place for me to set up camp if I wanted to. I sat and thought about it for a few minutes and as I did I suddenly felt very panicked and uncomfortable. I hadn't ever felt anything like that before, at least not for seemingly no reason, and I wasn't sure what was going on. The woods seemed to have suddenly gone completely quiet and eerily still, and the hairs on the back of my neck stood up. I shivered a bit and looked around but I didn't see anything out of the ordinary. I decided to hike back to the truck and grab my camping gear. I was going to stay the night, despite how strange and creeped out I was feeling at the time. I figured maybe I was just fatigued and needed to rest for a bit. I hiked back to my truck.

The whole way there I had an overwhelming feeling of fear, dread and panic and it wasn't going away. The crazy part was, at least for me, there was absolutely no reason for me to have been feeling that way. It didn't make any sense and while I know now that those feelings were my intuition telling me that something was very wrong and I should get out of there, I had no idea about any of that back then. I was twenty eight years old and thought I knew it all. I felt like I could just walk or sleep it off. The feelings only intensified with the closer I got to my truck and by the time I was there and unloading my gear I was having a full blown panic attack. I had to stop and sit and try to wait for the feelings to subside. They did, at least a little bit, but not before I thought I heard someone walking up behind me. I turned to look but saw no one there. I threw up and then, feeling somewhat better, I grabbed my stuff and hiked right back to where I had just been. I set up my camp, got a fire going and had something to eat. While the terrible feelings of doom, dread and general uneasiness never went away completely, they did subside enough for me to have convinced myself that maybe it had been something I had eaten while out there. I hung out by the fire for a little while and noticed that the sounds of the forest never really returned, even after I had significantly calmed down. Finally, at around midnight, I grabbed a book I had been reading and sat by the fire to read before I called it a night altogether. I figured it would help me to relax a little bit. I was still somewhat nervous and knew I wouldn't get any sleep if I didn't find a way to either calm down or make my eyes so tired that I wouldn't be able to keep them open anymore. Within minutes of sitting there with my book, I heard branches snapping under someone or something's feet and the sound of something coming up from behind me from the woods.

I was in the middle of nowhere and hadn't seen another human being the entire time I was out there and it wasn't only true then, but all of the other times I had been out there as well. There shouldn't have been anyone there and never had been before. Sure enough though when I turned around there was a young kid standing there. He just stood there at first, looking at the ground. I jumped at the sight of him because it was the last thing I had expected to see and honestly thought that I had been being stalked by a bear or some other predatory animal the whole time and that I was going to have to fight for my life because I thought it was what had been creeping up behind me. I had absolutely no idea how right I was about all of that. At that moment though it was just a young kid, no more than sixteen years old, with short blonde hair. He wore raggedy clothes but they weren't old fashioned or anything. They looked like the usual hand me downs the third or fourth child in the family received that had long since been new and that had ceased to be fashionable a few years before. He had his hands in front of him and he was ever so slightly swaying back and forth. I asked him if he was okay and what he was doing out there in the middle of nowhere. He responded by saying, "please sir, I need your help." I asked him again what he was doing out there and where his parents were. I also asked who he had come there with. He only repeated exactly what he had just said. Once he said he needed my help a second time, I realized I was almost paralyzed with fear. I was sweating profusely and it had nothing to do with the fire I was standing next to. I kept thinking that it was only a scrawny little kid and that I shouldn't have been so frightened.

His voice was weird, too. It didn't have any inflection or affect to it. He sounded almost robotic. He spoke again, "we are going to go to your truck." I was taken aback at that. How in the world did he know I owned a truck? I couldn't fight the panic and everything inside of me was telling me to get away from this kid; as far away as humanly possible and without waiting another single second. I kept my composure. "What truck?" I asked him. He responded by telling me he needed me to bring him to my red truck and let him in. I told him I would do no such thing and that he needed to leave me alone. I threatened to shoot him! The words came tumbling out of my mouth before I had even realized what I was saying. I had just threatened to kill this young, seemingly harmless but also somehow seemingly dangerous CHILD! That's when he looked up at me, and I finally saw his eyes. They were completely and totally black. They were glassy and reminded me right away of the aliens in all of the science fiction movies I watched and even today when I think back to what happened, they remind me of the eyes of the grays. They weren't overly large or anything but they were pitch black and soulless. He smirked when heard me gasp at the sight of them. "You're going to let me in your red truck and we are going to take a short ride. It won't take long. It's not like I'm going to kill you or anything." That last part almost gave me a heart attack. He hadn't had any change in the tone of his voice until he emphasized the word kill. I told him to leave me alone and get away from me. He just stood there, staring at me and smirking. He spoke one more time and said, "Mister, it's just a short ride and I'm just a harmless young kid. Won't you please help me?" Before I knew what I was doing I was nodding my head in agreement with him and he turned and started walking away, expecting me to follow. I dutifully started to follow him.

Even as I was walking behind him my mind was telling me to stop and to turn and run as fast as I could to get as far away from him as possible. It was like I wasn't in control of my body and watching myself following him along the trail towards where I had parked my truck and there was nothing that I could do to help myself. I stopped walking. He turned and looked at me, still with that amused little smirk on his face that made me feel like he knew something I didn't and that he wasn't going to tell me. The smirk told me that I would soon know whatever the secret was and that I wouldn't like it. He spoke again after turning around once again to face me and said, "Come on mister. It's just a short ride." I don't know what came over me as I dropped to my knees, my hands in praying position at my heart and I started to loudly pray in the name of Jesus. I wasn't even religious at the time and hardly even knew what I was saying. The boy immediately went from looking amused to looking extremely angry and his pale skin seemed to become even more pale as I prayed. It started to look like his skin was fake. Almost like he was wearing a human suit or something. It looked droopy all of a sudden, his face, and he angrily yelled for me to stop praying. I refused and closed my eyes. I kept praying as hard as I could to a God I wasn't even sure existed in the first place. After I didn't even know how long, I opened my eyes and the kid was gone. The feelings of panic, fear and dread that I had been feeling all day were totally gone and the forest had once again come to life with all of the usual sounds.

I jumped up off my knees and looked around, wondering if he was going to jump out from somewhere and attack me or something. But somehow I knew he was no longer there. I looked around some more, just to be sure but the feelings I had been feeling were totally gone and only then did I connect those feelings with that black eyed kid. I knew somehow that he had been following me around those woods all day long and just waiting for the right time to approach me. Waiting for the right time to strike is more like it. I was still scared, don't get me wrong, but I just instinctively knew it was over. I also knew somewhere deep down inside that it was only over for the night. I crawled into my tent to wait for the sun to rise so I could get the hell out of there and never look back. I slept a little bit but it was a restless sleep that was full of nightmares about that kid and all of the hellish things he planned on doing to me. Of course I can't be sure what his intentions were but I am absolutely sure they weren't good and were definitely downright evil. As soon as the sun came up I packed up my things and got out of there. I started feeling apprehensive about what I was going to find when I got to my truck but I figured it was broad daylight, so there shouldn't have been any reason for him to have been there waiting for me. Turns out they approach people in the daylight too. As I was about to learn. I walked up to my truck and started to immediately panic. I had looked all around and had even looked inside of the truck before I unlocked it but the kid was nowhere in sight. At least not at first, anyway.

As I was loading my bags into the cab of my truck, I turned around and once again I was face to face with the black eyed kid. He didn't try to hide his eyes from me that time and just stated, once again in that monotone and robotic voice, that I needed to help him by inviting him into my truck and bringing him on "a short ride" so that his mother wouldn't have to worry. I backed away, got into the truck and slammed the door right in his face. He immediately became angry and started pounding on the windows right next to my face. He was yelling, his voice twisted and demonic. "Let me in! Don't you dare drive away! You must LET ME IN your truck." I pulled away as quickly as my old, beat up truck would go. I heard a very loud and animalistic scream or howl, it sounded almost like a bobcat or something similar, but when I looked back in my rearview mirror, there was no one there. It's possible he walked back into the woods but he would have had to have been super fast because it had only been a matter of seconds from when I pulled out of there, heard the scream and then looked in the mirror. I was terrified and had a hard time paying attention to the road because I kept on looking in my rearview mirrors. I thought he was following me somehow but I never saw him again. I never had another visit with a black eyed kid again but I never stopped trying to find out what it was, exactly, that I had encountered that day. Up until the late nineties I hadn't really ever heard any similar reports from people who have come into contact with these entities. I use that word very purposefully there because whatever he was, it certainly wasn't a teenaged boy. I know that for an absolute fact and no one could ever convince me any different. Throughout the years I've told the story to anyone and everyone who would listen, in the hopes of perhaps gaining some insight but for the most part people told me I was crazy and/or that I was paranoid. They suggested it was maybe a kid who had some sort of eye disease or something. Well I've looked into that and IF someone were to naturally have eyes like that, they would be completely blind. Also, that explanation discounts all of the terrible things I had been feeling while in his presence and also while leading up to it. It wasn't human, at all. It seemed evil but it also seemed robotic and even like it might have been some sort of extraterrestrial and robot hybrid. I've learned a lot about the black eyed kids in the years since my encounter but I still have no idea why I was chosen. Maybe I was in the wrong place at the wrong time or maybe it had picked me out purposefully at some point in my life, I don't have a clue as to when, how or why. None of it makes sense and there's still something, deep down inside of me, that feels sometimes like it's still watching me and waiting for another chance to strike. I believe with all of my heart and soul that it still has plans for me and that one day, sometime soon, that entity and I will meet again.

CHAPTER FIFTY-TWO

MY ENCOUNTER STARTED off simply enough. I merely wanted to go on a weekend camping trip in some woods I had been in a hundred times before in order to clear my mind and let go of the pressures of everyday life. I was in my early twenties and while I know now that the things I was dealing with then were petty compared to other things I had gone through later on in life, things were getting overwhelming at that time in my life. It was the early nineties and I had a corporate job working for a family company right out of high school. I was in school to further my education in order to move higher up in the company and all that. I won't bore you with the details but to say I was super stressed out would be a major understatement and nothing had ever been able to refresh and revitalize me like a few nights in the woods could. I had parked my camper in the usual spot at the edge of the woods because the forest I planned on camping in was far too dense and the trails way too narrow to be able to drive it in. I didn't mind though and had a nice sized tent I planned on setting up somewhere, once I found the perfect spot. I used my intuition a lot when I went camping and it was a lot easier than when the noise and all the other nonsense of the world outside of the forest would get in the way and cloud my judgment. I picked a spot based on where it felt right, I don't really know how else to explain it.

I finally found my spot for the night without much time to spare before it was fully dark out there. The trees were high and so even the moonlight wasn't going to give me much illumination to be able to set up my tent and things before that happened. I managed to get it all done in time and I had something to eat by the fire. I still don't know why I decided to go walking along a trail at night and it wasn't anything that I had ever done before but I would definitely live to regret it. I was just sitting there by the fire, sort of zoned out when the idea to go to one of the trails to my left and follow it popped into my head. It was almost an overwhelming urge and I couldn't shake the feeling that I needed to do it. I knew it was a bad idea to be wandering around out there in the darkness but managed to convince myself that the flashlight I had was enough for me to be able to get around and so, without giving it another thought, I got up and walked over to the trail. I kept thinking that I didn't remember seeing that particular trail when I had first started setting up but the sun was just setting and it was possible that it had been there all along and that I just wasn't paying attention to it. It seemed reasonable, actually because trails don't just appear out of nowhere. They aren't supposed to anyway.

I was in a good mood when I started walking the trail and I was even whistling for the first few minutes. Something changed in the air though about ten minutes into my little hike and I was becoming extremely uneasy for no reason. I felt like there was electricity in the air or something and all the hairs on my body were suddenly standing on end. I was in a state of heightened awareness and before I knew it I was having a full blown panic attack. It was crippling and though I had only been walking on that trail for about ten minutes, there was no way I could have turned and gone back even if I had wanted to. The thought crossed my mind but I knew that, whatever was happening to me and all around me, I needed to have my wits about me in case I ran into some sort of predatory animal. My mind was racing but it was all for seemingly no reason. I sat down underneath a very large tree so that I could try to calm down and get myself back in shape enough to get back to my camp and lay down. I was becoming scared that I was going to have a heart attack out there or something and that no one would find me. I hadn't told anyone where I was going because the truth is I didn't have very many people that I was close with in my life at that time. I tried to take a few deep breaths. It seemed to be working.

Within five minutes of sitting under that tree I was starting to feel better. I was relieved because I had been really scared for a few minutes there and it had been completely incapacitating. I was just about to stand up when I saw what looked like a bright pink light over to the left and in front of me a little ways. It didn't look like anything natural and I thought that maybe, for the first time ever, there were other people camping in the area that night too. I had been going to that spot for as long as I could remember, at first with my dad and grandfather and then once I was old enough I would go all by myself but I hadn't ever come across another human being. Not that far out in the woods anyway. I was feeling better and had calmed down significantly and my curiosity had definitely gotten the better of me as I went towards the light to explore it a little more. I honestly thought it was coming from someone else's camp. Once I got closer though I could tell it was something not of this world. It started out looking like a giant pink orb just floating there but the closer I got to it the more I realized it was huge, about my height and I was almost six feet tall at the time. Also, I could see inside of it with the closer I got to it. Instead of being a ball of light it had wavy edges all around it and looked like some sort of holographic picture frame. The "picture" inside of it was a place with bright colors and where it was broad daylight. I took a few steps closer in order to get a better look and couldn't believe what I was seeing!

There were people, far off in the distance, gesturing and waving for me to come and join them. I walked around the image, walked around the light, and the only thing that was behind it or on the sides was more woods like the ones I was in. I didn't know what was happening to me but I started to feel giddy and something like a sense of peace started to come over me like a warm blanket on a freezing cold night. The people were smiling and seemed to be almost glowing. They were gesturing and their mouths were moving. It looked like they were smiling and saying, "Come on! Come with us!" I smiled too and before I knew what I was doing I started walking towards them. They looked excited and encouraged me with more waving. I couldn't hear them or anything but I knew what they were saying. Suddenly the pink light surrounding the scene started to flicker a little bit and I stopped for just a second when I noticed it. Suddenly what looked like lightning flashed across the sky inside of the portal and the people were suddenly really angry looking. They each had their own sort of illumination and so despite the scene having gone dark, I could still see them. Not only that but their faces were distorted and stretching out. It was like they were suddenly not friendly human beings but some sort of demonic creatures. Their faces were so distorted and went from looking somewhat human to demonic and back again, all the while stretching and undulating in strange ways. Where before, when they were smiling and waving for me to come to them, there were about ten of them, all separate human beings. Now there was just one big lump of darkness, fading in and out and where some of the faces were human and angry and others were that of creatures out of my worst nightmares. I backed away and another flash of lightning. It seemed to get darker and darker inside of the opening and the darker it got, the smaller the opening became. I turned and ran and heard whispering all around me the whole way back to my camp.

It wasn't regular whispering though, not of human beings speaking to me or to one another in hushed tones. It sounded like whispering screams of terror, torture and torment. It was horrific and I tried to run with my hands over my ears. I made it back to my camp safely but couldn't wrap my mind around what had just happened to me. I was absolutely terrified and thought that I was in the midst of some sort of nervous breakdown. I laid awake in my tent all night and things only got stranger and more terrifying from there. I remember hearing about portals and vortexes but in the early nineties things like that weren't common knowledge or something you just went around talking about. I only thought I knew what I had just seen and experienced because I was a huge fan of everything science fiction and had seen every single horror movie known to man at the time. I didn't know what to do but I knew I wasn't going to get much sleep. I tossed and turned but finally I had to get up and go use the bathroom. I tried to hold it in but couldn't take it anymore. I reluctantly crawled out of my tent and made my way into the woods a little bit.

As soon as I was done doing what I needed to do I turned and went to start walking back towards my tent. That's when I heard what sounded like something very large rustling around in the bushes and trees near where I was standing. It was directly behind me and seemed to be coming from right where I had just come from. I didn't want to turn and look but felt like I would have been attacked from behind or something if I didn't. I turned to look and at first I didn't see anything. I could still hear whatever it was moving though and so I strained my eyes to see a little bit better and that's when I saw what looked a little bit like a man. He blended in very well with the trees and tall grass. I could tell he was there though and I yelled out for him to stay away from me. I threatened that I was armed and would shoot him, knowing full well I had no weapons and would never have shot anyone anyway, even if I did have one with me. Suddenly a man stepped out from behind the trees. He was about my height and very thin. He wore a regular pair of jeans and a simple and plain white t-shirt. He had on boots that were appropriate for construction work or hikes in the woods. He was so incredibly nondescript that it struck me as odd right away. Plain brown hair, plain brown eyes, caucasian skin but not too pale nor too tan. There was nothing at all that stood out about him and I honestly almost didn't remember him at all, at least what he looked like, when I sat down to write this encounter down. He had his arms up, almost like he was mocking me and the fact I had threatened to shoot him. He wasn't actually worried about it though because he was also smirking playfully. He took a couple of tentative steps towards me as I kept stepping backwards. He leaned casually against the tree.

My mind was racing because I felt that weird energy shift again and was afraid of having another incapacitating panic attack. He smiled and told me to relax and that wasn't going to happen. I was shocked because he had so clearly just read my mind. I felt him, somehow, like he was poking around in there. I thought of the portal and the images inside of it next. He said, "Oh that! Yes, that was quite unfortunate. It seems they became a bit too overzealous a bit too soon huh?" I shook my head no. His voice was even and had no accent at all. He was "every man" and there was nothing memorable at all about him. I realized that was the point. He told me he figured he would give me another chance to go with him, to meet those other people who had been waving me towards them and trying to get me to go into the portal with them. I told him I wasn't going anywhere except home and that I would be doing that as soon as the sun came up. He suddenly looked extremely angry and with the expression of anger on his face, that's when his features became distorted and almost demonic, just like the other people's had done a few hours before. I cursed at him and turned to run back into my tent. I didn't get more than a few steps when I heard what sounded like some sort of bobcat howling right behind me, right where the man had been standing. I turned back around but there was nothing there except the vaguest glint of an exceedingly retreating pink light.

I didn't bother to look for the man, I knew he was gone and I didn't bother to wait until the sun came up to leave either. I packed up all my things right then and there and walked as fast as I could through the wilderness at night and risked being ripped apart by wild animals just to get the heck out of those woods. I don't know what I came across and witnessed that night and I have never seen anything like it since. It didn't keep me out of the woods for longer than a year and that was only right after it had first happened. Throughout the years I've kept the experience to myself and at first I merely thought that I had been having a nervous breakdown. However, I have done a lot of research in the decades since that night and I think I just happened to have come across one of those places where the veil or whatever you want to call it is thinner and got a glimpse of something I wasn't supposed to see. I think I was seeing some form or version of hell and "mister every man" was the devil or a top demon, who couldn't resist trying one more time for my immortal and already very compromised human soul. Luckily I had the presence of mind to resist and I've turned my life around. Maybe that's the purpose it served but I truly don't know.

I would have just stuck with the feeling that I was losing my mind but there have been far too many people who have experienced very similar things and who have had very similar encounters to mine, especially while out and all alone in the wilderness, all over the world, for that to be the most reasonable and logical answer. I don't know but maybe one day I'll find out. Until then, that's all I have.

CHAPTER FIFTY-THREE

IF YOU'RE a believer in other worlds and things that are paranormal in nature, as I have been my whole life, then it will come as no surprise to you that I had my first encounter with fairy beings in the woods. I know a lot of people who do believe in the paranormal and even those who believe in extraterrestrials, will draw a hard line at believing in fairies. I get it, I really do because I was one of those people up until the year 2000 when I had my first encounter with them. I was hiking up a mountain near my home with my dog, Bella, when it happened. I've since been seeing the fae nonstop and almost every time I go into the woods. I've even seen them in my backyard. I bring gifts and treats with me whenever I go into the woods now, even if it's only for a day hike. That's what I was doing that day. I was hiking during the day with my dog. It was the first really warm day of Spring after a particularly harsh winter where I live on the east coast of the United States. I was excited about the weather and eager to get back out into mother nature to spend some quiet time to myself. I had Bella for about five years at that point and she had accompanied me on thousands of walks through dozens of different types of woods all over the place. I even took her camping with me. She was so well behaved I didn't even need a leash, though I brought one with me just in case. Sometimes the mountain I was hiking on would be pretty busy on nice days and there are always those people who complain when a dog isn't on a leash.

Bella and I walked up the mountain and I saw a trail I didn't remember ever having taken before and so I led her over onto that trail. She was acting weird from the moment I discovered it and she was reluctant to follow me down that path. I laughed at her and egged her on a little bit and within no time she seemed to be her normally happy and goofy self again. She dutifully followed behind me which was a little odd because normally she would go bounding excitedly up ahead of me. I didn't think much of it at first and thought that maybe she smelled some sort of predator or something. Not that I thought it would be anything I couldn't handle but just maybe something a dog would be concerned about is all. We walked for about ten minutes and it occurred to me suddenly that we hadn't seen another human being or animal since we got onto that one trail. It also seemed like we had gone a lot farther than ten minutes into the woods because I could no longer hear all the noise of the other people up on the mountain that day. There are usually families picnicking in certain areas and there is a view that overlooks the whole city where people go to take wedding photos; things like that. That day had been no different but suddenly it was like everything had been put on mute. Again though I tried to rationalize and explain it all away as perfectly normal. Plus, I was happy for the rare moments of peace and quiet. It was much different than when Bella and I would go walking around or hiking in that same area in the winter time. The place was almost always deserted then. It wasn't anything I planned on worrying about for too long and decided to simply enjoy the day.

I picked up a little stick and threw it for Bella to go and catch. She did and returned it to me. I sat down on a large boulder and threw it again but instead of coming back with it I heard her growling ferociously at something. I immediately jumped up and called out to her because it was so unlike her it immediately scared me. Plus, I didn't want her to attack anyone and I thought that, for her to be behaving that way, some little kid must have been bothering or teasing her or something. She didn't even turn to look at me when I called her and as I approached her I saw that her hackles were raised and her fangs were bare. She was all but foaming at the mouth and growling at something that I couldn't see. I thought that maybe it was some sort of small forest critter that she just wasn't familiar with but I couldn't see anything or anyone around us at all. That in and of itself should have struck me as odd; that there were no squirrels or chipmunks, but I was so worried about Bella it didn't even register at first. I heard no insects or birds chirping either but before long I did start to hear what sounded like a very tiny and squeaky little voice saying something I couldn't quite understand. It sounded like it was coming from the direction where Bella was barking but I still didn't see anything.

I focused on trying to calm my normally friendly and sort of dumb dog down. I reached for her and she turned and tried to take a bite out of me. I pulled my hand back just in time and was absolutely shocked. That seemed to snap her out of it and she immediately whimpered and ran over to me. I petted her and told her it was okay and then I turned around so she would follow me back out of the woods. I didn't like how I was feeling and though I couldn't put my finger on what it was, there was something strange happening and I didn't want any part of whatever it was. Bella followed me for no more than two seconds when she turned again and took on the same aggressive stance and started barking again. She had gone right back to where she had originally been standing when she had first started showing that aggressive sort of behavior in the first place. I was frustrated and yelled for her to come with me. She looked at me for a second and growled, as if telling me where I could shove my yelling at her. I admit, I was worried about trying to forcefully remove her or pick her up because of how she had tried to take a bite out of my hand just a few moments earlier. I knew for a fact something was agitating my dog but I simply couldn't see anything at all that could be blamed. I heard the small voice again and it was once again coming from the ground where Bella was staring and growling at.

I moved closer but still didn't see anything. I took her leash out of my pocket and while she was distracted I put it on her collar and started pulling her with me. I wasn't rough or anything but she needed to be taken out of there because something was upsetting her pretty badly. She fought me like crazy and managed to break free from my grasp. She went running further into the woods and I followed after her. I was really concerned at that point and had no idea what in the world was going on or what I was going to do about it. I needed to get myself and my dog out of there. I somehow knew it instinctively but had no idea why I felt that way or what to do to convince her to come with me. Suddenly I heard Bella whimper up ahead of me and then I heard what sounded like a little child yelling in some sort of foreign language I had never heard before. English is the only language I speak and I wasn't familiar with how anything other than Spanish sounded. Whatever language the kid was yelling in I was unfamiliar with it. I was angry though because of how Bella had whimpered as though something had hurt her. I ran up to her and that's when I saw what she was doing. I saw it with my eyes but my mind hadn't caught up yet. It was almost comical and now that I think back on it I am actually giggling a little bit. At that moment I was scared out of my wits though, don't get me wrong. Bella was growling and shaking her head back and forth. She had something in her mouth and that's where the yelling seemed to have been coming from. I stepped towards her in order to get a closer look. She had what looked like a doll in her mouth and she had a firm grip on it with her teeth. The thing in her mouth had its hands up in the air and was yelling. It looked like a very tiny version of one of those garden gnomes people put in their yards. I couldn't believe my eyes and it all seemed very surreal. I began to question my own sanity.

Then, something red started flying all around as the thing in her mouth screamed and screamed. It didn't sound angry anymore but like it was in extreme and excruciating pain and it actually hurt to listen to it. My dog was ripping whatever it was apart. Despite the fact I didn't know what I was dealing with, it struck me she was about to kill something that was living and looked very much like a teeny tiny human being. I mean, the thing was a foot tall only, no more than a foot and a half, maximum. Finally, after yelling for Bella to "Drop it" numerous times and with the little creature still screaming and bleeding, I yanked my dog's leash for a second, really hard, and she opened her mouth just long enough to drop it out of her mouth. The thing laid there perfectly still for almost a full minute as my dog tried to get to it.

Bella was growling and barking again but I had a firm grip of her leash and wasn't going to let her attack the little being again. I got a closer look before it disappeared into thin air right before my eyes. It was wearing a little red hat, blue overalls with a blue shirt underneath, and had a long brown beard that went almost down to its feet. Its skin was pale white. It also had very rosy cheeks and was a bit on the chubby side. Bella looked at me, seemingly just as confused as I was, when the thing evaporated into thin air. That's when my dog yelped again, this time sounding like she was in excruciating pain.

I asked her what was wrong but she just kept on jumping and whining and whimpering. It was like she couldn't sit still and I thought maybe she was being repeatedly stung by a bee or that she was being stung all at once by several bees or something. I didn't see anything though and once again, probably due to the whole ordeal and the pain she was in, she lunged and bared her teeth at me. I held firm to her leash and tried to pull her away with me but she was too distracted by the pain she was so obviously in at the time. Finally I looked at the ground and saw about a dozen little beings jumping up and down underneath my dog. They were so teeny tiny as to almost be invisible. They glistened in the sunlight and that's the only way I was able to notice them. Bella also seemed to suddenly be aware of them and she growled and snapped her jaws at them as they seemed to be taunting her. I got on my hands and knees and within seconds one of them landed on my face and I felt a pin prick in that spot. I slapped at my face and the little being flew backwards and was hovering there in my face right before my eyes. I swatted at it and turned to run away. I would pull Bella if I had to but we were getting out of there right then. I tripped and almost fell and when I looked down another one of the gnome creatures had been standing there. It shook its little fist at me and was yelling in that tiny voice and gibberish language, just like the other one. Or, who knows, maybe it was the same one. I pleaded with them all to just stop and once I literally started to cry, they all stopped at once. The fluttering entities that had been poking my dog's under-belly disappeared altogether and the little gnome just stood there, next to several others who were standing next to it, and they all had their arms crossed defensively across their chests.

I don't know what made me think to do this but as my dog growled and snapped her jaws at the little creatures, each time making them jump until eventually they ran and hid behind the boulder, I knelt down and very deliberately said I was sorry. I then reached into my pocket and grabbed a dog biscuit, a stick of old gum and some pennies and put them down in front of the boulder. They all came running out from behind it and believe it or not, they actually bowed to me. They were dancing around in a circle and seemed to be celebrating. I stood up and they instantly stopped and looked from me to the "treats" I had just left them. They then began to gather up the items greedily, as if they thought I would take them back or something. I called for Bella and she finally came with me. She didn't stop snarling and she didn't take her eyes off the creatures for a single second though. As she walked by one of them whacked her with a stick and they sounded like they were laughing. I stomped my foot down hard and they all disappeared, along with the coins and everything else I had left there.

Listen, I don't know what I came across that day or why I was allowed to see it. I'm not nor have I ever been mentally ill, on medication, drunk or on drugs. I can't explain it and I've gone back to that same trail dozens of times, without Bella of course, and haven't ever seen them again. I can't seem to locate that big boulder either and I haven't been able to find it since that day. Bella has since gone on to doggy heaven but she was never the same again after the experience. She was terrified to go outside anymore, especially in the woods and her usually pleasant and dumb demeanor changed too. She became almost rabid in the presence of anyone but me and she would attack other animals she otherwise would have been excited to have around and to play with. I can't say that the experience is what changed her but I am almost positive that's what did it. As for me, I've seen fairies, gnomes specifically, many times since this all happened but never in that same spot. Despite not being able to find the boulder again I always leave jolly ranchers, an airplane bottle of whiskey and a little bit of rolling tobacco near the tree where I believe we encountered them that day. I'll write about the other encounters too. Thanks for letting me share this one.

CHAPTER FIFTY-FOUR

MY ENCOUNTER HAPPENED when I was about six years old in 1999. My mom used to drive my older siblings to all of their sports games and things like that and I always had to tag along because I couldn't stay home by myself and my dad worked late usually. She would take turns whose game she would watch because each sibling was in a different grade and therefore played different sports. It was time for my brother's soccer game and his team was playing in a field near some woods in our hometown. I wasn't supposed to wander off and had to stay with my mom while she sat and cheered him on from the bleachers unless there were other kids my age to play with. It was always so boring for me and sometimes I would ask her if I could just walk around. There were always a ton of people there and usually there would be some kids my age there too and we would all ask our parents if we could walk around the perimeter of the woods together. My mom never had an issue with it and though I didn't know most of the kids except from those games, where their older siblings were a part of a team as well, my mother knew most of their parents so I guess they figured it was safe. That day there were only two other kids around my age hanging out with their parents, which was a little unusual, and I remember thinking there weren't nearly as many people there as there normally was. It was just a passing thought but I've since wondered if that was merely my intuition being heightened and somewhat warning me that it was not a good day to go near the woods. Maybe it was something in the air or whatever that was keeping people away. The bleachers on both sides were less than a third of the way full than I had ever seen them and that they had ever been. I still don't know if what I saw that day had anything to do with it and I guess I never will.

I didn't see any of the kids I normally hung around with during the games but I saw two others who were playing together near the woods. It looked like they were playing tag and so I asked my mom if I could go and join them and she said yes. She was so wrapped up in my brother's game I don't know if she even looked over to see who the kids were before agreeing to let me go and play with them. I walked over and asked if I could play and the kids said yes. However, they said they were going to play hide and seek and that they were going to be including the woods in the boundary. I knew I wasn't supposed to be going into the woods under any circumstances. They were extremely dense and that's what it was like all over the small town I lived in. It was almost like someone carved out enough space for a soccer field right at the edge of them and that was it. There was nothing else around there and that was that. It was my turn to "Seek" first since those two kids knew one another and I was the new kid so to speak but I didn't mind and gladly counted to thirty. I was still a little worried about my mom being angry with me for going into the woods but I didn't want my new friends to not like me or think I was weird and so I didn't follow my gut which was telling me to stay as far away from the woods as possible. However, I didn't understand it all for what it was and my six year old mind thought the overwhelming sense of uneasiness was just not wanting to get into trouble. I dutifully counted and then ran into the woods to find my two new playmates. I looked everywhere and it seemed like I had been looking forever when I heard a little giggle coming from behind one of the trees near where I was standing. I was relieved because it had been almost fifteen minutes since I had been roaming around in those woods and looking for them. I was about to yell out that I gave up and couldn't find them.

I followed the sound of the giggling and I walked another five minutes into the woods. I was walking along a trail but kept getting off of it in order to check behind trees.

I heard giggling coming from behind one tree again finally and walked over and yelled that I had found them and it was my turn to hide now. However, the boys didn't step out from behind the tree, something else did. It was about five and a half feet tall and looked mostly human. At least as far as its body was concerned. It had two legs, two arms, a head, shoulders and even a neck. It was bipedal too but it had a tail and ears that looked sort of like those of a fox. It wasn't wearing clothes though and just seemed to be covered in very short fur that was light tan or sand colored. It did have hair on its head and it looked like human hair that was dark brown, wavy and shoulder length. At first it just smiled at me, not showing its teeth and then it took a step towards me. I was only six and so I had no qualms about asking what it was and what it was doing there. It told me, in a man's voice, that it lived there and that it couldn't tell me what it was because it was a secret. It then said to me, "you're not supposed to be here." I took a step back as I finally noticed its eyes were a bright golden yellow color and the smile on its lips didn't fit with how the eyes looked. The eyes looked like that of a predator and it took another two steps towards me. I thought about running but it seemed to have read my mind and asked me why I would want to go and do a thing like that. I was terrified and immediately peed my pants. The creature frowned and then looked at me and finally showed me its teeth. They looked razor sharp and deadly, it advanced on me again and I started running away.

As I ran I didn't bother looking back because I knew it was there. The same giggling I had been hearing that had led me to that tree where the entity had been lurking was very loud and following right behind me the whole time. The problem was I had been following the giggling thinking that it was the other kids I had been playing with and I hadn't been paying attention to where I had been going. Turns out I was deeper in the woods than I meant to be or had ever been before. I was completely lost and knew that if I stopped running, just for a second, that I would be at the mercy of that fox man creature. It was giggling and sounded just like a little kid. I was so scared and when I finally looked back I ran right into something in front of me. It turned out to be a tall man I recognized as one of my brother's friend's dads. I screamed but the giggling had stopped. I fell on my butt from the impact and the man helped me up. He told me a lot of people were looking for me and that my mom was a nervous wreck. He spoke into a walkie talkie and told someone he had found me and that's when I realized it was night time, but I didn't know what time it was and only knew that much because it was fully dark outside. That didn't make sense because from the time I had asked my mom if I could go and play to the time I ran into one of the people searching for me, it didn't seem like more than an hour at most. It turns out it was midnight and I had been missing for almost five hours. I was terrified and confused and just wanted my mom.

The man led me to my mother and father who were there along with my siblings and we all hugged. I thought for sure I was going to get into a lot of trouble but I didn't and my parents were just relieved to see me and that I was okay. My mother did ask why I had gone off into the woods and I told her the two kids I had asked if I could play with wanted to play hide and go seek. Just then a terrifying thought crossed my mind and I was wondering if the other two kids were okay or if the fox man had gotten them. I asked my mother if the other two kids were okay and she looked at my father and then back at me. She told me that it was okay and I wasn't in trouble but I needed to tell the truth. She urged me to say that there weren't any other kids and that I had maybe just wanted to explore the woods but knew that she would have said no if I had asked. I was confused but knew enough to just agree with her. There was no point in insisting that there were other kids or talking about the fox man/entity because she had already made up her mind. I didn't care. I wasn't in any trouble and so I let her believe that she was right. My dad carried me and suddenly I was very tired. Here is what I found out later.

I asked my mother if I could play with the other kids and she said that I could. I went to play with them and went into the woods thinking I was playing hide and seek with two new potential friends. When the game was over it was just starting to get dark and my mom looked up but didn't see me. It wasn't that she hadn't been watching me up until that point, or so she says, but she still swears she was watching me talk to myself over at the edge of the woods for two hours before the game ended, she looked up and I was gone. She asked other parents if they had seen me but no one had. She called the cops and my dad and everyone went into full search mode. It took four hours to find me because I had wandered into the forest several miles. I was so confused because it only seemed to me that I had not only been gone for less than one hour, but that it had only gotten fully dark when I bumped into one of the searchers. It's all so confusing and while I would like to say that through all of the research I've done that I've since figured out what happened to me that day or at the very least that I know what the creature was that I encountered but I would be lying. I can't find anything at all about what happened to me. The closest I came is when I researched something called elementals but even then there's no half fox half man entity anywhere in what I've read. I came across one or two other encounters with almost the exact same entity though and it always happened to the person telling the story when they were out in the woods alone. None of those people have any sort of explanation either though.

I definitely have missing time and wonder if I somehow wandered into a portal but I honestly don't know because it seems the little kids I was playing with didn't actually exist and that makes me believe that I was chosen and that the entity used images of those kids to lure me there. I haven't ever seen the kids again and when I described them to some of my closest friends once I got older, no one knew who I was talking about. It stands to reason they didn't really exist at all and were either a figment of my imagination or a lure by whatever that creature was to get me into the woods. It's all very frightening and still gives me nightmares because I still live in the same house in that same town and while I've always avoided not only sports but the woods like the plague, those same woods are still very prominent in the town and make up most of the land here. I have a feeling I'll see it again one day, or maybe I'll see both boys or just one of them. I'm not looking forward to it because I don't think it's something I will just be able to shoot and run away from. There have been times when I was walking past some woods in the town, they're all connected, and I've felt either something watching me or a feeling that something was trying to pull me into them again. I have no idea if that makes any sense or not but that's how I feel. None of it makes any sense and I've since tried to tell my mom what really happened that day but she just blows it off and says that I had an overactive imagination back then and probably made it all up and convinced myself of it and that's why I still remember it all so vividly. I'm pretty sure she doesn't believe that but she obviously doesn't like to talk about it so I guess my quest for the truth and knowledge about what I had encountered continues.

I have this strange feeling that I'm never going to feel safe again as long as I have no answers and no ideas as to what really happened to me that day. I don't know what else to say except that I haven't ever had any other encounters with anything supernatural, paranormal or otherworldly and that one time when I was six was it for me. But, I have had many odd feelings and intuition about those woods. They still call me sometimes when I drive by them and if I ever decide to pull over and explore what's reaching out to me and why, I'll write about that too. Provided that is, I survive it again.

CHAPTER FIFTY-FIVE

I USED to hunt elk along the Oregon Coast for years. I was introduced to this area by my uncle who passed a few years back. The place itself was a large farm, my uncle knew the owner and he gave us permission each year. What made this nice was it gave us privacy on opening day. It was just us, the elk and seventy-nine acres, mostly wooded but with several large fields. It was prime elk habitat as the elk would come down to the fields to graze at night.

Over the years my uncle and I noticed something strange about the area while camping one summer and another time in the fall while scouting for new places to set up for opening day. On our fall camping trip we gave the strange place a name, the dead zone. It was about a half mile from our usual camping site. The dead zone was creepy and we always got a bad vibe when we were there.

While the rest of the forest was teaming with life, the dead zone, was just that, dead. Yes, it had trees and under growth, but as far as wildlife, nothing. While the forest would be alive with game like, elk, pheasant, squirrel, coyote, you name; this area had nothing. Not a squirrel or even a game trail. The dead zone was not small either, it compromised a sizable chunk, about two acres of the seventy-nine acres. When we'd traverse the forest, we come up on the dead zone and boom, nothing, not even a bird, then when we left; all the animals would be around. There was a very defined contrast between a teaming forest with animals and nothing.

———

I arrived at the property the night before opening day. My uncle was running late so I was going to set up camp and get everything ready for the big day early the next morning. I had two hours of daylight left and put it to good use.

I unpacked my truck, and set up the large dome tent we'd both use. I cleaned up the site and started a fire. As I relaxed in front of the roaring flames I heard some commotion coming from the direction of the dead zone. I looked in the direction but didn't see anything. I faced the fire again and the hairs on my neck stood up. It felt like something was piercing my soul with its eyes. Everyone knows the feeling. I looked back over my shoulder but I couldn't see a thing. Mind you it's not quite dark so I could see into the woods a bit.

I shrugged it off and went back to enjoying the warm flames. A couple minutes later I distinctly heard a loud snap of a breaking branch to the left of my camp. I should mention that I had some music playing, not too loud, but loud enough so I wouldn't hear slight sounds. I got up and turned the music off. I listened intently for at least a minute then I heard a very light rustle of leaves and a twig snap followed by what I swear to today was a few footfalls. The sound came from the woods on the other side of a large grove of holly bushes which ended near some old growth trees. About a minute later I heard another soft footfall. Then another.

At the time it reminded me of my own sounds when quietly stalking game through the forest. For some reason I thought it was another hunter or someone playing a joke.

I called out "Hello, someone there?!"

Silence, nothing.

About another full minute later another couple of soft crunches. There is a game trail on the other side of the holly, so whatever is making the sound is on the trail and slowly coming closer to the old growth.

By this point I was getting nervous. I ran through several scenarios like a drunk hunter playing games or some kids playing a prank. Either one, if true, was stupid. When you're five miles from any civilization, you don't go playing games with someone, like me, who is armed. Not only did I have my rifle, but I also had my Smith and Wesson Model 19, it was my father's old police service pistol from the 1960s.

I heard a few more footfalls.

I had a mix of emotions racing through me. I was both spooked and annoyed. I drew my revolver and yelled, "Whoever is out there, quit fucking around, I'm armed, and not afraid to use it. Now stop this shit and make yourself known!"

No response, nothing.

About a minute later I heard my soft footfalls. Whoever this was wasn't done playing with me. It's closer to the gap between the holly and the old, perhaps thirty feet away now.

The sun was completely down now, so I dug through my pack and found my flashlight. I clicked it on and shined it in the direction of the sounds.

Nothing.

More soft footfalls.

I was getting really scared now. I began to imagine this was someone or something up to no good. I don't know what made me do it, but I made the loudest scream I could muster. It was so loud it echoed through the valley.

The footfalls stopped for a minute and then continued again.

I should tell you that I'm not a small man. I stand over six foot two inches and weigh in around 230 pounds. I'm not fat, but I'm not a string bean. I used to play football and I'm an avid weight lifter. I tell you this so you can get an idea that I'm physically capable and have some size to me. Plus, it's to provide some context for what I'm about to tell you.

The footfalls now placed whoever it was just on the far side of the holly and the gap between it and the old growth. I turned my flashlight in the direction and boom I see a head pop around the corner and pull back.

I recoiled at the sight and gulped hard. It looked like a man, but also didn't. I know that sounds crazy, but the head was covered in hair. I raised my revolver and yelled, "I'm sick of this shit, whoever is there, just turn around and leave me alone."

I couldn't have been more honest in that moment. I didn't want whatever it was to show itself, I wanted it to turn around and go back to wherever it came from.

My flashlight is still beamed at the sight and again this thing popped its head around the corner. The second time I got a better look at it. It looked like a gorilla or ape of some kind. I started to wonder if an ape had escaped from a zoo and ended up on the Oregon Coast.

It stared at me for a few second and pulled its head back.

As I tried to process what I was seeing, I then noticed that this thing had to be tall, like freakishly tall. The head was popping out at around eight feet off the ground, so either this thing was standing on something or it was that tall.

Fear fully gripped me now. I don't even recall thinking about firing warning shots, I just didn't it out of pure fear. I raised the revolver and let two rounds flied then shouted, "Turn around, I'm serious!"

The shots echoed for along time then silence. I stood there waiting for it to pop its head around the corner. I prayed it wouldn't, but today my prayers wouldn't be answered as it just didn't pop its head around the corner, it fully stepped out.

There in the bright white light of my LED flashlight stood this monstrous creature. I stood on two legs, was massive. It stood over eight feet tall, had these gargantuan shoulders and a barrel chest. Its arms were long and muscular, and the things legs were also thick and muscular. If this thing wanted to destroy me and tear me into pieces it could easily. I could see its muscles it was so ripped.

It was covered in thick brownish / black hair that was matted with leaves, mud, and twigs. What terrified me more than anything was this menacing look on its face. It appeared to be angry with me. The first two looks I had gotten it didn't have an expression, but this time it did. It grimaced with its thin lips and glared with its brooding eyes.

I lowered the revolver and aimed at its chest. When I did that it grimaced and showed me its teeth. This thing wasn't just mad it was pissed. I can't help but think now it knew I had a gun or what a gun was and that it didn't take kindly to having one pointed at it.

Based on its hulking size I wasn't even sure if my .357 rounds could even hurt it. I know this, it was thirty yards away and if it took off at me, I may have been able to get off a round or two, but would that really be enough to stop this thing was ending my life.

All I could think of was using my voice. I yelled again, "Go away!"

It stood and stared at me.

"Go away!" I repeated.

This time it did as I asked. It pivoted ninety degrees and as fast as it had appeared it was gone. This time it didn't slowly walk away, it let out a howl and ran. It tore its way through the forest, branches breaking the entire way.

With it gone, I took the opportunity to leave as well. I jumped in my truck and sped off. I called my uncle and had him meet me at the diner. I told him what I'd seen and told him I wasn't going back.

At first he laughed at me and told me to stop pranking him, but I insisted I was telling the truth. He finally stopped teasing me and asked what we were going to do about the gear. I told him I didn't care about my gear and that I wasn't going back...period.

After we talked for a bit, I drove three hours back to home shaking the entire time.

My uncle called me the next morning and said he found the site undisturbed. He packed everything up and dropped off the gear at my house. He urged me to reconsider going back out for the hunt, telling me I was giving up an entire years worth of scouting and planning because I 'think' I saw something.

I was pissed at him. I had been hunting with him all my life and he just couldn't quite bring himself to believe me. I found that and still do very odd. Like I'd make this shit up.

Since then I no longer go into the forest alone and I've never been hunting since.

CHAPTER FIFTY-SIX

MY ENCOUNTER HAPPENED VERY RECENTLY in the summer of 2022. I was hiking near my home which is close to the eastern Sierra Nevada mountains. This was nothing unusual for me and I had been camping and hiking all over the place near those mountains my whole life. I was supposed to be spending a weekend camping there by myself. There was no particular reason I was doing it other than it was something I loved to do. I always believed in the paranormal and have extensively researched all of the fairly recent disappearances in the woods and national parks of our country and around the world and believed very much so in the more supernatural explanations. However, like most humans with most things, I figured those types of things and those kinds of encounters only happened to other people. Boy was I naive. There is a really long, strenuous and treacherous trail near where I had set up my camp that I decided to hike when I got there, after I chose where I wanted to camp for the weekend. It led to a large rock slide and most of the time there were other people there but this time was different. It looked different too and for a minute I wondered if I had accidentally gone off the trail and somehow ended up somewhere else altogether. The rock slide was there but once I walked a little bit further after taking in the scenery a little bit, I came to a sort of clearing where the trees looked like they were interconnected or woven together. There was no one around and the woods were completely silent. I needed a break after the strenuous hike I had just taken so I sat down on the ground under the strange trees and took a drink of water and ate a snack. I was exhausted but knew the way back down the trail would be a breeze. I sat there for about fifteen minutes in silence that could really only be described as deafening. Finally I couldn't take it anymore and I got up to hike back down the trail and back to my camp for the night. The whole hike, there and back to camp, took me about four hours. It wasn't anything unusual for me to have done, like I said, and I made it back to my camp in one piece.

I have to admit I knew something was wrong the minute I saw how strange the trees were in that area. I had been there dozens of times before and had never seen them like that. It was almost like they had suddenly just sprung up or something but I reasoned with myself and told myself that I just hadn't ever walked so far past the slide before and that was the reason it looked so unfamiliar. I didn't want to think about it and I also didn't want to think about the creepy silence that still hung in the air or the fact that I felt like I was being stalked the whole way back to my camp. I wasn't alone after all, not really, because although I was there by myself, there were a lot of other people camping in the area as well and I had even passed some of them on my way up and back down the trail. They were mostly families on vacation or whatever and they all seemed friendly enough. I couldn't see anyone from my camp but I could smell the marshmallows roasting and whatever else they were cooking on their fires and barbecuing. I warmed up some food and sat back by the fire to listen to my radio on low. My cell phone didn't work out there at all but it didn't matter because for me that was the whole point; to escape the outside world and be off grid for a couple of days. I had an old boom box that was battery operated and a few compact discs I was happy to sit back and enjoy on that cool summer night. The air was a bit more stale than normal and I found myself not being able to shake the feeling of being watched. As night fell over the forest and my camp, I decided I would feel a lot better if I just got up, turned on my flashlight and searched the perimeter of my camp for people lurking or who otherwise didn't belong there.I didn't understand that the silence permeating the woods that whole time was a harbinger of something supernatural happening and still believed the threat was more than likely human. I felt threatened because I felt like I was being watched and that I had been for a while that day. It was really unusual and made me very uncomfortable. So, I grabbed my flashlight and searched all of the surrounding areas to my camp where I thought someone could be hiding and waiting for me to let my guard down and or go to sleep.

There was absolutely no one there, of that I was sure because I even looked up in the trees above my camp but still I saw no one. For a little while after I searched I felt better and the eerie feeling left me. I no longer felt like I was being watched and finally, at around one in the morning, I put out my fire and went to bed. The forest was still unnaturally silent all around me and it was still very eerie, lying there listening to the sound of nothing while trying to fall asleep. It was weird too that I hadn't heard any other campers. There's never been a time when I was out there for a weekend when there wasn't at least one person who had too much to drink and got a little too loud and rowdy. But, that night it was silent and still, you could have heard a pin drop. I got up in the middle of the night to use the bathroom and was shocked that the forest hadn't yet come back to life. I was scared, that I'll admit, but it was very frustrating because my body was having the usual fear reactions but my eyes couldn't see anything to indicate why. I couldn't quite put my finger on it but the very real feeling of being intensely watched was back. What was I supposed to do? I had to go to the bathroom, there was no avoiding it. I walked a little further into the woods and looked around to make sure that I wasn't where anyone could see me or where I would disturb anyone else who was camping there. I peed and turned to walk back to my tent but as I did I heard a wolf howling, very loudly, in the not so far off distance. It was even more frightening because the woods had been silent all day and now there was a wolf howling. I got chills all over my body and stopped when I heard the trees and bushes rustling beside me. I turned around and shined my flashlight into the darkness in that direction. I didn't see anything, well, not at first I didn't anyway. I didn't for a second believe it was the wolf because, although it sounded much closer than I would have liked it to be, it was nowhere near close enough that I would be encountering it by my camp at that time. It had been several miles away at least.

I stood there for a minute and scanned the perimeter with my flashlight and that's when I thought I saw something moving in the bushes. I shined my flashlight over in that direction and I saw a set of eyes that looked like they were glowing yellow. I actually breathed a sigh of relief at that point because I thought it was just a human being and their eyes looked like that because I had shone a flashlight right into them. Whoever it was didn't even flinch though. They didn't move and they didn't make a sound. They were just standing there watching me. I lowered my flashlight and told whoever it was that they had scared me. I let out a nervous laugh as I said it. They didn't respond and the fact that they were still somewhat hidden by the tree they were halfway standing behind was unnerving. I could see the eyes peeking out from behind the trees and I also saw the person was wearing a trench coat. That was very strange because it was at least seventy degrees at that point. There was a bit of a breeze in the air but for someone to be walking around wearing that heavy, long trench coat, it made me very nervous. I suddenly became super alert and very aware of my surroundings. I was sweating profusely and noticed my hand was shaking around my flashlight. Suddenly the stranger spoke to me and asked me, very politely, to not shine my flashlight in his direction. He said he needed help and that he was hungry. It was a male voice and almost came booming through the still too silent woods. This actually made me feel better because, though it was very creepy, it wasn't the first time a vagrant had made their way into the camping area and was looking for money and food. I thought for sure the person was going to rob me as he stepped out from behind the tree.

He was massive! He was at least nine feet tall. When I saw the eyes earlier I thought he had been standing on something. He had a hood up over his head and I couldn't really see his face. I raised my flashlight and he hollered at me not to do that. I told him I didn't have any food and if he didn't get the hell away from my camp I would inform the rangers and security and he could end up spending the night or some significant time in jail. He laughed at that and told me I misunderstood. I just stood there, stupidly staring at him and wondering what the hell he was talking about. That's when the hood dropped from his head and I was able to finally see his face. It wasn't a human being but a wolf and I immediately took notice of the hands I hadn't seen before as he took them out of his pockets. This is going to sound crazy but suddenly he howled and he must've flexed or something because the trench coat ripped right off of him. He looked like his body was in peak physical condition and I knew I didn't stand a chance. He was covered in gray and white fur all over his body and he was definitely more wolf than man. My mind didn't want to accept what I was seeing and I was experiencing a paralyzing and crippling fear I hadn't ever experienced before and that I didn't know what to do with. He had been turned to the side and leaning slightly up against the tree when he let out the howl and now he was turned and staring right at me. His fangs were long and looked sharp. They protruded from his mouth just enough for me to be able to make those observations. I slowly started to back away and sputtered and stuttered out a question. I asked him what he wanted. He responded that he had already told me and it hit me again and paralyzed me; the reality that I was having a real conversation and was face to face with what could only be described as a werewolf. However, he wasn't foaming at the mouth and crazed looking. In fact he seemed dapper and spoke in a dialect that sounded old fashioned and educated. Thinking back on it, he seemed more like how we like to show modern day vampires in the movies nowadays than what I had always thought of as a werewolf. He didn't seem threatening but the underlying threat of my life was always there, and we were both very aware of that fact.

I literally thought I was losing my mind and attributed it to the strenuous hike I had taken earlier in the day. I actually turned my back on him, thinking he was nothing more than a mere figment of an overtired and overworked imagination. Hadn't I been thinking of all the people who had gone missing in those same woods that I was camping in and all over the world for most of the day? Hadn't I just watched a movie about an alleged real werewolf who roamed the woods thirsty for the blood of humans? I had conjured this thing and it was nothing more than a figment of my imagination. I must have shocked him when I turned my back on him because he howled again and that time it sounded much more angry and fierce. I was sure that when I turned back around he would be gone but he wasn't and he had in fact gotten much closer to me than he had been when I first turned away from him. I blinked a few times, still sitting there on the ground in front of my tent where I had built my fire earlier in the night. I told him he couldn't possibly be real and he laughed again. He bared his fangs to me then and within less than a second he was on top of me. He had sprung and knocked me to the ground. I was pinned down underneath him and didn't stand a chance. Then and only then did it occur to me that he was in fact a real being and that I should have run when I had the chance. It was so strange as I saw my life pass before my eyes, I wasn't scared. I mean, I was frightened a little bit, sure, but it wasn't like how you think it would be when you're pinned underneath a real life, walking and talking werewolf in the middle of nowhere in the woods. No one would hear me scream and even if the other campers had heard me, they wouldn't ever in a million years know what happened to me. I laughed at how ridiculous it all was.

He was angry at that as well and his drool dripped onto my right cheek. He took a long, deep whiff of me and then pulled his head back and howled. He then sprang as fast as lightning up from on top of me and back into the woods. In the blink of an eye, literally, he was gone. I just laid there for a minute or two and then realized that suddenly I could hear insects, critters and even the owls all around me. The forest had come to life again suddenly and I knew it was because of the wolf-man. It had been him all along. He had stalked me, he had been the reason for the eerie quiet that settled over the forest that whole day, and he had been the reason for my seemingly irrational fear of the woods surrounding me that I had previously loved with all my heart and would have never thought to have been scared of. I jumped up when I remembered the trench coat and I walked cautiously over to where I thought it had landed. There was nothing left but a piece of the arm and I kept it. I honestly wasn't stressed out by the whole thing and I think that was something supernatural as well. Maybe the spirits of the forest were doing a good deed for me or maybe it was my guardian angels protecting me because it wasn't my time to go yet. Maybe, I was just in a deep and all consuming state of shock and my mind and body couldn't decipher how to react or respond to what I had just been through. Who knows? I wasn't feeling the fear, not at that time anyway. I went to my tent, laid down and went to sleep. I didn't wake up until late in the morning when I thought I heard someone was outside of my tent. I immediately thought of the wolfman and quickly got out of the tent to confront him. The sun was bright and I saw a man standing in the woods, right where the wolf had been the night before. He was with a blonde haired woman and they were both looking at me. I asked them how I could help them and what they were doing at my camp and they looked puzzled and a little put off by my rudeness. I quickly corrected myself and apologized.They nodded like they forgave me and then the girl said she was helping the man find his coat.

I looked at the guy and noticed something familiar in his eyes. He smiled, his teeth weren't fangs or anything but he did have very prominent canine teeth on both the top and bottom of his mouth. I told them I hadn't seen or come across a trench coat. He told me he had been on a walk the night before and had misplaced his trench coat. The girl was giddy with excitement and told me to be careful because there were rumors a wolf was on the loose near the camps and that many people had heard it howling the night before. The man thanked me for my time and they turned to walk away. But, not before the man turned back around and winked at me as he walked off arm in arm with the young girl. I didn't know what to make of it but I figured the less I know the better. The overwhelming fear I should have been feeling still hadn't gripped me and I finished out my weekend camping. It was uneventful. Once I got home I started doing some research into that particular area of the camp and saw that there had been many werewolf sightings there over the years but they were all the same; a crazed and beastly monster of a man/wolf was roaming around the area and showing itself to people. Several of them even claimed to have been attacked by it. So, what in the world had I witnessed and what could I possibly do or have done about it? I don't have the answers.

I think that maybe the fact that I wasn't showing fear was what saved my life. That thing wanted to drag me away and devour me but there was something about the way I smelled that turned it off and the only thing I can think of, based on all of my extensive research since the event took place, was more than likely the fact that I wasn't showing fear. As for the man and woman the next day I still don't know what to think about that either. Did the man just happen to put his trench coat down, have it stolen by the wolf and then just randomly come to my camp looking for it? That's almost as preposterous as I once thought a werewolf in the woods was. I don't know what to think about the blonde young woman who was with him the next morning either. She was either an accomplice or a victim and I honestly hope it is the former of those two options but I have no way of knowing, obviously. The encounter hasn't kept me out of the woods or out of that specific area but I've made a few changes to my camping routine. I now own a camper van and will only stay in it and I carry a firearm and am trained on how to use it properly. I've been to that same exact spot several times since then and haven't ever encountered the wolf man again. I've also never found that clearing with the trees that seemed to be woven together. I figure it's best to accept that there are some things out there we aren't meant to understand but that we should take seriously and learn to protect ourselves from. I've rambled on enough, that's all there is to my encounter story. Thanks for letting me share.

CHAPTER FIFTY-SEVEN

NEAR WHERE I LIVE, on the southwest coast of Florida, in the United States, there is a beautiful wilderness area that has trails that lead all throughout the town. The woods are dense and there's a lot of swampland mixed in throughout but other than those swamps, the scenery is absolutely gorgeous. One night I had an argument with my then boyfriend and needed to clear my head. The woods run all up and down the street, in everyone's backyards and all throughout the area wherever there isn't anything else standing. This was back in the last seventies so even less of the land had been built upon. I decided to drive my car down to the end of the block and park so that I could walk one of the trails. This wasn't unusual for me in that I walked those trails dozens of times throughout my life but I had never done so at night. Also, despite it being the same woods, technically, that I had grown up walking through, I lived in a different part of the town now and wasn't nearly as familiar with that part of the woods as the ones I had grown up exploring. Still and all I hadn't ever encountered anything scary while in the woods and I needed to get away for an hour or so. I had a flashlight in my car and that was all I figured I needed. I could have just as easily walked out of my back door, into my yard and then walked one of the trails back there but it was more dramatic for me to drive off like I did and make it look like I was leaving and actually going somewhere. I was down the street and parked within three minutes of leaving my house, that's how close it was but it was also far enough away that my boyfriend wouldn't have been able to see me pull in. If he had been watching it would have looked like I made the left hand turn onto the road leading to my parent's house. I tried to park inconspicuously and took a spot behind some tall shrubbery and bushes. I wanted him to worry and to regret some of the things he had said to me during the argument.

I grabbed my flashlight and put on a light jacket. Then I went and chose one of the three trails that led further into the woods. I wasn't thinking about wild animals and I know now that was stupid but it simply didn't cross my mind. I grew up in those woods, basically, and had long ago let go of any fears I may have had about the place, whether they were real or imagined. There was one legend of a swamp creature who roamed those woods and who was responsible for a bunch of unnamed people who had allegedly disappeared within them over the course of about a hundred years or so. I was taught at a very young age that it was nothing more than an urban legend, created by parents to keep their kids out of the woods or from roaming too far off into them at least. I was pretty angry and sort of talking to myself, under my breath, for the first half a mile into the woods. The trail forked and I just randomly chose to go off to the right. I noticed within a few minutes that something was very off with that part of the woods. It not only smelled strange but there wasn't any noise either. Normally I would hear the animals of the forest making all sorts of sounds as they ran around and hunted. There was nothing though and I tried my best to convince myself that it was because I had never been there at night. I just wasn't used to how quiet it was. I knew better though, somewhere deep down inside. The smell got more and more powerful with the deeper into the woods I walked. Don't get me wrong, the swamps always smelled horrible but this was something different. I don't know how else to describe it except to say it didn't smell like the swamps normally did, a smell I was more than familiar with. It smelled more like an animal or something; one that hadn't ever been in water or bathed itself.

I started to hear shuffling from behind me and immediately knew that I was being followed. My first instinct told me that it was a human being and that I was about to be attacked. I turned around to look but there was nothing there. Despite it being a fairly dark night, it wasn't pitch black, even without the light of my flashlight and that was unusual as well. It was almost like the forest had taken on some sort of eerie glow to it but I couldn't tell what the source of the illumination was though. I also noticed that to the left and right of me, as far as the other trails, they seemed to be pitch black. I felt lucky at first for having chosen the trail I had. Little did I know I would later come to regret that decision immensely. I walked for about a half an hour and the whole time I heard nothing at all except for the sounds of something following behind me but that I still couldn't see. I decided to turn back when all of a sudden I heard what sounded like a very loud splash coming from right behind where I had just sat down on a large rock to rest for a moment. I jumped up and immediately turned around and shined my flashlight directly onto that spot. I couldn't believe what I was seeing and terror gripped me and paralyzed me like nothing I had ever seen before or since.

There was what looked at first like a man, slowly walking through the swamp and directly towards me. It was about ten feet away at first and the closer it got to me, the more of it came into view. It wasn't a man, not really, it was an abomination. It looked like a gigantic, bipedal lizard man. It had arms and legs just like a human being but it was about nine feet tall. It had the same type of webbed feet and hands as a regular, smaller lizard and the face was hideous and terrifying. I couldn't move, even as it came towards me. The stench was unbearable and when I leaned over to vomit right there on the spot, it seemed like that's what finally broke the spell and I was able to move again. When I looked up again it was almost within arm's length and I somehow just knew that it planned on grabbing me and doing God only knew what with me once it had me in its clutches. I threw my flashlight at it and hit it in the face. It growled at me but honestly it sounded more like a roar, as its head was knocked to the left and before it looked back at me. It was even more angry after I had hit it and I was still only just standing there and not running away like you probably figure I would have been. Finally I ran. The creature was muscular and looked like a man would if he worked out and did stomach crunches at the gym for twelve hours a day, every day. I mean, it had twelve pack abs and its arms were gigantic. I ran for my life but I heard it behind me the whole time. I don't know how it didn't catch me or if perhaps it never really intended to catch me in the first place and was either just playing a game or was feeding off of my fear. I didn't dare turn around to look and tried to get to my car as fast as possible.

However, of course, I was lost. I couldn't hear the creature behind me anymore and I had no idea where I was or where it was. There was no light and I had stupidly thrown my flashlight at the swamp creature. I was full of adrenaline and fear and all I wanted to do was stop running and get out of those woods. There were still no normal sounds in the forest and I somehow just knew that meant the creature was still lurking around somewhere. Eventually I couldn't run anymore and had to stop to catch my breath and get my bearings. I stood perfectly still in the middle of the trail and listened to see if I could hear or see anything moving. At first there was nothing but then I saw what looked like two glowing, yellow eyes in front of me inside of some bushes, or perhaps hiding behind them. I was very confused at first because there was no way it could have been the lizard man because I hadn't noticed his eyes before and also, he was about nine feet tall and the eyes were at about the height of my ankles. I am five foot four inches tall and was the same back then too. As soon as it started to move out of the bushes it dawned on me and I realized it was the same creature only it was crawling around, like a lizard. It seemed like it was camouflaged in some way because it only became visible a little bit at a time until eventually it was in full view right in front of me. That awful stench and that dark green, scaly skin just stood there, looking at me. I could see it was wet from the swamp water it had originally emerged from and I started to cry. Suddenly, it stood up.

It stood up in one swift motion I can't even begin to try and describe for you and it was terrifying. I heard bones cracking as it moved and I swear a smile crossed its filthy lizard lips. Then it licked its lips and I saw it had a forked tongue and its teeth were yellow, green and razor sharp. I turned and ran and it followed behind me. I didn't know where I was or where I was going and just ran towards where I thought my car might have been. It was nothing more than sheer pure luck that I did make it back to my car that night. I saw the parking area and breathed a sigh of relief but I wasn't out of the woods yet, no pun intended, as the creature was still following very close behind me. I could hear it breathing and though I was extremely winded and felt like my chest would explode, it was breathing at a very normal and steady rate despite the adrenaline of the situation and also how far and long we had been running. I opened the door, which thankfully wasn't locked and got inside. I locked all the doors manually the second I got in and just in time. I turned the car on as the creature pounded on the windows. I knew it was only a matter of time before it broke one or all of the windows and dragged me out of my car through it. I had to act fast. I backed up, trying to run it over, but it just leaped right over my car and landed, on its feet, in front of the car. I watched it in my headlights as the reality of what I was being faced with suddenly and all at once dawned on me. It was monstrous and hideous and it was pure evil. It looked like it was grinning again as, with lightning speed and inhuman agility, it jumped onto my car, holding onto the sides as it laid flat on its stomach on the hood of the car. I screamed as it smashed its head into my windshield. I swerved onto the main road but it wouldn't let go. Finally I stopped short and it went flying off the windshield and into the middle of the road.

I should have just driven off and gone home or to the authorities but I didn't do either one of those things. I ran over it several times, back and forth, over and over its lizard body, again and again. Then, finally I started to drive in the direction of my house. I looked in my rearview mirror and saw something even more strange than everything else I had been through that night and up until that point. The lizard man/creature stood up, but this time it wasn't in one quick and fluid motion. It did so slowly and it looked like it was not only broken, but like it was glitching. It looked like it was fading in and out of existence or something but by that time I was just so happy and relieved to have gotten away from it and to be alive that I turned away from it to pay attention to the road ahead of me as I drove to my house. I heard an extremely loud roar like I had heard earlier in the night and with that it seemed like the night had once again come to life. I heard owls and birds and all sorts of insects again and it was very loud after the deafening silence I had experienced ever since I had walked into those evil and cursed woods. The night had exploded into a cacophony of all of the usual sounds and I had never been more happy to hear them in all my life.

I don't know what happened to me that night or why. There was some damage to my vehicle but I told my boyfriend it must've happened and been vandalized while I was on my walk. I knew with absolute certainty that if I had told him I had been attacked by a giant and evil lizard man he would have only heard I was attacked by a man and would have insisted on going into the woods to find the perpetrator. I knew I would never have been able to reason with him or stop him from going and therefore I never told him. I ended up moving out permanently and going back home to my parents a few months later anyway. Sometimes when he and I would spend time in the backyard or barbecue and things like that, I would feel eyes on me, watching me from the woods. There were other times when the night seemed to go unnaturally and eerily still and silent and I would always excuse myself and pretend to have a migraine when that would happen. I would go and lay down and pray I didn't hear my boyfriend or anyone else screaming as the lizard man attacked the party or whatever else was happening at the time. That never happened and I've not talked about it with anyone until now. Lately I've been having nightmares about that lizard creature and the more I research online about the race of evil reptilian extraterrestrials, the more I believe that they inhabit our planet as well in the form of not only hybrids but in the swamplands and wherever else reptiles can survive. I believe the land is cursed and wonder if, after all these years, that entity or whatever it was is coming back to finish the job. I still live in the same town surrounded by the same woods and swamps. I think about the last thing that I saw before I turned my focus back to the road and how it seemed to be phasing in and out of existence. I wonder if that's because it's an extraterrestrial and was somehow being beamed somewhere safe where it would be able to heal, before going back out into the woods to hunt for helpless and unsuspecting human beings to torture and feast on.

CHAPTER FIFTY-EIGHT

THIS ENCOUNTER HAPPENED to me and my son when he was two years old. He's five years old now but doesn't really remember it except that he won't go near the place where we encountered the little monsters. We live next door to a huge plot of land that has trails leading all through the county where we live but it's wildlife conserved and protected land and therefore no one is allowed to build on it. We moved here, my husband and I, about a year before I became pregnant with our son, who is an only child. I wanted to be a stay at home mom from the moment I found out that I was pregnant and luckily for me my husband wanted the exact same thing. He took on more hours at work in order to help make ends meet and to make up for the money I was pulling in with my part time job at the time. Once my son was finally old enough to start being curious about what's outside, our adventures together began. My husband and I own a little less than two acres and it's a beautiful property. However, the trails and woods next door to our home, that are connected to our house, always called to me and even before I became pregnant I would walk them at length all of the time on my days off. One day my son and I were playing outside when he looked over and saw a car pull into the tiny parking area where people could leave their vehicles when they went to ride their bikes or hike the trails. He kept pointing over there and so finally I relented and decided to pack a little picnic for us. I loaded him and our little lunch into his wagon and rolled him down a slight incline and into the parking area. There's a grassy knoll that sort of surrounds the parking area and I was planning on just staying there. My son hadn't ever been in the woods before and I thought it would be best if we just hung out by the main road to let him get used to it first and figured eventually we would make our way inside of the woods more. It seems something else had plans for us that day though.

We played and ran around for a while and finally I encouraged him to take a break and have something to eat. We sat on the little blanket I had packed for us and started eating our sandwiches and fresh fruit. My son hadn't started talking yet but could toddler babble all day long. I didn't mind, I enjoyed listening to him as he pointed out the birds and other little animals that live around this area of rural Illinois. He kept pointing up the small hill and into the woods and saying "boo." I thought that he was trying to say the color blue and that he had perhaps seen a blue bird or something. I figured it had landed in that spot a few times, for a couple of seconds each, and then flew off before I could see it but not before he had caught sight of it. Eventually though he was screaming the word boo and had jumped up, making his way as fast as his little legs could carry him up the small hill and trying to get to something in the woods. It didn't occur to me to be scared or apprehensive and so I just followed him. I helped him up the hill and then put him down and let him explore. He went right to one tree in particular and looked all around it and behind it but then he looked very confused. He looked up at me and asked, "boo?" and I said I didn't know and that maybe the birdie had flown away. This upset him and he stomped his little feet and crossed his arms, once again yelling the word and continuing deeper into the forest. It was the middle of the afternoon and broad daylight so I didn't mind exploring with him. He was clearly looking for something and far be it from me to try and stop him from finding it.

We had been walking deeper and deeper into the woods for about twenty minutes when I suggested we turn back. He didn't want to but I wasn't comfortable being that far in the woods as it was, not with my son and with nothing to protect us against the larger, predatory animals that roamed around in there. I went to scoop him up, knowing full well that he was going to have a temper tantrum but not caring at that point because it was a matter of safety and that always came first. I went to grab him and he ran behind a tree, then he started just running away from me in general. He was crying and still repeating the word, "boo" and didn't want to leave. I was getting frustrated and finally, once he ran behind one tree, I decided to sneak up on him instead of letting him hear me coming but when I got to where I could look around the tree and see him, he wasn't there. My heart sank into my stomach and I immediately started thinking of the water that ran through the woods in that area. I was sick to my stomach. I had just seen him go behind the tree seconds ago but he wasn't there. Where could he have gone and where could he have been? I was in a full blown panic. I heard snickering and when I looked over in that direction I saw what could only be described as a blue fox. It looked amused and while I know that doesn't make sense, it's just how it looked I don't know how else to explain it. It ran up one of the trails opposite where I had last seen my son and, defying all reason and logic, I ran after it.

I yelled for it to stop and eventually it did. The forest had changed though and we had only been running for about ten minutes. Suddenly I remembered my son, and it was as though I really had forgotten him for a moment there. I don't drink and have never done drugs. There's absolutely nothing that could explain the fact I had left the spot and the area where I had last seen my baby. I was devastated and thought for sure, due to my chasing that damn blue fox, that my son had wandered into the water. I bent down with my hands on my knees while still standing in order to catch my breath. I was crying and didn't know what to do. I no longer saw the fox but I did hear my son crying. It wasn't just crying like he was lost or scared but it was more like he was in pain and hurting. I ran to where the sound was coming from and ended up in a clearing. Right there in the middle of the dense woods there was an actual clearing and a circle of very large boulders. The rocks were taller than me and I am five foot seven inches tall. I would have had to climb them to get on top of them and they made a perfect circle all around that clearing. I heard my son but i couldn't see him. I started to panic even more and climbed to the top of one of the boulders. It started to shake underneath me and right there, in the middle of the boulder circle, an image started to appear. It was hazy at first and looked almost like heat sparkling off the ground and in the air on a very hot and humid day. It became clearer and clearer by the second and finally my son was sitting there. He was by himself and he was crying. I jumped off the boulder and ran to him. He screamed and kicked at me as though he didn't even recognize me and when I looked closer at him I saw he had tiny bruises all over most of his body.

He had only been wearing a diaper and a sleeveless shirt so a lot of his skin was exposed. Remember I hadn't planned on going into the woods that day and so I didn't dress him for that type of outdoor excursion. Finally he looked at me, as I held him there in my arms, and said in his tiny little voice, "Mom, Boo!". He started crying again with his head on my shoulder. I rubbed his back and asked where Boo was and he pointed even deeper into the woods. I didn't want to go and knew it was a bad idea but I was being compelled. I walked through the clearing and got onto one of the trails on the other side. I just kept walking. It had been about fifteen minutes and I was ready to turn around. That is until my son started screaming and crying, pointing to yet another very large rock, and yelling, "No Booooo!" The rock wasn't nearly as large as the giant boulders in the circle but they were about the size of my son. Of course I looked but I couldn't see anything. I wanted to just get out of there but something or someone had hurt my baby and I wasn't about to just let that go. I didn't want to bring him home and come back another time because I wanted to make sure I confronted whatever or whoever it had been who did that to such an innocent little boy. I walked over to the rock to get a better look and that's when I saw about ten little blue creatures. Their skin was blue and they wore blue clothes. They glistened in the sunlight and had blue wings but they were running around on the ground, not flying. I yelled for them to stop and they did. They looked up at me and then looked at my son and started pointing at him and laughing. I kicked one of them because at that point I think my anger was overriding anything else I was feeling. The rest of them attacked me and started pulling and biting my feet and ankles. I figured I should just get out of there and I turned to run. They tripped me by pulling on my sandal and down to the ground I went. I had still been holding my son but luckily he wasn't hurt in the fall. He ran a few feet away from me and just watched, crying the whole time as these little beings bit and clawed at my body. They were also poking me with what looked like sewing needles. I was terrified for myself but mainly was trying to get away from them so I could get my son out of there. Finally I broke away from them, brushed them off my body where they were hanging on and I was so angry I stomped on one of them. I lifted my foot in satisfaction but there was nothing there. In fact, all of the little creatures were gone and I grabbed my son and ran as fast as I could back through the clearing.

However, once I had done that I didn't know where I was anymore. I was extremely confused and disoriented. I was once again holding my son and needed to sit down before I fell with him again. He wasn't crying anymore and in fact he seemed to be having a great time, giggling the whole time I had been running. I started to panic when my son looked and pointed and said, "Kitsune." I SWEAR to you, he said it loud and clear. I know I hadn't just been hearing what I wanted to because I didn't know the meaning of the word before all of this. I looked and there was another fox, this time it was all white and beautiful, unlike the blue one that looked mangy and malnourished. Something in the eyes looked way too human and I wanted no part of it. However, my son was standing and I was sitting and he took off after the white fox like a bat out of hell. I swear he was running unusually fast right then. I chased after him but eventually, of course, I once again had lost sight of him. I saw the white fox and followed it and then my son jumped out from behind a tree, smiling and laughing as though we were both aware we were in a game of hide and seek. The fox made a strange noise that sounded like a human being clearing its throat and when I grabbed my son and looked up it was running away again. I ran after it.

Finally I realized the tree my son had just jumped out from behind was the one he had originally disappeared behind about an hour before, or so I thought but I'll get to that in a minute. I ran down the trail and it was immediately fully dark outside. I saw my husband's work vehicle parked there, down near the grassy knoll where I had originally left all of our belongings. I called out for him and he ran up and embraced me and our son. I tried telling him what had happened but he didn't want to hear anything other than that we were alright. He wouldn't have believed me anyway and so I told him I just got lost and was lucky to have randomly found my way out of the woods before I encountered a bear or some other predatory animal looking to devour my son and most likely me too. We had only been gone an hour, two at the absolute most and yet ten hours had passed. I looked back one last time towards where the little hill leading into the woods was and there was a blue, amused looking fox sitting on one of the fallen tree logs.

Don't ask me what happened because I don't know. I know the Kitsune is an animal but it's only supposed to live in Japan, not in the United States and certainly not in the middle of nowhere in the woods in Illinois. I don't know how my basically non verbal toddler knew the word or how he managed to say it so clearly. He must have been being enticed by the "blue fox" into wanting to play or something and it most likely, from what I understand from all of my research into what happened, was communicating with him somehow to go and play with it and its friends. I don't think it counted on the white fox helping me and I believe without that creature, what or whoever it was, my son would have ended up another statistic included with little kids who go missing in the woods right before their parent's eyes and are never found. I think the blue fox was a fairy creature as were the sparkling blue things and that they saw or sensed something in my son that made them want to keep him and bring them with him. I'm grateful it worked out the way it did, for obvious reasons, and though I haven't been back to that area ever since, I do leave candy and airplane bottles of liquor at the edge of the woods from time to time as a thank you. My son doesn't remember but for at least a year after the ordeal, whenever we would drive or walk by the woods, he would point and whisper "bad boo" to me and/or his father. My husband is still clueless and is content to stay that way. I have since armed myself with as much information as I could possibly retain about so-called fairytale creatures in the woods, just in case one should happen to roam into my backyard one day from the woods connecting my property to the forest we had gotten lost in that day a few years ago. My son isn't allowed to play out there alone and probably won't be until he is old enough to understand not to follow things into the woods and even then I'm reluctant because whatever those things were they wanted him and they didn't ever plan on returning him. That is the only thing about all of this that I'm absolutely sure of.

CHAPTER FIFTY-NINE

WHILE THE TITLE of this encounter has the word human in it, I want to say right from the beginning here that I am not entirely sure if what I encountered and witnessed that day was human or not. Once I get more in depth into it you'll understand that a little better. I was twenty years old in 1979 and I was having the time of my life walking some of the Appalachian Trail. I didn't really know how long I was going to be out there on that hike and was honestly just taking it one week at a time. I knew someone who lived near the area of the trail where I was planning on starting the hike and they let me park my camper there and agreed to bring it to me when I called and asked for it. There are parts of the trail where there's no way to get word to the outside world for a fairly long time but I wasn't planning on taking on any of those areas yet. I was young and while I was fairly inexperienced with that particular spot, I was not at all unfamiliar or inexperienced with camping and hiking in the woods in general. I am an only child and was raised by my father alone. Therefore I was by default a "tomboy" and everything my father enjoyed, like basically anything and everything having to do with the outdoors, I also grew to love. My dad had recently passed away and I was taking on the trail as a sort of homage to him. He hadn't ever been able to hike the whole thing because he had me so young. He had hiked parts of it, like I was doing at the time, but he never had a chance to get to all of the states and I wanted to be able to do that in his honor. I even planned to carve his initials on one tree in every state. I had no grand idea that I would be able to just walk nonstop for the entirety of the massive trail but I felt like if I could hike for a day or two in each state, even if I took a break here and there in between, he would be proud of me for that. So, that was my plan.

I started in Maine, which is my home state and really didn't have a plan, like I said. I hiked from when I got dropped off at six in the morning and then started looking for a place to camp a few hours before the sun was about to set for the night. I found a spot that looked like as good a place as any and set up my tent and built a small fire. I was physically fit and in the best shape of my life but I was still fairly tired. The only entertainment I had brought with me were a few books and I sat down and got comfortable and read some of the first one. By the time midnight rolled around I was exhausted and made my way into my tent to get some sleep. I figured I would sleep really well that night and was looking forward to seeing how far I could make it along the trail the next day. I hadn't seen a single other human being while out there that whole day and hadn't heard anyone else in the area either. I didn't think that was too unusual though given how huge the trail is and how massive the length of it is. I fell right asleep but was woken in the middle of the night with a start. At first I couldn't put my finger on what had startled me awake so quickly so I just sat there, sort of stunned and listening intently. I had a bad feeling from the moment I opened my eyes but after a few minutes of hearing nothing out of the ordinary I began to calm down. I eventually laid back down and started falling back asleep quickly. Just as I started to drift off, I heard a very loud scream that jolted me back awake and into reality.

It wasn't an animal and it sounded like a woman. The scream was one of pain and horror and it was echoing from somewhere in the woods. It sounded like it was coming from everywhere all at once but I knew that was impossible. It definitely sounded like someone needed help and was being attacked or something. I wasn't equipped or prepared to fend off an attacker and it's not like I could have just whipped out a cell phone and called for help. I didn't even know where the sound was coming from. It gave me chills and within a minute or two of the first blood curdling scream, there was another one. It sounded the exact same as the first one only the second time it sounded much closer. I remained in my tent, silent and stone still, while I decided what I was going to do. It stood to reason that if the female who was yelling and screaming like that was getting closer, so was her assailant. I should say here that I never was a big believer in the paranormal or supernatural and believed up to that point that everything had a logical and reasonable explanation. The issue sometimes was just figuring out what those explanations were. I immediately assumed a woman was being attacked or possibly even killed and that the assailant or attacker was another human being. I started to pray that maybe the woman would run the other way and that neither she nor her killer would come past or notice my tent or campsite. I prayed that she would escape whoever it was but also that she wouldn't come to me for any sort of help. It sounds terrible, I know but I honestly didn't know what I could have done for her. I didn't even have anything other than a small knife for carving my dad's initials in a tree and cutting fruit on me as a weapon and wasn't much of a fighter, not by any stretch of the imagination. For all the things my dad had taught me, self defense wasn't one of them. I listened for what seemed like forever but didn't hear anything else.

Instead of feeling relieved like I thought I would, I became even more nervous. What if the woman had been killed and now whoever killed her was simply roaming the woods, looking for his next victim? There was no one else out there for miles and I was just terrified beyond words at that point. I peeked out of my tent but it was the middle of the night and it was really hard to see anything beyond a few feet in front of me without turning on my flashlight. I didn't want to do that because then, if there were someone around the area, I would have been not only alerting them to my presence but also shining a beacon of light out that would lead them right to me. Eventually I laid back down. I looked at my watch and it was two in the morning. I fell back asleep soon after but woke up again about an hour later when I heard loud rustling that sounded like footsteps in the general vicinity of my camp. The footsteps sounded like they were still a ways in the woods yet but they were definitely getting closer as the seconds ticked by. I was shaking and knew there was someone out there. It didn't sound like an animal and although it could have been a bear or something similar, I somehow just knew deep down inside that it was a human being. I immediately started thinking about the woman I had heard screaming earlier that night and terror gripped me and pulled me into a state of total paralysis. I needed to snap myself out of it in case someone or something was out there and meant to do me harm. I tried not to be afraid and I listened carefully again to try and hear what direction the noises were coming from. The harder I listened the more I realized that whatever was coming down towards my camp and out of the woods sounded like it was moving really fast.

I grabbed my small knife and stepped out of my tent with my flashlight off but in my hand. I was either going to see what was out there or use it as a weapon but I couldn't just sit there all night in fear, waiting for whatever it was to come and get me either. Suddenly I was standing there with my knife in one hand and my flashlight in the other when I heard a short yelp. It sounded like someone was about to scream but was then silenced by someone else putting a hand over their mouth or something. That was it and I knew I needed to face whatever it was and was really hoping it was a bear. I figured I would shine my light out into the wilderness, see that it was a bear and then go back into my tent until it passed my camp up. I had followed all of the safety protocols concerning food and wild animals while out in the woods and specifically in that area of the trail and figured at the worst case scenario, I could just give it all of my food and make my way to a place where I could call my friend in the morning. I was seriously rethinking being out there alone anyway at that point. I took a deep breath and shined my light out into the woods, in the direction I heard the rustling coming from.

At first I didn't see anything and I kept moving the flashlight all around. Finally, it landed on something. I couldn't tell what it was at first and once I did clearly see what it was, it's like my mind couldn't comprehend it fully. It looked somewhat like a human female but she was crawling backwards and on all fours. It was a position we used to get into and walk as kids and we called it the crab walk. Dirty, sort of blonde hair hung over her face but it was greasy and stringy and therefore I could see a lot of her face. Her face was contorted in pain but also, she seemed to be smiling a little bit too. Many of her teeth were missing and those that weren't were stained brown and green in some places. She froze when the light hit her so I had more than enough time to take it all in. She was completely naked and from what I could see of her she had all the normal parts of a human female but her eyes looked like they were whitish-blue and dead. She had cuts and huge purple bruises all over her body and some of them looked like they were fresh and still bleeding. I think I was in shock because I didn't scream right away and I didn't lower the flashlight either. I couldn't because I couldn't move right then. She finally started moving towards me, still in the awkward and bent backward "crab" position and that's when it all hit me and I started to scream. I screamed at the top of my lungs over and over again while still standing there, shocked and trying to take in and understand what it was that I was looking at. After I had screamed a few times the thing stopped and almost seemed to tilt her head towards me.

Then, she began to stand up. She moved in slow, awkward and very jerky movements. I could hear her bones cracking and creaking and the sound was nothing less than absolutely sickening. Eventually she was standing upright and her head was awkwardly facing the forest floor. It looked like her neck was broken at first but eventually she looked up at me. She opened her mouth and I will never forget not only how wide her mouth opened but the sound of that scream. It was the exact same ear piercing and blood curdling scream I had heard before when I thought that someone was being attacked. I stared at her in horror and started to scream myself and we stood there like that, taking turns screaming, for at least a full minute, maybe even two. Eventually I stopped screaming and so did she but as soon as she did blood started gushing out of her neck and her mouth and she reached out her hand to me. The other hand leaned up against a tree that was right next to her. I slowly started backing away even though she was still at least twenty feet away from me at that point. Eventually I heard one more very loud scream pierce the air around her but blood was still pouring from her mouth so it seemed to be coming from the ether, despite also seeming like it was coming from her. She slowly faded out of existence over the course of the next few seconds. I turned from where she had been standing and puked. I was shaking uncontrollably and realized I had to pee. It was the last thing I wanted to do but knew I would soon go in my pants if I didn't take care of that. I don't know what I was thinking as I went and grabbed my toilet paper.

I had seen many horror movies up to that point and it dawned on me that perhaps she had been murdered in that area of those woods, along the trail, and maybe had some unfinished business. It sounds cliche I know but so was every single horror movie that came out around that time. It wasn't like it is today where the paranormal and spirits are popular topics of research and conversation. The adrenaline made me exhausted and I crawled into my tent to go to sleep. The next morning I woke up and immediately walked over to the tree where the woman had been standing. I carved my dad's initials in it before making breakfast and packing up my camp. I headed back in the direction from where I had originally come from and made my way into town to call my friend to bring my camper van to me. I didn't want to explain and just said I thought I had eaten something bad and didn't want to be out there alone if I was going to be sick like I was. He didn't ask any questions and I never went back to that area again. I did some research at the local library in that area but couldn't find any disappearances or murders that fit the description of the injuries or with victims who fit the description of the girl.

I still don't know what happened to me that night or why I was chosen to see what I saw. Was I chosen? Was I just in the wrong place at the wrong time? I have been considering going to a medium and possibly getting some answers because the girl has been in my thoughts and nightmares a lot lately and I hadn't even thought of her for a long time. I eventually made it through the trail and spent at least one night in every state but I never went back to that area in Maine. I don't have any more information and don't know anything else. That was my one and only experience with the paranormal and I really want to keep it that way. However, it seems like whoever that woman was, she may have other plans for me because of how often she has been making appearances in my thoughts and dreams the last few months.

CHAPTER SIXTY

MY ENCOUNTER HAPPENED in upstate New York in some woods near my house. Now, while these woods were in a very residential area and there were many houses surrounding them on all sides, once you went into them and started walking the trails there, you would never know there was any sort of civilization anywhere near the general vicinity. I had grown up playing in the woods and like so many other people I've come across who had a terrifying encounter of one kind or another, I hadn't ever even thought to be afraid of anything other than maybe some poison ivy or a bear. I was only eleven years old and my family wasn't religious or superstitious in any way and I hadn't ever given a thought to whether or not I believed in the paranormal because it was just something that hadn't ever come up yet at that point in my life. I was about to come face to face with something evil and it changed the course of my life. It was a Saturday afternoon in the middle of the summer and my older sisters had gone to some birthday party for one of their mutual friends. I hadn't been invited and therefore was left home with nothing to do and to my own devices. My dad was at work and my mother had gone to bring my sisters where they needed to go. I knew that she would more than likely just hang out with the girls whose party it was mother because they had also grown up together. The town I lived in was small and my mother was also good friends with some of my friend's moms and parents as well. I was bored but for one reason or another none of my friends were around to play or hang out that day and so I decided to go into the woods and do some fishing. I didn't like to tell people that I loved to fish because my friends would have made fun of me and because of that it wasn't very often that I got to do it. I grabbed everything I would need, packed myself a snack and headed out into the woods to a pretty large creek where there were usually plenty of fish.

The spot I was looking for was only about a fifteen minute walk into the woods and I had been there a hundred times or more. I always took the same trail and knew I would have about two hours to fish before I would have to head back home because it would just be getting dark by that time. I made it to the creek without any issues and set everything up quickly. I cast my line in and almost immediately I got a bite. I excitedly grabbed my fishing pole and slowly, very steadily, I tried to reel in my catch. However, the more I pulled the more I realized there was no way that what I had caught was a fish because it weighed so much. I was a small framed and thin little girl but I knew what a large catch felt like on the end of my line and this felt like it weighed as much as I did. Eventually my line snapped and while I was annoyed, I didn't really think anything of it. I sat there and fixed my line and baited my hook again but as soon as I casted out the line for the second time, it felt and looked like a bunch of dark clouds had settled over the woods. It was cold all of a sudden and windy. Not only that but it looked like it was dusk already and that full darkness was fast approaching. I checked my watch and it was only six at night. It shouldn't have even started to get dark until eight at night or later at that time of year in New York.

I suddenly felt like someone or something was watching me from the woods. I looked up into the sky and it was black. Despite that, it still looked like it was dusk outside. In other words, while the sky was dark everything else still looked like the sun was only beginning to set. I looked around because I was suddenly incredibly frightened but there was honestly no reason for me to have been except that maybe there was some sort of odd weather event happening all around me.

Something inside told me to pack up my things and get out of those woods as fast as possible. I obeyed and immediately started putting everything away. I wasn't dressed for the cold and the temperature seemed like it had dropped almost ten degrees in the few minutes I had been sitting there. I got everything together but when I stood up to leave I saw something directly in the path of the trail I needed to walk in order to get home. It looked like everything was blurry but it wasn't everything and was only in that little, hovering circular area on the trail. Everything around it still looked perfectly normal. Unfortunately I had to go to that exact spot and therefore didn't want to move towards it but couldn't go anywhere else. I stood there trying to figure out what to do next when suddenly something seemed to have either appeared out of nowhere or popped out of the little blurry circle in the middle of the trail. I wasn't sure which and either one was a scary thought. I immediately started to cry. It looked like a black blob and the moment it was out of the circle, the blurriness evaporated and everything looked normal again. Well, as far as the trail was concerned. I slowly started to back up but knew I was only steps away from falling into the creek. I watched in horror as the big black blob turned into two and then into three. There were three of them in total.

I considered making a run for it but again, I would have had to have run right past whatever those things were. I couldn't do anything but stand there and watch it all unfold. I was freezing and darkness was falling very fast all around me. The only way I knew to get home was that one trail and everything surrounding it was thick, lush and very dense woods. I couldn't even make a break for it. Suddenly, each blob expanded and stretched to be about nine feet tall and all three of them did this in perfect unison. Then there were two red dots near the top of each one. They morphed and changed very quickly and finally, standing there before me were three red eyed shadow figures. They were the shape of a human man only much taller. As soon as they were fully formed it seemed like darkness fell completely and I could hardly see anything around me. I had a flashlight, a very small one that I had always kept in my tackle box for emergencies but I couldn't take my eyes off of the beings before me for long enough to get it out of there. I was terrified and I knew somewhere deep down inside that I was in the presence of absolute and pure evil. I shivered and it had nothing to do with the cold. I looked at my watch and only ten minutes had passed. It was approximately six fifteen and pitch black outside already. With as dark as it was, however, I could still see the figures very clearly and it wasn't just their eyes. They stood out completely in the darkness and they were blacker than the night around us. I didn't know what else to do and so I screamed at the top of my lungs, several times. The beings seemed confused by this and I think that's what happened because they sort of cocked their heads to the side and looked from me to one another and then back at me again.

Finally I decided to just start running along the trail. No sooner had I thought to do that than they started quickly moving towards me. My mind was screaming at me to run and get the heck out of there but I couldn't move. It wasn't fear that had so completely paralyzed me either, I think the beings had something to do with it. I suddenly heard a loud splash coming from the creek behind me. The water was down about ten feet and there was a drop off right behind where I was standing. I looked down and in shock and horror watched as another being slowly and steadily climbed up the wall. I could see it pulling itself up and as I looked down I saw its hands and arms and then its head as it lifted itself onto the ground. The strange part is that it didn't look wet at all, despite having just come from the creek, but it was wet. I could see the water pooling at its feet. I started to feel very dizzy but I knew I couldn't let myself pass out right there because I just knew something terrible would happen to me if I did. I made a break for it and ran past the three beings slowly coming towards me and turned to run from the one that had come up from the creek behind me. They didn't make a sound and aside from that one loud splash, I realized I hadn't heard a single sound since I hooked that heavy fish that got away from me. I have an idea about that too but I'll save it for the end. I left all my stuff behind and ran as fast as I could through the darkness and prayed that I wouldn't stray from the trail accidentally. It would have been pretty hard to do that because of how dense everything around the trail was but as I had just seen, stranger things have happened.

I cried as I ran, I couldn't help it. I would see the red eyes pop up from behind a tree or lean out and peek from behind a shrub somewhere. The whole time I was running for my life back towards my house I saw the shadow beings but they never approached me again or tried to grab or attack me. They just kept making themselves known. I finally made it home and once I was in my own backyard I finally stopped to catch my breath. I had been running for a while without ever looking back and so I finally looked back and when I did I saw about ten sets of eyes in various places all over the woods. They were up in the trees and behind them too. They were everywhere. I ran into my house, locked all the doors and ran upstairs. Once I got to my room and looked out my bedroom window and back towards the woods, the sun was just about to start setting and it was dusk. I laid down and ended up sick with a very high fever for two weeks after that. I believe the creatures made me sick. I also believe they were making themselves known because they were feeding off of my adrenaline and fear. These theories and all of the other ones I have come from researching in all the years between now and then. I never stopped seeing the shadow entities either and I see them everywhere I go. They lurk in my homes, and I've moved many times trying to escape them. They lurk in grocery stores and parks and I see them in broad daylight more than I see them at night. I have almost nightly sleep paralysis episodes and they have made my life a terrifying, living hell.

I never told anyone about them until I met my husband because I was afraid people would think I was as crazy as I felt. Luckily for me he believes in the paranormal and supernatural and has even come up with a few theories of his own. He believes, for whatever reason, I happened to be in the wrong place at the wrong time and just happened to see them coming into our reality. They must have liked something they saw in me, or something that they tasted- like my extreme fear, and latched on to me somehow. As far as his theory about the creek and the large fish? He believes I had accidentally hooked the shadow person. Either that, or, the shadow person purposely latched onto my line in the hopes it could pull me into the water with it. If they truly do feed off of fear then imagine how much fear energy I would have produced should I have thought I was going to drown. Maybe when it didn't work it summoned its friends to come and help it. I don't know if any of this makes any sense or if it's normal or not, as far as paranormal experiences with malevolent shadow beings go, but I know what my experience has been and everything I've been through with these evil entities since it all started that day in the woods long ago. The weather anomalies aren't uncommon for paranormal activity, though I've yet to see it in anyone else's encounters with shadow people. Thanks for letting me share and I have plenty more encounters with them in the woods that I can write about too but honestly they've become so usual in my life, almost somewhat commonplace, that it hasn't ever scared or disturbed me as much as it did that very first time I saw them.

CHAPTER SIXTY-ONE

IT WAS 1985, around the beginning of January. My nephew and I had spent the day riding our ATVs on a piece of farmland, not far from my house. We had constructed a makeshift ramp in a small field adjacent to a larger stand of trees, opposite a hedge row that bordered another expansive field.

The field we were in was relatively narrow, spanning no more than 50 yards where we were situated. It opened up into a larger field surrounded by woods on three sides and the same hedge row on the fourth side. Earlier in the day, the weather had been warm, causing the snow to become compact and perfect for jumping our ATVs. With some persistent begging and pleading, our parents finally granted us permission to go.

We rode our machines to the spot with the jump and spent about an hour soaring over it. Eventually, we decided to take a break and turned off our engines. We began attempting to pack more snow onto the ramp, but it had become significantly colder, causing the snow to freeze and resist being compacted. As we sat there, quietly chatting, we suddenly heard noises emanating from the woods across the hedge row. The sound resembled a flurry of animals running through the now-crunchy snow, accompanied by the snapping of twigs. We fixated our gaze on the edge of the woods, unsure of what was about to emerge.

To our surprise, a small herd of white-tailed deer burst out from the southwest corner of the woodlot. There were perhaps 10 to 12 deer, not all appearing simultaneously but clearly in a hurry to escape the woods. We pointed and joked about their swift movement across the field, dispersing in various directions. After a few more minutes, we heard something else approaching slowly through the woods, following a similar path as the deer. It halted just before reaching the edge, and we strained our eyes to catch a glimpse of a shadowy figure, although we couldn't be certain. Nonetheless, an inexplicable sense of unease began to settle upon us.

By this time, we had risen from our positions and were cautiously inching closer to our parked ATVs, which were no more than ten feet away. Suddenly, a peculiar sensation coursed through my chest, as if I were leaning against a vibrating object. It then escalated into a long, loud, and sustained call that reverberated through the air. The duration was so extended that the only comparison I can draw is to a siren due to its length. The call maintained a medium-high tone for what felt like a minute before gradually fading away. The sound was so deafening that we instinctively covered our ears in an attempt to protect them.

In a state of panic, we bolted toward our machines, both equipped with pull-start mechanisms. After a few frantic pulls, accompanied by our continuous screams, we managed to get the engines roaring and swiftly descended the hill as fast as we possibly could. When we reached the bottom, approximately half to three-quarters of a mile away, we halted, gasping for breath, and exchanged bewildered glances. We couldn't help but ask each other what on earth had just occurred. It wasn't long before the sound echoed once more, seemingly coming from right behind us. Fortunately, we never laid eyes on what-ever was producing that haunting call, for which we were immensely grateful. We immediately accelerated at top speed, parking our ATVs in the garage and securing all the doors behind us. I remember my mom asking us what was happening because our commotion was impossible to ignore. Yet, we were both too rattled to offer much of an explanation.

We briefly considered returning the following day to investigate, but when morning arrived, neither of us possessed the desire to venture back. As far as I know, no one else had heard or witnessed anything before or after our encounter. To this day, whenever I venture into the woods for deer hunting, I dread that walk through the darkness. Thank you for reading my story.

CHAPTER SIXTY-TWO

I HAVE SHARED this story over the years on different blogs etc so it may seem familiar. I will say it did take me many years before I did because I feared ridicule and doubted anyone would believe me.

It was May 1982, and I was serving on active duty at Camp Pendleton, CA, I was temporarily assigned to a staff of Marines supervising a youth program. Our program involved conducting rigorous two-week mini-boot camps for teenage boys.

Camp Pendleton is situated between the Pacific Ocean on its western side and the Cleveland National Forest on its northeastern side. With three intersecting mountain ranges, I had become intimately familiar with every corner of the base, spanning over 200,000 acres of mountains, ridges, ravines, canyons, trails, and back roads.

On a calm night after an exhausting day of forced marches, displays, and demonstrations, we led all 300 boys to a bivouac site situated on a spacious meadow shelf above the Infantry Training School in the San Onofre/52 area. Despite their exhaustion, the boys eagerly set up their shelter-halves. However, they began to grow a bit too boisterous, so I took it upon myself to quiet them down and ensure they settled for the night.

Unbeknownst to me, the rest of the staff had already retired for the night, leaving me as the sole person awake, aside from the half-asleep individual on radio watch. The darkness had enveloped us, with only a faint glimmer of starlight offering some visibility. Finally, I managed to get the boys settled and quiet. I stood there for a few moments, ensuring everything was secure and not a single sound could be heard.

As I turned to face west, my gaze reached the closest edge of the perimeter, where I noticed a tall, dark, bulky figure standing about 15 meters beyond the last tent or 20 meters away from me. We appeared to be engaged in a silent stare, although it was difficult to discern any facial features. Nonetheless, a strong intuition told me that this figure was intently observing me since I was the only one moving in the vicinity. My heart began pounding, and my body felt as if it had anchored to the ground. There was an undeniable presence, something peculiar and potentially hazardous standing there, fixated on me. This entity possessed an imposing height, with broad shoulders that added to its stature.

Using my peripheral vision to confirm what I saw, I observed the figure slightly swaying its upper body from left to right, as though surveying the area in front of it. It stood at an imposing height of approximately 8 feet, but the darkness veiled any detailed features, leaving only a massive silhouette. Its broad shoulders and lack of a noticeable neck added to its powerful appearance.

Deciding to retrieve a flashlight from our vehicle at the top of the knoll and inform the staff about the situation, I proceeded cautiously and quietly, stepping backward to prevent the entity from charging or entering the bivouac area. I kept a watchful eye on the figure, which remained motionless in its original spot. As I made my way about halfway up the knoll, I lost sight of it momentarily, but I continued to move slowly, attempting to locate it. The darkness made it challenging to see anything clearly beyond the perimeter's fringes from the vantage point atop the knoll.

I retraced my steps back to the tents, scanning the area with the flashlight, but there was no sign of anything resembling what I had seen before. Clearly, the figure had shifted its position. Rather than waking everyone up and potentially causing unnecessary panic, I opted to stay awake and wait to see if anything else would transpire. I also hoped that the mysterious entity wouldn't suddenly appear behind me, especially since none of us were armed. The situation would have been far worse, possibly disastrous, had I alerted everyone without any way to verify what I saw. Fortunately, the rest of the night passed without any further incidents.

Just before daybreak, I made a beeline for the spot where I had seen the figure standing. However, there was nothing there—no pole, bush, tree, or reed. Absolutely nothing that could have simulated what I witnessed. We were positioned on flat, open ground, with the exception of the knoll and a tree line situated approximately 50 to 60 meters away, with a mountain looming beyond. I knew these features existed since I had observed them as the backdrop to the figure the previous evening.

The grassy ground had already been trampled and marked by the constant movement of feet and vehicles in that specific training area. I am certain that I saw something abnormal. It wasn't a hoax, nor was it any of the kids—I had accounted for all of them. Trusting my judgment, even at my current age of 62 with near perfect vision, I can confidently say that it wasn't any member of the staff either. I had seen them all sleeping when I ascended the hill. With nearly 11 years of active military service in the infantry and extensive experience in conducting nighttime observation posts, I knew how to utilize my eyes in the dark and distinguish between stationary objects and moving entities. I don't know what it was, but maybe your readers can help with that.

Thank you for your books and for allowing me to share my story.

CHAPTER SIXTY-THREE

I DECIDED to write my encounter down here after coming home from work tonight and seeing something that I had up to this point struggled with, wondering if perhaps it had all been in my imagination the first time I saw it a little over thirty years ago. It's really messing with me because the encounter terrified me and I spent most of my life just trying to convince myself that it was all in my head but seeing the entity again, this time in my home, had made that little fantasy come crashing down around me and I'm scared. Since my encounter, which happened in the early nineties, I have seen more and more people coming forward with encounters with shadow entities and all different types of them being reported as well. I saw what I think most people would call the hat man and I've had nightmares about it ever since. I wonder if those nightmares were actually just that, or if maybe they were something a lot more real that I've been completely blind to this whole time. I live in the house I grew up in. I was lucky and right out of college got a high paying job with a very famous company and by the time I was thirty I was earning a six figure income. I say that only because at the time of the encounter I was sixteen years old and living in my parent's home. When they decided to retire and move to Florida, I couldn't bear the thought of them selling my childhood home to strangers and so I bought it from them. I've since raised my family here. I've always thought there was something very creepy going on with and in the woods that surround the gigantic property but aside from that one encounter and a general but constant sense of overall unease when I'm anywhere near the tree line leading into the woods, I have never actually experienced anything. As far as I know, neither has anyone else like my parents, siblings, husband or kids.

I was born, raised and still reside in upstate New York. I love it here and wouldn't ever leave unless I absolutely had to. I was sixteen years old and I had a small group of friends. We were the so-called nerds and smart kids and didn't get invited to a lot of parties or places with our classmates. It was a Saturday night and my two best friends and I had been invited to a party at one of the popular girl's houses. We couldn't believe our good luck and didn't care at all that her mom was friends with my mom and forced her to invite me and my friends because my mother had embarrassingly called her daughter's snobbish and elitist behavior out and into question. My friends and I got ready at my place and my older sister was going to give us a ride because she was headed that way anyway to hang out with her friends. My curfew for the night was one in the morning and she said she would swing by and pick me and my friends back up at that time, and then the three of us would all spend the night at my house. This was a big deal for us because the best we could otherwise hope for on a Saturday night was if there was something good on HBO. Anyway it took us hours to get ready and eventually we were at the girl's house. We went inside and it was a good time. There were some snide remarks about why she had invited us and she wasn't very welcoming at first but it all went fairly well in the end. I mean, we didn't end up like Carrie from that Stephen King novel so that was a plus. There was a weird vibe in her house though and it had nothing to do with the snobs being so uncomfortable the "egg heads" were invited either. Her house was creepy. Eventually we all went outside for a bonfire and to listen to some music. I kept having mini panic attacks the whole time and for whatever reason I was terrified of the surrounding woods.

I guess I kept staring off into those woods to the point where it became noticeable and eventually the girl throwing the party pulled me aside and asked if I was okay. I told her I was fine and realized I probably looked even more strange than I already did to this girl and she wouldn't be inviting me over again. She looked somewhat disappointed and asked me if I was sure, and if I happened to see anything weird in the woods. It was my turn to look at her strangely and I reiterated that everything was fine. She walked off and that was the end of that. At around midnight, myself and all of the other girls there were gathered around the giant fire, trying to stay warm. It was cool outside, the beginning of fall, and in these parts it starts getting cold early on in the season. They all kept telling the girl who was throwing the party, meaning all of her regular friends, to tell the scary story about the dark man in the woods. She refused and after they kept trying to push her, she looked at me and then got angry and stormed off. At twelve forty five my two friends and I went out front to wait for my sister. As I turned at the door to thank the girl who invited us she just slammed it in my face. All of the other girls were sleeping over and very quickly all of the lights in the house were turned off. It was around one thirty in the morning when I realized my sister probably forgot to come get me again, for whatever reason. It was something she did a lot but she was only three years older than me so looking back now I can kind of understand it.

My friends and I didn't want to wait anymore and knew we could just take a shortcut through the woods. I don't want to waste too much time explaining the geography of the town but basically everything connects when you walk through the woods. We played in the woods near our homes many times and when we were little kids, before popularity mattered, all of us were friends and had played in the woods at this girl's house too. It wasn't ideal but it wasn't a huge deal either and I knew my mom would be mad enough that we walked home through the woods in the middle of the night that I would hear my sister getting into trouble for it eventually. That was just the icing on the cake for me. So, we cut through the backyard and started to walk. The strange part was, while we were away from the backyard, like in the house getting ready to leave and waiting on the front porch for my sister, I wasn't feeling that same creepy feeling but the second we were back within sight of the woods I was scared for seemingly no reason all over again. I kept thinking about the other girls trying to get her to tell a scary story about the so-called dark man in the woods. My friends picked that up too and asked me what I thought they were talking about. I had no idea and I told them so. I also told them the woods over there, near that side of town, creeped me out. We walked for a few minutes, with everything nicely illuminated by the moon and the stars, and at first everything seemed fine and we were talking about the night and how much fun we had. Eventually though, we were all scared and kept thinking someone was following us. We all said it at least once, that we felt like there was someone walking behind us, but every time we would turn around there would be no one there. Finally though, we did see something.

It wasn't behind us but up ahead of us a little bit. It looked at first like two glowing red orbs hovering in front of a tree at about ten feet up off of the ground. We all stopped short at the same time and asked each other if we were seeing that. We all agreed it was there as we were all looking right at it, but none of us could make out what it was yet. As we got closer we could see that it was a set of red eyes. We all stopped in our tracks at the exact same time. We didn't want to keep walking because we would have had to have passed whatever it was. This thing, we didn't know yet what it was at the time, just felt evil somehow. We knew we were in grave danger but couldn't put our fingers on or wrap our minds around how or why. We only had a few minutes to go before we would be safe, or so we thought, in my back-yard. I finally decided to just keep walking, figuring they would follow behind me eventually. I walked closer and saw what looked like the silhouette of a cowboy with glowing red eyes. It looked like it was an all black, cardboard cut out of the Marlboro man or something. It had a big hat and even looked like it was wearing a duster. I stopped again and almost giggled because for a minute I honestly thought that someone had left it in the woods in order to scare someone, just like we were scared now. It was looking right at us and it hadn't blinked or anything. I thought we were safe and it was a cut out but then it turned its head. It turned its head to look to the left, which is exactly the direction we had to go if we wanted to get to my house.

I didn't have to say anything once that happened and we all started screaming at the top of our lungs and we all took off running towards my house. I had never felt fear like that before and hadn't ever since until tonight. I looked back several times, mainly to make sure my friends were still with me and that they were keeping up with me too. Every time I looked back, I would see that the shadow cowboy or whatever it was had been moving right along with us. I saw it once peeking out from behind a tree, another time it looked like it was glaring upwards at me and tipping its hat. It was almost comical like it would keep moving into all of these crazy and somewhat silly positions so I would catch sight of it. Eventually we ran into my backyard and we all stopped to take deep breaths. I looked back one more time and saw it just standing there, glaring at us. It was so evil and I could just feel it all throughout my body and into my soul. Then, it lifted its arm, pointed right at me and winked. I screamed which made my friends scream and we all ran inside of the house. Of course my parents heard us and by then it was almost two o'clock in the morning. They came running downstairs to see three hysterical teenage girls in their kitchen. They were worried and we tried to explain what happened but they were so outraged that my sister had forgotten us, again, that they didn't seem to be paying much attention to what we were actually saying. Eventually they went back to bed and we all calmed down enough to go to sleep ourselves and eventually we all kind of just stopped mentioning it to one another. We certainly didn't tell anyone else what we saw because back then it wasn't cool or trendy to see shadow people or spirits and we were low enough on the popularity totem pole as it was without something like that following us. I never mentioned it to the girl who had the party though I did often wonder if maybe that was the, "man in the woods" she had seen and that her friends kept trying to get her to talk about when we were all standing around the bonfire that night.

I pulled into my driveway tonight and as soon as I got through my front door I realized no one was home and no one had let the dogs out in a while. I opened the back door, the one off of the kitchen, and let them run loose to do their business while I got settled in after a long day of work. I heard them going crazy and when I looked out of the window I saw that they were all barking and snarling at something in the woods. At first I didn't see anything but then, once I went and opened the door for them to come back in, I saw the cowboy shadow man and his glowing red eyes standing at the edge of my property, in the woods. He looked like he was tipping his hat to me but he was too far away for me to be sure. I don't know what I am going to do. Two of my kids live here and so does one of my grandkids. It's terrifying and might just end up being the reason I let go of this old place once and for all. Hopefully it won't show itself again, if it does I'll write about that too.

CHAPTER SIXTY-FOUR

MY BEST FRIEND and I decided to take a road trip across the country in a rented campervan right after we graduated from college. We met in kindergarten and we were friends all throughout school and even went to the same college. We are both the only child in our otherwise large extended families and therefore we were more like sisters than anything else. This was back in the late eighties and times were a lot different and a lot simpler back then, in so many different ways. However, what I've found while researching incessantly on the internet about the terrifying experience we had one of the nights during our trip, what I have come to realize is that the terrifying world of the supernatural has stayed relatively the same. Her name is Kelly and we are still best friends to this very day. I became obsessed with getting more answers to what happened to us, though I'll admit it's only been in the last ten years or so that any real information on all of it has become available, but Kelly never wanted anything else to do with it. We don't discuss what happened and the only person I share my research with is my other best friend, my husband Jim, whom I didn't meet until a few years after the terrifying experience. Let me bring you to the first day of our cross country adventure.

We had been planning this trip since our freshman year of high school and we were both over the moon to finally be able to get on the road. There were no cell phones but we were stopping in every state and using pay phones to call our parents and boyfriends. We stayed in the camper van because it saved us a lot of money but also because we both loved to camp and we wanted to incorporate that into our trip as well. We grew up in New Jersey and wanted to go all the way to California and back. We planned on taking a different route each way so that we could try our very best to see as many states as humanly possible. Neither one of us had ever been further than Florida and we hadn't stayed more than to just drive through when we went there either. We had been on the road for a few days, remember we were pulling off and camping in random spots, and we were driving through Arkansas. We decided to camp for the night. We pulled off the highway and went down a very remote and very long country road. It was surrounded by woods and not really much of anything else was around and so we thought it would lead us to the perfect place to pull into the woods and camp for the night. We had equipment in case we had to actually walk a trail and set up camp in the woods but we hadn't had to do that up to this point. It was a gorgeous night though and Kelly suggested that we bring the camper in but that we spend the night outside under the stars. I agreed and was actually more than a little excited about the idea. I don't want to waste time with logistics and directions so I'm going to skip over how we found the spot we did and get to what happened once we were there. We gathered everything we would need for a night under the stars and we set up our tents.

Luckily we had the lights from the camper because it was pitch black outside. It was a warm night with a very slight breeze. It was the perfect night to spend outdoors in Arkansas, or so it seemed. We were young and we hadn't even considered the dangers of what we were doing and didn't even bother to have a plan and familiarize ourselves with the wildlife in the area. We were absolutely winging it and having a great time in the process. We built a small fire because we weren't sure if the area we were in was legal to camp at but we felt like we were well hidden enough that we would be okay for just one night. We told stupid, somewhat scary stories around the fire and had something to eat. After that we each went into our tent and went to sleep. It was around midnight. My tent was on one side of the fire, closest to the camper van and Kelly's was on the other side, further away. We were surrounded by woods but at first it all seemed very peaceful. The forest didn't go silent or strangely dark or anything like that. In fact, we hadn't a clue as to what was about to happen to us. It was around two in the morning when I thought that I heard someone walking around our camp. I sat up and listened intently and heard the footsteps coming from near Kelly's tent. I figured it was just her using the bathroom or something and so I got out of my tent to do the same and say hello to her.

Once I left my tent though I didn't see anything. I went pee in the camper but when I came out I heard what sounded like someone struggling coming from Kelly's tent. I looked over and saw what looked like arms and legs hitting against the sides of it. It was like someone was in there with her and they were rolling around or something. We didn't have any weapons on us but I ran over there as fast as i could and planned on just leaping on top of and surprising whoever was in there with her. I snuck over to her tent but to my surprise, I must have missed it literally when I blinked. She was sleeping soundly and there was no more movement from her tent. I looked over and my tent looked perfectly normal as well. I was very confused but I was also very groggy and tired and just wanted to go back to sleep. The minute I crawled back inside of my tent and laid back down I heard Kelly scream. I was scared, but still found the courage to run to her. I found her smacking her body outside of her tent. Come to find out she found a large bug on her. She was done with the tent and wanted to now sleep in the van. I was annoyed but said okay, anything to get back to sleep. There was only one bed but it was huge and it was in the back of the van. We laid right down and went back to sleep.

Within seconds of dozing off I heard what sounded like someone opening the door of the camper and walking the ten steps or so to the back where our bed was. It was separated by a curtain so I couldn't see anything beyond that. I was frozen in fear but when I looked over at Kelly she was sound asleep. I listened but didn't hear anything else and I honestly convinced myself I was imagining things due to being so tired. I had done most of the driving and it was really wearing me out. I laid back down. Suddenly I felt Kelly start violently moving around. I rolled over and looked at her and there was some sort of creature, it almost resembled a woman, on top of her chest and strangling her. The beastly woman looked at me and smiled. Her eyes were red and her hair was straggly but the thing was, she wasn't anything more than a shadow and yet somehow she still had features. She had breasts that hung down and her shadowy hands were wrapped around my best friend's throat. Kelly's mouth was open in a silent scream as her eyeballs moved back and forth until finally they landed on me. She was terrified and I didn't know what to do. I kicked at the shadow woman and she let go of Kelly's throat, hissed at me and flew backwards into the corner of the room. She literally flew! She had giant black, shadow wings and she was all curled up. If she were standing she wouldn't have been taller than maybe four feet but she was kind of crouching there in the air, in the corner of the room nearest to Kelly's side of the bed. Kelly and I sat up and she gasped for air. I screamed and the hag woman mockingly screamed too. She sounded just like me, like she took my voice or something. Kelly asked me "what is that thing?" but i just shook my head that I didn't know. The woman once again mimicked us and she had used Kelly's actual voice. I don't know how to explain it except to say that if I wasn't looking at the creature, I honestly would have thought that it had been Kelly who was speaking. Kelly and I hugged each other in fear and terror as we sat there on the bed.

The corner where the hag was just happened to also be next to the only exit from the back room that held the only bed. We didn't know what to do. All at once the woman just vanished right before our eyes. We were still scared but breathed a sigh of relief. We had no idea our nightmare had just begun. Needless to say we didn't want to sleep anymore that night but we were in the middle of the woods and it was the middle of the night. We couldn't just drive off because we had left all of our stuff outside and it would have taken a long time to break it all down and pack it again. We both just laid there, trying to be calm and go back to sleep. We were supposed to take shifts and I offered to stay up first. Kelly accepted and, knowing I would be awake and watching, she managed to fall asleep within just a few minutes. I started to doze off not too long after but jumped awake because I felt like something was wrong. I don't know but the energy in the room had shifted again and I immediately thought the hag was back. As soon as I opened my eyes and looked up I saw a giant shadow man. It was who we would call today "the hat man" and his piercing red eyes were staring down at me. I tried to move and I tried to scream but I was having my first ever experience with sleep paralysis. I couldn't move. He leaned in and seemed like he was just staring at me, with his face about two inches away from mine. Then, he turned and left the room. I heard the door to the camper van open and shut again. I was able to move again after about a minute and I jumped up and ran to the door. I looked outside and saw several sets of glowing eyes, some red and some yellow, all over the inside of the woods and surrounding our campsite. I was terrified and seriously considered just getting out of there. They all seemed to be staring right at me, like they knew I was there and looking at them.

I didn't wake Kelly up and I sat up all night in the driver's seat of the camper van, waiting for the sun to rise. Kelly woke up the next morning bright eyed and bushy tailed. She had absolutely no memory of anything except there being a huge, black, shadowy bug in her tent. A bug we were never able to find or identify by memory. A bug that I don't think ever existed except in shadow. The way she described it didn't escape my notice. She had no idea what I was talking about and actually got pissed off at me because she thought that I was just trying to scare her. We got into an argument about it until finally I just let it go and stopped mentioning it. The rest of our trip, once we made up a few hours later and once we were on the road and far away from that demonic forest, we had a very exciting, fun and paranormally uneventful rest of our trip. A few years later Kelly recovered the memories of what happened that night, and she even eventually remembered that she had seen the hat man there in my face the way he was too. Both Kelly and I have had several encounters with the hat man and more sleep paralysis episodes than either of us could count but she never wants to discuss it and I respect that. I have come to understand that the hat man usually visits when there's a lot of negative emotion or something lower vibrational going on with someone's energy. That wasn't the case for us though, at least not that I'm aware of. I think maybe it had something to do with the camper van we rented. I feel like we were sort of forced to sleep inside of it that night so the old hag woman could have us trapped. As for why I named this encounter the way that I did, it's said that Lilith is a demon and while she is normally associated with the succubi, who exclusively are said to visit men, some think she also has dominion over the elusive and terrifying shadow beings as well. All of them, including the one who most people think leads them, the hat man.

CHAPTER SIXTY-FIVE

I WAS STAYING in a remote cabin in the woods in Alaska over the Christmas holiday one year. I was twenty one years old and it was the mid 1980s. The reason I was there was because I was meeting my parents and siblings in order for us to spend the holiday together. My parents have this really weird tradition where they like to travel to remote places where there's a lot of snow during the Christmas holiday. We have always lived in sunny California in the United States and my father is a very wealthy businessman. It started out with him ordering snow to be blown all over the outside property of our house when we were little. It sort of grew into this traveling adventure every year from about the time I was five years old. I'm the youngest and don't remember the artificial snow days too well but my siblings tell me it was amazing. Anyway, we hadn't ever been to Alaska before but my parents were tired of always going to the same old places and wanted to have a bit of an adventure. I was taking a year off of school due to some personal issues I was having at the time and therefore had the most free time out of everyone in order to stay at this cabin in Alaska. I asked my father if I could stay for a week before everyone got there and then for a week after everyone left if I decided I really liked it. I wasn't a very sociable person and the idea of a cabin in the middle of nowhere in Alaska was right up my alley. I couldn't wait to finish school so that I could move somewhere just as secluded. My dad of course said no problem and so I am starting this encounter on my first day in the cabin.

The cabin wasn't only in the middle of nowhere, it was in the middle of a very dense and very foreboding forest. I'm sure he had to pull some major strings in order to rent the place out for three weeks because it seemed like it was someone's year round home. The place was spectacular, at least as far as cabins in the woods go, and I was in love with it the moment I saw it. As soon as I stepped out of my car though, in order to hike through the snow and into the woods to get to the place, a strong and seemingly random sense of foreboding came over me. It was almost incapacitating. I told myself it was due to the fact that I was REALLY all alone out there and if something should happen to me, no one would know until my parents arrived the following week. I knew I was being silly but it dawned on me that there was no way off the island until the ferry came and it was only me, I was the only human being in the area, for miles and miles in every direction. The thought was terrifying and comforting all at the same time but I decided to make the best of it. I grabbed my backpack and one more rolling suitcase full of my clothes and other necessities and I started the hike through the woods. It would have taken only about fifteen minutes but it was snowing fairly heavily and therefore I didn't arrive at the cabin for a half hour. It was almost fully dark by the time I reached the place. The only thing I can say about the woods was the fact that it sounded like someone was rattling chains and following behind me for the entirety of my walk there. I kept turning around and looking all over the place but I never saw anyone. I figured it was something easily explainable but it dawned on me that the noises would stop when I would start to look for the source.

I let myself into the cabin and locked the door behind me. I walked through it and chose a bedroom. There were three bedrooms upstairs and all of them had their own bathroom. There was a kitchen, foyer and living room area downstairs, as well as a dining room. Someone had stocked the refrigerator and cabinets with all of our favorite things to eat and drink and after I unpacked I had something to eat. It was dark outside and I decided to make a cup of tea and go out on the back deck and look at the stars. They were everywhere and clearly visible in the sky, along with a full moon. I sat there and drank my hot tea and I had already put on my pajamas and my robe. The view all around me was of the wilderness and I couldn't think of anywhere else that I had ever been where I had felt more at home. As I sat there, after a few minutes, in the silence and serenity and as I watched the snow fall, I thought I heard those same sounds of rattling chains coming from the woods as I had heard earlier when I was walking through them. I didn't understand what the sound could be or where it could be coming from. It was disturbing for sure but it wasn't enough for me to have been scared or wanting to go back inside or anything. I went inside and grabbed a book and went back out onto the back deck in order to settle in and read until my eyes were tired enough for me to be ready for a shower and bed.

I had barely cracked my book open when I noticed the jacuzzi. I was excited and once I got it running, the amazingly hot and bubbly water against the chill of the snowy weather was so comfortable and relaxing. The entire time I was preparing the hot tub and the whole time I was outside, I was hearing those same sounds of rattling chains. I had been in the hot tub for about five minutes only when I heard something big moving around in the trees just at the treeline, about thirty feet in front of where I was sitting in the jacuzzi. I stopped reading and strained my eyes to see if there was anything there. I knew there was something there and it sounded like it was something very big. It didn't take long for me to see what was making the noise, kind of. I saw what looked like two yellow eyes peering out at me from the darkness. I gasped and as soon as I did I heard a loud howl and the eyes disappeared completely. The howl seemed to shake the ground beneath me and I saw the snow shaking off the branches of the trees surrounding me too. I looked all around and saw that it had reverberated and had the same effect on all of the trees, all around me and not just the trees in front of me where the howl had come from and where I had seen the eyes. I was scared and thought it was a wolf. I had no experience with wild animals at all but I knew enough to know that a wolf was a predator and that I should most likely get back inside where it was safe.

I went inside and made sure all the doors and windows were locked. I took a shower and went to bed. I was still trying to read my book and so before I turned off all of the lights in my room, I read for a little bit. The whole time I kept hearing chains rattling and it sounded like it was coming from outside of the bedroom window. I was too afraid to get up and look. You have to understand there were no other human beings around for miles and miles and the woods I was surrounded by were snow covered which seemed to lend to the eeriness of the quietude that surrounded me from the time I had gotten to the cabin or even before that when I first entered them. It was beautiful but the sounds of the chains and the previous sighting of what I thought was a wolf, along with that loud and seemingly vicious howl, I was on edge. I turned off the lamp next to my bed and the rest of the house was dark as well. I fell right asleep. At around two in the morning I got up to get something to drink from the kitchen. I immediately heard the front door knob jiggling and turning. I walked over to it and sure enough, someone was trying to get inside. I was panicked because I didn't have a phone in the cabin and cell phones didn't really exist then for the average person. I tried to be quiet and tiptoe over to the peephole to look out and see who was there. I did that and standing there, right on the other side of what suddenly seemed to be a very flimsy door, was a giant wolf. It had glowing yellow eyes and it stood on its two hind legs. Its fur was dark gray and looked very dirty. It was lowly growling and seemed to be getting agitated with not being able to open the door. Suddenly it stopped playing with the door and just stood still for a minute. I couldn't take my eyes off of it and continued to stare into the peephole at it.

It sniffed the air and made a face and then started to walk around the front porch. I ducked down and it looked through the windows. The shades were drawn but the curtains were open and I wasn't sure if I would be able to see my shadow if I were to move. I saw its shadow that's for sure, as it tried to get a glimpse of what or who was inside of the cabin. Finally it moved on and as it did I heard that distinct sound of the chains rattling again. It dawned on me right then and there that this strange monster had been what had been following me all day from the time I got there because it was somehow connected to the noise. I was hunched over and stooped down trying to stay hidden as I walked back through the kitchen. My plan was to go and hide under my covers and hope that it didn't decide to try and break the door down or come through one of the windows. It had been very muscular looking and super tall. It was definitely what I had come to know as a werewolf because regular wolves didn't stand and walk on their hind legs and they also weren't ten feet tall either. It looked like it was in peak physical condition as well. I was terrified because I knew I wouldn't have stood a chance. As I crept through the kitchen a loud bang scared me and I screamed at the top of my lungs. I looked over to the glass door where the noise had come from. That's when I saw the whole beast, in all of its terrifying glory, and it had seen and heard me as well.

I just stood there, staring at it and it did the same. It had some sort of shackles attached to its ankles and wrists and they looked like they had once been not only connected to each other but connected to something else. Someone had chained this thing up and tried to keep it locked away. That's what I presumed anyway, based on the shackles. It growled at me, low and deep and I still could only stand there staring at it. It started smashing its head into the glass door and I thought for sure that any minute then it was going to bust through the glass and devour me. It kept banging its head hard against the glass and it also kept looking up at me, furious that it couldn't get to me. It smashed its fists against the glass as well and oddly enough, it kicked it too. It had all the features of a wolf; the fur and paws, the wolf face, snout and ears too. It was a werewolf, of that I had no doubt. I had read about them in college in one of the elective courses I had been taking the year before. They weren't supposed to be real and yet, there I was face to face with one nonetheless. It had blood on its head and it began to howl and snarl at me; white foaming spit hung from its mouth. It then started to claw at the door. After ten minutes it stopped, but it still remained just outside.

I didn't know what to do and I certainly wasn't going to try and go near the door. It seemed calm at that point and while I did consider banging some pots and pans around to scare it off I didn't because I didn't want to agitate it.

Its face had a sort of human quality about it despite also looking like a wolf but I think that was the eyes. It made me feel bad, once it laid down and stopped snarling and honestly, without the chains and the ordeal it had just put me through when trying to get inside of the house and at me, I would have thought it was a simple wolf with the way it was calmly and very benignly lying there like that. I went back to my bedroom and got into bed because what else could I have done? Needless to say I didn't sleep too well that night and every time I dozed off I had nightmares of the werewolf and it had gotten inside and ripped me to pieces. I don't know when it left but when the sun came up and I went to check, it was gone. I went outside and checked the front porch too but it was gone. There were huge and deep claw marks not only on the front door itself but all over the side of the house as well. There was no other evidence that it had ever been there. I thought long and hard about what to do next and decided to see what happened before panicking and trying to get myself out of there. I liked the peace and quiet and I really didn't want to have to leave yet. I know it's hard for people to understand but I was going through a lot at that time in my life. I was terrified, don't get me wrong, but the light of day had dulled some of that terror and I went on about my day at that point.

I knew it was lurking somewhere in the woods though because every time I was outside that day I felt eyes on me. I had even heard the rattling chains at some points as well. I left out a huge, bloody steak on the back deck that night and when I woke up the following morning it was gone. I saw paw prints in the snow, only two at a time though and not four like you would see if it had been a normal wolf or some other animal. I left food out every single night I was there alone and it never bothered me again. I knew it was around though, always lurking, because of the rattling of the chains. My parents and siblings didn't believe me and thought that I was having a nervous breakdown. That is, until they had their own experience with what I believe was the same creature, in the woods on the third night they were there. I'll write about that one another time. I believe someone knew they were going to turn into the werewolf and either chained themselves up to try and not have to hurt anyone or someone else chained them, whether at their behest or not I am sure I don't know. I moved to Alaska, to that same island, once I graduated college and have lived here ever since. I have more encounters with more allegedly fake creatures and also with paranormal entities than I could count. It doesn't even phase me anymore and the week leading up to a full moon until two days after it's gone, I leave out red meat and other treats for the werewolves just in case. For the first twenty years I lived here those treats would always be gone in the morning and when there was snow on the ground there would be bipedal paw prints leading up to and away from the area. There was also a little something else that seemed to drag behind the prints and I always thought that those were the broken shackles. I still see those bipedal prints from time to time but not with the shackles anymore and sometimes the treats go untouched. Who knows what this is all about? Surely I don't and I also don't know why I was chosen but my research has been extensive since that first night and I must have found a very rare type of werewolf for a number of reasons, but, they aren't relevant to my story and I am still scared of running into one while out hiking or otherwise making my way through the woods. Thanks for letting me share.

CHAPTER SIXTY-SIX

I DECIDED to go on a three day long camping trip by myself in some mountains on the east coast of the United States back in the year 2000, when I was eighteen years old. I had just graduated high school and wanted to just take a break from life for a while. I hadn't invited any of my friends to go with me or anything because I really just needed some alone time; some time to decompress. This was only two weeks after graduating and I had made plans for basically the whole summer, right up until I left for college in California at the end of August. So, this time was reserved for me. I didn't have a cell phone, not everyone did back then, but I did have a digital camera. Before digital cameras, and all through my high school career, we had to use those disposable cameras that needed to be developed and if you were lucky you were able to get the pictures back from them within twenty four hours. The digital camera was a godsend because I absolutely loved capturing memories and had several murals all over the wall of my bedroom at home. It let me be able to see the photos and decide if they were worth the money to get developed before I went and did so. It was quite the exciting invention, let me tell you! I mention all of this because that digital camera was the beginning and cameras in general have been the epicenter of the phenomenon I started experiencing way back then and that I am still living with to this very day.

I left early and had decided that the best place for me to go was to a very remote and secluded spot that I used to go with my dad and older brothers all of the time. The place is nowadays known for paranormal activity and strange things happening but back then the internet was only just becoming a thing and therefore we didn't have access to the information like the teenagers and everyone else have today. We couldn't look up where we were going and see reviews, ratings and encounter stories so we were basically left to our own devices and to figure it all out for ourselves. About ten years before my trip my brother had a very creepy experience in the same spot but I had always just assumed that he was telling the story to try and scare me, the only girl. I've since asked him about it and it turns out he was telling the truth the whole time. I believe him now, definitely, based on what I went through when I was out there. The place was extremely remote and it was also private property. I'm not sure who owned it but my dad had a friend of a friend who was always able to get us permission to be there when we wanted to go. We always went right before school started in early fall but I was heading out there in the beginning of summer. My dad was able to get me permission and a pass for my car. So, when the security people would drive through the parking lot, expecting it to be empty and see my car there, they would just have to look at the pass in the windshield and then they would know I was supposed to be there and leave me alone. We hadn't ever had any issues. We were always the only ones there and I had asked my father if anyone else was going to be there at any point while I was there and he told me no. He was worried about me being out there all alone but I assured him I would be fine. I parked my car and hiked to a spot near a large man-made lake where I wanted to make my camp for the whole time I was there.

That spot was where my family and I always set up camp because the water was nice to swim in and the area was just a little bit removed from the trees. I set up right near one of the fire pits, it was probably one that we had originally built, and settled in. It was really warm out and I stripped off my clothes and jumped into the lake. I swam for a few hours and at first everything seemed fine. However, it was right around the time that I was getting out of the lake to dry off and eat something that things started to take a turn for the scary. I started hearing strange growling noises coming from the woods surrounding the lake. The woods were about twenty feet away from the lake and my camp but the growling was extremely loud and sounded almost like it was right next to me. But, I couldn't see anything. I had one of those digital cameras that also allowed you to record for a few seconds, even though I never knew what to do with the videos. I didn't know you could put them onto your computer until much later on. Anyway, I got out and quickly dried off. I grabbed my camera and started recording the sounds. I played it back and sure enough it sounded like something was growling at me, loudly. Actually, it sounded more like someone was growling because it didn't sound like any animal I knew of that would have been in that area at the time. It sounded like a human being who was trying to sound like an animal, if that makes sense.

It gave me the creeps and I kept looking around to see if I could see anything but after a few minutes the growling stopped and I was able to calm myself enough to move on with my day. After having something to eat I decided to walk around the perimeter of the lake. It was almost fully dark outside by the time I had decided to do this but I was in the middle of nowhere and all alone and there was almost no chance anyone else was out there with me. Also, I knew that security guards roamed the perimeter of the place and that they also walked through certain areas of the wilderness, in order to check for people who weren't supposed to be there, too. I didn't find any of that odd at the time and it was just how things sort of always were. I grabbed my flashlight and started to walk around the giant lake. It was peaceful and the full moon, along with all of the stars in the sky illuminated the lake so beautifully, along with everything around it. I had gotten halfway around the lake when suddenly I heard something large moving around in the bushes behind me. I stopped and listened and I could have sworn I heard a low growling noise again but I was determined to ignore it. I wasn't going to let whatever was happening around me ruin my good time. I knew I would end up working myself up into a frenzy if I gave it another thought. I will say too that I had already taken a whole bunch of pictures, including selfies, by the time I was walking around the lake. The whole time I was walking I kept hearing growling and strange sounds. It was like someone was gurgling and then they would growl. The bushes kept moving in certain places and it got to the point where I felt like I was seriously being stalked by something that was in those woods.

Once I made my way around the lake and back to my camp I made myself a fire and tried to forget about how freaked out I was feeling. I started to review my photos. At first I didn't notice anything out of the ordinary but after I looked through the first few pictures I started to notice that in every single picture from the fifth or sixth photo and on, there were two little bright red lights coming from behind me in the woods. No matter where I was in reference to my camp or the lake, these little orbs would be there. I was immediately terrified and filled with an overwhelming sense of dread as I realized they weren't orbs, they were eyes! I had to take a closer look and when I did I felt fear unlike anything I had ever felt before grip me. I immediately started looking around but I didn't see anything. I was scared but knew if I didn't at least check around my campsite I would never be able to go to sleep there and I was still sort of thinking that it could have been something else, something I could easily just explain away. That's what I was hoping for so that I didn't have to deal with whatever it was and also so that I didn't have to cut my trip short. Despite the feelings of being watched and followed that had been with me since the minute I got out of the lake and started walking around it and despite the strange growling noises I had been hearing the whole while too, I was trying to convince myself that it was all just one big misunderstanding and that I was scaring myself over nothing. I grabbed my flashlight and started walking the perimeter one more time before bed. I shined the light into the woods and at first I didn't see anything. I tried to force myself to look, and at least seem, as confident as possible.

After about five minutes, and the walk around the entire lake took about twenty minutes at a regular paced walk, I started to feel like someone was following me again. I immediately turned around and saw two sets of eyes looking at me through the tall trees in the woods.

I froze but I didn't take my flashlight off of them. They were the same red eyes I had seen in the photos but this time they were each connected to an entity. There were two shadow beings standing there and something deep inside of me just knew with absolute certainty that there were a lot more than that out there. I know that shadow beings aren't known to growl or to make any noises at all, not really, but I believe that perhaps there was something there with them too that was keeping itself hidden. I slowly backed away and with all the strength I could muster I turned my back on them. I was trying to play it off as though I hadn't seen them or like perhaps I had only seen the eyes. I've since learned they think human beings are mentally stupid anyway and I was hopeful they would just leave me alone. Unfortunately, this was only the beginning of the terror in my life. Something surreal and somewhat unbelievable happened. It was, at least, something that I wasn't aware of and that hadn't ever happened to me before, up until that time. I started to jog around the lake but kept stopping and shining my flashlight into the woods every now and again and each time I would do that I would see two shadow figures with glowing red eyes staring out at me from the woods. I finally made it back to my tent and put my fire out. I crawled in and prayed.

I didn't even consider sleeping and all of the strange noises coming from outside in the woods weren't helping sleep find me either. There was mainly growling and at other points I heard loud splashing in the lake. That, admittedly, could have been anything and I didn't have the nerve to look out and try to see what it was. I started to doze off at one point but the sound of something akin to a pig squealing in pain jolted me awake and back to reality. It was like that the whole night and as soon as the sun rose I got myself out of there. I had a nightmare and what we now have come to call sleep paralysis and one held me down in my tent while the other one sucked something that looked like smoke out of my open mouth. My mouth was open because I was fully aware of them and aware that they were doing something evil and possibly trying to kill me. My mouth was open because I was trying in vain to scream. No scream ever escaped my lips that night. There were two of them and they came out of the woods. They eventually switched places and the other started sucking what I believe was something akin to my life force out of me while the other held me down. That's what we now know is one of the things they like to do, right? They've been with me ever since and show up everywhere I go. I still go camping but never alone and have never been back to that particular spot either. I don't know what it all means but I still have the photos and they are in every single picture I took that first day. They even ended up being in the first few, but I just hadn't known what I was looking for and therefore hadn't seen them the first time I looked through them all. From the time I parked my car until the time I figured out what they were and stopped being in a fun mood and taking pictures, they could be seen somewhere in the photos. Even in the broad daylight.

While I didn't see them at all once morning came I knew they were with me as I walked as fast as I could through the trails and out of the woods. I felt their presence once I entered my vehicle and when I walked through the front door of my parent's home. I went to college at the end of the summer and they followed me there too. The sleep paralysis episodes on a regular basis started when I got to college as well. I don't know what they want but they have made my life almost unlivable and completely unbearable sometimes. I've lost many friends because of them and many relationships have ended too, because of the presence of these beings and their constant influence over my life. I have come to know myself spiritually and I do every-thing I can now to keep them at bay but unfortunately there seems to be no fully getting rid of them. I always expected them to torment my kids once they were born but they never did. They were always observing though and I have more photos of myself, my children and other family members, at events plus random photos in general where you can see the two eyes in the background. Sometimes you can even see the two beings. That's all I have, that's what happened to me and that's really all I know about any of it.

CHAPTER SIXTY-SEVEN

THE WORLD IS a strange and curious place, full of mystery and wonder. As a child, I had always been fascinated with the idea of extraterrestrial life. I would look up at the stars and wonder what civilizations could be out there. I think that is what fueled my passion and helped me grow into a writer. I've spent my life exploring the darker corners of the human experience, searching for the hidden truths that lurk just beneath the surface of our everyday lives. And yet, even though I have countless years of exploring, researching, and experiencing, I was unprepared for the experience that I'm about to share with you. A tale of terror and wonder, of the unknown and the unknowable.

My story begins just as all stories begin… it was a dark and stormy night, and I was driving alone on a deserted stretch of highway when I saw something that changed my life forever. I saw a UFO.

It began with a flash of light, a blinding burst of energy that lit up the sky like a thousand suns. I slammed on the brakes, my heart pounding in my chest, and watched as an otherworldly vessel descended from the heavens. It was like nothing I had ever seen before, a silver disc of impossible dimensions that defied all the laws of physics. It was as if time itself had come to a standstill and the very fabric of reality was unraveling before my eyes.

And then it was there - the UFO hovering just a few feet above my car. The sound that it made was like the roar of a thousand lions, a deafening howl that rattled the windows of my car and shook me to my very core. I was paralyzed with fear, unable to move or even breathe. The light that emanated from the UFO was blinding, a pure white radiance that seemed to penetrate into my very soul.

I don't know how long I sat there, staring up at the UFO in helpless awe and terror. It could have been minutes, or hours, or days. Time seemed to lose all meaning in the face of this cosmic visitation. And then, just as suddenly as it had appeared, it vanished into the night. The roar of its propulsion system faded away into the distance, leaving me alone on the highway, shaken and stunned.

I didn't know what to make of this. I wanted someone else to see it, but dang it, this was the first time in the history of humanity that I was alone on the road. There was always so much traffic on this stretch of the flat highway. Wouldn't you know it? The one time I wanted another car around, no, I *needed* another car around, but there was no one. No one for miles and miles. No one else saw what I saw, there was no one to validate my experience. Such is my luck in life.

I could feel my heart beating inside my chest, so wild, so hard. I knew I should pull off the road, regain my composure and try and calm down. It wasn't good for my blood pressure to be driving in such a fervor state. There were flashes of lights before my eyes. I knew my blood pressure was about to reach a dangerous high.

Looking over to my right, I saw an exit. The hour was late and there was no one around for miles. I thought it would be a good idea to pull over to the rest area. It sat on the edge of a lake. A lake, that's what I needed. Something calm and peaceful. Something to help me get a grip on reality again before I traveled on.

The storm clouds that cloaked this part of the road were beginning to break and I could see the stars. The moon, bright and full, began to peek from behind the clouds. The clouds. Just look at the clouds, how quickly they were blowing. There must be a storm coming through, blowing these clouds out of the way. I didn't care. The weather was clearing, the night dark and deep. The air was sharp with the fresh electricity of the ozone and my lungs were taking it all in, recharging my soul. I knew this was someplace I needed to be, at least for the moment, so I could get a grip on my sanity.

Pulling over, I parked near a large picnic table. I thought it was perfect. I could sit there on the table for a little bit, calm down, and try to process what just happened. Should I tell anyone? My friends never would believe me. Do I tell the police? Probably not. Maybe try and track down someone from MUFON? It happened so fast, I don't know if I can get any of the details right.

All these thoughts and more were running through my brain at a rapid pace. I decided to take a deep breath and to focus on the bright star shining over the lake. But then I noticed, the star was getting larger. How could that be? Hey, wait a sec… that star is *moving*! It was coming closer to me. Out of the night sky, it floated down, down to the earth, growing larger with each passing moment.

Before I had a chance to move, it was here again, right before me. I started to wonder, was the UFO following me? The craft was hovering over the lake like a luminescent jellyfish, casting an eerie green light over the water. I slid down from the tabletop and fell to the seat of the table, my heart pounding in my chest once again. I felt exposed. There was no place to hide. At least in my car, I felt protected a bit, but here, out in the open, sitting on the picnic table by the lake, I felt exposed. I had no other choice but to remain there, frozen, praying I looked like a shadow in the night. I sat there and watched in disbelief as the UFO descended closer and closer to the surface of the lake. There was some-thing hypnotic about it, something that drew me in like a moth to a flame. I sat there, transfixed, as the UFO moved closer and closer to me.

The sound that it made was like a thousand trumpets, an other-worldly howl that echoed across the lake and sent ripples through the water. Could this be the same thing as Ezekil's Wheel? Was this the same, the same sound that was described as the "trumpeting of angels" in the Bible? I could feel the vibrations in my bones, could feel the energy coursing through my veins. And then, all at once, it was gone. Vanished into the night like a ghost. Why? Was it taking on water? Did the UFO need water to travel? Or was it observing, studying what was below the surface? Or maybe it decided to pull off on the side of the road like I was? I had to wonder, is there a version of Google Maps for Space Travelers?

I drove home in a daze, my mind consumed with the image of the UFO hovering over the lake. I couldn't shake the feeling that something had been watching me, something that I couldn't see or understand. I spent the night tossing and turning, my dreams consumed by images of the UFO. I couldn't help but wonder what it was, where it had come from, and what it wanted.

For weeks afterward, I was plagued by doubts and fears. I became obsessed with this extraterrestrial encounter, obsessed with my UFO experience. I was like a madman, possessed, pouring over books and articles, trying to make sense of what I had seen. I couldn't shake the feeling that there was something out there, something that was watching me, waiting for me. I started to see signs and symbols everywhere I looked, signs that I couldn't explain. With a sudden epiphany, I realized something - I was an actual UFO Experiencer.

After that thought, I knew I had to try and find out more, more about the out-of-this-world visitors. I went for a drive, trying to clear my mind and think about what my next move should be. Is there a way I could ever experience this again?

I drove for what seemed like hours, trying to think, trying to relax my mind. When I finally started to reawaken and reimagine myself into this reality I noticed something. This area of the road began to look very familiar. Without realizing where I was driving to, I somehow managed to find myself staring at the highway sign for Exit 169, the exit that led me back to the lake where I saw the UFO.

I took the exit and saw the lake. Next to the lake was my picnic bench. Could lightning strike twice? I doubt it, but maybe there was a reason I was driving here subconsciously. Maybe there was a piece of the puzzle that I was overlooking. Maybe if I just return to the bench, a light of inspiration will be delivered onto me, like extraterrestrial divine guidance.

I sat there for an undetermined amount of time. The wind was light and cool, gentle to my face. It was easy to breathe and I began to relax. I leaned backward, resting my elbows on the table, and sat facing the lake. I closed my eyes and thought about the encounter. Thought about the green jellyfish UFO. I felt a stronger breeze on my face, the wind was beginning to shift. I opened my eyes and there, in the distance, I saw it again. The UFO was hovering over the same lake, casting the same eerie green light over the water. I stopped thinking and watched as it descended closer and closer to the surface until it was just feet away from me. And then, all at once, it was gone.

Again.

I searched the skies and tried to figure it out. What does it mean? But like a dusty memory, something from my distant past, I remembered something. I remember when I had seen this before. It wasn't something I had seen in the movies. I had actually seen this UFO before! With that realization, I started to search, began to really study, and honestly investigated, but nothing could have prepared me for the experience I was about to have, the night when a UFO from my childhood came to visit me.

I knew then that I was being called, that the UFO was trying to tell me something. I started to make connections between the signs and symbols that I had been seeing and the UFO. I started to believe that it was trying to show me something, to guide me on a path that I couldn't yet see.

Just as my mind began to piece it all together, something happened. I began to be plagued by nightmares and hallucinations. I couldn't get the image of the UFO out of my mind or shake the feeling that something had fundamentally shifted in my understanding of the world. I became obsessed with UFO sightings, spending countless hours poring over government documents and conspiracy theories, trying to make sense of what I had seen.

But the more I looked, the more I realized that there was no sense to be made. The UFO defied all explanation, all rationality. It was a reminder that the universe is vast and unnerving at times, full of things that we can't even begin to understand. It was a reminder that there are forces at work in the world that are beyond our control, beyond our comprehension. I decided that no one would believe me, short of a MUFON Field Investigator. I closed that chapter of my life and had no plans of ever reopening it. But you know what they say about the "best-made plans"...

It took me years of research and exploration to understand what the visitor from another world was trying to tell me. It was a warning, a message from a higher power that something terrible was coming. An event that would change the world as we knew it, something that we couldn't possibly comprehend.

I came to accept that my encounter with the UFO was something that I would never fully understand. It was a glimpse into a world that lies just beyond the borders of our own, a world that is simultaneously beautiful and terrifying. And yet, even now, years after that fateful night, I can't help but wonder. What else is out there, lurking just beyond the edges of our reality, waiting to be discovered? What else will we see, when we look up into the night sky?

And now, as I sit here writing this story, I can feel the weight of that message bearing down on me. The world is changing, and we are powerless to stop it. We can only watch as the UFO hovers over the lake, casting its eerie green light over the water, and wait for whatever comes next.

CHAPTER SIXTY-EIGHT

I DON'T KNOW if there's a single person in my life who I've told about my encounter who fully, truly believes me and most of them flat out call me a liar and think I'm trying to pull their legs or something. Yes, I pride myself on being able to make people laugh but something like what I saw isn't something anyone should be joking about because not only was it terrifying, the implications of what it means for the world are scarier than anything I've yet to see on television. Nothing cooked up by Hollywood or allegedly based on true events comes close to the terror most people who know about such things will feel when they understand the implications of what I'm about to tell you here, provided that is, that they believe me. Now, that isn't to say it isn't scary as all hell in and of itself and that's why I decided to finally talk about it publicly, kind of. I am keeping my real name out of it and changing a few minor details but the events are one hundred percent real and they happened to me way back in 1995. I decided I wanted to move across the country and I really didn't want to tell anyone where I was going for a while. I had always been the odd man out in my family and while I would tell people I was leaving, I wanted them to be discouraged from reaching out to me for a while. I sold most of my possessions and bought an old camper. I traveled from state to state starting in my home state of Washington and traveled all the way across and around the country, stopping in every single state and staying in each state for as long as I possibly could. I planned on staying in every state at least a week before deciding which one I liked best and possibly wanted to settle down in. My camper wasn't state of the art or anything but it had all of the basic amenities and sometimes I would stay in a motel if I had had enough of feeling so confined. The state of Mississippi is the state I spent the least amount of time in and I haven't been back ever since. It turned out that it didn't matter because the phenomenon just followed me and I've been dealing with it on and off ever since I visited there almost thirty years ago. Because it was the first place it happened though I just associate that place with horrible things and I don't ever intend on going back there again.

It was the summer time here in the United States and I arrived in Mississippi a couple of hours before the sun fully set for the night. I had been put on to a place where I could park my camper for the week, for a small fee, and I had scribbled the directions down on a diner napkin. I found the place easily enough but it was in the absolute middle of nowhere and I don't know that I had ever been in more dense woods in all of my life up until that point. I was more of a beach and serf type of guy but I knew the camper would make my life a lot easier on the road, and save me a ton of money. It was inevitable that I would end up in the woods with it at one point or another due to the fact I was relying on word of mouth from total strangers at randomly chosen truck stops in order to find places to put it for a week or two at a time. This person owned a small cabin in the woods and I guessed they could use the money. At least, it sure looked like they could. I opened the screen door to knock but when I did I saw a small piece of paper fall out from between the screen and the door and it was addressed to me and told me where I should park and that they would be back soon. That was it. I knew the name signed on the bottom because that was the guy I had met at the truck stop a day earlier. He was a trucker and I guessed he hadn't made it back home yet. It was a simpler time but that has nothing to do with the encounter. I wasn't one of those people who believed in ghosts and spirits, things we call the paranormal nowadays but I did always wonder if extraterrestrials actually existed. Something about the thought of that always made me very scared, like if they existed then what else was out there that our government was probably keeping from us? I shuddered at the thought.

I parked the camper by the cones where he had instructed me to but I was a little bit put off by how far off into the woods they were. I mean, I understood it if he didn't trust me to be too close to his home while he slept, with me being a stranger and all, but I was way out there and he probably wouldn't have even known I was there once he got home unless he checked. He certainly wouldn't see me from where he would have pulled in and parked. I set myself up for the night and made myself something to eat. It was a beautiful night that night and something about those southern states I will say is that their skies are absolutely beautiful when the sun goes down. I went and set up a chair outside of my van and put my little radio on low volume to listen to some tunes. It was gorgeous and I hadn't been more glad since I had left Washington to have done so than I was at that moment. I was just singing along in my head and looking up at the stars, which were very clear that night and all over the place, when suddenly my radio started going in and out like I was picking up some sort of static station or something. I slapped at it a few times and that seemed to correct the issue but only for a minute or two. Suddenly there was a very high pitched frequency blaring through the tiny speakers and it seemed like the volume had been turned up extremely loud. It seemed louder than it was actually supposed to be able to go. I covered my ears and turned the knob to turn it off as quickly as I could. I suddenly had a pounding headache and I was agitated because I felt like that high pitched squealing was what had done it to me and had ruined my otherwise peaceful and beautiful night. I sat back for a minute, still looking at the stars, when all of a sudden a brilliant blast of blue light came shooting down into the woods from somewhere in the sky. I heard a very loud crashing sound somewhere off in the distance but from where I saw the light go out it seemed to have landed about a hundred yards away from my camper. I'm not good with math or distances but I had 20/20 vision and I couldn't help but follow the extremely bright blue light down into the trees. It landed and immediately blinked out. I stood up and was about to investigate when suddenly the radio started blaring out that frequency, high pitched squealing again. It was turned off and so I turned around and kicked it. It fell to the ground and, a bit freaked out, I grabbed it and my chair and went back inside to go to sleep for the night.

My camper had one of those little black and white televisions that sucked battery from somewhere or another in the van's power system. It came in fuzzy but most of the time, but with the little antenna I had that I could put on the roof, I could get at least one decent station. I went ahead and set that up and lounged back on the pull out sofa and laid down to watch some television. My head was still hurting pretty badly but I wasn't quite ready for bed yet. After a while I started to doze off and as I did I would keep jumping up for what seemed like no reason. Finally I decided to go to bed. I opened my eyes and everything had gone dark in the van except for the television. I had left one light on in the front by the driver and passenger seats. Something immediately felt wrong and I was scared from the minute I saw those lights had gone off. That wasn't a typical reaction for me. The television screen filled with static and I became concerned. I didn't stick around to figure out what was going to happen next. I jumped up and turned it off and then went to make sure the doors were locked. I laid down on the couch and after some time I fell asleep. I don't know what it was but something deep down inside of me somehow knew to be scared. I didn't recognize it as fear and thought it was merely agitation at the headache I had. It was slowly dulling and going away though. I woke up and tried to see what time it was on the watch that I was wearing. Since everything but the television had gone out earlier, the big red numbers on my alarm clock were blinking at twelve. It was two in the morning.

Something told me to look outside but when I did there didn't seem to be anything amiss at first. I just had a creepy feeling overall and couldn't relax. Something was nagging at me so I got up off the couch and looked out the front windshield. There wasn't anything there either. I told myself to stop being a moron and to go back to sleep. I hadn't meant to leave the curtains open where I had looked out of the window while still lying on the couch but I guess I had because after I came out of the bathroom I screamed like a little girl. There was something staring in through the window. It immediately looked over at me and stuck out its tongue. The tongue was forked and the being attached to it was the ugliest damn thing I have ever seen in my entire life. It actually looked like a badly made costume of a giant lizard man or something that you would have expected to see in one of those just as poorly made horror movies about outer space and its creatures from the nineteen fifties. I stumbled backwards. The creature had its hands up against the window. Four long and wide fingers that looked like the hands and feet of your average pet iguana. It was bald headed and the shape of the head wasn't quite round but almost. It had what looked like bumps instead of hair, its eyes were gigantic and bright yellow and looked like the eyes of a regular lizard. Its mouth looked purple and while I couldn't see too clearly what color it was because it was so dark, it looked like it was a mixed shade of dark green and dark blue. It just stared at me. It showed me its teeth as well, which were yellow and razor sharp. There also looked like there were too many of them in its mouth or something but I don't really know how to explain why I thought that. I closed the curtains and just stood there, looking at the window. I couldn't see it anymore. Suddenly, the television went on by itself.

of transport itself in front of the screen and then move off to the side until it was directly behind where the driver and passenger seats were in the front of the van. I sat down on the sofa so I didn't fall down. I felt very dizzy and extremely confused. Just as though they were coming out of the tv screen, two beings crawled out of the static that had just come from it. They crawled out just like someone or something would crawl out of a box and once they were fully in the van, the circle expanded and was tall enough that they could have just turned and walked back through it. I was face to face with two of the exact same creatures as the one I had just seen looking through the window. One of them was very obviously a female and had breasts as well as other human-looking parts. I was terrified and thought I would have a heart attack right there on the spot. The entities didn't say anything to me, not verbally or telepathically, they just stood there for a minute, looking around. Then they came towards me and one of them, the male entity, quickly grabbed my ankle. I screamed and started kicking but it was trying to drag me back through that portal and it had tremendous and inhuman strength. I screamed and clawed at the floor until finally I grabbed the bottom of the sofa. The creature pulled and pulled while the other one did something in the front of the van near the driver's seat. I don't know what it was doing and I still have no clue to this day. They were going to pull me into that portal with them and I knew that meant certain death or worse for me. My life was flashing before my eyes and I knew that no one would ever know what really happened to me.

There was a very loud banging at the door and the creatures, the female was crawling back into the portal and the male was still trying to pull me through with them, stopped what they were doing. I jumped up and ran to the back of the van. I heard a man's voice booming through the camper, coming from outside. The voice was calling my name. It was the guy who lived in the cabin. I cowered in fear but he didn't let up. I finally answered the door and I must have looked really scared but he was drunk and therefore didn't realize what the emotion was. He laughed and asked if I was okay. I told him I was and that I had a nightmare. He asked me if I had seen any strange lights in the woods earlier in the night and I told him no. He didn't seem to believe me but he asked for his money next and I invited him in while I went and looked for it. He apologized for showing up so late but told me he had to be back out on the road early in the morning. He told me to stay for as long as I wanted and not to worry about paying him more money right away. I think he was lonely and looking for someone to hang out with. I told him I would see him around and I would think about staying, knowing fully well that neither of those two things were true, and he smiled and walked out of the van. I looked out the window and saw him look back at the side of the van one more time before he called out to me again.

I opened the window and asked what was wrong and he asked me what the hell was on the side of my van. I looked down and right below where my head was, on the side of my van and exactly where the creature outside had been standing a few moments earlier, was some sort of radioactive looking, glowing green goop like substance. It was perfectly shaped like the webbed hands of a giant lizard. Luckily he was too drunk to have seen that. I told him I had no idea and tried to laugh it off like it was nothing. I said goodnight to him again and waited for the sun to rise. I left the second it was light enough for me to see where I was going and didn't stop until I was two states away. That didn't stop the visitations though and in fact, those lizard men were just getting started with me.

CHAPTER SIXTY-NINE

MY ENCOUNTER HAPPENED BACK in 1995 when I was a college student. I went to school in Pennsylvania, and I was working towards getting my Master of Fine Arts degree in filmmaking. I had always been fascinated by video cameras and I even had a penchant for regular photography. Back then we had those gigantic video recorders we would have to put on our shoulders, and we had to bring our film in, out of our cameras, to get developed. There weren't even digital cameras at that time. Anyway, I bring all of this up because my major was the reason why I ended up in the woods for an entire week. I was assigned to directing a short film as a big part of my final and I won't bore you with the details because they're basically irrelevant, but I had several tasks I needed to get done to make it all work. I had plenty of friends who were more than willing to help but the bulk of the work, the behind-the-scenes stuff, had to be done by me. My favorite genre of movie is horror movies, and I was determined to blow my professors away with how scary my film was. I gathered up a ton of supplies and was able to get a great deal on several campervans because I was a student and it just so happened that someone in my family knew someone else who was able and willing to help me. I packed up all my gear, along with my equipment and four campervans, and headed off into the densest and creepiest woods I could find in the area. I had other people who were driving the vans and leaving as well.

There's a spot that's locally known to be haunted by demonic entities and I thought that would be the perfect place for the setting of the film. It was in the middle of nowhere and there wasn't any civilization around for miles and miles. I didn't know who owned the land, but I assumed it wasn't private property because there weren't any signs posted telling trespassers to keep out of anything like that. Plus, I had gone there when looking for locations and found other people camping in campervans there as well. I talked to them a little bit about what I was planning to do, and they thought that it was cool and, they told me about some scary experiences they had while they were there. I thought it would be cool to incorporate those stories into the movie a little bit. I was excited. From the moment we entered the forest there was nothing but trouble though. It immediately started to downpour which, while it isn't unusual for it to rain heavily in Pennsylvania, was a bit weird because the weather hadn't called for any rain at all for several days. That's specifically why I chose that time to be there. The crew wasn't hanging out with me until a few days later, they just came with me to help me bring all the equipment there. They wished me luck and told me they would see me in two days' time. I was upset about the rain but figured I would use that time to try and capture b-roll and to plan how to bring the whole drawing board of the script to life. I was extremely optimistic. I got my camper set up and went for a walk in the rain, just to get a feel for the area. It was creepy and with the sky being so gray and overcast and the rain pouring down it was even scarier. I was happy that there weren't any other people around but a small part of me was nervous about that because I was alone with nothing but miles and miles of woods surrounding me in every direction.

I walked around for about an hour until it felt like my rain slicker couldn't handle any more water and started to head back to the campsite. I felt an odd sensation come over me like I wasn't alone anymore, and I was feeling a terror growing inside of me unlike anything I'd ever known before. It wasn't long after I started heading back that I heard the first of the growling. It sounded like it was right in my ear and if it weren't clearly growling that I was hearing, then I would have swatted at the side of my face, thinking perhaps it was some sort of bug or something that was making the noises. I was scared, I'm not going to lie, but I tried to pretend I wasn't hearing it and get back to the camp as fast as I could. It was starting to get dark and though I had a flashlight, I obviously didn't want to be stuck out there in the middle of the woods without the relative safety of the van around me. I was a fan of horror movies and books, and I was out there with the specific intention of filming a scary short film in an allegedly haunted wood but up until that very moment it hadn't occurred to me that there could possibly have been anything of substance to the long-standing rumors of what went on inside of them. Before I knew it the rain had started trickling down to a drizzle, but it was fully dark, and I wasn't sure of the direction I was headed in. I needed to stop and get my bearings.

I was more than afraid at that point, but I knew I had to keep a cool head. No matter what happened there was no calling off the shoot that would be starting in those woods in a matter of days. I needed it for my final, had already gotten at least a dozen people to help out with it and there was no turning back. I prayed with all my might that I didn't run into anything scary or demonic, not only at that moment in time but throughout the whole shoot. I would not get my prayers answered on that one. It was about a minute or two after I stopped that I heard more growling, only this time it was much louder, coming from behind me somewhere. I immediately turned around to look but saw nothing. I needed to know what it was, and I was also trying to convince myself that it was something with a reasonable explanation. I set out to prove that and maybe I shouldn't have. I am alive and well, writing this down today so it didn't end too badly for me but at that moment I was beyond terrified. I shined the flashlight all over the place and started walking around the area I was in. I somehow knew it wasn't just an average wild animal and I know that now because I had no fear of something like a bear jumping out at me. Under normal circumstances that would have been my initial thought immediately when I heard the growling and I would have gotten the heck out of there fast, not stayed to investigate as I was doing right then. After a few minutes of searching for the source of the noise I didn't hear it anymore and didn't see anything that it could have been coming from so I turned once again to head back to the camp. I heard something breathing. It sounded big and scary, and it took everything I had not to run away and never look back.

I turned around and was face to face with bright red eyes. They looked like they were peeking out from behind a tree, and they were about nine feet up off the ground. I honestly thought for a second that maybe it was some sort of bird or something, just hovering there, watching me. I knew that wasn't the case though because before I could even form another cohesive thought on the matter, whatever it was stepped out from behind the tree and revealed itself to me in all its glory and terror. It was nine feet tall, and the glowing red eyes belonged to it. It seemed to have no problem at all with me shining a light on it to get a better look and it just stood there, staring at me. It was covered in gray and white hair; mostly gray but with patches of white all over the body. The arms and legs were extremely skinny but also very muscular and the feet and hands looked like something between an animal and a human. I instantly thought "who's afraid of the big, bad wolf" and instantly regretted it. I was looking at a were-wolf. Something deep down inside of me told me as well that it wasn't alone. I got strange flashes of insight and started gaining knowledge of things I had no business knowing. I knew it had more with it but I also knew it was a man placed under a curse and that something demonic in the woods controlled him. It was ancient and it was pissed off that I had intruded on its territory and land. The wolfman huffed at me and it sounded almost like a sneeze or something. It took a step forward.

I put my hands out in a gesture I was hoping would mean that I meant it no harm, but it didn't seem to care. It was approaching me cautiously, or so it seemed, and it hadn't just leapt on top of me to devour me. That was a plus, I guess. I turned and ran, and I thought for sure it would take off after me, knock me to the ground and kill me. But that didn't happen, and I ran all the way back to the camp without looking back. I immediately got into the driver's seat and was about to drive away when it dawned on me that I could use what had just happened to me in my scary short for my final. I locked the doors and closed the little curtains on the one window I had in the camper. I sat and rewrote the whole script, and it was much better than anything I could have made up, though I did make up most of it. It's like the encounter had somehow inspired me. I was just about done when I heard what sounded like nails scraping across the entire right side of my van. It went from the back where the bed was, around one side, to the front where the windshield was and over to the other side. It did those numerous times. I saw the door handle jiggling and I swear my heart skipped a beat. I decided to call it a night. I put out all the lights and went to lay in my bed in the back, with the privacy curtains drawn so I felt like I was in a safe little space, and I turned on my flashlight. I kept it under the covers with me and stayed awake listening for more noises. The van rocked a little bit, and it was being rocked from both sides which told me two things right away. The first was that there was more than one of those things or at least more than one thing out there and two was that whatever was out there wasn't trying to tip over the van but just trying to scare me. Maybe it was trying to scare me out of the campervan and right into their path but if anything, it just made me more terrified and less likely to leave before the sun came up. After about two hours the noises and the rocking stopped and I fell asleep eventually, at some point. I woke up several times that night to what sounded like very loud howling.

I didn't tell anyone what had happened to me out there, but I did call some of my crew the very next day to come and stay with me out there for the final night or two that I would be scouting locations. Everyone wondered why and was a little annoyed that I had changed almost the entire script, seemingly on a whim, but I stood firm and kept the reasons why to myself. Eventually we got everything we needed and about a week later we all cleared out of the forest. I captured one scene where there were glowing eyes peering out from behind a tree in the background and it wasn't anyone in my crew. It was one of the wolfmen or maybe it was their demonic leader, I really don't know. I know I experienced something supernatural while I was out in those woods, but I honestly don't know why. I've been a believer ever since though and it threw me even deeper into my obsession with horror and making movies. Nowadays my ambitions aren't as lofty and I've settled for being an author, writing about the supernatural and the paranormal, in a nonfiction format. I've been thinking about telling my family what happened to me out there and what inspired me to write my first book, which is basically the story of what happened to me but with me swearing it was something that happened to an old friend. I've learned so much from and since that experience, but I haven't personally encountered anything else ever since.

CHAPTER SEVENTY

I'M A BEAUTY INFLUENCER, and my followers mean everything to me. For privacy reasons, I won't tell you my name but you can call me Barbie. Ever since I was a little kid, I've always wanted to look like a Barbie doll. I was fascinated by their perfect features, their long blonde hair, and their flawless bodies. As I grew older, that desire only intensified. And when I became a beauty influencer, I saw it as my chance to finally achieve that dream.

I started getting plastic surgery - first a nose job, then breast implants, then lip fillers. I spent hours in front of the mirror perfecting my makeup and hair, trying to recreate that iconic Barbie look. And my followers loved it. They praised me for my beauty and my dedication to the craft.

But deep down, I knew that something was wrong. I was never satisfied with how I looked. There was always something else that needed to be fixed, something else that needed to be perfect. And the more surgeries I got, the more I felt like I was losing myself.

One day, during a live stream, a viewer asked me why I was doing all of this. Why did I want to look like a Barbie doll? And at that moment, everything clicked. I realized that I had been chasing an impossible standard of beauty - one that wasn't even real. I decided that it was time for a change.

I started to embrace my natural features - my brown hair, my imperfect nose, and my small chest. And to my surprise, my followers loved it even more. They appreciated my authenticity and my willingness to be vulnerable. But others weren't so nice. It began a long trail of bullying which led to a drop in numbers that I wasn't happy with. I decided to take things a step further and make it a life makeover.

But there was still one thing missing - a healthy lifestyle. All of the surgeries and makeup in the world couldn't make up for bad eating habits and lack of exercise. So, I decided to make some changes. I started eating paleo - cutting out processed foods and focusing on whole foods like meat, vegetables, and fruits. And I started doing yoga - not just for the physical benefits, but for mental clarity and peace of mind.

It wasn't easy at first. I had to retrain my taste buds and my body to crave healthy foods instead of junk or worse, no food at all. And yoga was a challenge - I was used to pushing myself to the limit, not finding stillness and calm.

But over time, I started to see the benefits. My skin cleared up, my energy levels increased, and I felt more centered and grounded than ever before. And my followers noticed too - they appreciated my dedication to a healthy lifestyle and my willingness to share my journey with them.

I documented every step of my journey. My viewership started to continue upward and I'm feeling overall better about life in general. Nowadays, I still love makeup and fashion - but it's not about trying to look like someone else. It's about expressing myself and having fun. And while I'll always have a soft spot for Barbie dolls, I know that true beauty comes from within - not from a plastic surgeon's office.

When my views started to plateau, I knew I had to do something drastic. That's why I rented an Air BnB in the middle of nowhere. I thought that the isolation would give me a chance to connect with my followers and create some buzz. But I want to tell you how I ended up in this situation, to begin with. So, a little backstory first.

As an influencer, I'm used to getting attention. I have thousands of followers who like and comment on my posts, and I'm always getting messages from people who want to collaborate or work with me. But there's one person who's been giving me attention that I don't want - a stalker. It started innocently enough. I noticed that someone had been liking all of my posts and leaving comments on them. At first, I thought it was just a fan who was really into my content. But then the messages started coming - dozens of them, every day. At first, they were just compliments and requests for more content. But then they started to get more personal - asking about my family, my friends, my daily routine. And then they started getting super creepy - talking about how they wanted to meet me in person and how they couldn't wait to see me.

I tried to ignore it at first, thinking that it would just go away on its own. But it only got worse. The stalker started showing up at events that I was attending, always staying just out of sight but close enough for me to know that they were there. I started to feel like I was being watched all the time. Every time I left my house or went out in public, I felt like someone was following me. I couldn't sleep at night, always checking the locks on my doors and windows and jumping at every little noise.

I knew that I needed help, but I didn't know who to turn to. I didn't want to tell my followers or my friends - I didn't want them to worry or think that I was being dramatic. I contacted the police and told them everything. They took it seriously and started investigating, but it was a slow process. Meanwhile, the stalker was still out there, still watching me, still waiting for their chance to get closer.

It's a scary situation to be in, but I'm trying to stay strong and not let it control my life. So, I figured it was time to get out of dodge and get back to the one thing I absolutely loved, making content and getting views.

I figured a week in the woods was something that I needed to do something solo and destination-orientated. That always upped my views before and this time I decided to tackle the Appalachian Trail. It was very deluxe, red and purple hues flooded every soft surface with alternating cotton and velvet. It was a total dream and the perfect style for fall.

I arrived early and set up the best room with my rigs. I chose the one closest to the forest so I could get the best light and the best view. I thought I had everything planned and nothing could possibly go wrong. I was super wrong.

On the second day during the sixth live, I had the most disturbing thing happen. During one of my live streams, viewers started telling me that they saw a terrifying figure in the window behind me. Others had said that they had seen antlers. At first, I thought it was just a prank. But then I saw it too - a dark, shadowy figure lurking in the background.

I ended the live stream, convinced that it was a crazed fan who had somehow tracked me down. I was terrified and didn't know what to do. I looked out my window and saw something moving through the woods. I couldn't get a good enough look at it. Maybe it was a deer but the next night I was proven very wrong.

The next day, I was sitting in my cabin, enjoying the peace and quiet of the forest around me. It was a chilly night, and I had a fire going in the fireplace to keep warm. As I sipped my hot tea and read my book, I heard a strange noise outside. At first, I thought it was just the wind rustling through the trees. But then I heard it again - a low growl that sent shivers down my spine. I got up from my chair and walked over to the window, peering out into the darkness.

That's when I saw it - a figure standing just beyond the tree line. It was tall and thin, with antlers on its head and glowing eyes that seemed to pierce through me. It couldn't be! This must have been what my viewers had seen.

I froze in terror, unable to move or even breathe. The wendigo stared back at me; its mouth twisted into a grotesque grin. I could feel its hunger and its thirst for human flesh radiating off of it like a palpable force. For what felt like an eternity, we stood there staring at each other. And then, as suddenly as it had appeared, the wendigo vanished back into the forest.

I collapsed onto the floor, shaking with fear and disbelief. Had I really just seen a Wendigo? Or was it just my imagination playing tricks on me? I'm losing it. I have to be losing it. I questioned my diet, my yoga, Korean made cosmetics-anything- for what I had just seen.

But deep down, I knew the truth. The wendigo was real - and it was out there, waiting for its next victim. And from that moment on, I knew that I could never let my guard down in these woods again.

At first, I was even more scared. But then I noticed that it wasn't attacking me. Instead, it seemed to be protecting me from something else. It would leave dead animals on my porch as gifts, and I started to realize that it was trying to help me. Weren't they supposed to be cruel and vicious demons? I guess it was better to have things like this on your side rather than against you.

On the fourth day, I was running low on food and decided to drive back to town. I heard the townies talking about strange sightings in the woods. They warned me not to overstay my visit and I agreed, telling them that my time would be up in a few days. They seemed leery of my time but decided to say nothing else. That's when the storekeeper, Sally, told me about her most recent encounter that happened about a month ago.

"I've always loved hiking in the woods near my home. There's something about being surrounded by nature that makes me feel alive and free. But one day, my peaceful hike turned into a nightmare when I spotted a wendigo." Sally looks genuinely shaken. "At first, I didn't know what I was seeing. It was just a dark shape moving through the trees, too far away to make out any details. But as it got closer, I realized that it was something that shouldn't exist - a creature with antlers and glowing eyes, with skin stretched tight over its bones." My mind flooded with the image through the woods. I asked her to continue.

"I froze in terror as the wendigo passed by me, not even noticing my presence. It moved with unnatural grace like it was gliding over the ground instead of walking. Its eyes were fixed on something in the distance, and it didn't even glance my way." She paused to take a sip of her Coke. "As soon as it was out of sight, I turned and ran back the way I came. My heart was pounding in my chest, and I could barely catch my breath. I knew that I had just seen something that most people would never believe. I started researching Wendigos online, trying to find some explanation for what I had seen. The more I read, the more terrified I became. Wendigos were said to be unstoppable hunters, with an insatiable hunger for human flesh. They were said to be able to mimic human voices, luring their prey into traps. I knew that I had been lucky to escape the wendigo's notice that day. But I also knew that I could never let my guard down again. The woods were no longer a place of peace and freedom for me - they were a place of danger, where something ancient and hungry lurked in the shadows."

Her words chilled me to the bone, but I wasn't altogether certain that this creature was a danger. After all, it hadn't done anything to harm me. What was it guilty of? Looking scary and acting scary? It didn't seem fair to judge something based on looks alone.

I mean that's how I got in this situation to begin with. Putting my looks first and becoming someone, I wasn't, to begin with. Maybe it was the same case with the creature. Maybe it was truly kind, but no one ever gave it the chance to prove itself.

Eventually, I found out that the person who the police had investigated had made bond and left town. I was so scared. He had been watching my live streams and had tracked me down to the Air BnB. But the wendigo had been keeping them at bay, preventing them from getting too close with the gift of dead animals.

When I found this out, I started packing everything up early, but it took a long time to tear down as I had multiple sets and didn't want to be charged an excess cleaning fee. By the time I had finished, it had almost been dusk. I bought the last box for the car when I saw that my tires were flat. I ran up the stairs to safety when I saw my stalker sculking out of the shadows with a knife. I screamed at the sight and quickly opened the door and slammed it. Much to my terror, my phone was in my car and I was trapped. I tapped an emergency code into the security pad, but I knew it would take the police too long to get here and it might be too late. The stalker's face was pressed against the window telling me to let him in. I started crying and screaming for him to get away.

That's when I saw it. The wendigo charged out of the woods screeching in chaotic bellows. My stalker looked as terrified as if the devil himself was chasing him. He disappeared into the woods with the creature chasing hot on his tail. A half-hour later the police arrived. I changed the story from a wendigo to a black bear praying that they wouldn't notice my lie. Thankfully they didn't. They never did find my stalker either. They figured he must have run away in fear, and they were correct.

I have never been contacted since by this stalker and all I do is thank my lucky stars that I had that strange creature on my side. In the end, I think the Wendigo saved my life. It may have been a terrifying experience, but it also showed me that there are good things in this world - even in the most unexpected places.

CHAPTER SEVENTY-ONE

I NEVER THOUGHT I'd be the type of person to take a week off to go camping. But after months of non-stop work and endless stress, my therapist suggested that I take some time to unwind in nature. I step out of the car and take in the sight before me. The luxury wooden cabin stands tall and proud, with its warm honey finish contrasting beautifully against the silver, gray, and black tones of the open porch. The porch is adorned with comfortable couches and an open fireplace, inviting me to sit down and relax.

As I walk closer to the cabin, I notice a hot tub on the ground floor, beckoning me to take a dip and unwind. Further, down the way, I see a fire pit made of stone with wooden beach chairs surrounding it. The thought of sitting by the fire pit with a glass of wine in hand sounds like the perfect way to spend my evenings.

I make my way inside and notice a separate area for a wine bar. This is my idea of roughing it - being away from the hustle and bustle of city life, but still having access to all the luxuries I need. I start thinking about what my therapist says about falling back in with myself. She suggested I take myself on a get away and maybe even take myself out on dates. Laughable. At least it was at first.

I start to plan dates. In the mornings I will do yoga and tai chi on the porch, taking in the fresh mountain air. And at night, I'll go for a run to clear my mind before settling down by the fire pit for some much-needed relaxation and a glass of wine. Everything that I would want to do with a partner.

I work a very stressful job. Working in marketing is a fast-paced and exciting career. Every day is different, and there's always a new challenge to tackle but that's what I love about it. As a marketer, my job is to create campaigns that will grab people's attention and persuade them to buy our products or services. One of the best things about working in marketing is the creativity involved. I get to come up with new ideas for ads, social media posts, and other promotional materials. It's a thrill to see my ideas come to life and have an impact on our target audience.

But despite the challenges, I love working in marketing. It's a field that rewards creativity, hard work, and innovation. And at the end of the day, there's nothing quite like seeing a successful campaign come together and knowing that you played a part in its success. A job in marketing can be stressful for several reasons.

Here are a few possible reasons why; tight deadlines, high expectations, constant change, balancing creativity and data. Finally, collaboration: While collaboration can be a positive aspect of working in marketing, it can also be stressful if there are communication breakdowns or personality conflicts among team members.

And this is where things go wrong.

I've been working in marketing for a few years now, and I've always enjoyed the creative environment. But recently, something unexpected happened - I fell hard in love with my coworker. His name is Alex, and he works on the same team as me. He was the most handsome man I had ever seen in my life. He had dark chestnut hair that was so thick and full that even Fabio would be Jealous of its luxury. He was tanned from many summers he had spent in Greece with his family as a teen and muscular from countless nights sailing and I was smitten. Not only was he sexy but he was clever and funny. A triple threat as far as I was concerned.

We've always gotten along well, but it wasn't until we started collaborating on a big project that I realized how much I enjoyed spending time with him. We would bounce ideas off each other, share funny stories, and generally have a great time working together.

As the project progressed, I found myself looking forward to our meetings more and more. I would get butterflies in my stomach when I saw him walk into the conference room, and I couldn't help but smile whenever he made a joke or complimented my work. One day, after we had finished a particularly challenging part of the project, Alex asked me if I wanted to grab a drink after work. I said yes without hesitation, and we ended up spending the whole evening talking and laughing over beers.

From that point on, we started hanging out more outside of work. We would go to concerts, try new restaurants, and take long walks around the city. It was like we were in our own little world, separate from the stresses of work and deadlines. He was everything a gal could have wanted. I started to wonder, could I actually have it all?

But as much as I enjoyed spending time with Alex, I couldn't help but feel nervous about what our coworkers would think if they found out about our relationship. My nerves were becoming frayed. I decided to start seeing a therapist. Between the stress of the job and the uncertain future, I had to do something before I broke down. I couldn't help thinking about my work environment and my coworkers. Would they judge us? Would it affect my professional reputation?

Despite my worries, though, I knew that I couldn't keep my feelings for Alex a secret forever. So, one day, after we had been dating for a few months, I decided to talk to him about it. To my relief, he felt the same way. We agreed to be open about our relationship with our coworkers, and to do our best to maintain professionalism in the workplace. However, things started to change when a higher-up position opened in our department. Alex started working longer hours and seemed more focused on his career than our relationship. I tried to be supportive, but I couldn't shake the feeling that something was off.

One day, I decided to surprise Alex at work with lunch. When I got to his office, I found him kissing another woman. I was devastated and confronted him about it. He admitted that he had been cheating on me with her and that he had done it to get the promotion. He said that he felt like he needed to prove himself to the higher-ups and that he didn't think he could do it without cheating.

I was heartbroken. I had never felt so betrayed in my life. I couldn't believe that someone I loved could do something so terrible. In the end, I decided to break up with Alex and move on with my life. It was painful, but thanks to a prescription and my therapist; I knew that I deserved better than someone who would cheat on me for their own gain.

It was painful and messy, but I knew deep down that I couldn't be with someone who would put their job above everything else. It took me a while to move on, but eventually, I found a new job and started dating someone who valued me for who I was - not just as a coworker, but as a person.

I woke up early and decided to treat myself to a yoga date with myself. I had always wanted to try yoga, but never had the time or motivation to do it. But today was different. Today, I was going to take the time to connect with my body and mind. I rolled out my yoga mat and put on some calming music. I closed my eyes and took a deep breath, feeling the tension in my body slowly melt away.

As I moved through the different poses, I felt a sense of peace and tranquility wash over me. Each movement felt like a gentle hug, reminding me to be kind to myself and listen to my body. I focused on my breath, inhaling deeply and exhaling slowly. With each breath, I felt more grounded and centered. As I flowed through the different poses, I felt a sense of strength and empowerment. My body was capable of so much more than I had ever given it credit for. Maybe my therapist was worth her money after all. The immense density of the forest gave me the privacy I so desperately needed, and I felt less silly as I got into more poses.

After an hour of yoga, I lay on my mat in savasana, feeling completely relaxed and at ease. I opened my eyes and smiled at myself in the mirror. I realized that this yoga date was not just about connecting with my body and mind, but also about connecting with myself. It was a reminder that self-care is important, and that taking time for myself is not selfish, but necessary. As I rolled up my yoga mat, I felt grateful for this experience. I knew that this would not be the last time I would go on a yoga date with myself.

Hours later I am sitting in my cabin in the middle of the woods. I'm trying not to think about work. Did I leave enough information? Should I have taken my laptop? Ugh, here I go again fixating. I'm trying to relax and forget about all my problems but all I can think about is Alex or the work I am not doing. The woods became eerily quiet. All I could hear was the wind. But something strange is happening out here. I decided it was now time to move my self-date night indoors because clearly, I was tired. I locked the house, closing all the windows except for my bedroom window. After brushing my teeth, I crawled into bed and looked forward to a much-needed deep sleep. I couldn't shake this feeling like something wasn't right. I chalked it up to my nerves needing something to fixate on.

At first, I thought it was just my imagination playing tricks on me. But then I started hearing strange noises - rustling in the bushes, footsteps that seemed to come from nowhere. I tried to ignore it at first, telling myself that it was just the wind or some small animals. But as the night wore on, the noises grew louder and more persistent. At first it started with low whistling rustling through the night air. Then, a child's voice crying for their mother in the woods. At first, I criticized my cowardice and hid under my covers like a child. Somehow I managed to fall asleep.

It wasn't too long after when I woke up in the middle of the night to a strange smell that filled my nostrils. It was a putrid odor, like nothing I had ever smelled before. It was so strong that it made me gag and I had to cover my nose with my hand. My stomach churned with the wine that I had earlier nearly spilling out on my bed spread. My mind filled with images of decayed flesh dripping into small, dark putrid puddles outside my window.

I saw a shadow with long tendril like hands caressing the windowsill. A gasp caught in my throat. Air battled for space in my throat. I felt as if I was a helpless child wondering about the toxic terrors out in the dark. Imagined those long claws causing strawberry gashes across my face and I covered my mouth with my hand to stop myself from crying out.

But then, I heard something even more terrifying. It was the sound of a voice, mimicking that of my ex-boyfriend, Alex. The voice was coming from outside my window, and it was calling out to me, beckoning me to come outside. I felt a sense of relief wash over me. I could jump into his arms and forgive him for everything if he would save me from the things that lurk in the dark. As quietly as I could manage my way to the front door and then the porch door before I was absolutely certain that I was out of the view of the window.

That's when it hit me, I knew that it couldn't be Alex. He had moved away weeks ago and we hadn't spoken since. Especially not since the tonsil hockey incident with Tracy in accounting. But the voice sounded so much like him that it sent chills down my spine. I cautiously approached the porch door and peered outside. I decided against going outside. That's when I saw it, standing in the darkness, was a wendigo. Its eyes were glowing red, and its mouth was twisted into a grotesque smile.

The smell grew stronger as the wendigo approached my window. It was like the stench of death and decay, mixed with the scent of rotting flesh. The smell was so strong that it made me dizzy and disoriented again. But the voice continued to call out to me, urging me to come outside. I knew that I had to resist its call, or else I would be lost forever.

With all my strength, I slowly and safely retreated to my bathroom. The smell lingered in my room for hours, but eventually dissipated. Relieved I cut my trip short. I quickly packed up all my belongings and made my way to my Tesla.

I turned on a deserted road in the middle of the forest. I loved the feeling of driving fast, and the silence of my electric car made it even more enjoyable. The silence was drowning out the insanity of last night. But as I turned a corner, I saw something that made my heart skip a beat. A wendigo was standing in the middle of the road, its eyes glowing red.

I slammed on the brakes, but it was too late. The wendigo was too close, and I hit it with a sickening thud. I sat there, frozen in fear, as the wendigo got up and started to approach my car. Its eyes were fixed on me, and I could feel its hunger and rage emanating from its twisted form.

But then something strange happened. The wendigo recoiled in pain as if it had been electrocuted. I realized that my Tesla had hit the creature with such force that it had activated the car's autopilot system, which had delivered an electric shock to the wendigo.

The creature stumbled back, disoriented and weakened. I saw my chance and hit the accelerator, speeding away from the wendigo as fast as I could.

As I drove away, I couldn't believe what had just happened. I had hit a wendigo with my Tesla and survived. I knew that I had been lucky, but I also felt a sense of pride and empowerment. From that day on, I knew that I was capable of facing any challenge that came my way. I had faced a creature of legend and come out on top. I didn't need Alex or a therapist, I have my bad ass self! What more could a girl ask for?

CHAPTER SEVENTY-TWO

MY SCARY AND strange encounter happened back in 1983 when my church held a children's retreat for middle school children whose parents were a part of the congregation. There were four chaperones, including myself, and about ten children present. The kids all ranged in age from eleven to fourteen, or something like that, and I was in my mid twenties at the time. I can't remember the exact ages of the kids but they were a calm and innocent crew of misfits in their own schools who had formed deep bonds with one another during all of the church functions throughout the year. This wasn't the first time we held a retreat like this but it was the first time I was chosen to chaperone and I was super excited by it. It was also the first time we had been to this particular spot. It was a little eerie right from the get go. I mean we already lived in the middle of nowhere in Texas but this place was way out in the middle of the wilderness. It was a tiny little cabin with only two bedrooms. We had the kids using sleeping bags and had the girls in one of the bedrooms and the boys in another. The four adults slept in sleeping bags on the floor of the tiny living room. None of us minded though and the kids were having a blast. It was a week-long event, sort of like Bible camp and it was our third night there when the first sighting/encounter happened. We built a fire and roasted hot dogs, made s'mores and told all of the silly "scary" stories that usually go around at these types of places. The kids were bored though and it wasn't quite Bible and bedtime yet. Two of the other adults were ready to go inside and I later found out they were feeling uncomfortable in those woods but at the time they just said they were tired and would meet us inside in an hour for the before bedtime study group. I shrugged it off and jokingly told the kids they were stuck with just me and Ted and then asked them what they wanted to do. By the way Ted had a crush on me, I met him at the camp then and there and we ended up marrying several years later. He still remembers that night too and he is just as confused about it all as I am.

I asked the kids what they wanted to play and they said police and hostage. It sounded like something I should probably discourage but they explained it just meant that they would split up and half of them would take one of us adults into the woods and hide us as a "hostage" and the other adult and the rest of the kids had to find them. It sounded a little scary but I set boundaries that didn't go further than a few feet into the woods and that no one was allowed to be alone at any time. Most of the girls went inside to gossip and talk about whatever middle school girls talked about at that time but there were two left who decided to come with me into the woods. The logistics of the game don't matter, the fact that I ended up alone in the wilderness and then had my encounter is what's important. When the girls and I were finally ready to go and find Ted, within five minutes they were tired out and wanted to go inside. Some of the boys were too and so I announced that after I found Ted it would be time for all of us to go in. By the time we figured it out and they hid him somewhere in the forest, we had about twenty minutes left until we had to be inside. It was just me and I was looking for Ted. The boys who hid him stayed with him but they were out of sight so I didn't spot any of them first. I had a small flashlight and that's it. I'll admit, it was scary right from the first steps I took into the forest. I felt like I was being watched but I brushed it off because I figured the boys and Ted were watching me from somewhere.

I looked for a good ten minutes but it was hard to see, even with my flashlight. I wandered around inside of the designated area for at least ten minutes before I announced that I was giving up and it was time to go back inside. I thought I heard giggling coming from behind me and so I decided to try and sneak up on the boys. I walked one of the few trails but I didn't see anyone and instead kept walking deeper and deeper into the forest. I don't remember much of this and I think I was being compelled somehow. I know most people think that cryptids are some sort of mammals, but I believe they're something far more intelligent and far more terrifying. Suddenly two of the boys jumped out of the bushes and scared the life out of me. I screamed but quickly composed myself and laughed along with them. Everyone gathered around but when we went for Ted and saw him, he wasn't hiding behind a tree like he was supposed to be and was instead focusing very hard on the dense wilderness around us. He had his sights set on something and his flashlight aimed at it as well. I asked him what he was doing and he responded by asking me to make sure everyone was with me. I took a very quick head count, believing that would reassure him. However, it only seemed to make him more confused looking and seemingly more nervous. I asked him what's going on with my eyes but he just shook his head no. We walked back to the cabin and the boys giggled and jumped around the whole way .Ted looked very nervous.

We got to the cabin just in time and we all did our bible study and got ready for bed. Once the kids were all tucked in, Ted and I made cups of tea and went out front to sit under the stars and drink them. There wasn't a porch or anything but we turned some crates upside down for chairs. He told me he had seen something strange in the woods and was having a lot of trouble processing it. I asked him to explain and he took a deep breath and told me he had seen a strange, tall figure lurking around. It had glowing red eyes and stood at about ten feet tall. It kept going from one tree to another but it looked like it was trying to hide behind them, as he was, but one after another. It was almost playful, like it wanted in on the fun. He said as soon as he shone his flashlight on it, it froze. Before he could finish the pastor came out and told us it was time for lights out. We told him we were finishing our tea and would be right in. Ted didn't want to talk about it anymore and he abruptly got up and went inside to go to bed. I was scared but when I got up to follow him I heard something moving around in the woods right in front of where we had just been sitting. There was a somewhat small but wide open area where there were no trees and taller grass. I looked and shined my flashlight on it. It froze and turned to look at me. Its hands were at its sides and it just stared. Its eyes glowed bright red and I knew it was the same thing Ted had just been telling me he had seen earlier in the night. I didn't know what to do and I just froze and stared right back at it. It didn't even flinch when the bright light hit its face.

It had greenish gray skin but it didn't have scales or anything and other than the fact that it was bald, how tall it was, the color of its skin and its obvious eyes, it looked no different than a human. It looked like it had once been wearing human clothing but they were just tattered pieces hanging off of its skin all over its body at that point. It reminded me of that old show The Incredible Hulk, when the guy would Hulk out his clothes would rip and tear to shreds. It smiled at me and then got down on all fours and started slithering towards me on its stomach. It moved so quickly that I almost didn't have time to react. I screamed at the top of my lungs and ran inside to lock the door. I immediately ran over to the window, ignoring everyone who was now out of their sleeping bags and asking me what was wrong. I didn't have the heart to tell them. It would have terrified the children and ruined their whole experience. I looked at Ted and gently nodded but to everyone else I laughed and told them that I had seen a bat and it swooped a bit too close. The adults didn't look amused but the kids thought it was hilarious. We all laid down for bed but for obvious reasons, I couldn't sleep.

I finally fell asleep for a few hours but the next morning I got up at around seven, knowing the kids weren't required to get up until nine. None of them ever did and it was more like ten by the time they were all up and moving and ready to get on with their days. I woke Ted up and he didn't ask any questions. We checked the area where I had seen the entity the night before and sure enough there was what looked to be one long and wide drag mark going all through the grass and dirt. The day was uneventful but I was scared and kept looking over my shoulder. Ted didn't leave my side for a second but no one really noticed. It was all about the kids, you know? That night the kids wanted to play the same hostage game and it ended up being the same couple of kids, me and Ted. I tried to say no but they didn't understand and they were having fun so i didn't want to ruin it. I laid the ground rules though and told them to make sure they didn't leave Ted's side. My tone was much more serious than normal. However, once we broke apart and I was looking for them, I heard screams of terror coming from a little way ahead of me. I ran and there were the boys, they were crying hysterically and screaming and Ted was trying his best to console them. He took the boys and started walking ahead of me, expecting me to follow but I didn't, at least not right away. They didn't notice and that was okay with me and actually it was preferable. I was scared but I was angry it had scared the children more than anything else. I called out to it and suddenly there was movement in the trees.

It was definitely humanoid and it stood there again, with its hands at its sides like it was just casually waiting for me to join it. I approached it, hoping to learn what it was and praying, deep down inside, that it was something totally ordinary and easily explained away. It began to slither away again and I followed it for a few minutes. However, something told me to turn around and go back to the cabin. I felt like it was my guardian angel or the voice of God or something like that and so I turned and hightailed it out of there as fast as I could. As for the children, well, they got over it and we were able to convince them it was some sort of exotic bear or something like that. I remember how confused I was but when I was face to face with the creature I didn't notice and I think the kid's memories may have been jumbled up as well. I spoke to two of them recently on social media and they have absolutely no memory of that event. They remember the camp fondly and have all of the other memories, but not of that night. It's a blank. I've searched far and wide and all over the internet to try and figure out what we encountered in the woods all those years ago but nothing I have ever come across even comes close. It was like a serpent but also like a man and Ted is convinced it was some sort of lower level demon. However, in my opinion, it was most likely some sort of unknown cryptid that not enough people have come across yet.

I think if we give it a few years enough people will be reporting sightings and encounters and it will end up having a name. I can't explain
the confusion away though or the fact that it terrified me but I couldn't
run from it right away. It's all a mystery and I still have nightmares to
this very day.

CHAPTER SEVENTY-THREE

I STEPPED out of my old Ford pickup truck, squinting against the blinding sun in the sky. I'm a journalist searching for the strange and bizzare, and I'd come all the way to Point Pleasant, West Virginia, to investigate the strange sightings of some creature locals were calling the "Mothman". I wasn't sure what to expect, but I took a deep breath and made my way down to the main street, notebook and recorder at the ready.

As soon as I arrived, I could feel the eyes of the people upon me. They knew who I was and why I was here. They were curious and yet cautious, as if they didn't want to share their secrets with an outsider. But I was determined to uncover the truth.

I quickly found myself at the local diner, and I ordered a black coffee to help shake off the long drive. That's where I first heard the stories - about the red-eyed creature with wings that had been spotted around town. Some had seen it in the sky, others on the ground, but everyone agreed on one thing: it was no ordinary bird. The hairs on the back of my neck stood up, and I knew this was going to be a story worth telling.

I began my investigation in earnest, talking to the locals and gathering information about the Mothman sightings. The more I dug, the more convinced I became that there was something deeply unsettling about this creature. The red eyes, the dark wings, the eerie prophecies - it all added up to something out of a nightmare.

One man I spoke to claimed to have seen the creature up close and personal. He described it as no bird or animal he had ever seen before. It moved with an otherworldly grace, almost like it was gliding through the air. And its eyes - he shuddered at the memory - those glowing, red eyes that seemed to stare right through him, as if seeing into his very soul.

As I continued to investigate, strange things started happening. I would hear rustling in the bushes behind me, or catch a glimpse of something moving out of the corner of my eye. I tried to shake it off, telling myself it was just my imagination, but I knew deep down that something wasn't right. It was as if the Mothman was watching me, waiting for me to get too close.

But I couldn't stop now - I was in too deep. I had to find out what the Mothman was and why it was here. I had to know what it wanted. And I was willing to risk everything to find out.

The prophecies. They were the thing that made the Mothman truly terrifying. At first, I thought were just the ramblings of a few crazies, but then I started hearing them more and more often - whispers of doom, of death, of destruction. And the worst part? Some of them were coming true.

One prophecy in particular stuck with me. It was whispered by a young girl in the town square, and it sent shivers down my spine. "The river will flow red with blood," she said, her voice barely above a whisper. "The skies will fill with fire, and the town will burn." And then she smiled, as if it was all some kind of sick joke.

I tried to dismiss it as just a child's vivid imagination, but then the river did turn red - the result of a toxic spill, the authorities said. And then the fire broke out, a massive inferno that engulfed half the town. I knew then that there was something truly sinister happening in Point Pleasant.

I continued to investigate, even as the prophecies continued to mount. The Mothman was no longer just a creature of myth and legend - it was an omen of death, a harbinger of doom. And yet, I felt that there was something more to it all - some dark secret that was lurking just out of sight.

I spent sleepless nights pouring over my notes, looking for any clues that might explain the Mothman's presence in Point Pleasant. And then, finally, I found it. A mention in an old newspaper article of a creature that had been spotted in the area almost a century ago, a creature with wings and glowing red eyes that had caused a panic amongst the locals. It had been dismissed as a hoax at the time, but now I wasn't so sure.

Armed with this new information, I began to piece together the truth behind the Mothman's prophecies. I dug deeper, ignoring the warnings of the locals who told me to leave town before it was too late. But it was already too late - the Mothman had marked me as its next victim.

It was a dark, stormy night, the weight of humidity hanging in the air. That was the night that it finally revealed itself to me. I was walking back to my truck, my head down against the rain, when I heard wailing in the bushes beside me. I turned, heart pounding, just in time to see the Mothman emerge from the shadows. I froze, unable to move as it loomed over me, its red eyes glowing like hot coals.

And then it spoke. Its voice was like nothing I had ever heard before - a deep, guttural sound that seemed to come from everywhere and nowhere all at once. "You should have left when you had the chance," it said. "Now, you're mine."

I sat straight up the next morning in my motel room, covered in sweat and trembling all over. It was obvious I had been tossing and turning. The sheets rapped around my legs and pillows tossed to the floor. Had that entire thing been a really bad dream? Was it an omen? A Prophecy?

As far as I was concern, the Mothman was still out there, still watching, still waiting. And I knew that my investigation had only just begun. I sat up in bed, heart pounding, the memory of the Mothman's glowing eyes burned into my mind. I knew then that I couldn't back down - not now, not ever. I had come too far, seen too much, and I couldn't let the Mothman win. I was a journalist, damn it, and I would get to the truth no matter what the cost.

The rain was still pouring down outside as I got dressed, the sound of it battering against the motel window like the drums of some other-worldly creature. But I didn't care about the rain - all I cared about was finding the answer to the question that had been haunting me for so long: what was the Mothman, really?

I stepped outside, determined to face whatever lay ahead. The air was thick with a sense of foreboding, as if the whole town was waiting for the other shoe to drop. But I wasn't afraid - not anymore. I had a mission, and I would see it through to the bitter end. And if that meant facing the Mothman head-on, then so be it. I would do whatever it takes to uncover the truth.

I made my way to the local hardware store, my boots splashing in the rain-soaked pavement. I needed supplies, and I needed them fast. I wasn't sure what I was up against, but I wanted to be prepared for anything.

The store was a dimly lit, cramped space, filled to the brim with tools and equipment of all kinds. The owner, an old man with a weath-ered face and a gruff voice, greeted me with a nod. "What do you need?" he asked.

I rattled off a list of items - a flashlight, a knife, a can of spray paint. I wasn't sure what use they would be, but I wanted to be ready for anything. As the old man rang up my purchase, I couldn't shake the feeling that I was in over my head. But I was determined to see this through, whatever the cost.

I stepped out of the hardware store, supplies in hand, and made my way to my truck parked out front. The rain had tapered off a bit, but the air was still thick with an ominous mist. I loaded up my gear and started the engine, revving it to life. The sound echoed down the street, and I could see the locals peering out of their windows, curious but tight-lipped.

As I drove down the main street, the locals lined the sidewalks, watching me with a mixture of curiosity and suspicion. They didn't say a word about the Mothman, but I could sense their unease in the way they avoided eye contact and crossed their arms defensively.

I decided to stop at the local diner before venturing out into the wilderness. It was deserted, save for the old waitress who greeted me with a smile. "You heading out to find the Mothman?" she asked, her voice hushed and conspiratorial.

I nodded, not sure what else to say. The waitress didn't seem to want to talk about the Mothman, but I could sense that she knew more than she was letting on. As I finished my coffee and got up to leave, she whispered one last thing to me. "Be careful out there," she said. "It's not just the Mothman you have to worry about. There are things in these woods that nobody talks about."

As I drove deeper into the wilderness, my mind raced with all kinds of possibilities. What was the Mothman? Some kind of demon, sent to punish the town for its sins? Or was it a creature from another world, come to Earth to claim it for its own? Whatever it was, I knew that it was something beyond my wildest imaginings - something that might drive a man mad if he looked at it for too long.

But I was determined to face it. I had to know the truth, had to uncover the secrets that the Mothman was hiding. And if that meant venturing out into these dark woods then so be it. I had no choice - the Mothman had marked me, and I knew that it was only a matter of time before it came for me. But I was ready. I was armed with my supplies, my trusty notebook and recorder, and a fierce determination to get to the bottom of things. The woods may be dark and foreboding, but I was not afraid - not anymore.

I remember the day I found the Mothman like it was yesterday. It was a chilly autumn evening in West Virginia, and I was on assignment for my newspaper to investigate reports of a mysterious creature spotted in the area. The woods were dense and misty, and the only sound was the crunching of leaves beneath my feet. I had been walking for hours, my nerves on edge, when I saw a figure in the distance.

As I approached, I could see that it was a large, dark creature with wings, perched high up in a tree. The smell was overpowering; a mixture of damp earth and rotting flesh. I stood frozen, staring up at the creature, wondering if it was real. The Mothman's eyes seemed to glow in the darkness, and I could feel its gaze piercing into my very soul.

Fear consumed me as I continued to observe the creature. Its wingspan was enormous, and I knew that if it flew down, I would have no chance of escape. But I couldn't leave. I was a journalist, and I had to get the story. I pulled out my notebook and began to take notes, trying to steady my shaking hand.

As I wrote, the Mothman made a sudden move, spreading its wings and taking flight. I screamed and fell to the ground, certain that it was coming for me. But as it flew past, I could see that it wasn't interested in me at all. It had its own agenda, its own purpose.

I lay on the ground, paralyzed with fear, I watched as the Mothman took flight. But as it soared through the air, I could see that it wasn't leaving me behind. It circled back around and landed on a branch above me, staring down with its glowing red eyes. Its wings were still outstretched, and I could feel the wind from its flapping, beating against my body.

I was terrified and helpless, completely at its mercy. But instead of attacking, the Mothman seemed to be studying me, as if I were a specimen it had never encountered before. And then, without warning, it spoke. Its voice was guttural, inhuman, and it spoke words that I couldn't comprehend.

I screamed and tried to crawl away, but my body was frozen with fear. I could feel the Mothman's gaze upon me, and I knew that I was in grave danger. But just as suddenly as it had spoken, the creature took flight once again, disappearing into the darkness.

I was left alone in the woods, shaken and traumatized by the encounter. But as time passed, I began to realize that the Mothman's presence wasn't just a chance encounter. It had chosen me for a reason. Perhaps it saw something in me that made me a target for its dark machinations.

I spent the rest of the night in the woods, too scared to move. I lay on the cold, damp ground of the forest, staring up into the darkness above. The sound of rustling leaves and snapping twigs echoed through the trees, but I couldn't move. Fear had taken hold of me, and I was trapped in a nightmare that refused to end.

Hours had passed since I first spotted the Mothman, and still, it lingered above me, watching and waiting. I could feel its presence, even though I couldn't see it. Its scent, a mix of rotting flesh and damp earth, hung heavy in the air.

I tried to crawl away, but my limbs refused to cooperate. I was paralyzed, helpless, and at the mercy of a creature I couldn't even begin to comprehend. Its glowing red eyes seemed to pierce through me, and I could hear its deep, guttural voice speaking words I couldn't understand.

The night was endless, and as the hours ticked by, my fear only grew. I wondered if I would ever see the light of day again, or if I was doomed to spend the rest of my life in this forest, waiting to be devoured by the Mothman.

As the first light of dawn began to filter through the trees, I heard a sound that filled me with hope: the flapping of wings. And then, with no warning, the Mothman was gone, disappearing into the shadows once again. I lay there for a few moments longer, too scared to move. The first light of dawn began to filter through the trees, I knew that I had to leave. I pulled myself up, my limbs trembling with fear, and stumbled out of the forest.

The walk back to my truck was a blur. Every rustle of and snap of a twig seemed louder, more ominous. But I made it back to the truck, and as I climbed inside, I knew that I had to get out of there. Fast.

With shaking hands, I turned the key in the ignition and peeled out of the parking lot. I didn't stop to look back; I couldn't bear the thought of seeing the Mothman one more time.

As I drove down the deserted road, I knew I was being watched. Every shadow seemed to move, every tree branch reaching out to grab me. I gripped the steering wheel so tightly that my knuckles turned white.

As I approached the nearest town, I knew that I had to make a decision. Part of me wanted to stop, to find someone who could help me, but another part of me knew that I couldn't risk it. What if the Mothman was following me? What if it was waiting for me in the town?

With a sense of dread, I pushed down on the gas pedal and kept driving. The town faded into the distance behind me, and I was once again alone with my thoughts and my fear.

As a journalist, I pride myself on my ability to explain the unexplainable. But the encounter I had with the Mothman left me speechless, with more questions than answers.

The Mothman was not just some creature of legend, but something much more terrifying. It was as if I had come face to face with a being from another dimension, something beyond our earthly understanding. Was the Mothman an interdimensional traveler?

As I researched more about the Mothman, I realized that it was not just some random creature. It was a harbinger of death, a warning of impending doom. I couldn't help but shudder at the thought that it had targeted me for a reason.

I began to wonder if the Mothman was a tulpa - a manifestation of our collective fears and anxieties - a warning about the darkness that lurks within us all. Or perhaps it was something even more sinister, a being not of this world that had come to remind us of our own mortality.

Whatever it was, I knew that I could never forget that trip to West Virginia. The Mothman had left its mark on me, and I couldn't help but feel like it was still out there, watching and waiting for its next victim.

As a journalist, I know that sometimes the truth is stranger than fiction. And in the case of the Mothman, the truth was something that I could never have imagined in my wildest nightmares.

Years have passed since that night, and I am still haunted by the memory of the Mothman. I've since come to realize that there are some things in this world that we can never truly understand. But I feel I have a duty to try. And so, I continue to search for answers, no matter how terrifying they may be.

I can't help but wonder what would have happened if the Mothman had decided to take me with it that night. Perhaps I would have become one of its many victims, forever lost in the shadows of the unknown. The memory of that encounter will stay with me forever, a reminder that there are things in this world that are beyond our comprehension and our control.

CHAPTER SEVENTY-FOUR

I AM NOT your average traveler. I like to think of myself as an urban explorer who seeks out the most remote and isolated parts of the country, driven by a deep sense of curiosity and a desire to uncover mysteries that have been hidden away for centuries. To me, there is nothing more thrilling than embarking on a new adventure, hiking through rugged terrain, and setting up camp in the wilderness.

My passion for exploration has taken me to some of the most remote parts of the country, from the dense forests of the Pacific Northwest to the desolate plains of the Midwest. My goal has always been the same - to uncover unsolved mysteries that have been forgotten by time. There is still so much that we can learn about our world and our history, and I have always been determined to be the one to uncover those secrets. There is no greater reward than the feeling of discovery, of pushing beyond the limits of what we know and venturing into the unknown.

This trip was no different. For months, I had heard rumors of a hidden village nestled deep within the forest, a place where time seemed to stand still. Some said it was a magical place, others that it was cursed. But all agreed that it was near impossible to find, and that few who ventured into the woods ever returned. Together with a few friends of mine, we plotted, planned, and finally set out on the adventure of a lifetime. We were in search of a lost civilization, deep in the mountains of the Catskill. If Rip Van Winkle could find a hidden band of time shifting dwarfs, surely we could find something equally as exciting!

My group ventured deeper into the forest, the trees grew taller and the path grew more narrow. Mist clung to the ground like a thick veil, obscuring my vision of what lay ahead. My heart pounded in my chest, and I could feel the sweat beading on my forehead despite the cold air. The team wanted to rest, break and make camp for the night. I told them I'd keep on, there was so much daylight left. I would stay on the path and check in every few hours. I'd go ahead and set up our next camp. When they arrived we'd be ready to jump in and begin our research. I pressed on, driven by a sense of curiosity that bordered on obsession.

After a few feet, I turned to wave to my group, almost taunting them with the fact that I was going forward. It was then when I turned I saw the mist that was beginning to creep across the trail. Mists in these parts were not uncommon and I wrote it off as such. As long as there was daylight and the path ahead was clear, I was good to go.

Checking my pedometer, I saw I walked a few miles. Still on the trail, the surrounding path was clear and full of light. I decided to sit down for a moment, catch my breath, and have a bit of water. I found the nearest large rock and leaned up against it. That was the moment when I first heard it, when I heard the first whispers. They were soft and insidious, flickering through the trees like ghostly fingers. At first, I tried to ignore them, telling myself that they were nothing but the sounds of the forest. But as they grew louder, I began to realize that they were following me, taunting me with their secrets.

I had heard whispers before, of course. The kind that come from the mouths of others, carried on the wind like a distant echo. But these whispers were different. They were ancient and sinister, as though they had been waiting for me for centuries. I looked to the sky and saw the sun was beginning to drop lower and closer to the horizon and decided I would move over to the clearing and set up my camp for the night.

At first, I thought it was just my imagination playing tricks on me. But then I saw them - dark shapes lurking in the shadows, their eyes gleaming like those of a predator. For a moment, I froze, the whispers growing louder and more insistent.

I knew I had to find the source of the whispers and confront them head-on. There was no way I could rest for the night if there was someone whispering around me. I've seen enough bad movies to know that is not the situation you want to be in. The whispers continued; it was as though I was being drawn towards something, a force that I could not resist. Putting my pack back on, I knew I had to find the source.

The trees grew thicker, the path more treacherous. But I continued on, my senses heightened by the thrill of discovery. And then, suddenly, I saw it - a clearing in the forest, with a small village nestled at its heart.

At first, I could hardly believe my eyes. The village was like something out of a fairy tale, with huts made of woven branches and thatched roofs. There was no sign of life, but I could feel the presence of the villagers all around me. The trees had eyes and I knew, they were watching me.

The whispers grew louder, and as I stepped closer into the village, the hairs on the back of my neck stood up. I could feel the villagers watching me, their eyes following my every move.

And then, I heard a voice. It was soft and feminine, but its words were laced with a cold, menacing tone. "You should not have come," it said. "This place is not for outsiders."

I turned to face the speaker, but there was nothing there. The whispers grew louder, and I felt a sense of unease creeping over me. It was as though the forest itself was warning me to leave. But I refused to be intimidated. I had come too far to turn back now. And so, I walked deeper into the village, searching for answers. There was no one to be seen and I had no idea where the whispers were coming from. It was almost like a mental download, something that was just put in my pineal, allowing me instant understanding.

As I explored the huts, I could feel the presence of the villagers growing stronger. They were watching me, their eyes boring into my soul. I could hear their whispers all around me, their voices rising and falling like the tide. Looking into one of the last huts, I found it. A small, ancient book, hidden away in a corner, almost obscured and half hidden. It was written in a language I could not understand, but its pages were filled with drawings of strange symbols and rituals.

As I looked through the book, I felt a sense of dread creeping over me. Why did I insist on going on ahead without the rest of my group. That's Safety 101. Don't go alone! The villagers were not just watching me - *they were waiting for me*. Waiting for me to play my part in a ritual that had been repeated for centuries.

Putting the book in my backpack, I decided to run, but the forest had closed in around me like a cage. The mist that divided my friends and I was here, surrounding me too. The whispers grew louder, their voices like a chorus of the undead. And then, I felt a hand on my shoulder.

When the hand touched my shoulder, I felt the hairs on the back of my neck stand up. Standing before me was an old woman, with skin as withered and dry as the bark of a dead tree. Her eyes gleamed with a fierce intensity, and I could feel the weight of her gaze upon me.

There was something about her that sent a shiver down my spine, something otherworldly and ancient. As she spoke, her voice was like a whisper in my ear, as though she were speaking to me from another realm.

I later learned that the woman who touched me was a member of the village hidden in the forest, a place forgotten by time and untouched by the modern world. She was one of the last surviving members of her tribe, a keeper of secrets and ancient knowledge. Her tribe was fierce, often taking matters in their own hands, doing what needed to be done to protect themselves from the outside world. At times that included acts so vile, she could not even bear to recount them. As a teen, she had fled the village, leaving behind her family and her past, and creating a new safe haven for those who were lucky enough to have escaped. But the memories of the ritual had haunted her for decades, and she had spent the latter part of her life warning outsiders to stay away from the forest and the ancient secrets that lay within. It was a warning that I should have heeded. Alone, she was searching for someone to carry on the knowledge. She had spent her entire life in the village and it was her time to pass on.

"You should not have come," she said again. "But now that you are here, you must stay. You must take part in the ritual, carry on the work. It is your duty now."

And then, the whispers rose to a crescendo, their voices like knives in my ears. I knew I had no choice. I could feel the villagers closing in around me, their hands grabbing at my clothes. Voices pounded in my ears like the timpani of the damned. The energy was growing stronger and I was growing weaker.

And then, everything went black.

When I awoke, I was back in my own bed, drenched in sweat. It was as though the entire experience had been a dream, but I knew it was not. After I woke up in my bed, I felt disoriented and confused. I tried to shake off the feeling of dread that had clung to me since my encounter with the woman in the forest. The entire experience had to have been a dream, a product of my fevered imagination and late night buffalo wings.

Just like every day, I ran for the bus, taking the first available seat. About ten minutes into the ride, I realized that something was off. My body felt heavy and sore, as though I had been put through the wringer. Then I began to feel it, a long scratch down my back, deep and red against my skin. I had no memory of how it got there.

Despite the strange occurrence, I was determined to go to school and forget about the bizarre encounter in the forest. No matter how hard I concentrated in school, I couldn't shake the feeling that something had changed within me. The memory of the woman's voice, her warnings, and the whispers echoed in my mind like a never-ending nightmare.

I tried to ignore it, but the feeling refused to go away. I had stumbled upon a secret that was not meant for human eyes, and that knowledge would haunt me for the rest of my life. But what did I see? What did I witness? I don't remember anything at all. What secrets lie in the depth of the Catskills? There must be a reason why the story of Rip Van Winkle takes place there. Was that story really a warning? I wondered if they were connected, his experience and mine?

The bus shifted and jerked, making the last turn as we entered the school property. The bus came to a screeching halt, narrowly missing a handful of students. *If I wanted a life a danger, I could just ride the school bus.*

As I made my way off the bus, I couldn't help but feel that something was watching me. It was an unnerving feeling, like blazing eyes stabbing through the back of my head. And then, as I glanced back at the fence line dividing the school parking lot from the street, I saw her - the woman who had touched me on the shoulder. She was standing at the edge of the property line, watching me with those piercing eyes. My heart began to pound, my breath stopped and I froze in fear.

And then, just as suddenly as she had appeared, she vanished into the shadows, leaving me to ponder the mysteries of the forest and the secrets that lay within. I pulled up the sleeve of my hoodie, wiping my eyes and hoping for clearer vision. I couldn't shake the feeling that what had happened was real, that I had stumbled upon something ancient and otherworldly.

Since that trip with my friends, I haven't had the heart to go back and explore anymore. I know something happened and it is trapped in the catacomb of my mind. I know it was real but I can't face that fact. Part of me still clings to the belief that it had all been a dream. But no matter how hard I tried to push the memory away, I knew that it would stay with me forever, a reminder of the mysteries that lurk just beyond the veil of our everyday reality.

CHAPTER SEVENTY-FIVE

I GREW up in Upstate New York on the east coast of the United States. I was fourteen at the time of my encounter and my friends and I had been having a fairly typical day up until the point where it all went bad for me and I saw something I still can't explain and have a hard time wrapping my head around. It was the late eighties and as anyone who grew up back then will probably tell you, it was a much simpler time. I won't bore you with the details of life back then and I will try to just get right to the point of my encounter. I lived in a very small town and most of us were what were called latchkey kids. That meant that we were left alone and to our own devices a lot and we practically raised ourselves. I had a core group of three friends but we all lived on the same block. On that block there were several families who all had kids around the same age. So, while it was normally just me and my best friends, every once in a while a whole group of us would get together and go into the woods and play a game that was our own spin on the manhunt game that was so popular back then. The idea of manhunt is basically like hide and seek but when it's dark outside and also, there is a home base. Another element was the use of walkie talkies but only some of us had ones that worked or had them at all and so we didn't use them that night. There were ten kids and we broke up into two groups. If you found someone from the other person's group you had to walk them to your own home base. The other team could free their people from your base if they could touch them on the hand or arm, or really wherever, but that was easier said than done because one person was left there to watch those who were "taken captive." It's all a bit complicated to write out but it was a lot of fun and we would play in the woods down at the end of the street from us to make it even more interesting. It was scary, sure, but not the terrifying type of scary that you get when you watch horror movies or come face to face with something like what I ended up seeing that night. It was more thrilling, if you will.

We broke up into teams and walked down to the end of the road and about a half a mile into the woods to establish our home bases. I was chosen to be the guard which means I didn't hide or hunt but just waited for one of my team members to bring back someone from the other team. Once all the kids from one group were in the other's home base area, the game was over and that group won. Then we played again. It started off really fun and completely normal. I waited for my teammates to find the other kids but it always took longer in the woods because it was nighttime but also because there was much more space for us to hide. When we played on the street there were narrower boundaries. The boundaries were the points where we couldn't step outside of without forfeiting the game. No one ever did that on purpose because we all enjoyed playing so much. I remember it had already been about ten minutes and I still didn't hear anyone anywhere near me. I could hear the other kids in the distance but for the most part it was a quiet game that required stealth. You had to try and not only find the other team's members but sneak up on them as well. I waited and waited until finally fifteen minutes had passed and I had to go pee. I decided to just go somewhere in the woods, out of sight of anyone who came back to the base area, of course. So I walked a little bit further into the woods and did what I had to do. It would have been super embarrassing for me to have been caught out there with my pants down, especially because several of the kids playing that night were female. I walked for about five minutes before stopping, to make sure that no one would see me.

As soon as I was done I heard what sounded like someone sneaking up behind me. I was immediately embarrassed and yelled out that I was going to the bathroom and it was time out. I informed whoever it was that I would be right back to the base and that they needed to leave me and give me some privacy. I had already pulled up my pants but was still nervous whoever it was had seen something already. I didn't hear anyone turn and walk away though but I did hear a very odd noise instead. It sounded like dripping. It was almost as if someone had just stepped out of a pool or something and water was just dripping off of them and into a puddle at their feet. It was really odd and I had chills all up and down my spine. The hair on the back of my neck stood up and something told me not to turn around at all. I stood there, frozen with fear and staring straight ahead while whatever it was stood about five feet behind me, apparently dripping into a random puddle in the middle of the woods. It didn't make sense but like I said I was too scared to turn and face it. I listened and that's when I realized I also couldn't hear any of the other kids anymore. I hadn't walked that far and so that was even more frightening. After a few seconds, which seemed like an actual eternity, the dripping noises stopped and I waited a few seconds before catching my breath and turning around. There was nothing there. I breathed a sigh of relief and turned to start walking back to the base so I could wait for my friends, who I was sure would be returning at any moment if they weren't already there waiting for me. It was only a short five minute walk from where I had used the bathroom to where the base was but the whole way there I kept hearing the dripping noises behind me again. It would start and stop, over and over again. I didn't turn around and vowed not to until someone else was there with me. I was trying to convince myself that it was something that was easily explainable but I just couldn't make sense of it or place the sound. It scared me very much and I wasn't an easily scared kid, none of us were.

Once I got to the home base area I waited for another five minutes before I turned around but there was once again nothing there. I felt like I was being watched though and so I called out for the others to come back and relieve me. I suddenly didn't want to play anymore, I didn't want to be in the woods either and in fact I just wanted to go home and be inside where I felt safe. I didn't receive a response from my friends but I heard something move, quickly, in the woods right near me somewhere. I looked all around and shone my flashlight all over the place. It landed on something that looked like it was hiding between some trees and behind some very tall and overgrown grass. I kept my light on it and asked who was there. As soon as I saw whatever it was I immediately became angry because I was convinced that it was one or more of the other kids and that they were playing some sort of joke on me. I yelled at them to come out from hiding but instead, something else revealed itself to me. It crawled out on all fours and looked somewhat like a human being. Its skin was pale gray and had no hair anywhere, including on its head. Its arms and legs looked sickly and so skinny that it was almost like a crawling skeleton. Its mouth hung open disgustingly and I could see its yellow, very sharp teeth. Its mouth was bright red, like it had blood or lipstick on it and it was totally naked. It looked like it had very long talons or overgrown and razor sharp fingernails. Other than that, it looked somewhat human. I was shaking so badly it was everything I could do just to not drop the flashlight at that point. The thing just stayed there like that for a full minute or two and I didn't move either. I remember telling myself to try and not even breath lest whatever it was attack me. Its eyes were all black and soulless. I backed up so much I eventually backed into a tree, which made me jump and let out a little, pathetic yelp.

That seemed to agitate the entity and it started making a horrific shrieking noise. It was horrible but I couldn't cover my ears because that would have meant taking the flashlight off of it. I kept shaking my head no and blinking my eyes, hoping it would just disappear and end up being a figment of my imagination. I knew that wasn't possible, I was too young to have been having a stroke or something like that, but I felt like that would have been preferable to that thing having actually been there. Suddenly it stood up and I kept looking around because I couldn't believe how long it had been since I had seen or heard any of the other kids. They had to have still been out there and there seemed to be no way that no one had found anyone else yet. In reality it had only been about twenty minutes and while that is a long time in a game of manhunt, it isn't unheard of, not really. The person who is captured can try to break free and run away, it's a whole thing. The creature stood up in quick, jerky movements and once it was fully standing I noticed a couple of things. First, it was soaking wet and dripping. That meant it had been following me and had been behind me that whole time earlier when I was relieving myself in the woods. The second thing I noticed was that its joints, like its elbows and knees, looked like they had been put on backwards or something. It was awkward and grotesque. It started coming at me but it moved slower than a snail but in jerky, chunky sort of movements. It wouldn't get anywhere near me within the next five minutes, despite being only a few feet away from me. I couldn't take it anymore and turned to run. I heard a loud shriek coming from the creature behind me just as I crashed into another kid. There were a few of them and they were all laughing.

They asked me what I was doing but I was crying by that time and shaking so badly I couldn't stand up straight let alone talk. I ran right past them and kept right on running until I made it out of the woods. I then ran half a block to my house, went inside and locked the doors. I went into my room, got ready for bed and cuddled up under the covers. I heard my parents come in a little while later but I pretended to be asleep. I slept with a night light on that night and it was only the first of many nights I had to do that. I was terrified. After all, those woods surrounded my house, for the most part, and my bedroom faced the backyard and was on the ground floor. I never saw the entity again but I think I've heard it a few times. I stopped playing manhunt in the woods but I only told two or three of my closest friends why. They didn't ever tell anyone and would always try and back me up when the other kids on the block wanted to move the game into the woods. If they succeeded, the majority always ruled, then I would just go home and not play. I didn't get to talk to any of the other kids about what I saw in the forest that night but I know my friends who I did tell told me they hadn't ever seen or heard anything. That night, too, no one heard that strange and horrible howling noise that came from right behind me as I ran into those kids. There's no way they couldn't have heard it, but they swore they hadn't. They hadn't heard the incessant shrieking before that either.

I believe what I saw is the creature known as the rake that I keep seeing encounters with all over the internet nowadays. I believe creatures like them, other cryptids for example, walk between worlds, with one foot in theirs and one in ours. I think that's why no one else heard it that night but also why no one else has ever seen it either. I think conditions have to be just right and maybe it even has to want you to see it, I don't really know. That's it on this encounter though, thanks for letting me get it out. It's been a very long time but I can still remember every single detail and I will probably be the only grown man I know who is sleeping with a night light on tonight, after having written about all of it and brought it front and center to my mind again.

CHAPTER SEVENTY-SIX

I WAS twenty-two years old when I had my encounter in 2005. I had just graduated college but still wasn't really sure what I wanted to do with my life. I moved back to Ohio to stay with my parents while I figured it all out. I went to college in southern California. I love the wilderness and all of mother nature is awe inspiring to me so it wasn't a big shocker to anyone when I decided to go camping for an entire month in some remote wilderness near where my parents lived. It wasn't near their house or anything but it was two towns over and still in Ohio. I had been camping and hiking before on my own but never for that long and I even surprised myself when I finally made the decision to go out there and stay for that long. My parents agreed to restock me every week and I showed them a map of where I was going so they would be able to meet me at my car on Fridays to refresh my supplies. I know that they were worried, especially when I told them I would not be bringing my cellphone but I reassured them by telling them that they would see me once a week at least and know that I was okay. It just felt like something I had to do, sort of like a rite of passage or something, and I was hoping that by the time my camping excursion was over I would have a better idea on where my life was headed and what was next for me. My psychology degree just didn't thrill me

445

the way I thought it was going to and I was starting to feel like I had wasted all of that time in school just to get a degree in a field that didn't make me feel excited. Little did I know those woods would change the course of my life for the better. It was terrifying, don't get me wrong, but it is the entire reason why I am a parapsychologist today, loving what I do and every minute of my life.

I left on a Friday afternoon with enough time that I would get there before it got dark and be able to set everything up. I was a heavy packer, so to speak, and I brought a lot of things with me I probably didn't need. The way I see it is, it's better to have something and not need it than the other way around. I got to the area I planned to stay at around five thirty at night and knew I had about two hours until it was fully dark outside. I parked my car in the unofficially designated parking area and hiked about two miles into the woods. I was going to change the place where I was camping every week after my parents came and met up with me. I had a digital camera with me because I also loved taking pictures. Photography has always been a hobby and passion of mine. I always believed in the paranormal and extraterrestrials too but I stood alone in my family on those particular beliefs. It didn't matter or make any sort of difference but I feel like being out there alone made me vulnerable enough but I truly believe that my strong belief in the paranormal might have been what drew whatever this was to me. I had many experiences throughout my life, but I still don't know if what I saw and what happened to me was paranormal or not. I don't know if cryptids are really considered paranormal entities but I guess it would depend on who you ask. I believe that what I saw was not only some sort of so-called mythical creature and a cryptid too, but also, that it was extremely malevolent. I set up my camp and got a good fire going. I had something to eat and just sat by the fire thinking and not really paying much attention to my surroundings at first.

It started with the sound of leaves crunching and branches snapping as though someone were walking around near my camp but more so in the woods surrounding it. It wouldn't have been unheard of for there to be other people out there but because it was almost one in the morning by the time I started hearing those strange noises, and also because I hadn't seen another human being or camp the whole way there throughout my hike, it definitely made me pay more attention. It sounded like whoever it was, they were trying to sneak up on me. The whole forest suddenly went silent and when I say suddenly, I mean it in every sense of the word. It was like one second an owl was hooting in a tree to the left of me and insects were buzzing and chirping all around and the next second someone was sneaking up on me and those were the only sounds that I could hear. I was immediately scared and looked around to see if I could catch a glimpse of anyone. I didn't see anything out of the ordinary or anyone lurking around but just to be sure I went into my tent and grabbed my flashlight and my digital camera. It had a flash on it and because of something I had seen on one of the many paranormal shows I watched almost incessantly, I knew that snapping pictures when you feel like there is something lurking around you gives you a better chance of catching a glimpse of what it is. So, the camera was functioning for the paranormal like the flashlight was in case it was perfectly normal. I didn't know what I would have rather done because if it was a human being they couldn't have had good intentions, sneaking around a lone woman's camp in the middle of the night. The alternative, that it was a creature or entity, even a wild animal, wasn't a much more desirable situation.

I walked around my campsite a little bit, being sure to never stray too far from the light of the fire despite having my flashlight on and aiming into the woods around me. When I couldn't see anything and all the sounds had completely stopped, I sat in front of the fire and held up my camera. I snapped photos of whatever was behind me. It was almost like taking a selfie but I wasn't in the pictures. Finally, the owl started hooting again and even though the insects were still way too quiet, I decided to go to bed. I was exhausted in more ways than one and had managed to almost convince myself that I had been imagining it all along. Almost, but not quite. I crawled into my tent and fell asleep almost immediately. I woke up at around three thirty in the morning feeling disoriented and somewhat dizzy. I got up to use the bathroom in the woods but had a terrible feeling that something was watching me and it was so quiet I could have sworn I heard something breathing. Again, the woods had gone eerily silent. I didn't understand why I felt almost drunk but again I tried to be reasonable and I chalked it up to how tired I had been when I finally went to sleep. I got back into my tent and fell right back to sleep.

I woke up suddenly and it felt like something was on top of me. I opened my eyes as I tried to struggle but I went completely limp almost immediately. It wasn't that I physically couldn't move but that I was so filled with terror at what I was seeing that I didn't know what to do. I immediately saw some sort of figure and its red eyes were staring straight into mine. It had me pinned down but it wasn't a sexual thing. The entity or whatever it was looked shocked that I had woken up and even backed up a little bit when I opened my eyes and screamed. For a split second we were just there, staring at each other in shock, horror and confusion. The thing, whatever it was, seemed almost embarrassed that it had been caught. I somehow knew intuitively that it was scanning me. I know that doesn't make much sense, or that it probably won't for a lot of people because even I don't really understand it. That's just what my mind was telling me what was happening at that moment. I started to scream and struggled against it. It sort of rolled backwards and off of me and took off into the woods. I don't know how I had the presence of mind to grab my camera but I did and just started taking random pictures with the flash, aimed outside of my tent through the flap in the direction the entity had gone. I immediately scrolled through not only the photos I had just captured but the ones from earlier in the night, from behind me while I sat by the fire as well. I couldn't believe what I was seeing and a part of me wished I had looked at the other photos as soon as I had taken them, although I honestly don't know how or if that would have changed anything. There were bright red eyes staring at me, from directly behind me in the trees. Whatever it was couldn't have been more than fifteen feet away from me. The image was a little blurry because of the light of the fire and the flash and I could only see a weird black shape other than the red eyes. However, what I saw from the photos I had just taken, of whatever had attacked me while I was sleeping, was a whole other story.

I saw what looked like the hooves of a deer in the air as though it were running away from me. I also saw what looked like a black cape blowing in the breeze. You'd think I would have wanted to get the heck out of there but I was more intrigued at that point than scared. After all, it could have easily hurt me while I was sleeping or when it had me pinned down but it didn't. It actually ran from me. I went back to sleep and a part of me hoped it would return while the other part of me prayed that it wouldn't. The next day I went about my business as usual and hiked a bit like I had planned. I fished a little bit too but I was distracted the whole day. I was constantly looking over my shoulder and listening to see if the forest would go silent again. I didn't see anything unusual but still there weren't any other humans anywhere either. That was odd too. I went to sleep at around midnight and while I didn't wake up to anything inside of my tent, I knew something was out there, in the woods, just lurking. I got up and out of my tent. I walked to the edge of the woods and that's right when something stepped out from inside of some tall grass. It had the face and head of a human being. It had a stomach, a neck and two arms and hands. However, it had what looked like deer legs and ears. I hadn't noticed the ears the night before. The hands and face had some fur on them but they weren't covered. It immediately reminded me of Mr. Tumnus from the book The Lion, The Witch and the Wardrobe. I couldn't believe it. I knew that I should be scared but I was also fascinated. It just watched me with those terrifying red eyes. It looked like it had stepped out and showed itself in order to watch me panic or something. Something about the way it stood there was aggressive and like it was protecting or marking its territory. I told it I was sorry for encroaching on its space and that I would move the next day. With that it backed up slowly until I could no longer see it. I heard a swishing noise like it had taken off running again but I knew it wasn't gone until five full minutes later when the owl started hooting and the insects started buzzing and chirping again.

When I woke up on my third morning there I packed everything up and moved my camp to a mile away from where I had seen the entity and deeper into the woods. I didn't experience anything else the whole time I was out there. My parents came every Friday as promised and like clockwork. I didn't tell them what happened to me or what I had seen because they would have either thought that I had gone crazy or they would have been worried sick. Either way they would have insisted I come back home with them immediately and I wasn't ready to do that yet. I didn't fully enjoy myself or get to relax at all because I was always afraid that thing would come back and finish whatever it started in my tent on the first night. It's weird because I knew it was evil and had malicious intent, I felt that to the core of my being. Why it didn't hurt me I will never know. That's it for that encounter but I have so many now because of my job that I am seriously considering writing about a lot of them. I've personally had encounters with the paranormal before and since but never in the woods.

CHAPTER SEVENTY-SEVEN

I REMEMBER THE MOMENT VIVIDLY, when I realized that the only way to salvage my crumbling manuscript was to escape to a remote cabin tucked away deep in the heart of the dense woods. Thankfully, my publisher had such a place!

Surrounded by towering pines and the haunting melodies of nature, I knew this seclusion would be my saving grace. The deafening silence promised an escape from the cacophony of everyday life, a respite from the endless distractions that had held me hostage for far too long. In that small, weathered cabin, I would rediscover the writer buried within.

With a mix of anticipation and fear, I stood at the edge of the cabin's porch, watching as my publisher's car disappeared down the winding gravel road. The engine's fading hum marked the beginning of my isolation, a solitary confinement I had willingly embraced. As she rolled down the window, a fleeting smile graced her face, and she called out, "See you in three days!" Her words hung in the air, a gentle reassurance that I would not be forgotten. And with a final wave, her car melted into the distance, leaving me standing there, alone, ready to immerse myself in the wilderness of my own imagination.

Alone, without the ever-present distractions of modern technology,

I found myself stripped down to the essentials: a desk, a typewriter, and my thoughts. Gone were the incessant demands of the buzzing phone or the flickering allure of the television. Instead, I was left with the sheer power of solitude, where creativity thrived in the depths of silence. Surrounded by the raw, untamed beauty of nature, the only voices I heard were the whispering winds and the rustling of leaves, urging me to delve deeper into the recesses of my imagination.

Hunger started to gnaw at my stomach like a relentless beast, its claws digging deeper with every passing moment. Desperation drove me to rummage through the cabin's sparse pantry, hoping for any semblance of sustenance. Just as my patience waned, I stumbled upon a room adjacent to the pantry, its door creaking open with a foreboding invitation. My eyes widened as I witnessed an eerie sight: chains, thick and rusted, adorned the walls, their massive shackles dangling ominously. A shiver danced down my spine, the air turning frigid as a sudden wave of unease washed over me.

A chill wind whispered through the room, rustling the chains as if they possessed a life of their own. My heart pounded in my chest as I took a hesitant step forward, drawn to the unsettling presence that emanated from those ancient restraints. I could almost hear a faint echo of tortured cries, carried on the wind, intertwining with the eerie silence of the cabin. Shadows danced on the walls, contorting into grotesque shapes, as if mocking my curiosity. Something sinister lingered in the air, a malevolent energy that seemed to awaken with my every breath.

My hand trembled as I reached out, compelled by an inexplicable force, to touch one of the chains. Cold metal met my fingertips, sending a jolt of primal fear coursing through my veins. Panic overwhelmed me, urging me to flee, but where would I go? I closed the door and hurried back to my typewriter. "The faster I finish this, the faster I can go", I thought to myself.

I hastily prepared a meager meal, my trembling hands struggling to steady the knife. The taste of the hastily devoured food did little to satiate my hunger, as my thoughts were consumed by the unsettling encounter with the chains. However, with the feeble light of the setting sun casting long shadows through the cabin's windows, I knew I had to steel myself for the task at hand. As I gathered my notes and settled down at the worn desk, I tried to dismiss the haunting image of those menacing shackles. But my mind couldn't help but wander back to the chains, their cold touch lingering in my memories like a lurking nightmare.

I tried to convince myself that the chains belonged to a long-gone pet, perhaps a massive dog that had once roamed these desolate woods. Yet, doubt clawed at the edges of my sanity, as a chilling realization seeped into my consciousness. What if that creature, whatever it had been, had never truly left? What if it lay in wait, a remnant of forgotten horrors, biding its time in the depths of this isolated cabin? The hairs on the back of my neck prickled, and the comforting rays of sunlight seemed to wane, eclipsed by a growing sense of unease. As I stared into the encroaching darkness beyond the cabin's window, I couldn't shake the disquieting thought that something far more sinister than a mere dog had once been bound by those chains.

Hours blurred into a haze of frenzied writing, my fingers dancing across the keys like a possessed conductor orchestrating a symphony of words. The manuscript had consumed me, driving me to the brink of madness as I poured my soul onto the pages. In the hushed sanctuary of that cabin, I battled my inner demons and wrestled with the blank pages that previously mocked my ambition. With each keystroke, the words flowed like a river unleashed. The cabin became my cocoon, protecting me from the distractions that had plagued me before. The outside world ceased to exist as my thoughts intertwined with the story, my surroundings fading into an ethereal backdrop. But as the sun descended on the horizon, casting long shadows that stretched like grasping fingers, a realization pierced through the creative frenzy. I needed a break, a moment of solace before the encroaching darkness swallowed the landscape whole.

I emerged from the confines of the cabin, the weight of my literary obsession still heavy upon me. The fading light painted the surroundings in eerie hues, the trees whispering secrets among themselves as a chilling breeze rustled through their branches. The path to the lake beckoned.

As I reached the edge of the lake, the setting sun cast a crimson glow upon the rippling water. I remember thinking, this must be why people move out here, to get away from it all. I could live like this. I wasn't aware, but shadows began to dance beneath the surface, elongated figures that twisted and writhed, hiding secrets below the waterline. An unnerving stillness hung in the air, broken only by the distant cries of nocturnal creatures, their calls carrying a mournful echo through the encroaching darkness. The beauty of the view was now tainted with an unshakable sense of dread; I couldn't shake the feeling that I was being watched, that unseen eyes bore into the core of my being.

I stood at the water's edge, my feet sinking into the damp earth, as the last remnants of daylight dissolved into a veil of darkness. The lake lay before me, an inky expanse that mirrored the night sky above. It was a sight of haunting beauty, but an indescribable unease settled deep within my bones. The moon, a pale specter, began to rise, casting a glow upon the waters.

Time seemed to stretch, as if caught in the clutches of a mystic force, as I watched the moon climb higher, its cold light illuminating the surrounding landscape. Shadows danced in distorted patterns, their forms twisting and contorting with an otherworldly rhythm. A chilling breeze whispered through the trees, carrying with it a melody of disembodied whispers that sent a shiver cascading down my spine. The water lapped against the shore with an eerie rhythm, each ripple hinting at hidden creatures lurking just beneath the surface.

Minutes quickly turned into a hour as I stood there, captivated by the moon's ascent, unable to tear my gaze away from the haunting spectacle. The world around me grew hushed, the nocturnal creatures silenced in fearful reverence. An oppressive stillness settled upon the air. I became acutely aware of a presence, an unseen entity that watched with a malignant intent. It felt as though the moon itself was a gateway, opening the doors to an ancient darkness that sought to envelop everything in its grasp. In that moment, as the moon reached its zenith, I realized I had trespassed into a realm where the boundaries between reality and nightmare had blurred, and I was but a vulnerable spectator in a cosmic play.

Quickly I turned for the cabin. Thankfully, it was a short walk.

Even shorter when you walk quickly. With a sense of urgency born from primal instinct, I hurried back to the cabin, my heart pounding in my chest like a frantic drumbeat. The once inviting refuge now seemed like a frail barrier between me and the encroaching terrors that lurked in the night. I bolted the door shut, my hands trembling as I turned the key, as if it could fortify the flimsy walls against the impending horrors that threatened to breach my sanctuary.

Inside, I was engulfed by an overwhelming need for light, an instinctive longing to banish the encroaching darkness that clawed at the windows. *There is no darkness in the light*. Fingers fumbling, I flipped every switch, illuminating the cabin in a blinding glow. The incandescent bulbs hummed with an eerie resonance, casting elongated shadows that danced upon the walls. Outside, I switched on every exterior light, hoping their weak glow would ward off the encroaching darkness that seeped through the trees.

But even as the cabin radiated with light, a chilling realization seeped into my consciousness. The brightness served only to accentuate the looming shadows that stretched and twisted like sentient entities. The glow cast distorted shapes on the walls, morphing innocent objects into grotesque caricatures. Every creak, every whisper of wind, sent shivers down my spine. The very fabric of the cabin reverberated with an unseen force. In that moment, I couldn't shake the feeling that the lights, rather than repelling the darkness, only exposed the vulnerability that lay within.

With a trembling hand, I retreated to the pantry, my heart pounding like a desperate drum in my chest. Amidst the meager supplies, my eyes fixated on a dusty bottle of wine, its crimson contents calling to me in a desperate attempt to drown out the encroaching terror. Normally I do not drink, but I would make an exception that night. I paused for a moment, staring at the chains in that little room. Quickly I slammed the door, locking it, just in case something was going to show up next to them.

The act of pouring the deep red liquid into the glass felt both comforting and unsettling, as if I were imbibing an elixir that would open my senses to the horrors lurking just beyond my fragile sanctuary.

Returning to the safety of the cabin's dimly lit interior, I sank onto the worn sofa, the weight of my fears settling upon my shoulders like a suffocating blanket. The wineglass trembled in my grip as I brought it to my lips, the liquid sliding down my throat with a bittersweet taste that mirrored the ominous ambiance of the night. Shadows danced in the corners of the room, their twisted forms mimicking the strands of darkness that crept closer with each passing moment.

As I sat there, the eerie silence enveloped me, broken only by the distant howl of the wind and the faint rustle of unseen creatures. Every creak of the floorboards sent a jolt of adrenaline coursing through my veins, as if the very foundations of the cabin whispered secrets of impending doom. The wine failed to offer solace, its intoxicating warmth unable to drown out the paralyzing fear that clung to me like a cheap pair of pantyhose. In that moment, I realized that I was not alone. There was something moving in the shadows outside.

I sat alone on the worn sofa, the dim light casting elongated forms that danced across the room. Silence reigned, broken only by the faint crackling of the dying fire and the distant rustle of leaves outside. Suddenly, a chilling howl pierced through the stillness, the sound carrying on the wind with an otherworldly resonance. Dread washed over me, for I knew that howl was no ordinary cry of a nocturnal creature. It was a call that spoke of a lurking terror drawing closer, its hunger growing with each passing moment.

With bated breath, I peered through the window, my gaze fixated on the horizon where the full moon began its ascent. Its pale light bathed the surroundings in a glow, illuminating the twisted forms of the surrounding trees. But as the moon climbed higher, its light revealed a horrifying truth. Silhouetted against the moon's radiance, a figure emerged from the shadows, its shape contorting with bestial ferocity. It looked like a werewolf, but not like what I'd seen in Hollywood movies. It had a man's body, but a dog or wolf like head. It snarled and bared its razor-sharp fangs.

*For lack of a better way to describe the creature, I'll just
   say werewolf from now on, but I have since also
   heard about a creature known as a dogman.

My heart pounded in my chest, each beat a desperate plea for escape. The werewolf's piercing yellow eyes locked with mine, its gaze filled with a primal hunger that chilled me to my core. It prowled closer, its steps as silent as death, its monstrous form growing more grotesque with every passing moment. Fear rooted me to the spot, my muscles paralyzed with a primal terror that defied reason. I could feel the presence of imminent danger closing in. I knew I had a date with death.

The room seemed to shrink, the walls closing in as the creature's presence loomed larger. Its howls reverberated through the cabin, a haunting symphony that echoed throughout the rooms. A putrid stench filled the air, a combination of wet fur and decay, as the creature's proximity intensified. I could hear its labored breathing, a guttural sound that sent a shiver cascading down my spine and through my soul. The light cast elongated shadows upon the creature's hulking frame, accentuating its grotesque transformation and revealing the raw power that lay beneath its fur.

Time slowed to a crawl as the werewolf approached, its menacing silhouette now filling the windowpane. Its feral eyes bore into my soul, as if savoring the terror that radiated from my very being. With a snarl that echoed through the cabin, the creature lunged, its claws slashing through the air with a horrifying swiftness. Instinct kicked in, and I dove for cover, seeking refuge in a darkened corner of the room, trying to escape the monster's onslaught. The sound of the creature hitting the side of the cabin echoed.

I huddled in the darkest corner of the cabin, my breath shallow and rapid, my heart thundering against my ribs. It lunged again as the heavy sound of its weight colliding with the wood siding of the house shook the cabin.

A bright light shined suddenly shined through windows from the driveway. I peeked up and saw someone had just pulled in front of the cabin. My heart leapt for joy. It was as if a guardian angel had appeared.

The creature stopped its assault on the cabin. I heard it race off and crash into the woods. I got to my feet and looked out to confirm it was gone. Suddenly a knock on the door startled me. I immediately went to go find my publisher. She said she had forgotten her handbag. I didn't know what to say, I didn't recall seeing it.

She suddenly looked at me and could see the fear on my face. She asked if I was okay, my response was, "NO!"

I immediately packed my things and said I needed to leave.

She kept peppering me with questions but I had nothing to offer. I knew no one would believe me, hell I still hadn't come to grips with what I'd seen.

I grabbed my things, she found her handbag and within ten minutes of her arriving we left and I never looked back. I have since reserached the type of creature and I know werewolves are things of fiction but there is some lore the fictional accounts are based upon. I have even read my people's stories about dogmen. What came at me that night was something out of this world and from nightmares. I know if my publisher hadn't returned, it would have gotten into the cabin and killed me. I pray you reading this never encounter such a creature and if you do, you have the means to defend yourself.

CHAPTER SEVENTY-EIGHT

AS I CROSSED the threshold of Shadow Hollow, a shiver slithered down my spine like a lingering phantom touch. The town was nestled deep within the bowels of an ancient forest, its trees looming tall and ominous, their branches swaying in a macabre dance. The air felt heavy with secrets, and a palpable sense of foreboding hung like a thick fog over the streets. I knew, in that moment, that this place held stories, dark tales etched into its very essence.

The townsfolk of Shadow Hollow wore weary expressions, their eyes haunted, as if they had glimpsed things best left unspoken. Their whispers permeated the air, carried on gusts of wind that echoed through the barren streets. Legends and rumors thrived here, tales of vanishings and the unknown. Every nook and cranny concealed a sinister secret, lurking just beyond the veil of perception.

It was the disappearances that plagued the town that piqued my curiosity. The enigmatic cases of those who had ventured into the depths of the surrounding forest, only to vanish without a trace. The fear in the eyes of the locals hinted at something more sinister, a presence that stirred in the darkness, its malevolence palpable. As I delved deeper into the mysteries of Shadow Hollow, I could feel the tendrils of the unknown tightening around me, whispering of untold horrors lurking in the shadows. And I, foolishly perhaps, was drawn to uncover the truth that lay beneath the surface of this eerie town, to face the darkness head-on and unveil its secrets.

Rumors of mysterious disappearances danced through the town like phantoms, whispered from one trembling lip to another. The tales carried the weight of fearful speculation, their details embellished with each telling. Faces grew pale as they recounted the vanishing of loved ones, their voices trembling with a mixture of grief and dread. The town became a breeding ground for paranoia, as neighbors eyed one another warily, questioning who might be the next to succumb to the unknown forces that lurked in the shadows. In Shadow Hollow, fear was a constant companion, clinging to the fabric of existence, waiting to ensnare the unwary.

Shadow Hollow's dark history unfolded before me like a macabre tapestry, its threads woven with tales of horror and despair. The town's origins were steeped in ancient rituals and sacrificial rites, whispered in hushed tones by those who dared to speak of them. As I dug deeper into its past, I unearthed accounts of a blood pact made with an other-worldly entity, a sinister bargain that bound the town to an eternity of suffering. It was said that Shadow Hollow had become a cursed place, its very foundation soaked in the blood of innocents.

Legends whispered of a vengeful spirit that roamed the streets, its ethereal form drifting through the darkness. Locals spoke of spectral figures that materialized at the stroke of midnight, their mournful cries echoing through the abandoned alleyways. The ghosts of the town's tragic past still lingered, forever trapped in a purgatorial dance of anguish and torment. The streets bore witness to countless unspeakable acts, the residue of malevolence seeping into the very soil upon which the town stood.

But it was the ancient woods that surrounded Shadow Hollow that held the true heart of its darkness. The gnarled trees reached out like skeletal fingers, their branches clawing at the night sky as if desperate to escape their roots. Whispers carried on the wind, tales of encounters with unseen creatures lurking among the twisted undergrowth. The forest held secrets so vile that the very air seemed to shudder, and those who ventured too deep were said to become forever entwined with the enigmatic horrors that dwelled within. In Shadow Hollow, the darkness thrived, its insidious influence creeping into the souls of all who dared to call the town their home.

I will forever be grateful for my magazine, for connecting me with locals who had more knowledge and experience in this phenomenon than I could ever care to have. The magazine found a crew for me, braver than any I had ever known, for this voyage. I arranged to meet the crew at the local diner, our first meet and greet. I was praying that this wasn't going to turn into a "met and regret" assignment.

On my team was Detective Samuel Collins, a weathered man with eyes that held the weight of countless unsolved mysteries. His grizzled beard and worn-out trench coat seemed to blend seamlessly with the ominous atmosphere that clung to the town. Rumors whispered that he had been haunted by a case from his past, one that had taken its toll on his sanity. I could see it in the way he carried himself, a mixture of determination and a flicker of vulnerability. He had dedicated his life to unraveling the truth, driven by a relentless need for justice. The lines etched deep into his face told stories of sleepless nights and the relentless pursuit of answers, even in the face of the inexplicable.

Also joining us was Emily Reynolds, a young woman with an insatiable curiosity. Her fascination with the paranormal had led her to Shadow Hollow, where she hoped to uncover the truth behind the town's mysteries. She carried a worn journal, filled with dog-eared pages detailing her encounters with the supernatural. Emily had always been different, an outsider drawn to the macabre. Whispers in the night and ghostly apparitions had been her constant companions since childhood. Despite her own haunted past, she possessed an unwavering determination to shine a light on the darkness that plagued Shadow Hollow, a resolve that burned brightly in her stormy gray eyes.

Mark Davis, a local historian and the town's reluctant guide, had spent decades unearthing the secrets of Shadow Hollow's past. His research had consumed him, blurring the line between historian and fanatic. Mark's once-vibrant spirit had been drained by the weight of his discoveries. He had delved deep into the annals of the town's history, unearthing forgotten tales of malevolent spirits and cursed bloodlines. It was said that Mark's obsession stemmed from a personal tragedy, tearing his family apart and leaving him forever changed. The haunted look in his eyes spoke volumes about the horrors he had encountered, and yet, he clung to the hope that exposing the town's dark past would somehow grant him redemption.

For local flavor, Doris Thompson, an elderly widow with wisps of gray hair framing her lined face, joined our table. She was known as the town's oracle, her home a haven for those seeking solace from the encroaching darkness. Doris possessed a deep connection to the supernatural, her veiled insights often providing guidance in times of uncertainty. Many believed that her gift came at a great personal cost, a sacrifice she made willingly to protect the town she loved. Despite her frail appearance, there was a fire within her, a determination to safeguard the innocent from the clutches of the unknown. Doris said she had her reasons and would help in any way, but she refused to go back into the woods with us and politely rose from the table and walked out of the diner and into the night.

That was the cast of characters that joined me. Oh, who am I? I was a writer seeking inspiration, drawn to Shadow Hollow by the allure of its dark tales. I had always been fascinated by the unexplained, driven to capture the essence of fear and weave it into the pages of my writing. As an outsider, I felt a peculiar kinship with the residents of Shadow Hollow, all bound by a shared sense of unease. My own past held its share of shadows, secrets that I had buried deep within my soul. In the face of the town's mysteries, my own demons stirred, hungry for acknowledgment. Little did I know that my journey into Shadow Hollow would test the limits of my courage and plunge me into a darkness far more profound than I could have ever imagined.

As I soon came to realize, strange occurrences had plagued Shadow Hollow recently, each one an unsettling piece in the puzzle of terror that gripped the town. Ominous howls echoed through the woods, tearing through the night with an otherworldly intensity. The haunting sound spoke of ancient beasts lurking in the darkness, their hunger and fury echoing through the ages.

We gathered in the dimly lit corner of the local diner, Samuel Collins, Emily Reynolds, Mark Davis, and myself. The air was thick with anticipation as we huddled over the worn wooden table, maps and journals spread before us. Samuel, the seasoned detective, wore a stern expression, his eyes flickering with determination. With each word he spoke, his voice carried a weight that demanded attention. We were preparing for an expedition into the heart of the cursed woods that surrounded Shadow Hollow, a journey that held both the promise of answers and the looming specter of unimaginable horrors.

Emily, her eyes shimmering with excitement, reached into her bag and pulled out a weathered journal, its pages filled with her hand-written accounts of the supernatural. Her voice trembled with anticipation as she spoke of the ancient rituals and the whispers that had guided her to this moment. She was our guide through the shadows, the one who would decipher the cryptic clues and lead us to the heart of the mystery. Her presence radiated a strange kind of energy, a mingling of fear and exhilaration that infected us all.

Mark, the historian burdened with the knowledge of Shadow Hollow's dark past, shared tales of the town's previous expeditions into the woods. His words were tinged with caution, his voice carrying the weight of unspoken warnings. He warned us of the restless spirits and the malevolent entities that lurked within the ancient trees. His fingers traced the lines on the map, tracing a path that we would follow, a path that seemed to have been etched by the hands of fate itself.

We made plans and gathered supplies, a medley of flashlights, ropes, and protective talismans, each item chosen with a mix of practicality and superstition. Our resolve solidified with each decision, our shared purpose forging an unspoken bond between us. We knew that the expedition would test our limits, that it would unearth truths too horrifying to comprehend, but we were prepared to face the unknown, to confront the darkness that had ensnared our town. As we left the diner, our footsteps carrying the echo of determination, we were ready to step into the realm of nightmares, bracing ourselves for the horrors that awaited us within the unforgiving woods.

We agreed to meet back here the next day, at dawn. This was our last chance for a good night's sleep and I wasn't going to miss it.

The next morning we gathered, a motley group. We took two trucks and together, we set off to search, try and find what the mystery was all about. It wasn't long before we were at the end of the road. Gathering our gear, we began to set off into the woods.

As we ventured deeper into the woods, claw marks on the trees greeted us, a grotesque graffiti left by an unknown entity. The marks were deep and jagged, claws of unimaginable size had raked across the bark. They defied any explanation, mocking the limits of reason. I could almost envision the creature responsible, a primal force that prowled the depths of the forest, its presence leaving a trail of destruction in its wake.

Whispers in the wind filled the air, chilling us to the core. The voices seemed to emerge from the very fabric of the town, intertwining with the rustling leaves. They carried secrets, tales of forgotten horrors and unspeakable acts. The whispers beckoned us, their ethereal tendrils reaching out as if to lure us deeper into the heart of the darkness. I strained to discern the words, catching fragments of desperate pleas and maddening incantations, but the full extent of their message remained just out of reach.

Shadows danced on the periphery of my vision, their movements hinting at hidden figures that vanished when I turned to face them. A pervasive sense of being watched settled over us, unseen eyes peering through the veil of reality. Every gust of wind carried a chilling presence, whispered my name, promising an encounter with forces beyond my comprehension. The very fabric of the town had become a conduit for nightmares, a realm where the boundary between the tangible and the supernatural blurred, leaving the residents of Shadow Hollow forever on edge.

We ventured further into the foreboding forest, our footsteps muffled by the damp undergrowth. The silence was broken only by the rustling of leaves and the distant hoots of nocturnal creatures. As we delved deeper, the atmosphere grew suffocating, the air thick with an unnatural fog that obscured our surroundings. With each step, a sense of unease settled upon us, a premonition of impending doom that clung to our skin.

Suddenly, horrific screams pierced the stillness, tearing through the woods like anguished wails of the damned. The sound reverberated in our ears, striking a chord of terror deep within our souls. We exchanged alarmed glances, the realization dawning upon us that we were not alone. The legend of the Wendigo, an ancient, cannibalistic spirit that stalked its prey with unrelenting ferocity, echoed through our minds. The forest had come alive with its malevolent presence.

As the fog thickened and darkness encroached, our senses became hyperaware, hearts pounding in our chests. Shadows danced in the periphery of our vision, teasing our sanity, while sinister whispers slithered through the mist, their words barely discernible but laden with a malicious intent. We pressed on, driven by a combination of curiosity and dread, determined to uncover the truth that lay hidden within the heart of the cursed woods.

With nightfall imminent, we halted our progress and set up camp, our hands trembling as we secured our tents and kindled a fire. The crackling flames cast dancing shadows upon the trees, their gnarled branches reaching out like skeletal fingers. Each flicker of light seemed to awaken a chorus of unseen eyes, glinting with an otherworldly hunger from the depths of darkness. We huddled around the fire, its soft glow offering a fragile barrier against the encroaching night. The weight of the unknown surrounded us.

Throughout the night, the forest seemed to come alive with a symphony of chilling sounds - an orchestration of whispers, phantom footsteps, and bone-chilling howls. The Wendigo's presence was palpable, its breath grazing the nape of our necks, its icy grip tightening around our hearts. Sleep eluded us, replaced by a restless vigilance as we clung to the flickering embers of the fire, desperately seeking solace in its dying light. In the depths of the forest, we were morsels, caught in the crosshairs of a primal predator, aware that our every move had placed us one step closer to the brink of annihilation.

No one slept that night; the shadows whispered their sinister secrets. We huddled around the dwindling campfire, our eyes fixed on its flickering glow. It held the last vestiges of our fragile sanity. Fear clung to the air, thick and suffocating, while the unknown encroached upon our unguarded sanctuary. We dared not close our eyes. In the depths of that cursed forest, sleep was an invitation to the horrors that prowled just beyond the reach of the fire's warmth. We stoked the

flames with trembling hands, determined to keep the campfire burning, knowing that it was our only defense against the encroaching
night and the unspeakable terrors that lurked within. And there we
stayed, for the longest night of our lives.

As the first rays of light stretched across the horizon, we hastily
packed up our camp, our movements fueled by a combination of
urgency and terror. The forest, still shrouded in a foggy haze, seemed
to hold its breath. Each rustling leaf and distant snap of a branch sent
shivers down our spines, for the Wendigo's hunger knew no boundaries. We knew we had to find a safer haven, a place where we could
regroup and fortify our defenses against the predator that stalked us.
With sweat-soaked brows and trembling hands, we shouldered our
packs and pressed on, haunted by the knowledge that our every step
could be our last.

And then, in the distance, we spotted it, an abandoned cabin, its
weathered facade a bleak refuge from the terrors of the forest. The
sight of it brought a glimmer of hope amidst the darkness that threatened to consume us. We hurried towards it, our footsteps quickening
with a mix of desperation and cautious optimism. As we crossed the
threshold, the air grew heavy with the weight of forgotten memories
and untold tragedies. The cabin's dilapidated interior was a graveyard
of broken dreams, its walls seemingly whispering tales of unspeakable
horrors. But we pushed aside our trepidation, seeking solace within
the decaying shelter, convinced that even in the embrace of decay, we
would find respite from the Wendigo's relentless pursuit. We hadn't
slept in two days and I suggested we all take this time, while the
Wendigo is gone, to rest. I knew we had a long night ahead of us, and
we needed to be at full strength.

Emily, driven by an insatiable curiosity and an unwavering determination, ventured deeper into the shadows of the abandoned cabin.
Her footsteps echoed on the creaking floorboards, a testament to the
silence that enveloped the air. It was in the corner, amidst stacks of
decaying tomes, that her searching hands stumbled upon an old book,
its leather-bound cover cracked and faded. Dust danced in the beams
of light that pierced through the cracks in the cabin's walls as she deli-
cately opened the ancient pages.

As Emily pored over the yellowed text, her eyes widened with a mix of anxiety and hope. The book revealed a ritual, a forgotten incantation passed down through generations, that claimed to hold the power to banish the Wendigo back into the deepest recesses of the forest. The words on the aged parchment seemed to vibrate with an otherworldly energy, and as she read them aloud, the air crackled with a palpable sense of both danger and possibility. We gathered around her, our gazes locked upon the ancient script, our hearts pounding with a desperate belief that this could be our salvation.

The ritual required us to venture deeper into the heart of the cursed woods, to a sacred clearing where the boundary between our world and the realm of the Wendigo was at its thinnest. There, beneath the moon's chilling gaze, we were to recite the incantation, our voices united in a symphony of desperate hope. It was a treacherous path we would tread, risking our very souls to confront the embodiment of our nightmares. But in that moment, as we clung to the knowledge found within the aged pages of the book, we knew we had no choice. The ritual held the key to our survival. With grim determination, we prepared ourselves to face the final confrontation with the Wendigo, praying that the ancient words whispered through the ages held the power to seal its monstrous fate.

Darkness fell upon the cursed woods, enveloping us in its inky embrace. The air grew heavy with a sinister anticipation. A bone-chilling wind swept through the trees, carrying with it the anguished screams of the Wendigo. The wails pierced the night, threatening to shatter our resolve. We huddled together, our breaths mingling with trepidation and a flicker of fading hope, knowing that the time for the ritual had come.

In the heart of the sacred clearing, Emily took center stage, her voice steady yet tinged with a mixture of fear and determination. The words of the ancient incantation spilled from her lips, resonating with a power that transcended our mortal understanding. Her voice rose and fell, each syllable laced with a desperate plea, an invocation to banish the abomination that haunted our steps. We joined our voices with hers, the echoes of our shared conviction intertwining in a haunting chorus.

As the last verse of the ritual hung in the air, a hushed silence descended upon the clearing, broken only by the distant rustle of leaves. The Wendigo, a monstrous entity born of nightmares, stood before us, its eyes glowing with a malevolence that threatened to consume us all. The beast hesitated, seemingly transfixed by the power woven within the ritual's words. And then, with an unearthly scream, it recoiled, its form dissolving into the shadows. The Wendigo vanished into the depths of the forest, its howls echoing in our ears as a final testament to its defeated fury.

We stood in awe and disbelief, our hearts pounding with a mix of relief and lingering dread. It worked. It actually worked. We gathered our supplies and prepared to leave the clearing. We had faced the Wendigo and emerged victorious, yet we knew that the echoes of its presence would forever haunt us, a reminder of the darkness that lurked within the depths of the human psyche.

We retraced our path back to the safety of camp, our souls scarred but strengthened by the encounter. The woods, now shrouded in an eerie calm, whispered secrets that would forever remain locked within. Even though the Wendigo had been banished, we knew that its memory would forever dwell in the shadows of our minds, a chilling reminder of the indomitable forces that lurked just beyond the veil of our understanding. We returned to our camp, exhausted, and immediately fell asleep.

Dawn broke, its light casting long shadows upon the forest floor. We gathered our gear and prepared to leave Shadow Hollow. The encounter had forever changed us, leaving indelible scars upon our minds and souls. The horrors we had witnessed, the malevolence we had faced, had reshaped our very essence. We were no longer the same people who had entered those cursed woods. Our innocence had been shattered, replaced by a dark knowledge.

As we departed from the woods that had borne witness to our ordeal, a somber silence settled upon us. The weight of our shared experience hung heavily in the air, a bond forged by the crucible of terror. We carried the memory of the Wendigo with us, a constant reminder of the fragility of our world and the horrors that lie just beyond the veil of perception. The encounter had stripped away the illusions of safety and exposed the raw truth of our vulnerability. We had glimpsed into the abyss, and its chilling gaze had left an indelible mark on our souls.

Forever changed, we scattered to the winds, seeking solace and redemption in the farthest corners of the world. Yet, no matter how far we roamed, the memory of the Wendigo lingered, a haunting presence that refused to be erased. It whispered in the depths of our dreams and haunted the recesses of our waking thoughts. Our encounter with the cryptid had become an indissoluble part of our identity, forever tethering us to the darkness, forever reminding us of the thin line that separates our reality from the realm of nightmares.

CHAPTER SEVENTY-NINE

I WAS CAMPING in southern New Jersey while visiting some family a few years ago. Most people know that area as where the Jersey Devil is said to lurk and a lot of people who I have told my story to have insisted that's what I saw but I really don't think so. I looked into the Jersey Devil and it isn't said or known to look anything like what I saw and it seems the only thing what I saw and the JD have in common is the location and the fact they both have wings. I grew up in northern New Jersey and my wife is from New Hampshire. When we got married I moved to her hometown with her because it just made more sense at the time because of our jobs and some other things going on with her family. This particular trip was one I had taken alone because she was going on a cruise with some friends and it seemed better than staying home all alone. I went to visit my family and some old friends but before I headed to their houses up north, I wanted to get a weekend of camping near the Pine Barrens. I had always gone camping there and to summer camps as a kid and I just loved it there. I had heard all the crazy stories of not only the JD but of a lot of super-natural and paranormal happenings taking place there, as well as a lot of extraterrestrial activity. However, I had never seen anything person-ally that would have led me to believe that any of that was true and I was very comfortable in those woods all alone. I didn't believe in those types of things anyways and so it was just going to be a nice, comfortable and relaxing weekend for me before all the hubbub and drama that always accompanied spending any time with my Jersey people. I got there on a Wednesday, late in the evening, and I planned on leaving Friday morning for the hour and a half drive to my parent's house.

I found a great spot to set up my camp and did the usual things someone does while camping. I built a fire and set up my tent and then I took a little night swim in this somewhat obscure area that had what we always called when I went to camp, the swimming hole. The water was nice and warm, it always was, and I was just enjoying the peace and quiet of mother nature all around me. The moon was full and there were tons of stars. I hadn't seen any other people while I was out there but I wasn't surprised because I went a little further than what was considered the accepted place to camp but I always had, that's why I knew about the swimming hole. It is a hidden gem in that area, trust me. Nothing seemed creepy or out of the ordinary until about twenty minutes into my swim. I kept hearing what sounded like loud clapping sounds but they seemed to be coming from the sky and over a little bit, more inside of the woods. There was a bit of a clearing where the swimming hole was and then the woods began again. Every time I would hear the loud clapping I would feel an extremely strong gust of wind. It was making me cold but not too creeped out yet. It was loud and spaced apart enough that I thought it may have been some sort of weird thunder. Areas like the Pine Barrens are somewhat known for weird weather events. After about twenty minutes of listening to the loud claps and feeling the cold gusts of wind, I decided to get out of the water. I dried off and took the short trail back to my camp to build my fire some more and hang out. The whole ten minutes I was walking back to my camp I felt like I was being followed. I couldn't put my finger on why I was feeling that way though. I didn't hear anyone walking behind me but it just felt like there were eyes on me the entire time. Once again I chalked it up to something perfectly normal, convincing myself some animal had caught my scent. I figured once I got back to my camp it wouldn't get too close and I wouldn't have to worry. I eventually went inside of my tent to sleep.

I have a tent that has a part of it on the top that you can unzip and see the sky. It's nothing but a small rectangular piece but I love star gazing and so I unzipped it for the night. I woke up about an hour later because I had to use the bathroom. I opened my eyes and when I looked up I thought I saw some sort of gigantic bird or something fly past my tent. It seemed extremely low to the ground and it scared me and made me jump. I got out of my tent and looked up but didn't see anything and I began to think I had simply imagined it. I went pee at the edge of the woods but again something didn't feel right. I still felt eyes on me and I had a strange and unusual sense of doom and danger. I shuddered for seemingly no reason. Something told me to look up but I ignored whatever it was. I wanted to get my flashlight and search around my campsite because at that point I was positive that something was watching me. Honestly I thought it was going to end up being a person and that they were going to try to hurt me or rob me or something. I had my shotgun with me but never expected I would have had to use it. I went into the tent and grabbed my flashlight and turned it on. Just as I turned on the light I heard the trees above me rustling and while normally that wouldn't have been anything to think twice about, there was absolutely no wind that night and the air was perfectly still. There was something above me, in the trees.

There was a part of me that didn't want to know what it was but my curiosity eventually got the better of me. I shined the flashlight all around my camp but nothing looked out of the ordinary and nothing had been disturbed at all. Whatever was in the trees had been moving around the entire time and I could tell it was massive. I couldn't imagine what sort of animal or bird could be making that much noise and then I heard a faint clapping of wings. It all started to make sense to me as I remembered the gigantic wings I had seen fly past my sky flap in my tent, the clapping and wind gusts at the swimming hole and now the loud rustling and light clapping right above my head. I took a deep breath because I was on the verge of panicking. I was convinced without even having to see whatever it was that it was the Jersey Devil and that it was going to attack me. I shined the flashlight into the trees above me. I didn't see anything clearly but knew something was up there because as soon as the light hit the one tree one of the branches seemed to bounce upwards and then a large branch from the tree next to it bent towards me. It was too high up though for me to be able to determine what was going on. I stupidly yelled out for whatever it was to get the hell out of there. I basically tried to shoo it or scare it away by being loud. Then, there was total silence. The problem with that was the fact that it was way too quiet because I should have heard whatever it was taking off and leaving the area. The large branch at the top of the tree still looked bent. I decided I didn't want to know and turned to climb back into my tent. I figured if what I had seen and sensed was really there, it would be far too big to get inside of the tent with me anyways and if it tried to then I would shoot it. I had the shotgun in the tent with me and within arm's reach.

Before I could walk the few steps back to the tent though I heard an extremely loud noise that, honestly and don't ask me how, sounded like a sheep. It made the same sounds a sheep makes but much louder and it made the ground shake. It also seemed to be coming from much closer than the top of the trees above me. I shined the light all over the trees again and that's when I saw it. Its eyes are what stood out the most at first because the light seemed to reflect off of them. As soon as the light hit it, it made the loud sheep noise again. I backed up in fear and fell over. I was lying there, half sitting and half lying anyway, on my behind and looking up. The flashlight had rolled a little bit to the side but it was still within arm's length of me and so I grabbed it and shined it again into the trees. Then the sheep noise penetrated the air again and I looked over to my left where it seemed to have been coming from. The entity just stared at me. Its eyes were bright and seemed like they were glowing because my flashlight was right on them. It was about eight feet tall and looked somewhat scrawny. I'm a big guy at six feet tall and I work out and am in great physical shape. I was agitated that I was so fearful of this scrawny little thing but it was terrifying.

It was crouching down a little bit and had its one arm up, grasping the low branches of the one tree. It had no hair and was extremely pale. It looked like the face was human but not human. I mean, it had human features like eyes, nose and mouth but this thing was definitely not a human being by any stretch of the imagination. I just don't know exactly how I knew that. Maybe it was its skin? It looked like it was made out of leather and when I yelled for it to get the hell away from me, it then started to make bird sounds. It sounded like it was imitating a bunch of daytime birds, and it wasn't very good at it at all. I jumped up because I felt very vulnerable in the position I had fallen in and I slowly started backing up. My thought was to grab the gun and shoot at it but then it spoke. It sounded like a bird but it spoke human words. It was like a parrot that had been trained to speak. It said "Don't grab that gun Jim, don't do it." I was like eff this and dove into my tent for the gun. I heard a strange noise like flapping and I grabbed the gun and turned to face it again. It said, again in the bird voice, "don't do it JImmy." I was dumbfounded, confused and terrified all at the same time and I honestly felt like I was going to pass out at any second. Then, I saw the wings. This thing had wings that looked like ripped up bat's wings but they were twice the size of the entity itself. It smiled at me and the eyes went red. I screamed and almost cowered against the tree farthest from whatever this thing was. It once again made the sheep noise and it seemed to me like it was mocking me. Then, just as I gathered the courage to aim the gun at it, it took off into the night, making sure to fly directly above me so I could see its belly. It was daring me to shoot it.

I don't know how I knew some of the things I mentioned here but please understand I simply knew them. I knew them with all of my heart at that time. I've since tried to convince myself I saw the Jersey Devil and that's normally what I tell people now, after years of my telling the truth and them trying to convince me otherwise. It was the most horrifying and surreal encounter of my life but it wasn't the only one. I don't know what I saw and the only thing that I've come across that makes any sense is something called a mimic but the problem with that is, depending on who you talk to or where you are in the world, the definition of and parameters for that changes so I don't know. I tell the story of my encounter around the campfire a lot and at parties and I pretend like it was no big deal. I'm sure ninety percent of the people I tell about it don't believe me anyway and the ones who do are impressed I came that close to the Jersey Devil and survived. It wasn't the Jersey Devil. It was some kind of evil creature who I think was only showing me one of its forms that night. It seems now looking back like it had been toying with me the whole time and knew exactly what it was doing. Mimics feed off of your fear. They're energetic vampires so that still makes the most sense to me. I don't know why it chose me, if it chose me or if I was just in the wrong place at the wrong time. I guess I'll never really know and for now, that's all I have.

CHAPTER EIGHTY

MY NAME IS Sharon and this is the first time I have ever mentioned what I witnessed in the woods near my home in Texas, back in 1993. I was always afraid that people would think that I was crazy or something because back then you just didn't discuss things like this. There wasn't any reality television yet and discussions about the paranormal didn't take place that often except in the context of maybe watching a scary movie or reading a book about the supernatural. I only decided to write about this now, after all these years, because my daughter came home hysterical last night and described something she saw on the side of the road, just outside of a very densely wooded area near my house and I'm sure it was the exact same creature I had seen when I was camping out there in my youth. I didn't even tell her yet but it just reinforced to me that what I saw was real and that whatever it was, it's still lurking around in those woods.

I was twenty years old and didn't have a care in the world. My friends and I spent most of that summer partying in the woods. We weren't heavy drinkers, even at that age, and when I say we partied I mean listened to music and smoked cigarettes. We didn't do drugs and we just liked the peace and quiet of the woods. We also liked the fact that we didn't have to deal with our parents while we were out there.

We all still lived at home and I was attending a local community college at the time. I had been camping in those woods tons of times with my friends and their families and with my family as well. It was a familiar place and I never thought anything could ruin the tranquility of those woods for me. I was about to be proven very wrong about that though. We were hanging out like we normally would be and then we realized none of us had any cigarettes. We pooled our money together and had come up with just enough to get the cheapest brand there was. We all had money, we just didn't have it on us and none of us felt like walking home to get any. I was with my two buddies, Gene and Nader and each one of them offered to go to the store for all of us, so we all didn't have to take the trek out there. We had gone into the woods on two four wheelers. They had their own and I didn't so I always rode shotgun on one of theirs. Let me preface all of this by saying it wasn't unusual that we would all be in the woods well into the middle of the night. It wasn't anything new for us to have been out there in the dark though none of us had ever really been alone out there once the sun went down. It was creepy and we just thought it was smarter to all be together. I didn't realize how late it was or how dark it was getting when I told them both to just go and that I would wait right there for them until they got back. They took the ATV's because there was a trail that if they traveled it far enough it would come out right behind the only convenience store in town. They each did the gentlemanly thing and offered to stay with me but I reminded them I wasn't a princess and didn't need protecting and so they gave up and left. It was nice being there for a little while alone with my thoughts and my favorite music.

I liked 80s love ballads but couldn't tell them that and so once I couldn't hear the quads anymore I blasted my favorite eighties station that played the most popular slow songs of the decade and knew I had about a half hour or so to listen to them and sing at the top of my lungs before the boys got back. My joy only lasted five minutes though because that's about the time the sun started setting and I knew they wouldn't be back before it became fully dark outside. They should have been but I knew them, they would have a smoke and chit chat first and probably flirt with the girl behind the counter at the convenience store. It would more than likely take them forty five minutes to an hour to return instead of a half hour like it would have if they had just gone and come right back and waited until then to have their smoke. The woods got really quiet and super eerie when the sun had finally fully set and I felt extremely uncomfortable. It seemed like there was nothing alive out there, in the vastness of the dark forest. No owls hooting or small rodents running around. It was creepy and the chills I was experiencing throughout my body had nothing to do with the weather. It was a really warm night in the middle of a hot Texas summer. I turned the radio down to low and just sat there, alone with my thoughts. I had brought a backpack with me that held some snacks, a couple of juice boxes and my sketchpad and pencil. I began to sketch random things that popped into my mind. It was something I always did and at that point I was doing it almost absentmindedly, as a distraction.

I turned the radio completely off and tried to listen for the sounds of the quads so I wouldn't have to be alone anymore and because I was sort of really needing a cigarette at that point. I didn't hear anything though and I had one of those book light things attached to my sketch pad so I could see. There were flashlights in my bag and I grabbed one of those out as well. Suddenly I heard what I thought was crying and it sounded like it was coming from somewhat close by, like fifty feet in front of me and through some taller trees and grass. There was a strange area in that forest and it was right near all of the boulders and rocks my friends and I always hung out near and on which I was then sitting. I listened closer and sure enough it sounded like a little kid was moaning. I have two younger siblings who are much younger than me because my parents adopted them when I was twelve years old. The crying sounded like it was coming from a five or six year old. I was immediately concerned and had forgotten all about how creepy that one area was, how we had always made it a point to stay as far away from it as possible and never take that one particular trail. However, whoever was crying was directly on that path and I knew I couldn't just sit there, doing nothing. It was early in the evening still but I couldn't imagine leaving a lost little child to fend for itself out there and more than likely it was someone I knew or their child. I took my flashlight and hesitantly walked the trail to see if I could help the little kid who was obviously in some sort of trouble. I called out but received no answer.

I'll admit I started to almost immediately become creeped out again and I was getting agitated because my friends weren't back yet and should have been, more than an hour ago. I kept walking towards the low crying and I kept calling out and asking if anyone needed help. The soft crying continued but no one was answering me. Eventually, I thought I saw a little kid standing near a tree, facing it with its head in its hands. I could only make out the general shape of it though and as I got closer I saw it looked like it was kneeling there. I called out but didn't approach the child because I didn't want to scare it in any way. When it didn't answer me I called out again but the only response I got was a giggle and then it ran away. I followed after it, once again annoyed, and asked them if they needed any help. I told them if they ran from me again I wouldn't be able to help them but the crying started up again and I wholeheartedly thought that I had caused that by saying I wouldn't help them anymore. I didn't know if they were trying to play or if I had mistakenly heard giggling when really it had been something else. I was confused and something about the whole situation just didn't seem right. I walked up a somewhat steep hill and came to a clearing. I wasn't familiar with that area because like I said my friends and I had always avoided the trail that led there because it just didn't look right to us. I used to think that we were just very superstitious or something but I've been back in those woods many times since the night I am telling you about now when I had my encounter and while I still won't go near that spot because of what I had experienced, no one else who I am ever with seems to want to take that particular path either. There's something wrong with the energy and it's obvious from the minute you lay eyes on it.

Anyway I saw the kid again and it couldn't have been more than four feet tall. It looked very dainty and ultra thin. I once again immediately felt bad for it. I called out again, trying to sound gentle and not wanting to take my eyes off of the child because I was afraid it would run away. I approached him or her, very slowly, announcing that I was a friend and just wanted to help as I did so. I didn't dare aim my flashlight directly at it because I thought it would run again. Once I got within three or four inches of them, they were still facing the tree and had their back to me, they turned around. To do this they needed to stand up and that's what I have such a hard time understanding. It turned and stood up so fast and all at once the thing I was looking at was not a child at all but was some sort of ghoul or something. It grew to be about seven feet tall and let out an incredibly loud shriek. It looked sort of like what we know nowadays as the rake entity but I just don't know. I would have otherwise believed it definitely was the rake, had it not been for the fact it had seemed, sounded and looked like a dainty, sickly little child just seconds before and up until that point. It hovered over me and I couldn't turn and run away from it fast enough. It shrieked again. It was hairless with grayish white skin. It had yellow and jagged teeth and normal looking legs and arms, albeit they were super skinny. The eyes were pitch and pure black and the hands looked like the talons of some oversized bird of prey. Before I made a run for it I suddenly heard the sound of my friend's quads come rumbling through the woods and the creature seemed very frightened by the sounds. It screeched again but then turned and crouched back down again. I could see its backbone sticking out grotesquely and the shape of its spine was terribly crooked as were its knee and elbow joints. It grabbed something off the ground in front of it, turned to me, shrieked loudly and aggressively one more time and then bounded off on all fours back into the wilderness. It was gone by the time I had opened my eyes from blinking once.

I turned and ran, screaming out for my friends the whole time. I was crying and shaking and I cursed at them for leaving me there alone for so long. They said they had run out of gas and that they had to convince the girl at the store to let them have some gas that they would pay her back for the following day. I was so angry I started pounding Nader in the chest and they both looked at me like I was insane. They kept asking what happened but I demanded they take me home. I didn't speak to them the entire way and once we got to my house I wordlessly hopped off the back of one of the quads and went inside. I went straight to my room and cried myself to sleep. I woke up the next morning thinking it may have all been a nightmare until

Nader called and asked if I was okay and if I wanted to talk about what had happened. I knew I had two choices, I could either embarrass myself and tell them it had been some perfectly normal thing that I had mistaken for something else and have them laugh at me or I could tell them the truth about what I had really seen and hope they didn't laugh at me. I thought if I chose to tell them the truth they might just believe me and then, knowing how they were at the time, they would have wanted to go searching for it. I didn't want any part of that and so I laughed and told them I had thought I saw a huge bear and it had freaked me out. I was right, they both laughed and never actually let me live it down either. I laughed along with them but I was always terrified of that one spot in the forest ever since and I still am to this day.

My daughter told me she was driving home from work and saw what looked like a little child on the side of the road and so she had stopped. She pulled over to the shoulder and yelled out her window, asking the little kid if they were okay. She thought it odd that the kid wasn't facing her but when it turned around and ended up being a seven foot tall, grotesque humanoid being instead of a child, she drove away as fast as she could. I guess I should tell her now what I saw all those years ago. Those woods connect to the backyard of the home I live in with my daughter, her son, my husband and our two other children. Also, where she saw it was only a half of a mile down the road from us. I am more than petrified and pray to God none of us will ever have to deal with whatever it was again. Something inside of me though is telling me we haven't seen the last of it.

CHAPTER EIGHTY-ONE

MY ENCOUNTER with the black eyed children happened in the eighties but lately, like in the past twenty years or so, there's been so much about them online that it has validated my experience enough in my own mind that I feel like I can finally talk about what happened to me. I have incessantly searched through encounter stories and read every book imaginable on the phenomenon and I haven't seen anything exactly like what I experienced but the one difference, that being what they eventually asked me for, might explain a lot when it comes to understanding these so-called children. Maybe it won't make a difference at all and might even further confuse the issue, I honestly don't know but what I do know for sure is that my story needs to be heard. I need to get it off my chest for once and for all. I was twenty five years old and had just bought a bunch of land in the middle of nowhere in Mississippi. I got the land at a really great deal and even I was a little skeptical as to why that was, even way back then. However, I didn't want to ask too many questions or as they say, "look a gift horse in the mouth" and so I just paid the money and then set about building on the property. While the land I purchased was just enough to build myself a little cabin out there in the middle of nowhere and have a few nice acres of backyard, once it was all cleared out, the place itself was surrounded by the densest woods I had ever been inside of. I mean, there didn't seem to ever be a way out other than where the woods met my new property. I spent hours walking, for miles and miles, in every possible direction over the years and I still have no idea where those woods end. I still live in the cabin and let me tell you I fully understand now why the land was such a bargain. I have had more experiences with all different types of entities than I could write about in several books. The scariest one, by far, was the one I am telling you about right now. It was also the very first time I realized it wasn't my new home and it wasn't me, and that all of the phenomenon and terrifying things that were happening to me there, were the result of something inside of the woods.

Yes I believe the black eyed kids who visited came from the woods but I believe there's something more than that going on here. Something like perhaps an ancient curse or maybe just some very old evil that was somehow unleashed. Whether I did it with all of the clearing and construction or whether it was always active is a question I've never been able to answer. I've tried and have had one expert after another come one after the other but no one ever has any clear answers for me. Such as it always is when dealing with this type of thing though, right? The cabin took almost a year and a half to build, including furnishing it and clearing out my acreage for the backyard but finally it was ready for me to move in. I was ecstatic because I had worked so hard for so long to have this dream come true and the cabin really was that for me. I lived by myself and didn't know when or if that was going to change anytime soon. The place was small but it had enough room to accommodate one more adult and a child, just in case. I worked for my father and was able to do most of what I needed to do from home. That was perfect because I don't know how I would have made a "regular" job work for me with how far off the grid I was living. This place was like if you were at a summer camp or renting a cabin somewhere because you wanted to escape reality and pretend you lived among the trees and with the animals, all alone in the wilderness. Well, I really did and I couldn't have been happier. That is, until the activity started. I don't want to get too much into other things here because I need to focus on the black eyed kids but there were other phenomena happening in my home from the day I moved in. I had a haunting, if you will. It was uncomfortable but never felt dangerous and so I honestly just ignored it as best as I could and went on with my life.

I would hike in the woods all the time and didn't even own a vehicle. I couldn't really because there would have been nowhere for me to park it. I went out for my nightly walk one night at around dusk. I planned on walking about a mile into the woods and then turning and heading back home. There was so much ground to cover but I wanted to familiarize myself with my surroundings and so once a week I would choose a new path. That night was one of those nights but within minutes of being on that one path I felt like I had somehow gotten lost or completely turned around because a dense fog settled over the woods and I couldn't see much in front of or around me. I stopped to try and get my head together because I felt very disoriented. I heard what sounded like little kids talking in hushed tones but something sounded off about it. I decided to head right back the way I came and forego the rest of my walk that night. The whole time I was heading back to the cabin I heard those same hushed voices and there were also a few times when I thought I heard someone walking behind me. I never saw anyone though and once I got back home I locked all my doors and windows because I felt inexplicably terrified. I couldn't pinpoint what was making me feel that way but it was almost primal. The feeling didn't go away as I took a shower and put on my pajamas. It was still with me and had reached almost a fever pitch when I got comfortable on the couch to try and watch some television before going to bed for the night. Within minutes of turning on the tv I heard people talking in my backyard. Now, please understand my nearest neighbor was several miles away and it was a hell of a trek to get to them too. There shouldn't have been anyone there and I cautiously made my way to the kitchen window in order to look out and see who was there. It looked like three kids who were huddled up in a little group and talking in low voices. The hushed tones sounded exactly the same as they had in the forest earlier in the night and at that moment my anger overwhelmed the primal sense of fear and dread that had been with me ever since I stepped into that fog. I yelled out my window for them to get the hell out of my backyard and off of my property.

They turned all at once and they almost seemed to move in unison. I saw their black eyes immediately and couldn't move away from the window because I was so struck with terror. I just stood there staring at them as they made their way towards me. I was inside and they were in the yard. I knew all of my doors and windows were locked but somehow that didn't make me feel any better. They were walking quickly and all three of them were staring right at me. They made no attempt to hide their eyes either. Their skin was pale but it was more ashen than white and they all had short, black hair. They were all male and wearing black hoodies and blue jeans. They moved in unison, were dressed exactly the same and they all had the same dark and soulless orbs where eyes should have been. I don't know why I was immediately gripped with terror like I was. I mean, I still hadn't really calmed down from earlier but this was a whole new level.I tried to tell myself to relax and that it was just a few kids trespassing. Maybe it was the eyes. I knew I was in some sort of extreme danger and so I turned off all the lights and turned off my tv. I then went to the front door and looked out the peephole. The porch light was on but other-wise the house was completely dark. They were out there and as soon as I went over to the door, despite my having been so incredibly quiet, they were all looking at me through it. "Let us in!" The one standing a little closer to the door demanded. I could see their lips looked strange, almost like they had been painted on with lipstick. Also, as he said this, his lips weren't moving in time with what he was saying. It was almost like there was some sort of delay, kind of like when you're watching movies in a different language and your language is dubbed over the person who is talking? It was like that. I was shaking and I started slowly backing away from the door. I didn't know where I planned on going but I knew I had to get as far away from the door as possible.

As I backed away they banged on the door and yelled for me not to run away. Only one kid was speaking and his tone was monotone and robotic. It was without a recognizable accent. It sounded like really good AI that we have nowadays sometimes in narrations and things like that. The fact that they not only knew I was there but that they immediately knew I had backed away from the door was too much and I ran into the living room where there were no windows and no door and sat upright on my couch just praying they would go away and never come back. However, that didn't happen. Anyone who knows about these "kids" knows they are nothing if not persistent. The one doing the talking then lowered his voice and tried, I think, to sound less demanding and more innocent. He asked me if I had any food and said he and his brothers were starving. I didn't answer. Then he switched tactics and said that his one brother needed to just use my bathroom quickly. I didn't answer. Finally it had been about five minutes and I hadn't heard anything so I crept back over to the door. As soon as I looked through the peephole I saw them and the one kid once again started speaking. He knew I was there, again! He then said the most terrifying thing anyone has ever said to me in my life, "mister, just give us the blood, Quick and painless. You won't die and then we can go and you never have to see us again." I thought I was gonna pass out. I turned and ran upstairs and locked myself in my bedroom. They kept banging on the door for another entire hour before finally I couldn't take anymore and crept back downstairs to grab my cordless landline phone. We didn't have cell phones back then and I threatened them that I was going to call the police if they didn't leave. The kid said, "no, I don't think you will be calling anyone tonight." I ran back upstairs and they kept banging on the door to my cabin. I was just about to dial 9-1-1 when I happened to glance out my bedroom window which looked out over the backyard where the woods were. The fog was back and the kids were all standing in a row and staring up at me. It was like they could see me which was absolutely impossible. Well, it should have been impossible, had they been human.

I turned the phone on and was about to start dialing but when I looked up again they were gone and so was the fog. They had vanished and taken the fog with them in a matter of a split second. I didn't leave my room or sleep that whole night. I had a little seat that lined up with the large bay window in my room and I just sat there all night long looking out the window. Every time I fell asleep I would jump up, thinking I heard banging on my front door. Like I said that wasn't the only time I ever had a terrifying paranormal experience in this cabin and I still live here and still have them. It's on a monthly basis but I never saw those kids again except in my nightmares. It's strange because in my nightmares they're knocking on the door and asking for my blood. They never get in and every single time I wake up there's a dense and unexplainable, seemingly random fog in my backyard, coming from the woods. I'll write about some more experiences soon. I don't know what they are or what any of it means but I am one hundred percent certain that it has to do with the woods surrounding my house. I stopped the nightly walks for about a year but then I started up again and still take them to this day. Nothing can scare me anymore, not after my experience with those black eyed kids. Well, maybe that fog, but I'm not sure yet.

CHAPTER EIGHTY-TWO

I GUESS I was like every girl growing up in the South, not that that was always a good thing. I have seen things in my life, things I cannot explain and things I wouldn't *want* to explain. Each time I witnessed something, I always buried it inside. Being ridiculed constantly is not something you want to go through all the time. In the beginning, I tried to tell others about all the wonders I saw, but no one ever believed me. After years of people not believing me, I decided to keep them just to myself. The things I have seen are not what I would consider "normal", so I had no choice but to bury them deep inside me.

My family fought a lot, over things that couldn't be controlled. Eventually, my dad had enough, and one day I came home from school and found my sister in tears and on the floor. My dad had walked out on us while we were at school. We had only been home for about an hour and in the distance, I heard his truck coming up from down the road. He had returned to get a few more things.

Mom and Dad got into one more argument before he turned to storm off. Before leaving he paused to tell me he was leaving our mother, not me. Well, the way I saw it, if you're not taking me with you, then you're leaving me too. It's just easier when you tell yourself that. You don't feel as guilty. He came back to get his bowling trophies. He wanted them. He wanted the trophies and not his children. I was 8 years old and the most important man in my life just walked out on me. I was devastated.

Mom didn't take it very well and as a result, she lashed out at us constantly. Often she became belligerent, so I stayed outside as much as I could. "Staying out of arm range", we used to call it. If she can't touch us, she can't see us. Outta sight, outta mind. Life had a way of being peaceful when we were invisible. As a result of growing up outside (raised by wolves I used to joke), I learned to appreciate nature in so many different ways. I would spend hours in the forest behind our house in the mountains.

The forest was always my escape. The trees always had a way of hiding me, of buffering the sounds of the world. I started walking down the path I made; inside the lush forest, the crisp scent of pine filled my lungs, invigorating my senses and made me take a deep breath, finally feeling alive. The trees towered above me and created a canopy overhead, casting dappled sunlight onto the moss-covered ground. With each step I took, a song of nature was played. It was the song of a soft crunch of fallen leaves, harmonizing with the symphony of singing birds and rustling leaves. It was here I felt most at peace. It was here I felt the safest.

One day, I found I needed to escape. The tension was fierce at home and I craved to be back in the forest, to be back in the arms of the mother I loved. When I saw a break in the arguing, I made a dash for the door. I ran as hard and as fast as my little feet could carry me, slamming through the screen door in the kitchen. Running across the yard, I could hear my mom yell for me to get back in the house, but I never stopped. The only thing I could hear was my heart beating in my ears, my breath as it escaped, being pumped by my arms like it was an old water pump. Finally, I made it to the treeline of my forest and I slowed to catch my breath. I was back home. I was in my forest.

As I walked deeper into the woods, an ethereal glow caught my eye through a gap in the tree line. I was intrigued. I had a feeling that the light was calling out to me, calling and asking me to follow it. There was an enchanting aura about the light, a radiance, that drew closer to me. I was mesmerized by all its allure. I was aware that the air was becoming tinged with magic. I felt myself beginning to fill with a sense of anticipation and wonder. I felt accepted and loved, possibly for the first time in my life. I lost my bearings; the trees above were thick and braided together and I could not see the sun. Only filtered light fell down from above.

After a few minutes of traveling through the forest, I saw the light growing brighter. I don't think I had ever walked this deep into the forest before. People were always telling me they were afraid of the things that lived in there. I didn't fear it. I had seen the face of evil as a child and I was forced to face it every day. This was, well, like a walk in the park.

I kept walking, the path leading me down a gentle slope. The path had turned into a dirt footpath. I could tell many had walked this way before me. I kept going and lost all sense of direction. The footpath was growing larger. I stopped for a moment and dug my big toes into the dirt and quickly flicked them up and forward. I loved to play in the dirt. It was the way I came back to nature. It was the way I grounded myself. I continued down the path, noticing how deeper the green was getting and how much cooler it was. Suddenly, I stumbled upon a hidden clearing, lit from above. The sunlight sparkled in a way I had never seen before. I know now that the light was reflecting off the drops of dew that were clinging to the pine needles.

Suddenly I was hit with a sense of vertigo. I stumbled a few feet and fell to my knees. A sense of nausea overcame me and I then heard a loud buzzing sound. I couldn't make sense of any of it. My vision blurred and before I knew it I fell forward face first into the dirt.

———

I woke and it was still daylight, but something was different, I don't know how to explain it. It was as if the light from the sun was brighter and the colors around me were more vibrant. I sat up and looked around. I was still on the trail, but all the trees, leaves, and grasses were a brighter shade of what they were before. I rubbed my eyes, wiped my mouth from the bit of vomit I had expelled and got to my feet. I brushed off my clothes and looked around. To my left, just off the trail and in the middle of the meadow I saw something I hadn't seen before. A small trail led to the spot and I had this urge to investigate. I made my way down the small and narrow side trail.

The sight that began to unfold before my eyes stopped me in my tracks and took my breath away. It was here, in this clearing, I found a miniature village, bustling with activity, lying nestled within the meadow. Delicate mushroom houses with tiny wooden doors stood before me in tiny neat rows. The tiny houses were adorned with vibrant flowers and gossamer curtains, exactly as I had seen in the storybooks. I couldn't help but stare in disbelief, looking at the tiny, intricate pathways, lined with pebbles and petals, that wove their way through the enchanting settlement, from house to house and door to door. I rubbed my eyes for a moment, not really believing what I was seeing. Fairies. Fairies are real. *Fairies are real!*

With stealth-like steps, I approached the fairy camp. I didn't want to scare them or frighten them away. Then again, I have heard that fairies could be mean and steal babies when you are not looking. I knew that wasn't true. I was able to look at this tiny hamlet and I knew, that was a story made up a long time ago. They must have made it up to keep people away and therefore it protected the fairy village. It was actually a brilliant idea. I laughed at the thought of fairies having their own PR firm, but I suppose they need something to help protect themselves from outsiders. When people are afraid, they won't come looking for you. And people feared fairies in this town. Not me, of course, I always wanted to believe in them.

With cautious steps, I slowly moved closer to the ground. I did not want to disturb the magical inhabitants. I stepped back closer to a tree. From behind a blossom-laden branch, I caught a glimpse of the fairies in their intricate attire. Their dainty wings glimmered in the sunlight; their dresses were made of petals and leaves. From my vantage point, I could see them as they flit about gracefully, their laughter echoing through the forest like tinkling bells, creating an enchanting symphony that danced in the air.

Curiosity began to overtake my initial trepidation. I decided to explore the fairy camp further so I crouched down and became nearly invisible amongst the shrubbery. I could have stayed there for hours. Now that I think about it, I *may have* stayed there for hours, observing the fairies as they engaged in their daily routines. It was Fairy Life! It seemed as if each fairy had a job to do. Some tended to delicate flower gardens, coaxing vibrant blooms to life with a touch of their magical essence. Others gathered dewdrops in tiny crystal vials, capturing the spirit and the feel of the forest in a shimmering liquid.

I was mesmerized and I really do not know how long I stayed there, hidden in the shrubbery. It only seemed like only a moment but I knew I had been hiding longer. I noticed a gathering at the center of the camp. There before my eyes were a group of fairies, circling around a small pond, the surface reflecting the kaleidoscope of colors from the surrounding flora. The fairies did not notice me because they were engaged in a lively conversation. Their voices were like a delicate song, a harmonious blend of musical tones. Eager to discover more, I began to slowly inch closer, careful not to disturb their spirited discussion.

I watched with pitched curiosity for I don't know how long. I wish now I had a camera but of course I didn't bring one. My leg began to fall asleep due to my position and I shifted my weight. Upon doing so I snapped a branch on the ground. It was so loud it might as well as been a banging drum or cymbal.

It was then I saw them look at me and like before I felt this wave of vertigo and nausea overcome me. I sat back and touched my head in a vain attempt to steady myself, but I was done. I could feel the crushing weight of unconsciousness coming. I fell backward this time, my head hitting a rock.

I woke and it was almost nighttime. I sat up abruptly. My head was pounding. I looked in the direction of where I'd see the fairy village but there was nothing there except a barren spot. I knew what I'd seen before or had I? Was this all some weird dream? But how did I fall down, then end up thirty feet away after another fainting episode. I walked to the clearing but there was nothing there. No houses, nothing. Not a sign that a fairy or village had been there.

Had I gone through some portal? I have so many questions and if you or anyone reading this can help me, I'd appreciate it. I know this story sounds fanciful, but I saw it. And if it wasn't, it was the most vivid and lucid dream I'd ever had.

CHAPTER EIGHTY-THREE

IN A TINY TOWN nestled among the rolling hills of Washington State, a small and mysterious paranormal podcast was once produced. Born of the light but drifting slowly in to the darkness, the fledgling podcast lived, struggling for any life on the airwaves it could possibly get. Gasping like it was in the town of Silent Hills, finding no life of its own and dying a slow death from lack of entertainment, the podcast was slowly fading away from the reality of this world. It wasn't a well received podcast; the host thought he was going to be a ParaCeleb, but looking back now I realize the Universe had a different plan for him.

Only in his delusional mind was he popular. Its host, Mick at the Mic, thought he had a knack for storytelling, delving into the eerie, spooky tales of the supernatural. Try as he might, Mick could never break the "fourteen viewers" mark of his podcast. Mick at the Mic saw himself as a "personality". Maybe it would have been better if he actually had one, but he didn't. Watching paint dry on a summer afternoon was more exciting than Mick's slow paced, monotone voice. But little did he know that soon, one of his stories, one of his tales of the wild and terrifying supernatural world would unleash an encounter, one that made all of our blood run cold.

As all stories begin, it was a dark and stormy night. Mick sat in his dimly lit home studio, or as we called it, his parent's basement. Determined to be the next greatest thing, Mick was researching for his next episode. I have to give him that much - he tried to find interesting topics to discuss, stories to tell. These stories, his tales, all fell upon deaf ears. But at least he tried.

I am able now to look back and see where the end started, now that I have put time and distance between us. It began this night, the night after we drove past the abandon Willoby Manor. The end began with Mick.

Mick had no life, not one really. He was fixated on the podcast. Every sentence he spoke, every word from his mouth was about the podcast. There was a metamorphosis of Mick, one that mutated the guy with the big heart into a person no one knew. The change in his personality began to drive a wedge through our paranormal team. No one wanted to be around him, much less investigate with him. It was like the podcast took on a life of its own and began to possess Mick the Mic.

As his ego began to grow, his self-deluded importance took over every conversation and our team, not wanting to be near him or even investigate with Mick, slowly began to break and drift away. Mick was becoming an island of one, and we all know what happens to the odd guy out in the horror movies.

For whatever reason, Mick had a publicist and thought he was on the road to stardom. He had a good heart, I am sure it was buried inside there... somewhere. Mick never realized, the publicist was just someone taking him for a ride and liberating him from his money. As his friends, we all tried to gently talk him down, off this self imposed cliff, but Mick swore he was leaping into fame and fortune. Only from the outside can I now see you can't leap anywhere, when you're down in the basement of existence.

The team and I began to drift apart and no one tried, not even in the least, no one tried to keep us together. One by one, we stopped wearing our matching black shirts and began to strive for independence. Some began to strike out on their own, others joined forces with other, more established teams, and then there were a few of us who turned and walked away from the paranormal field. The bitter taste of

Mick's constant narcissism left a sour taste in our mouths and we no longer wanted anything to do with it. I was in that group. I turned and walked away, stopping only when I was at a safe distance. I began to look at the dynamics of the group.

Feeling like I was the person on the Eight of Cups tarot card, I began to finally turn with the staff in my hand and walk away from a life that no longer satisfied me. Our drama free group had drowned in despair and disappointment. Like the cemeteries we so often visited, our Paranormal Group was finally dead, never to be resurrected again. At least, not while Mick was there. Mick did not care about our group, not really. He had changed. His only care was for himself, about his fourteen fans, and about the ParaCeleb he thought he was destined to become. Little did we know, this was the last time we'd ever see this incarnation of our friend, Mick the Mic. He was on a path that would change his life.

The night we drove past Willoby Manor particularly stands out from all the others. After an uneventful investigation, we all went back to Mick's parent's house and down into the basement. The way he saw it, it was an honor for us to be in the same room, in the room where the podcast lived. But to us, it was just our way of decompressing after an investigation, laughing and joking about events that had just transpired.

As we all sat around the 1970s wagon wheel shaped table flanked in the room of wood paneling, I noticed Mick feverishly clicking away on his computer, browser tabs popping open at a hurried pace. Searching through the internet, Mick thought that if he could find the one story, the one twist, find a tale never heard before, he would at last break the "fourteen viewer" mark that had plagued his entire, non-illustrious podcast career.

Speed reading and grunting, Mick's eyes glazed across open tabs. It wasn't long before he stumbled across the story of an old folktale. It was a story about a vengeful ghost. "A vengeful ghost" he muttered to himself. "Maybe that would be the one thing that would up my viewer count." Collectively, the team rolled our eyes and groaned. How was it that he could not see that he was destroying the group? We started as a drama free group, all of us equal, all of us wanting to research into the world of the paranormal. Mick's obsession with himself and the podcast was the beginning of the end for our little group. The more he over-inflated himself, the more space his ego took. There wasn't room for a "star" in our group and it was only a matter of time before his ego super nova'd.

That night after our last investigation together, as we sat around the wagon wheel table, Mick was quickly doing a Google search, looking for more information. This was going to be the next subject for the podcast. Mick was pushing into his early 50s, still living at home, and had no job. The Podcast was all he had. When he felt the need, and also at his publicist's urging, he did several podcasts a week, at random times.

Having more than our fill of Mick the Mic, we left all decided to leave and to go home. That didn't stop Mick. He was at least nice enough to look up from the laptop and tell everyone good-bye, but then instantly began tapping away at the computer keys again. Only folklore could be found on the open tabs, and Mick decided that it was going to be the truth. At least that was the way he was going to tell it.

The vengeful ghost was said to haunt an old dilapidated and abandoned mansion on the dark outskirts of town. Intrigued, he couldn't resist sharing the chilling tale with his listeners. Mick had the entire hour now, hours of life ticking away to the sound of his own voice. He was alone now, having driven away his co-host with his inane rambling about how great he was, how he could walk between the dark and light of life. Looking into the broken mirror of reality, Mick was fine with being a lone podcaster. I mean, after all, it gave himself more time to talk and that's what his listeners really were interested in - listening to Mick talk. Or so he imagined. It is dangerous when you live in a house of mirrors and you never stop to look at yourself. Take a honest and real look at yourself, for better or for worse. Accept what you see, for accepting is the roadmap to recovery. We all knew Mick was in deep denial and there was a long road ahead of him, a road to redemption. Even though he broke our team apart, we were still there for him... but just maybe this time, we were a bit further down the road, still willing to support him.

Tuesday night arrived. Like a demonic grandfather clock, time ticked down and finally, it was time for Mick to start the podcast. And so it began.

Unbeknownst to Mick, his voice droned on, and reached far beyond the realm of the living. The dull, monotonous, slow-paced cadence resonated within the spirit world, angering and awakening the very ghost he spoke of - the tormented soul of the long-forgotten resident of Willoby Manor. Filled with rage and desperation, the ghost materialized like he was the ghost of Bloody Mary appearing in a mirror, eager to seek retribution.

The following night, Mick the Mic resumed the podcast, oblivious to the supernatural entity that had been awakened by his tedious tales of unstimulating monotony. As he recounted the ghost's tragic story, strange occurrences began to unfold around the clueless podcast host. Lights, positioned in a three-point lighting fashion flickered on and off, fabricating shadows that created a distorted view of Mick's face, making his cherub-like cheeks appear sinister. Objects took on a paranormal life and moved on their own. An icy chill permeated the room, creating a breathy mist in front of Mick's lips as he spoke.

Unnerved, but committed and dedicated to his craft, Mick pressed on. After all, Mick was a podcast host and in his mind, that was the same as being a superhero. Not realizing the peril he had unwittingly invited into his life, Mick continued on. His voice carried into the void, emitting a infrasound so low, human ears were not able to detect it. It was with this low vibration Mick was able to reach the spectral being, annoying the entity with each passing word. The ghost began to shift dimensions, leaving his reality and began to grow stronger, drawing into the 3-D world and nearer to Mick's physical plane.

Not long into the podcast, Mick began to experience the presence of the entity firsthand. Whispers echoed in his ears, even louder and crescendoing to a deafening pitch when the room was silent. A frigid, cold breath lingered on his neck, like a kiss from a long dead lover, sending shivers down Mick the Mic's spine. Always in prime form, the podcast host sensed a malevolent force lurking nearby, just beyond the superhero's field of vision.

As the encounters intensified, Mick's resolve wavered. Fear gripped his heart sending waves of terror down his spine and into his solar plexus. Mick was frightened to his core. He had never experienced fear such as this and for the first time in the podcast host's tenure, he considered abandoning his podcast all together. Mick took a deep breath and knew that was not an option. His fourteen fans were counting on him, counting on him to provide the stability of another podcast from the depths of the basement of Mick's parent's house. He had an obligation to continue on with the podcast, but deep down, he knew that he had to confront the source of this paranormal torment. Looking back on the events of the night, no one can remember how he managed to do it, but Mick continued on with the podcast.

For the first time in his life, he was relieved when the podcast was over for the evening. He knew what had to be done before he could continue on with another show. Driven by determination, Mick took matters in his own stubby hands and started to actually research the history of the abandoned mansion, hoping to uncover the key to appeasing the vengeful ghost who haunted the halls of Willoby Manor. After hours of research, he learned of a tragic love story that had unfolded within its walls... an unrequited romance that had led to despair and eventual death. Mick was not a stranger to unrequited love and felt that he must persevere and move beyond his fear, finally revealing the truth. After all, he was a podcast host.

Armed with this knowledge, Mick hatched a plan of epic proportions. Zoinks! The gang from those Saturday morning cartoons would surely be proud of Mick the Mic. Alone and with out a team of "Black Shirters", he returned to the mansion, arriving back and equipped with digital recording equipment, IR Cameras, electromagnetic meters and cat balls, all in hopes of communicating directly with the spirit. It is common knowledge to those of us who work in the paranormal world that all entities love to play with cat balls. Never mind the scientific equipment and documenting in any scientific way any paranormal activity, if the cat balls light up that is a sign that a ghost is present.

Admittedly, it is thinking like this that helped me with the decision of walking away from a team. It is better to stand alone in your truth. As Mick stepped into the decaying structure, he realized he was standing alone in his version of the truth. The ghost's presence grew overwhelming.

In the darkness, Mick spoke directly to the ghost, his voice trembling but filled with empathy. Recounting the tale of lost love, remember what the feeling is like, and expressing his understanding of the spirit's pain, Mick pleaded for forgiveness, promising to spread awareness of the ghost's tragic tale to the living. It would be a great story for the podcast.

Gradually, the ghost's anger subsided, replaced by a sense of sorrow and longing. It recognized Mick's deep knowledge of unrequited love and genuine compassion and saw an opportunity to share its story, to be remembered and acknowledged once more. I firmly believe that is a reason why entities continue to walk the earth. It is not due to "unfinished business". They continue to walk in this dimension because they have a story that wants to be heard, they want to be validated and also because they still seek love.

Over the following weeks, Mick dedicated several of the podcast episodes to the ghost's tale. He recounted its tragic love story, capturing the attention and sympathy of his fourteen listeners. The ghost found solace in being heard, finding a sense of closure as its story resonated with people from all walks of life.

In the end, the ghostly attacks on Mick ceased, and a newfound peace settled upon the halls of the abandoned Willoby Manor. Mick's podcast continued, with the mystery of the ghost of Willoby Manor becoming one of its most popular episodes. Unfortunately for Mick the Mic, his viewership did not increase. In fact, it dropped by a few loyal viewers. The town's residents, once skeptical of the supernatural, began to acknowledge the existence of a world beyond their own. And this is what most entities really want... to be heard, to be validated, and to be loved.

And so, the ghost's vengeance transformed into a lasting legacy - one that reminded the living to tread carefully in the realm of the supernatural, while also emphasizing the power of empathy and the importance of listening to the unheard voices that linger in the shadows.

CHAPTER EIGHTY-FOUR

I WAS ten years old and it was the summer of 1978. I was ten years old and had spent much of my life exploring the woods near my house. I was a typical ten year old from that time, meaning if I could get out and not be home I would. I didn't have video games so I found fun in hanging with my friends, building forts, playing war, and other assorted games or simply riding our bikes all around the county. This particular story I'm about to tell happened to me while I was heading to see a good friend. I could have simply hopped on my bike and rode to his house, but that would have taken three times as long versus taking the short cut through the woods.

The sun was setting, casting a warm glow over the trees. The birds were singing their evening songs, and the leaves rustled in the gentle breeze. It was peaceful and serene, and I felt at ease. The magic of woods was absolutely in the air. I was enjoying the hike, my mind fixed on the fun games I'd be playing at my friend's house when I heard something that made my blood run cold. It was a sound like no other, a mix between a howl and a scream far off in the distance. It echoed through the trees, sending shivers down my spine. I tried to ignore it much like tonight. I kept thinking it was just an animal, but then I heard footsteps.

The footsteps were heavy and deliberate, like someone or something was stalking and circling me. I turned around, but there was no one there. I tried to walk faster, but the footsteps followed me, getting closer and closer.

That's when I saw it. A wolf came out of the woods. However, this wasn't really a wolf, this was something else. It looked like it was trying to have the appearance of a wolf. I looked into its yellow glowing eyes, there was something wrong with them. They looked like a reptiles pupils.

Its giant jaws opened into a wide yawn but instead of a yawn a twisted voice whispered my name, "Jooooeeeeeyyy." I froze in terror as it approached slowly. Like any 10-year-old boy, I was ready to piss myself. Its fur was dark as night, and its teeth were sharp as knives. It circled me, sniffing at my scent, sizing me up as its prey. I knew I had to run, but my legs wouldn't move. The thing lunged at me, its jaws snapping shut just inches from my face. I stumbled backward and fell to the ground.

The wolf thing stood over me, its eyes gleaming with hunger. I closed my eyes, waiting for the inevitable, but then I heard a voice creep out of its jaws, "Joooeeeeyyyy."

I was about to scream when a strange voice and language echoed through the woods. I turned to look and it was an old Navajo woman in the distance. She shouted something in her native tongue, and the thing recoiled in fear. It turned and ran back into the woods, disappearing into the darkness.

The old woman kept her distance. I got to my feet and ran back towards my house. I made it home safely, no wolf or woman in pursuit.

My mother could see the fear written all over my face and asked me what happened. I stuttered that I'd see a wolf. She consoled me and told me it was probably a large dog. My dad was in the other room and came in to ask me a few questions before leaving with his shotgun. He said it was probably some feral rabid dog and having it roam around was dangerous for all around. (I laugh, these were the days when people took care of business themselves. Now people would call the police or animal control. My dad was a strong and tough man. I miss him.)

I didn't want my dad to go alone, I offered to go with him, but he insisted I stay home.

The entire time he was gone my mind spun with images of him being torn apart by the wolf. That never occurred. He returned home an hour later and said he hadn't seen anything, but did say something I won't forget. He said he did hear a woman's voice in the woods and that it was speaking in a language he wasn't familiar with.

It was the woman, she was still there protecting people.

My dad dismissed the woman's voice as just someone's voice carrying from a house and said he'd venture back out tomorrow to look for the 'dog'. He called some of his friends and told them.

He did go back out the next day, but like the night before didn't find anything. He also didn't hear the woman's voice.

No one ever reported seeing a wolf or rabid dog in the area and soon it was forgotten.

———

I don't know if anyone will believe my story. But I know one thing for sure: that thing is out there. I believe it was a skinwalker or wendigo, and the woman, was a Navajo spirit who came to my aid and saved me. I believe to this day that if she hadn't appeared I would have been dead for sure.

It had been thirty years since that fateful night in the woods, but the memories still haunt me. Every time I close my eyes, I see the creature's glowing eyes and can hear the bone-chilling way it said my name. I had tried to forget about it, to move on with my life, but it has always been there, lurking in the back of my mind. That's why I will never go back to the woods.

CHAPTER EIGHTY-FIVE

DURING OUR ANNUAL ELK HUNT, which we go on during the last week of August and early September in central Idaho, we encountered something unusual.

The first two days were normal with no activity. We were just glassing for elk and fishing. On the third day my friend, Bob shot his elk.

It was that night that things started to get...weird.

We put some loins on an old saddle rack (about 4' high) for lunch the next day. The next morning they were gone with no trace of anything climbing or dragging them away. The rack would not of held up to anything of weight climbing on it. It was like something had picked them up and walked away.

The next night one of the hunters was awakened by something pushing on his feet through the tent wall. He asked his son if he was pushing on his feet but his son said denied doing so. He mentioned it the next morning to us as well, but none of us, while pranksters now and then, hadn't done anything like that. The last thing you want to do is scare people who are armed.

The next night I was awakened about 2:00 am by something dragging my tent. I thought I was dreaming at first but realized I wasn't. I grabbed for my light but the tent quit moving as I rolled over. My first thought was a bear was trying to break in but I could not hear any breathing like a bear which would be easy to hear at two feet. Something else strange was I couldn't hear moving outside the tent.

I kept my light on and laid there until morning. At daylight I exited my tent and found an old elk jaw at the doorway and the tent had been moved about three feet. I checked the elk jaw and tent for teeth marks or tears but there was none. Whatever had moved the tent would had hands, there weren't claw marks or tears on the tent.

I asked my friends and of course everyone denied. I pressed them but they all were adamant it wasn't them.

Everyone was now feeling a bit off. Each had their own odd incident.

We went hunting again and Brad got himself an elk. We dressed it and had it hung on a tree just feet from the campsite. That night was the crescendo of the trip.

While we were sitting around the fire telling stories and laughing. We all heard rustling near the hanging elk. Already on alert we jumped to our feet.

Brad was first to step forward. He wasn't about to have some animal carry off his hard earned elk. He flipped on his flashlight and there towering over the elk was the hulking figure. I saw it for a few seconds before it raced off.

A couple friends went to their tents and grabbed their rifles while I stood there in awe of what I'd just seen.

The creature, whatever it was, crashed through the forest. It sounded like it was tearing the trees and anything in its path apart.

Brad checked on the elk, it was fine, but around it he found large footprints.

We all agreed to create a watch through the night and agreed we'd end the hunt in the morning and head home early. None of us openly admitted it, but we were a bit scared.

We woke in the morning, packed, and headed home. We have since joked about it, but I'll tell you this, we never went back to that hunting location again.

CHAPTER EIGHTY-SIX

IT WAS 2009 during West Virginia's late antler-less deer season when I had this extraordinary sighting. Arriving at the area just after 3:00 pm, I parked my vehicle in a parking area about a half mile from the area I wanted to go to.

Eager to get into the field as swiftly as possible, I embarked on what seemed to be an old logging trail right behind the parking lot. Aware of my late start, my goal was to traverse the logging trail until I reached the deeper sections of the river bottom.

After about 30 minutes of hunting along the trail, I gained a clear view of the expansive river bottom to my right. Encouraged by the possibility of deer emerging from the dense thickets along the river at dusk, I decided to venture further into the bottomlands. As I left the logging trail, I came across another path, which I followed, delving deeper into the valley.

The road ahead was frozen and encrusted due to the chilly temperatures, making it impossible to move silently. Realizing this, I traveled a short distance until I discovered a small group of trees a few yards away from the trail. Taking advantage of the cover, I settled among the trees. Not long after finding my spot, I detected what resembled the sound of brush breaking roughly 150 to 200 yards below me, towards the river. Anticipating a group of deer moving into the flats to feed, I readied myself. However, despite my hopes, no creatures materialized. Minutes passed, and I heard the sound again, but once more, no sightings. Determined to investigate further, I repositioned myself in another group of small trees, approximately 100 yards below my initial location. It was within this grove of saplings that I remained for 5 to 10 minutes until I noticed movement in a cluster of trees situated roughly 80 to 90 yards below me and to the left. Even without the aid of my scope, I could discern the motion with my naked eye. Intrigued, I peered through my scope, only to be taken aback by what I beheld.

Initially, my mind registered it as a large man—a vague silhouette emerging as the first image through my scope. However, as my focus sharpened, I found myself staring at what appeared to be a primate-like creature, standing upright and locked in direct eye contact with me. Breaking its stillness, the creature would slightly sway its upper body in an up-and-down motion, as if contemplating sitting down but deciding against it. This peculiar behavior persisted for what felt like over a minute. Finally, the creature departed from the group of trees, moving to my left (its right), heading towards the mountainous terrain behind me. It traversed an expanse of river basin, spanning an estimated distance of 70 to 80 yards, before vanishing into the woods beyond my field of view. Throughout its movement, the creature remained fixated on me, only momentarily breaking its gaze to peer straight ahead.

Initially, I entertained the idea of tracking its footprints, but my nerves got the best of me. Overwhelmed by a rush of emotions, I swiftly made my way towards the parking lot. While the creature had never displayed any overtly threatening behavior, I felt uneasy and decided it was not safe to continue hunting or linger in the valley after sunset any longer than necessary. I promptly vacated the area, encountering no further incidents on my way back to the vehicle.

CHAPTER EIGHTY-SEVEN

I'M a 45-year-old director of human resources residing in East Texas with my wife and three teenage children. Although I was born in the city, I've spent most of my life in the countryside, cultivating a deep passion for the outdoors, much like the rest of my immediate family and relatives. Now, let me share with you the astounding encounter I experienced in the pine woods of Northeast Texas—a story that remains etched in my memory.

———

It happened in late November 1992 when my wife and I went deer hunting with my aunt, uncle, and niece in a nearby 9,000-acre hunting lease. This particular area, bordering the Sabine River for five miles, stands as one of the most remote and secluded forest lands I've ever encountered. To us, skilled outdoorsmen, the thrill lies in finding these inaccessible hunting spots, and this one was no exception. It demanded a six-mile drive down old logging roads followed by a 15-minute ride on a four-wheeler, deep into the Sabine River bottomland. Our hunting excursion took place during the evening hours. After dropping off my wife at her tree stand, I walked for about 10 minutes down an old fire lane to reach my own perch. The silence of the woods struck me that evening, hinting at the presence of a formidable predator nearby. Three hours later, just before dusk, I heard the familiar crack of my wife's rifle. Curiosity piqued, I headed back to investigate. When I arrived at my wife's location, my aunt, uncle, and niece were already there, having heard the shot as they were making their way towards us on the four-wheeler for our planned rendezvous and the journey back.

My wife recounted how a group of four deer had appeared within close range of her tree stand. She successfully shot the largest one, causing the remaining three to flee into the woods. However, to her dismay, the wounded deer struggled to follow its companions. Rather than taking another shot, she reasonably assumed the deer wouldn't go far and waited for my arrival. The deer had sustained a fatal injury, leaving a noticeable blood trail. Even though the sun had already set when I arrived, we easily followed the trail using flashlights. Armed with two fresh flashlights and a high-powered rifle, my uncle and I left the rest of our party to track the deer. Based on the tracks in a damp area, we estimated the deer's weight to be between 160 and 180 pounds.

After approximately 100 yards into the woods, we reached the spot where the deer had made its final resting place. We discovered a significant amount of blood but no deer in sight, nor an immediate continuation of the trail. Instinctively, we circled the area, searching for any sign of the trail's continuation. When we finally picked it up again, it had become faint. Despite the trail dwindling to occasional drops of blood, it remained fairly easy to follow due to its straight trajectory through open woods.

About 15 minutes into tracking the new trail, we encountered a fallen tree that appeared to mark the end of the trail once more. It was a sizable sweet gum tree, too large for us to step over. However, after maneuvering our way across, we managed to find the faint trail again. As we moved forward from the fallen tree, the trail grew more sporadic. Eventually, we crossed a shallow creek with steep banks and picked up the trail on the other side. Roughly 50 yards past the creek, we reached a point behind a large white oak tree where the ground was heavily stained with blood—but still no deer. It was at this moment, when the previously direct and deliberate trail took a sudden 90-degree turn, that my uncle and I silently reached the same conclusion: someone or something was carrying the deer. It had to be a creature large enough to overcome the obstacles we had encountered, momentarily pausing behind the tree to ensure we were still following.

By now, it was well past sundown, and we had been trailing the deer for a good 45 minutes. The moon, shining brightly, illuminated our path, while my flashlight started to fade. Since my uncle's light was larger and brighter, we decided to switch mine off and conserve its remaining power. It was around this time that the entity decided to confront us.

It's not what we saw that struck us, for we never caught sight of it, despite being within 50 yards and separated only by a small clearing. Rather, it was the sound that left an indelible impression. Having experienced everything from panthers screaming to the charge of a 400-pound wild boar hog, I can confidently say that I had never heard anything like the noise this creature produced. To this day, I struggle to find adequate words to describe it other than "big."

The incredibly loud, roaring howl it emitted was unmistakable, leaving no room for misinterpretation. It was a clear message that the chase was over, and it was time for us to depart. The sound resonated so intensely that our party waiting on the fire lane heard it and assumed we were on our way back, playfully attempting to startle them. In response, this mysterious entity growled back at them, challenging their presence. The entire exchange rattled me to the core, taking me at least 30 seconds to realize that I was the one holding a semi-automatic high-powered rifle and a flashlight. Nevertheless, I remained alert and focused on pinpointing the source of the sound across the clearing, where the bright moonlight provided excellent visibility.

My uncle and I, having spent countless hours together in the woods, shared an unspoken understanding of our next move. I immediately flanked to the downwind side of the clearing, hoping to compel the creature to release the deer and flee, or perhaps drive it into the opening, where we could witness it in the moonlit night, or even force it to confront me in the tall, open timber, granting me a clear shot.

Perhaps it was my unwavering determination not to let this deer be the first one we ever lost, or some other subconscious motivation that propelled me. Nonetheless, our plan didn't yield the desired results. Whether this outcome was for the better or worse, only time would tell. I circled all the way around the edge of the clearing, eventually reuniting with my uncle. Regrettably, neither of us caught a glimpse of the creature. At that point, we concluded that it was time to head back.

As we commenced our journey back, about ten minutes into the walk, our party started calling out to us again. Before we could respond, something else decided to join the chorus. We continued our progress through the dense underbrush in the direction of the fire lane. Each time our party let out a call, the entity would respond in a challenging tone, and it was drawing nearer. As we approached the fire lane, the underbrush thickened, except for a single opening approximately 100 feet wide. Acting on instinct, my uncle and I took our positions on opposite sides of the opening. For whatever pursued us, it would need to pass directly between us before entering the fire lane.

Crouching in wait behind two substantial trees, we heard one of the four-wheelers start and drive away from our location down the fire lane. This prompted us to spring into action, heading for the opening and briskly making our way down the fire lane toward our party. When we reached them, my wife informed us that they had heard me exiting the woods and heading in the opposite direction along the lane, seemingly carrying something heavy. It's worth noting that I am a sizable individual myself, standing at 6'1" and weighing 240 pounds. However, it became apparent that it wasn't me they had heard emerging from the woods and walking down the fire lane, covered in dry leaves. I swiftly mounted the other four-wheeler and caught up with my niece before she unknowingly encountered whatever lurked ahead. We all rode home in silence, with little conversation. We had experienced enough hunting for one day.

Despite returning for several subsequent days, hoping to find vultures or any signs of the deer or its captor, we discovered nothing. The mystery remained unsolved, leaving us with only our vivid memories of that extraordinary encounter in the Northeast Texas pine woods.

CHAPTER EIGHTY-EIGHT

MY ENCOUNTER HAPPENED when my two best friends and I were visiting a lake and camping in the woods that surrounded it. It was the nineteen eighties and things were a lot different back then. The lake was a place where a lot of people would go and visit during the summer but once the fall rolled around it was normally very deserted. It was located far out of the way in the middle of nowhere and I think most people didn't think about how great it was to camp in because they only thought of that spot as being where the lake was. I hadn't seen too many people camping there in all the years I had been visiting that spot but it's not like there was never another human being doing so once summer was over. It was a big tourist spot in the summer though and that's why there were always so many more people around. My friends and I had just graduated from high school the previous summer and we were all attending the same community college. One weekend right after school had started again we all decided to go out to the lake and camp. There were dense woods all around the area except for one trail that was cleared out for the visitors. There was a lot to park your vehicle and a well worn trail that led from that lot to the lake itself. During the summer you would have to pay in order to camp there but once that season was over then it was basically first come first serve and the information center wasn't even open anymore for the rest of the year. My friends and I camped all the time growing up and so we were all very familiar with that spot and with the woods in our town in general. We were excited to be getting some down time because ever since we started college, we had all been struggling a lot.

We parked my friend's car and unloaded all of our equipment. We hiked into the woods and set up our tents and our camp. The weather was unusually warm and so we decided to go for a swim and the following day we planned on going fishing as well. There were a few places to do so in those particular woods. After we swam for a little while, built our fire and had something to eat we just relaxed. Eventually it was time to go to sleep and the three of us were very tired and looking forward to getting some rest. Our first night there was uneventful and we all slept fairly well. It did strike us as odd that we all had the same scared feelings like we were being watched and followed the whole second day we were out there. We were determined to make the most of it though and so that's what we did. We went fishing as planned but it was too cool to swim again on the second day. It didn't stop us from having a ton of fun and the whole time we were out there we didn't see another human being. Like I said, that wasn't too unusual but the fact that we hadn't seen a single animal either was a bit strange. I mean, it stood to reason there would have been small animals running around at the very least. There was nothing though and while I wouldn't exactly describe the forest as silent or anything, there definitely seemed to be a lot less activity than there normally should have been for that time of year. We tried not to think about it and convinced ourselves it was all just our own imaginations. That night though, we would learn that we weren't wrong and that something terribly odd and very scary was going on. We went to bed at around midnight and I fell asleep almost right away.

Each of us had our own little tent and we were all feeling a bit jittery by the time bedtime rolled around. This must have crossed over into my dreams because I had nightmares from the moment I closed my eyes until finally, at around two in the morning, I jumped up and felt fear and panic rising up inside of me. I peeked outside of my tent to try and see if my friends were awake. It looked and sounded like they were sleeping though and I had to go to the bathroom. I grabbed my toilet paper and walked to our designated spot in the woods. Everything was normal, except for the eerie silence that had been over the whole area since we got there. I started to walk back to my tent. That's when I noticed very bright lights inside of both of my friends' tents that made them almost look like they were glowing from the inside out. The light's seemed to be filling the entire tent with them inside and therefore it was much more than what our small flashlights would have been exuding at that point. Something about the lights struck terror right into my soul and I didn't want to go and investigate any further. I went back into my tent and prayed until I fell back asleep. I wasn't a religious person and can't tell you the last time I prayed before that moment but I was really scared. I had some nightmares again and jumped up in a cold sweat at around three in the morning. The minute I opened my eyes I knew something was wrong. I immediately had to shut my eyes again in order to block out the bright light that was inside of my tent. It was absolutely blinding and I imagined that's how it would have looked had the sun itself left the sky and floated down, somehow, into my tent. I heard a very soft voice in my head saying, "Shh! She's awake." I opened my eyes, squinting against the brightness, and when I did I saw a strange looking figure. It looked like a human being's face but it had a bald head and I couldn't tell if it was a male or a female. It had very small ears and the eyes were a dark and very piercing blue color. I wanted to scream but quickly realized I couldn't and that I couldn't move either. I was absolutely panicked and was starting to believe that someone was in my tent with me and that whoever they were, they were shining a bright light into my eyes.

I laid there, unable to scream or move for a minute or two and then finally I began to struggle. I heard a strange, soft and somewhat soothing humming noise that I somehow knew was meant to calm me down. I tried opening my eyes again and that's when I got a clearer picture of what was in my tent with me. It looked like a human, as I said, but the light looked behind it instead of all around it and me, as it had looked before when I opened my eyes for the first time. The entity looked like it had white wings of which I could only see the tops of them as it leaned in and stared at me, directly into my eyes. It had bright red lips and no nose but it wasn't scary looking at all. The skin was very pale white and it had no wrinkles. The skin was incredibly smooth looking and flawless. For a minute or two it just stared at me. It looked like it was leaning into the tent and staring directly at me. I felt like I was quickly falling into some sort of trance and despite my being terrified and having no idea what was happening, I kept falling in and out of sleep. Every time I would wake back up I wouldn't be able to move and the being would still be there, just staring at me. I tried to ask it what it wanted but my mouth wouldn't move and no words would come out either. I asked it telepathically though, I guess, just by thinking about it, and the entity smiled at me without revealing its teeth and told me to just relax. Then, it put its hand on my face and stroked my cheek. I shivered at how cold the touch was and I started fighting again because I didn't want that thing touching me. I stared at it, fearful and wondering what it would do to me next. I started making the connections about the lights I saw inside of both of my friends' tents earlier in the night and realized they must have also been visited by this same entity. I don't know if I passed out or just blinked but when I opened my eyes the sight was one of horror and terror and something I won't ever forget.

The bald and angelic looking being that had been in my tent with me the whole time had morphed into something else entirely. Perhaps it was another entity altogether, I honestly still don't know. It was suddenly evil looking with black eyes and dark gray skin that looked like it was peeling off in chunks. Underneath the gray color of the skin there was pink and red and it looked like where the chunks were coming off the skin there was nothing but blood and muscle. I tried once again to move so I could get away and I also tried to scream but it was in vain. I was paralyzed and silenced. I saw the wings had turned black and what I could see of them just by the creature leaning into my tent the way that it was, they looked all tattered and ripped up. It leaned in like it was going to kiss me but then stroked my cheek and smiled at me. Its teeth were disgusting, rotten and very sharp. Its eyes were black and the nose looked like it had been broken off and all that was left of it was the skeleton part. It was suddenly holding me down and its hands looked like a dark gray skeleton and where it was touching me burned as if I had been thrown into a fire. I started struggling and finally I was able to let out a blood curdling scream. The entity looked angry but disappeared in a brilliant flash of bright white light. My friends were soon climbing into my tent and asking me what was wrong. I told them and they couldn't believe what I was saying.

Both of them told me they had experienced the same things but they thought it had been a nightmare. Where the entity had held me down, and because my friends had the same experience, where it had held them down too, we all had burn marks in the shape of a large hand with long fingers in those specific spots. We were freaking out and we all got out of the tent. We looked around the camp with our flashlights but didn't see anything. All of the feelings of weirdness and the strange silence had disappeared altogether. Everything seemed very normal again, very suddenly. We were stunned and terrified and we didn't know what to do next. We decided to stay inside of one tent for the rest of the night and leave as soon as the sun came up in the morning. That's what we did. To this day I don't know if what happened to us was real or some sort of shared hallucination. It's unlikely it would be the latter because we didn't drink or do drugs, have no history of mental illness between the three of us and we were otherwise very normal girls. None of us were overly religious and none of us believed in the paranormal. Well, that night changed everything and for the most part we have all lived in fear of whatever that thing was returning for one or all of us. As far as I know neither of my friends have ever seen it again but they don't want to discuss it and they don't want to search for answers for fear it may stir something up and bring it to us again. I have gone along with them for all these years but recently one of my grandchildren told my daughter that she saw a bad man in her room, leaning over her bed. My daughter described for me what my granddaughter told her and it was the exact same thing that I experienced with my friends in those woods so long ago. When asked to draw the creature, my grandchild did and she drew the dark entity, the one we all saw second to the angelic type being. What does it all mean? I'm sure I have no idea but I can't imagine it's anything good. That's all I have to share on the matter now but I'll write again if I get any answers or have any more experiences with it or anything else.

CHAPTER EIGHTY-NINE

DURING THE FALL of 1981 and the following winter, while living in Washington State, I experienced three unusual events.

One incident occurred in August or September when a shack that some of us had built was mysteriously destroyed. It was a simple structure made of poles and trees, covered with plastic. Britt Jones, one of the guys who helped construct it, informed me about the wreckage. When I went to see it, I found the main poles snapped like toothpicks, chairs and the table broken, and a foul smell lingering in the area. I also noticed reddish hair around the trees, about three inches long.

The second event happened around October or November during a nighttime gathering on the hill above the football field. The fog was thick, and the full moon provided an eerie ambiance. Suddenly, the entire group fell silent, and we all turned our attention to a large bipedal figure within 30-50 yards of us. It was too big and muscular to be a human, and the moving fog created a fluctuating visibility. Some of us decided to approach it, while others ran in the opposite direction. Strangely, as we moved closer, I found myself unable to go any farther, and the figure disappeared into the fog within a couple of minutes.

The third incident occurred during a severe snowstorm one winter evening. Two students rushed into the camp, visibly frightened, but reluctant to share details. As the dorm leader, I followed them to their bunks, and one eventually admitted that they had been smoking on the football field when something scared them. Intrigued, I decided to investigate and headed out into the deep snow towards the field. However, when I reached a certain point, I felt compelled to stop and was drawn to a clump of blackberry bushes near the situp station. I could not move forward but could retreat without any issues. This peculiar sensation lasted for a while until I decided to return to the camp.

I don't have further details or know the current status of the camp or the individuals involved. These incidents left a lasting impression on me, particularly the inability to move beyond a certain point and the clear boundary it created. While I can't explain what caused these experiences, but I'm sure many of your readers will be able to come to a logical conclusion.

CHAPTER NINETY

BACK IN THE EARLY 1970S, I purchased a house in South Lake Tahoe, located just south and east of the South Lake Tahoe airport. One day, while standing on my front porch and gazing in that direction, something caught my eye. It appeared to be a figure wearing a hooded, brown, long-sleeved jumpsuit. Given that there were only a handful of houses in my neighborhood, most of which were vacant vacation homes, I felt quite alone. In an attempt to engage with the individual, I whistled loudly, shouted, and waved in their direction. To my surprise, the person became startled and quickly retreated, backing into a pine tree situated approximately 150 feet away, close to the river. I frequently took walks in that area, and at the time, those pine trees reached just above my outstretched palm. To put it into perspective, I stand at 6 feet 3 inches tall and can comfortably touch an 8-foot ceiling. When this person backed into the pine tree, the top of the tree barely reached the tip of their right shoulder. In a swift motion, the figure spun around and dashed toward the river with a speed that rivaled the quickness of startled deer.

Upon realizing that the figure was taller than the tree, I immediately dashed off the porch, fixated on the tree to ensure I was heading toward the correct one. When I reached the pine tree, there was no evidence of anyone or anything present. The ground was hard-packed, leaving no discernible footprints. I confirmed the tree's height to be slightly over 8 feet, with a difference of approximately an inch. Curious, I made my way to the riverbank in search of footprints, but there were none to be found. It was broad daylight, adding to my frustration and disbelief. I muttered to myself, knowing that no one would likely believe my encounter. Determined to find answers, I got into my car and drove to the other side of the river, where a few homes were located. I began knocking on doors, hoping to find someone who could validate my experience. Two individuals refused to engage in conversation, but one person responded, saying, "Oh, you've seen them too." Taken aback, I asked, "Them?" The person admitted that although they would deny it if asked by others, they had also witnessed similar sightings, particularly during the springtime.

Four decades have passed since that incident, and it is only this year that I have decided to share my story with someone. The person I spoke to back then would be well over 110 years old if they were still alive, so I can't seek verification from them now. I have revisited the area since then, and with the multitude of homes now present, the chances of encountering such a creature in the vicinity are slim.

To further analyze the figure's size, I measured my own shoulders, which were a little over 2 feet wide. Comparing that to where the figure's shoulder touched the tree, it was evident that they were much larger, nearly double in width. I ran an imaginary line across my shoulders at the same height as where the tree made contact with the figure's shoulder. From the midpoint between my chest and shoulder, I measured the distance to the top of my head, which came out to be between 15 to 16 inches. Assuming the same measurement on the figure, it would be at least 18 inches or more. This estimation would make them approximately 9 feet 6 inches tall. Such a towering height, combined with the reported deer-like speed, defies what we consider typical of any human. Unfortunately, the figure was too far away for me to discern any details of their face.

I'm not someone who seeks attention for what I've seen. I simply wanted to let you know your readers know that they are not alone. I was only 23 years old when all this stuff happened. However, this sighting hasn't deterred me from camping or significantly altered my life. Instead, it remains a testament to the fact that I was fortunate enough to witness something that very few people ever get the chance to see.

CHAPTER NINETY-ONE

I REMEMBER GOING CAMPING in 2005 like it was yesterday. It was a warm summer evening, and my friends and I were excited to spend a weekend in the great outdoors. We arrived at the campsite just as the sun was setting, and we quickly set up our tents and started a fire. We sat around the flames, roasting marshmallows and telling stories late into the night. As we crawled into our sleeping bags, I remember feeling a sense of peace and contentment. The only sounds were the gentle rustling of leaves and the occasional hoot of an owl. But as the night wore on, things started to change. I heard strange noises coming from the woods, like twigs snapping and branches rustling. I tried to ignore it, telling myself that it was just a raccoon or a deer. But then I heard something that made my blood run cold - a low growling sound, like an animal in pain. I sat up in my tent, heart racing, trying to figure out what was happening.

My friends were still asleep, so I decided to investigate on my own. I grabbed a flashlight and slowly made my way towards the source of the noise. As I got closer, I saw a pair of glowing eyes staring back at me from the darkness. My heart skipped a beat as I realized that it was a wild dog, snarling and baring its teeth. I backed away slowly, trying not to make any sudden movements. The dog followed me for a few steps before turning and disappearing back into the woods.

I returned to my tent, shaken but relieved that nothing worse had happened. As I lay back down in my sleeping bag, I knew that I would never forget that night in the woods - the fear, the adrenaline, and the realization that maybe it was sleep in my eyes or just your run of the mill over reaction to a wild dog. I went back to my tent deciding to take my simplest explanation.

We spent more time hanging out and we enjoyed ourselves listening to music. We enjoyed fishing and swimming. It was better than normal, it was amazing. By the time the sun had started to set we cracked opened some beers and started winding down around the campfire. I am a master of campfire foods. There was never a better time to show off than this but as I cooked, we all eventually settled down around the fire. We had begun telling ghost stories and roasting marshmallows.

As the night wore on, we heard a strange howling in the distance. At first, we thought it was just a coyote or a wolf, but the howling grew louder and more intense. We all huddled around the fire, trying to ignore the sound. But it was too eerie to ignore. We argued about whether or not to investigate the source of the howling. Finally, we decided to go look for it. We grabbed our flashlights and headed towards the riverbank. As we got closer, the howling became more intense. It was coming from across the river. We shone our flashlights in that direction and saw something that made our blood run cold. Was that the thing I had seen last night?

Standing on two legs like a man but covered in fur like a dog was a creature unlike anything we had ever seen before. Its eyes glowed in the darkness, and its teeth were sharp and pointed. We all froze in fear as the creature continued to howl. It seemed to be calling out to others of its kind. We knew then that we were in danger. We turned and ran back to our campsite as fast as we could. Had I not been so frightened, I would have clocked our time running.

We spent the rest of the night huddled together in our tents, too scared to move or make a sound. The howling continued throughout the night, but eventually it stopped. The next morning, we packed up our things and left the campsite as quickly as we could. We never spoke of that night again.

Over the years, more stories of dogmen sightings in Villisca have emerged. Some say that they are the result of a secret government experiment gone wrong. Others believe that they are ancient creatures that have lived in the woods for centuries.

Whatever the truth may be, I know one thing for sure – I will never forget the night that I came face to face with the Dogmen of Villisca. And I will never camp by that river again.

Despite our fear and reluctance to talk about what we had seen; we couldn't help but be curious about the Dogmen of Villisca. We started researching and talking to locals, trying to find out more about these mysterious creatures. We discovered that there had been numerous sightings of dogmen in the area over the years. Some people claimed to have seen them lurking in the woods, while others reported hearing their eerie howls at night.

One local farmer even claimed that a pack of dogmen had attacked his livestock, leaving behind a trail of destruction and blood. As we delved deeper into the lore surrounding the dogmen, we began to realize that there was more to this story than just a scary campfire tale. Some people believed that the dogmen were actually shape-shifters, able to transform from human to animal form at will. Others thought that they were a type of cryptid, a creature that existed outside of our understanding of the natural world.

We even heard rumors that there was a secret government facility hidden deep in the woods, where scientists were conducting experiments on these strange creatures. Despite our curiosity, we knew better than to go looking for trouble. We had seen firsthand how terrifying these creatures could be, and we didn't want to risk encountering them again.

And we knew that the Dogmen of Villisca would continue to haunt our dreams for years to come. As time passed, we all went our separate ways and started families of our own. But the memory of that night in Villisca stayed with us, like a dark shadow that we couldn't shake.

Every time we heard a strange howling in the distance or saw a shadowy figure lurking in the woods, our minds would go back to that fateful night by the river. We tried to convince ourselves that it was just our imaginations playing tricks on us, but deep down, we knew that there was something out there that we couldn't explain. Years later, I returned to Villisca for a family reunion. As I drove through the familiar streets and past the dense woods, I couldn't help but feel a sense of unease.

I decided to take a walk by the river, hoping to confront my fears and put the past behind me. But as I approached the water's edge, I heard a familiar sound that made my blood run cold. It was the same howling that we had heard all those years ago. And as I looked across the river, I saw a pair of glowing eyes staring back at me from the darkness. I knew then that the Dogmen of Villisca were still out there, lurking in the shadows and waiting for their next victim. And as I turned and ran back to my car, I knew that I would never be able to forget the terror of that night by the river.

CHAPTER NINETY-TWO

I REMEMBER the night I encountered the Mothman like it was yesterday. I was driving home from work, tired and ready for bed. But then something caught my eye - a figure perched on a telephone pole, watching me with glowing red eyes. I was driving with my wife in the back roads of West Virginia. At first, I thought it was just my imagination playing tricks on me. But as I got closer, I could see that it was real - a creature unlike anything I had ever seen before. It was tall and thin, with wings like a moth and eyes like fire. Its body was covered in fur, and its claws glinted in the moonlight. I tried to keep driving, but something compelled me to stop. I got out of my car and approached the creature cautiously, unsure of what to do.

That's when it spoke to me - not with words, but with images in my mind. It showed me visions of destruction and chaos, of a world torn apart by war and disease. I tried to run, but the Mothman followed me - always watching, always waiting. It seemed to be everywhere at once, stalking me through the night.

As the days went on, I became more and more obsessed with the creature. I started seeing it everywhere - in my dreams, in the shadows outside my window. I tried to tell people about it, but no one believed me. They thought I was crazy - that I had lost my mind. But then something strange happened - a bridge near my town collapsed, killing dozens of people. And in the aftermath of the tragedy, eyewitnesses reported seeing a creature that matched the Mothman's description.

I was just a young man when the bridge collapsed in 1964. I remember it like it was yesterday - the screams, the chaos, and the overwhelming sense of loss that hung over our small town for years to come. I was working at a nearby factory when I heard the news. At first, I didn't believe it - how could a bridge that had stood for decades suddenly give way? But as the reports came in, I knew that something terrible had happened. I rushed to the site of the collapse, along with dozens of other concerned citizens. The scene was like something out of a nightmare - twisted metal and broken concrete littered the riverbank, and rescue workers were frantically searching for survivors.

I joined in the effort, wading through the murky water and calling out for anyone who might be trapped. But as the hours passed, it became clear that there was little hope of finding anyone alive.

The days that followed were a blur of grief and mourning. Families held funerals for their loved ones, and our town came together to support one another in any way we could. But as time went on, questions started to arise about what had caused the collapse. Some blamed faulty construction or neglectful maintenance, while others pointed to the heavy traffic and weight of the vehicles that crossed the bridge every day. I became obsessed with finding answers. I spent countless hours poring over blueprints and interviewing witnesses, trying to piece together what had gone wrong.

And finally, after months of investigation, we discovered the truth - a critical support beam had been weakened by rust and corrosion, causing it to buckle under the weight of a passing truck. The findings were sobering, but they also gave us a sense of closure. We knew what had caused the tragedy that had rocked our town to its core, and we could take steps to ensure that nothing like it ever happened again. I watched as a new bridge was built, stronger and more resilient than the one that had come before. And though the memory of the collapse still haunts me to this day, I am proud of the way our community came together in the face of tragedy, and of the work we did to make sure that our town would never have to suffer like that again. But then that's when the sightings came out. Apparently, I wasn't the only one to experience these sightings.

I knew then that I wasn't crazy - that the Mothman was real, and that it had come to warn us of something terrible. But what could we do? How could we stop the destruction that was coming? I never found out. One night, as I was walking home from work, the Mothman appeared before me one last time. It showed me a vision of my own death - of a fiery crash on the highway.

And then it was gone - vanished into thin air, leaving me alone in the darkness.

I don't know what happened to the Mothman after that. Maybe it was just a figment of my imagination, or maybe it was something more. But I do know that I'll never forget that encounter, and the fear and uncertainty it brought with it. The Mothman may be gone, but its message still echoes in my mind - a warning of things to come, and a reminder that we are never truly alone in this world. After that encounter, I couldn't shake the feeling that something terrible was going to happen. I became paranoid, constantly looking over my shoulder and jumping at every sound.

But then, it happened. I was sitting at my desk in the office when it happened. The ground began to shake violently, and I heard the sound of glass breaking all around me. I tried to stand up, but I couldn't keep my balance - the shaking was too intense. As I looked around, I saw my coworkers scrambling to get to safety. Some were hiding under their desks, while others were trying to make their way to the door. But the shaking was so intense that it felt like we were all being thrown around like rag dolls. I remember feeling a sense of panic rising in my chest. Was this the end? Was this how it all ended - crushed under tons of rubble and debris?

But then, just as suddenly as it had begun, the shaking stopped. I looked around, dazed and disoriented, trying to make sense of what had just happened. That's when I heard the screams.

Outside, chaos reigned. Buildings had crumbled to the ground, and people were trapped under piles of rubble and debris. The air was thick with dust and smoke, and the sound of sirens filled the air.

I knew that I had to get out of there. I grabbed my bag and made my way towards the door, dodging falling debris and broken glass as I went.

As I emerged onto the street, I saw a scene of devastation that will stay with me forever. Buildings had collapsed in on themselves, and people were frantically digging through the rubble in search of survivors. I joined in the effort, using whatever tools I could find to try and free those who were trapped. It was grueling work - we were exhausted and covered in dust and sweat - but we knew that every second counted. In the days that followed, our city was transformed. The streets were lined with tents and makeshift shelters for those who had lost their homes, and rescue workers from all over the country descended on us to help with the recovery effort. But even as we worked to rebuild, the memory of that day stayed with us. We knew that we had been lucky to survive, and we were determined to honor the memory of those who hadn't been so fortunate.

And though it was a long and difficult road, we eventually emerged stronger and more resilient than ever before - a testament to the human spirit and our ability to overcome even the most devastating of tragedies.

I couldn't believe that just a few weeks earlier after my sighting of the moth man a massive earthquake struck my town, destroying buildings and killing hundreds of people. In the aftermath of the disaster, I couldn't help but think back to the Mothman and its warning. Was this what it had been trying to tell me? Had it known that this was coming all along? I tried to tell people about my encounter with the Mothman again, but this time they listened. They started to believe that there was something more to the creature than just a myth or a legend. But even as we tried to make sense of what had happened, I couldn't help but feel a sense of dread in my gut. What other horrors lay in store for us? And would the Mothman be there to warn us again?

Years passed, and life slowly returned to normal. But I never forgot about the Mothman and its warning. And sometimes, on quiet nights when the wind howled through the trees, I swear I could hear its wings beating in the darkness - a reminder that we are never truly safe from the unknown forces that lurk in the shadows.

CHAPTER NINETY-THREE

I WANT to say first of all that I believe I had an encounter with absolute evil and though I believe the entity was something similar or akin to a skinwalker and perhaps maybe even a werewolf, it seemed to be neither one or the other and yet both at the same time. Stay with me because it's a really strange one. I live in Arizona and though my parents don't really embrace the Navajo culture and haven't for a long time, my mother was born and raised on a reservation or "the rez" as we like to call it. My father is a Christian and one hundred percent Irish and one of them had to do what needed to be done for harmony in the relationship because it wasn't going to work if they both held onto their family's traditions. It's not really important except to say that my maternal grandmother still lived on the reservation in Arizona and believed in all of the lore and superstitions that go along with the culture. Also, my mother allegedly turning her back on those same traditions and legends is what my grandmother and many of the other elders on the rez believe is the reason I encountered what I did. It was 1999 and my mom and I were visiting my grandmother's house on the rez which was located two towns away and we were staying for the whole weekend. I think it's necessary to explain that my grandmother has three dogs but in her culture and standing with the traditions of the tribe, she doesn't allow them in the house, especially not overnight. The dogs are super friendly golden and chocolate labs and I think one of the chocolate labs has some shepherd mix in it. There are some stray dogs and other animals, cats too, in the neighborhood and on the reservation but I wouldn't say the area surrounding her home is "overrun" or anything like that. We arrived at my grandmother's house at around seven at night on a Friday evening. My mother had plans to go and see my aunt who lived on the rez, about fifteen minutes away from my grandmother. I was perfectly happy to stay and spend some time with my grandma and we decided that after we had a snack and I got settled into the room she set up for me at her house, we were going to just chill and watch some DVDs.

Grandma realized she forgot to feed her dogs so she went outside and put some food out for them. As she was coming inside of the house I heard her telling something or someone to get away from the house and leave us alone. I immediately jumped up and ran to the door because, though I knew how unlikely it was, I thought that someone was bothering or harassing my grandma. I got to the door and saw her shooing a somewhat large, all black, mutt-looking dog away with her broom. It struck me as odd right away because normally if there was another dog or another animal in general hanging around outside of her house, especially in the backyard where her dogs stayed, they would normally bark at it or at least otherwise alert us to its presence. My grandmother's house is surrounded by very thick woods and she doesn't have many neighbors. There's a ton of wide open land on the rez and my grandmother got very lucky when she and my grandfather were able to build the house in the middle of all of that relatively untouched wilderness. I loved the woods and my bedroom at her house faced the backyard and the woods too. The strange dog ran off and we thought that would be the end of it so grandma came back inside and we got our snacks together and picked out a movie. Grandma and I both loved horror movies and because no one else in our family liked them too, she and I normally spent our time together watching both our favorite classics and anything new that she would have picked up from the local rental store in anticipation for my weekend visit. She put the dvd in the player and we turned the lights off. Her living room had a large bay window in it that faced the backyard and surrounding woods. She kept her dogs right there as well, near to the window because she liked to keep an eye on them. No sooner had she sat back down next to me on the couch than I looked up and saw that same, strange looking, black dog standing on top of a crate and looking into the window at us. I jumped because it startled me so much. My grandmother looked up and said a few curse words under her breath and then went and banged on the window to get it out of there. She said if it came back she was going out there with the broom again and then if it still didn't leave she was going to try and scare it off with a gun. I was freaked out because number one, a dog that close to my grandmother's house should have set her dogs off barking and growling. They always did when there was an unknown animal around and secondly, it was just bizarre, the way it was looking at me. There was something weird about the eyes and though they were typical dark brown dog eyes, there somehow seemed to be a lot more to them than that. Like I said it was really odd that when it came to that particular dog, her dogs didn't even seem to notice it was there at first and I asked my grandmother if it maybe belonged to someone who lived nearby and that's why it seemed so calm and well behaved. It didn't make any noise and something about the way it positioned itself on top of that crate to be able to look directly through the window and stare at us kind of creeped me out and I could see my grandmother was a little worried as well. She didn't say anything though except to tell me that she didn't know of any neighbors anywhere near her who had dogs and even if they did it was miles before you would even come across another residence so if it did belong to someone, it had traveled quite a distance. We decided we would check the next day and see if anyone was missing their pet.

Something about that dog really got to me and I had a hard time concentrating on the movie. I could tell my grandmother was very upset as well but I didn't know why at the time and just figured she was upset because I was so upset and for the same reasons as me. Its behavior was really strange and the way her dogs seemed to not even notice it let alone alert us to its presence was worrying. We watched two movies without further incident and right as the last one was ending, my mom came home. Grandma and I were planning on going to bed and when my mom came in she said she heard the dogs growling out back at something. We had been so engulfed in our movie and grandma always had the volume so loud, we hadn't even heard it. I went to look out the window and saw the same black dog and it was just sitting and staring at my grandmother's dogs and the moment it looked at them, they all ran and whined, each one cowering inside of its dog house. It was very bizarre behavior for her dogs as well and something about the whole situation was starting to feel not only very wrong but also really frightening as well. My grandma grabbed her broom and went outside to chase the dog off again. When she came inside she said that it wasn't a dog but a skinwalker and that it had its eye on her and she was scared. She told me not to look out of my bedroom window or any other window in the house at night for the rest of the time I was there and if I saw the dog to let her know because she was going to have to kill it before it killed one of us. I had heard my grandmother talk about skinwalkers before but it was extra creepy that time because the dog was behaving rather oddly. However, it looked like a perfectly normal dog to me and I honestly thought that it was someone's pet. I agreed not to look out the windows and rolled my eyes when she wasn't looking and then I said goodnight to her and my mom. I went into my room and laid down and within minutes I was asleep. That night passed by uneventfully and everything was normal until the next night when my grandmother went with my mother to my aunt's house. They invited me but I didn't like my aunt's bratty kids and so I decided to stay behind. That was nothing unusual and they said they might be home late but to keep the doors locked and don't answer the door etc. I agreed and they left.

At around ten o'clock that night I made myself a snack and sat on the couch to watch some television before going to bed. I heard what sounded like someone trying to come in the front door. The doorknob was jiggling and turning and I immediately knew that something weird was going on because my mother and grandmother both had keys and there was a spare key hidden right under the welcome mat in front of the door. There was no way they forgot their keys and couldn't get in. I was scared and immediately remembered what my grandma made me promise about looking out the windows at night while I was visiting with her. I thought someone was trying to break in, maybe thinking no one was home or something and so I felt like I had no choice and had to look out the window. I decided to try to see through the peephole first because technically that isn't a window and therefore I wouldn't really be breaking my promise to my grandma. I couldn't believe what I was seeing and I backed up and creeped over to the window where I would be able to see who was at the door and tried to peek without being seen to get a better look. When I looked through the peephole it was that black, mutt dog and it was standing on its hind legs and had its paws wrapped around the doorknob, turning it. As soon as I moved the curtain to get a better look, though I made no noise at all and all of the lights were out except for the one that was coming from the tv in the other room, its head immediately looked over at me. Its eyes were all white and terrifying. They had not looked like that on any of the numerous occasions we had seen it the night before. I backed away from the window and started to pray. I wanted to call my mom and tell her what was happening but she wasn't superstitious like my grandma and I knew my grandmother would be worried sick. I toughed it out and the "dog" ran off the front porch after getting back down on all fours and behaving normally again. I watched it disappear down the street. I just kept thinking, over and over again, that I never should have looked out that window. I turned off the television and all the other lights and went to bed. I thought that being in the dark would make it less likely I was seen or noticed by anyone or anything that might be lurking outside in the woods or beyond.

I fell asleep rather quickly and woke up around midnight when my mom and grandma were coming in from my aunt's house. My mom peeked in to check on me and I pretended to be asleep because I didn't want her to know anything was wrong until the next day. I heard each of their bedroom doors close about ten minutes later and fell back asleep again. I woke up to what sounded like light tapping on my bedroom window and when I looked at the clock it was three in the morning. I didn't want to get up and check to see if I was actually hearing anything and hoped with everything that I had that it had been a dream or something. Maybe I had imagined it because of how scared I was of the white eyed dog creature that was trying to break into the house earlier in the night. Even saying it now I know how ridiculous it sounds, believe me but I know what I saw. I heard the light tapping again but just rolled over, away from the window, and tried to ignore it. The next thing that happened is so terrifying I don't know if I can accurately convey the absolute fear and terror I felt in those next few moments. I heard what sounded like a man pretending to be a dog. It was a human man, one with a very deep voice, saying "ruff ruff, woof grrr ruff" etc. I think everyone who reads this will know what I'm talking about even if I don't know how to properly explain it or literally spell it out. It was definitely not a dog and in fact as soon as it started, my grandmother's dogs started moaning lowly and somewhat under their breaths. I had to look out the window because I wanted to make sure her dogs were okay and thought I was prepared for what I was about to see I really wasn't. Her dogs weren't outside which meant they were probably cowering in their dog houses and sure enough the black dog was there, standing on its hind legs, still in dog form. Understand this wasn't a werewolf and there was NOTHING human about this animal at all except for the voice and aside from the voice the only thing about it that didn't look perfectly normal for a dog were the fully white eyes. The eyes stared at me as the dog's mouth moved. The man's voice came out of it again and as I watched it said, "woof woof, woof woof." Then, it smiled and bared weird fangs that looked like they belonged in a human being's mouth but still the thing looked like a regular dog otherwise. It knew that I knew what it was and it was there to kill me. As it stood there it started to slowly transform and the front paws started morphing into two hands with talons where the nails should have been. The whole time the thing kept blinking almost in and out of existence and stretching as though it were being pulled up like a piece of silly putty. While that was happening I could still see the moth moving, repeating, "woof

542

woof, woof woof" perfectly like a human being but now it was only speaking the words over and over again and didn't seem to be trying to mimic the sounds of an actual dog anymore.

I ran back to my bed and heard a very loud and angry sounding howl as I closed my eyes and began to pray. My grandmother came running into my room seconds later and as soon as she flipped on the light I jumped up and ran to her. I was crying hysterically and shaking uncontrollably. She sat with me on my bed and asked me what was wrong. I told her what happened and before long my mother was in the room too, listening to what I was telling my grandmother. I told them about earlier in the night while they were gone and about what had just happened a few minutes before outside of my bedroom window. My grandmother grabbed her shotgun and ran outside while my mom and I yelled after her, protesting the whole time. We were terrified she would get hurt but she fired the gun in the air a couple of times and then came back inside. She was very upset and felt like maybe it was something she had done to bring the creature to the house and the reason its attention seemed to be focused on me. I highly doubted it and still do to this day. My mom and I tried to convince my grandmother to come and stay with us for a little while but she refused. My grandmother claimed to never have encountered the entity after that day but I was never sure if she was telling the truth or not.

I don't know anything else to really say about what I experienced that weekend except that I never had any similar experiences either before or since. I have no idea what in the world I encountered and though I have a feeling it was a skinwalker I honestly haven't seen or heard anything quite like it either in real life or while researching and reading through thousands of encounter stories online. I asked my grandmother about it many times after it happened but she would yell at me for even bringing it up. My mom didn't want to discuss it any further either and my father wouldn't even hear of "such nonsense." I was basically on my own in my search for answers and all these years later I still am not one single step closer in identifying what it was I saw. It could have been some sort of extraterrestrial who got its disguise mixed up or any number of other things I'm sure I can't even begin to imagine that exists out there in the wilderness of our world. I do know one thing, whatever it was came from the woods and I know that for a fact because I've seen a lot of strange things in those woods behind my grandmother's house and also, I always heard strange howling sounds coming out of it at night, specifically on the nights of the full and blue moons.

CHAPTER NINETY-FOUR

I HAD BEEN LOOKING FORWARD to this yoga retreat for months. It was supposed to be a chance to relax, unwind, and connect with my inner self. Just for the record, I was what you would call a yoga junkie. I lived it and breathed it. I became a very stereotypical image of your pumpkin spice latte toting, blonde, skinny legging wearing, Goop reading white woman. When I look back at myself, I cringe. I figured I would have a chance to unwind and work on my form at this retreat.

But as soon as I arrived at the resort, something felt off.

It wasn't anything specific - just a feeling of unease that lingered in the back of my mind. But I tried to push it aside and focus on the yoga classes and meditation sessions. Everything went smoothly for the first few days. I met some wonderful people, learned some new poses, and felt more relaxed than I had in months. But then, on the fourth night of the retreat, everything changed. I woke up in the middle of the night, feeling like something was watching me. At first, I thought it was just my imagination playing tricks on me. But then I heard a rustling outside my cabin. I had thought it was the wind or someone going for a late-night walk. I tried to convince myself that it was just an animal - maybe a raccoon or a deer. But as the rustling grew louder, I felt more and more ill at ease. I peeked out the window and saw a figure moving through the trees. It was tall and thin, with long arms and legs that seemed to bend in unnatural ways.

At first, I thought it was just a person - maybe someone who had wandered onto the resort by mistake. But then it turned its head towards me, and I saw its eyes. They were glowing yellow orbs that seemed to pierce right through me. And as soon as I saw them, I knew that this was no ordinary person. It was a skinwalker - a creature from Native American folklore that could take on the form of any animal or human it chose. I tried telling myself it was a refraction of light, or I had seen an animal? I tried to stay calm and rational, but my heart was pounding in my chest. I knew that I needed to get away from this thing before it saw me.

I crawled under my bed and waited there until morning. When I finally emerged, I told the retreat leaders what had happened. But they just looked at me with pitying eyes and told me that I must have been dreaming. I knew that I hadn't been dreaming. I had seen the skinwalker with my own eyes. And even though I tried to convince myself that it was just a trick of the light, I knew that it was real. The rest of the retreat passed in a blur. I couldn't focus on anything except the fear that lingered in the back of my mind. And even though I tried to tell myself that it was over, that the skinwalker was gone. After the retreat ended, I couldn't shake the feeling of unease that had settled over me. I tried to go back to my normal routine, but every time I closed my eyes, I saw the glowing yellow eyes of the skinwalker.

I started doing research on skinwalkers and found out that they were known for their ability to track and hunt their prey. I couldn't help but wonder if it was still following me, waiting for the right moment to strike. I tried to talk to people about what had happened, but no one believed me. They thought I was just being paranoid or that I had imagined the whole thing. But I knew what I had seen, and I knew that the skinwalker was real. I started carrying protective charms and doing rituals to ward off evil spirits, but nothing seemed to ease my anxiety.

Months passed, and eventually, I started to feel like maybe I had overreacted. Maybe it had just been a strange dream, or a hallucination brought on by stress. But then one night, as I was walking home from work, I heard a rustling in the bushes. My heart started pounding in my chest as I realized that the skinwalker had found me. I tried to run, but it was too fast. It chased me through the streets, its long limbs stretching out in impossible ways as it closed in on me.

Just when I thought it was going to catch me, a group of people appeared out of nowhere and started chanting in a language I didn't understand. The skinwalker let out a blood-curdling scream and disappeared into the night. I never saw it again after that night, but the memory of its glowing yellow eyes still haunts me. I know now that there are things in this world that we can't explain or understand, and that sometimes it's better not to mess with them.

After that terrifying encounter, I started to research more about the group of people who had saved me from the skinwalker. I found out that they were a local Native American tribe who had been practicing traditional rituals and ceremonies for generations. I reached out to them and asked if they could teach me more about their culture and beliefs. They welcomed me with open arms and taught me about their connection to the land and the spirits that inhabit it.

Through their teachings, I learned that skinwalkers were not just creatures of myth and legend, but real beings that could cause harm to those who didn't respect the natural world. I also learned that there were ways to protect oneself from these malevolent spirits, such as carrying protective talismans and performing rituals to honor the spirits of the land. Over time, my fear of the skinwalker faded as I gained a greater understanding of the world around me. I started to see the beauty in nature and the interconnectedness of all things.

I even started practicing yoga again, but this time with a newfound appreciation for its connection to spirituality and mindfulness.

Looking back on my experience at the yoga retreat, I realize that it was a turning point in my life. It forced me to confront my fears and opened my eyes to a world beyond what I had previously known. While I still feel a sense of unease when I think about the skinwalker, I also feel grateful for the lessons it taught me about the power of nature and the importance of respecting it. As I continued to learn from the Native American tribe, I became more and more interested in their culture and traditions. I started attending their ceremonies and partici-pating in their rituals, and I felt a deep sense of connection to the land and the spirits that inhabited it.

Through my experiences with the tribe, I also learned about the importance of community and the power of coming together to support one another. I had always been a bit of a loner, but being part of this community gave me a sense of belonging that I had never felt before. Eventually, I decided to leave my job in the city and move closer to the tribe's reservation. I wanted to immerse myself in their culture and learn as much as I could from them. It wasn't an easy tran-sition, but over time, I started to feel more at home in my new surroundings. I made friends with people in the tribe and learned more about their way of life.

I also continued to practice yoga, but now it was infused with a deeper sense of spirituality and connection to nature. It wasn't just about physical exercise anymore; it was about connecting with some-thing greater than myself. Looking back on my journey, I realize that encountering the skinwalker was a pivotal moment in my life. It forced me to confront my fears and opened my eyes to a world beyond what I had previously known. But it also led me down a path of discovery and self-discovery that ultimately brought me closer to my true self. And for that, I will always be grateful.

CHAPTER NINETY-FIVE

WHEN I WAS twenty-two years old I moved from Indiana to Alaska. I was offered a really great job working with some of my family members who ran a business there. Everyone who worked for the company who had to move a long distance, like me, lived in a little apartment complex in the middle of nowhere while we looked for permanent housing. It was a rough job and I usually worked twenty-hour days, six days a week and then on the fourth week I would only have to work two days. My point is, it was an exhausting schedule. For a young and unencumbered guy like me though, the money was amazing, and it was enough that it was all worth it. It wasn't like I wasn't already used to freezing cold winters and densely wooded areas. We had those in Indiana, but I wasn't prepared for Alaska, that's for sure. First, the other people who lived in the complex with me all lived there with their families. I was the only bachelor in the whole place and even though the company was run by my family, I wasn't given any breaks or favors, not that I wanted any. I would have liked to have stayed at my aunt's house though cause my granny lived there and she was my favorite person in the world. My mom's side of the family all lived in Alaska but whenever I would see them when I was growing up, they always came and visited us, so this was my first time in a new and strange place. It was all good though, or so I thought. My first month there went by easily, aside from the loneliness. This complex was out in the middle of nowhere and there were no stores around or any public transportation. I didn't have a vehicle yet as I sold mine, along with a bunch of other possessions, just to pay for the ticket to get there and things I needed to start the new job. I called my mom and dad back home often but at the end of the day I felt that I made the right decision. I knew I could move up in the company, that there was plenty of room for advancement, so I was looking forward to the day when I no longer was left doing the grunt work. So, that's my backstory, not let's get to the encounter.

The apartment complex was small and there were only about twelve tiny apartments in the whole place. It was surrounded by woods on all sides and sometimes it got creepy. However, I was used to the woods, as I already stated and sometimes, I would take a walk in them to clear my head or relax my mind, especially when I couldn't sleep. The walls were thin and the people who lived upstairs from me fought often and had a very little baby. The baby cried all night long and when he or she was finally quiet and settled down, that's when the parents would start yelling and screaming which would wake the baby up and it would start all over again. Honestly though, those neighbors were my only complaint. I noticed quickly that the people there kept to themselves and weren't very neighborly. I wasn't used to that and so the loneliness would start to weigh me down after a while. One night it was about two in the morning and the people upstairs were at it again. I didn't want to complain about them to my uncle who owned the building because I had to work with the guy and, I was worried my uncle would evict them and they had that little baby, you know? So, I went outside to smoke a cigarette. I always carried a little flashlight with me because it was just something I was used to from growing up surrounded by woods with wild animals roaming around. That night though I had a lot on my mind and instead of just standing in front of the door and smoking my cigarette, I decided that I wanted to walk a little bit. I still think back on it and feel like I might have been compelled to walk further into the woods but I'm not sure. I knew it could possibly be a little dangerous to follow that trail into the woods, but I did so anyway. I didn't plan on going that far into them and was just going to smoke a couple of cigarettes and head back to my apartment. It didn't quite turn out that way.

I walked along one of the trails that looked like it was well worn. I saw a lot of the couples and families in my building walking along those same trails and into the woods all the time during the day. It was bright outside considering what time it was and the moon was completely full. I remember looking up at the sky and thinking how beautiful the stars looked. I hadn't ever seen anything like that before and I was somewhat in awe of it all. I was watching where I was going but for the most part I was looking up. Finally, I came to a little clearing and decided to sit underneath a tree for a few and just stargaze. I had terrible insomnia back then but in the eighties that wasn't really a thing, and it was just called being overtired. I sat down and leaned against the tree, and no sooner had I done that then I heard a very loud sound that was extremely unfamiliar to me. It's hard to even describe now but it sounded kind of like the flapping of wings. However, I thought there was no way it could have been that because of how loud it was. I also felt a very strong breeze on the top of my head and a little bit in my face at the same time. I jumped up quickly and looked up into the tree. Standing on one of the branches was some sort of strange and evil looking creature. It oozed malevolence and I somehow just knew that it was happy to have come across me and that it had negative and downright evil intentions with me too.

The creature had glowing red eyes and gigantic black wings. The wings looked pristine and were almost shining. It stood at around seven feet tall, and the wings looked like they were at least ten feet tall but they sprouted out and the wingspan was like nothing I had ever seen before. They had to have covered twelve feet when they were fully sprung like that, easily. It could have even been more. The creature was all black, including its mouth and it had arms that were somewhat fat and talons for hands. The feet looked huge and far too big for the body, even at that height. They also looked like talons. The nose looked like what I would imagine a human being's nose would look like if someone just broke the tip off it and left it like that. I remember I kept focusing on the fact that the foot talons were wrapped around the tree branch and if the thing wanted to it could swing upside down and not fall, the grip was that tight and secure. I was terrified and started to back away from it. It smiled and its teeth were sharp and extremely white. I didn't expect it to have such white and seemingly perfect teeth, but it did. Its skin looked slick, like it was covered in slime or soaking wet or something and it was very wrinkly all over the place. It just stood there on top of that tree branch, which by the way didn't look like it should have been able to hold the weight of that thing. It was holding it though. I smelled something akin to sulfur, kind of like when you light a match, and it goes out; that smell. It was so strong though that it made me start to gag and I felt like I couldn't breathe. It rocked gently back and forth and just stared at me straight in the eyes, somewhat smirking at me with its giant black mouth.

I was afraid to run because I knew that when you run from predators and turn your back on them, they almost always give chase. I had no weapons on me, not even pepper or bear spray and I didn't know what to do. I felt like it was just waiting for me to make a move. I was desperate and so I grabbed my flashlight out of my back pocket and shined it right in the thing's eyes. It howled as though it were burning alive or something and the light wasn't even that bright. I thought that maybe I had just stunned it and it hadn't been expecting me to do that. I threw the flashlight as hard as I could at it and prayed, I didn't miss. I didn't and it smashed the creature right in the face. I heard it growl loudly and howl like it was in pain again, but I didn't see anything after the hit landed because I was already running in the opposite direction, back to my apartment complex. I heard a loud whooshing noise again and loud growling right behind me. I didn't want to turn around, but I honestly didn't have to because I could hear how close it was to me. It didn't seem to be able to fly very fast, either that or it wasn't trying very hard, because I outran it and I never thought I would have been able to do that. Eventually, right before I was almost out of the woods, I didn't hear anything behind me anymore. I stopped, turned, and looked and saw that the creature was up in another tree, this time on a higher branch, just glaring down at me. I walked out of the woods and ran inside my apartment.

I locked all my doors and windows and found it almost impossible to stop peeking out my blinds for the rest of the night. That thing tormented me for the entire year or so that I lived there, and it didn't take me long to find out that I wasn't the only one. I mentioned it to my uncle the next day and he told me that I should speak to my neighbors. I tried but only one or two of them would open to me. I don't blame them; I was a stranger and all. They said they nicknamed it "the batman" and that it sometimes tapped on the windows with its talons or swooped down at them when they least expected it if they were outside at night for whatever reason. The one guy said he had his encounter when walking back from the laundry room which was in a very small building on the other side of the complex. I was shocked and terrified. As far as they knew it had never actually harmed anyone, but legends and rumors abounded about it swooping down and grabbing small children and grown adults alike. I don't know what to make of all that and in all the times I had seen it, it never touched me or even really tried to hurt me. It seemed to enjoy the fear and I wonder if maybe it wanted to feed off that. Like a so-called energy vampire or whatever. I've investigated it a little bit and maybe it was the so-called batsquatch or maybe even the mothman. Maybe it was a mixture of both. After all, Alaska really is an extremely strange place, no matter where you live and even if you're only visiting. There's just something about the energy here. I moved from that building about a year later, got married and started a family of my own. My wife and I and all our kids still live in Alaska but let's just say none of us are outdoorsmen, that's for sure and it's mainly because I was open and honest about my encounter with all of them and none of them ever want to experience something like that. I haven't encountered that entity since I moved out of that place a little over thirty years ago. But, like I said, I stay away from the woods altogether.

CHAPTER NINETY-SIX

WHEN I WAS ABOUT twelve years old I went camping with two friends and my dad near a very large reservation where we lived in New Mexico at the time. We weren't directly on the reservation but we were really close to it. I always got a really weird feeling when either traveling through them or even being near them and I didn't really know why. I think it was all of the legends and superstitions my friends who had families that lived on them would tell me about. It always seemed like the reservations were places where a lot of evil existed. At only twelve years old I was too young to realize that evil exists everywhere but the Natives are simply more aware of it than most other people. I remember we were all sitting around the campfire and had just gotten done eating dinner. Us three kids decided to start telling scary stories to try and creep one another out. I was creeped out enough for all three of us already but I wouldn't have ever admitted that and so I played along and when it was my turn I had what I thought was a great idea. I had heard legends of skinwalkers from the grown ups in the area and again, from friends who would retell the legends of their relatives and ancestors still living on the reservations. The stories always scared me and so I thought for sure I would be able to scare my friends with the stories as well. I retold an encounter another friend allegedly had while delivering something to the reservation where he claimed a skinwalker morphed from a rabbit to a coyote and then to a human man, all while running alongside the truck they were driving in and keeping up with it the whole way. I realize now that story or encounter is very common and actually happens a lot more than most people would like to think it does. As soon as I made it halfway through my story though, my father seemed to know where I was going with it and stopped me right away. He told me I shouldn't speak about things I don't know the power of and that even talking about skinwalkers could bring them to me. Of course, me and my friends thought that was absolutely ridiculous but my father seemed really scared and I had never seen him like that. Just to prove he was wrong and I wasn't about to do exactly what he had thought I was going to, I changed the story to something stupid and not scary at all. My friends and I went to bed in our individual tents, laughing the entire time. My father put out the fire and went to his tent too.

During the night we were all woken up several times by strange noises coming from the woods surrounding us. It wasn't the normal howling of the wolves or braying of coyotes, it was something different. It actually sounded like the mewling or growling of a very large cat. Growing up in New Mexico, we all knew what bobcats and mountain lions sounded like and while the noises we were hearing were somewhat similar, they weren't exactly the same. It was creepy but my father managed to convince us that we were letting our imaginations get the best of us and that one of those predators, or something else entirely natural and normal, was in fact what we were hearing. We had trouble sleeping but only because of how loud whatever it was kept being and it went on all throughout the night right up until the sun finally rose. Despite being a little bit more tired than normal, we were all excited about getting our day started. We had some breakfast and hiked to a nearby lake, in the middle of a really dense part of that particular forest, and did some fishing. We were there for about four hours, just laughing, joking, fishing and even swimming. I couldn't shake the feeling that something or someone was watching us from the surrounding woods but it was a bright and sunny day so I did my best to put the feeling out of my mind. At one point I asked my friends if they really thought that the sounds we had been hearing the night before had been coming from the usual predatory animals we were all used to. They both said they thought it was skinwalkers but I knew they were only saying that to scare me and then they started saying some really vulgar and extremely disrespectful things about skin-walkers in general. It made me uncomfortable but the more upset I got it was like the more they were egged on to continue. Finally the subject was dropped and it was time to go.

We packed up our catches for the day and started hiking back to the camp to have some lunch and hang out a little bit more. We were going to hike the half hour back to the lake after lunch because it was a really hot day and we wanted to keep swimming. As we were making our way back to the camp, I thought I saw something move, very quickly, to the side of me out of the corner of my eye. I turned to look but kept walking as I did so and before I knew it I twisted my ankle. I couldn't walk anymore right then and my dad told my one friend to stay with me and he and my other friend were going to walk the fifteen minutes left to get back to the camp to get me some ice. He said it wasn't broken but was sprained and that I needed to put ice on it and keep it elevated for the rest of the night. I was bummed that I wouldn't be able to go swimming. I told my friend after my dad was out of earshot that I thought we were being watched and possibly followed through the woods. My friend laughed at first but then we heard laughter coming back at us, echoing through the air and the trees. We were scared at first but immediately chalked it up to our other friend having convinced my dad that he wanted to stay with us and then coming back to play a prank on us. The friend that stayed with me said he was going to follow the laughter and go and scare him instead. He told me to sit there and act scared and like I hadn't known where he had gone. I was scared, I didn't have to act and I told my friend I thought it was a really bad idea for us to separate at that time. He couldn't have cared less because he was more concerned with getting the better of our other friend. I didn't really have a choice but to sit there and sure enough, I was able to breathe a sigh of relief when, just a few moments later, both of my friends came out of a patch of woods with their arms around one another and laughing. I asked what was going on and they said the one friend had convinced my dad to go to the camp alone so he could come back and try to scare us. I was relieved immediately and said we should just sit and wait for my dad to get back with my ice.

My one friend, the one who had initially gone with my dad but then turned back said he had a surprise for me and pulled a bag of ice out of his back pocket. I was confused and asked him where he had gotten it from. He said my dad wouldn't let him come back unless I brought the ice and that he had agreed. Now, I didn't put together right away that that made no sense at all especially when compared to what he had just told me but I was relieved to have that little bag of ice and gratefully took it when he tossed it to me. I caught it and immediately put it on my ankle. It was a huge relief and after only having had the ice on my ankle for two minutes or so, it felt completely better. It was as if I hadn't ever hurt it at all. I started to move it around and my one friend asked how it was feeling. I said it was odd because it had hurt so bad and the ice seemed to have completely taken all of the pain away. I was a twelve year old boy who needed ice on sprains quite often because I played sports in school. My friend looked at the other friend and said "imagine that" but he said it with a weird smirk on his face. The two of them still had their arms around one another which was something they never did before and seemed really weird to me and I asked them what was so funny. They acted like they didn't know what I was referring to and I honestly thought the two of them had hatched some sort of plan to scare me on the way back to the camp. I didn't want to walk behind them. Something told me, something coming from deep down inside, that I definitely should NOT walk in front of them. So, I didn't. I motioned for them to lead the way and pretended the ankle was still just a little bit sore and therefore I had to walk slowly.

I noticed they kept turning around and looking at me and I asked them what they were looking at but they didn't answer me. Eventually it seemed like we had been walking for a really long time and yet hadn't reached the camp which at that point should have only been about fifteen minutes away, twenty because of how slow I was walking. They didn't answer me again and I felt something sinister in the air. Both of my friends turned around and once again had their arms around each other's shoulders and they looked at me. Their eyes were no longer brown but bright green and they looked like a cat's eyes and not the way a human being's eyes look. I was immediately terrified and almost stumbled backwards onto my behind. I caught myself on a tree and that's when my one friend asked me what was wrong. However, it wasn't his normal voice anymore, as it had been when he had handed me the ice about forty five minutes earlier, and this time it was almost like an echo underneath it or something. It sounded like movies always make people possessed by demons sound. I was stunned but a little part of me was still convinced they were playing some sort of elaborate prank on me or something. I knew in my heart there was no way they could have pulled this off. This was the early nineties and contacts like that, had they even existed at all- I'm not sure, would have been a lot more money than those two had put together. Also, he wasn't holding anything up to his mouth when he spoke to me. I sat down on a nearby fallen tree trunk and refused to move. My other friend held out his hand to me and his skin was noticeably yellow and his fingernails were also yellow, sharp like talons, and very dirty. I recoiled in horror and when he asked me what was wrong, again in that evil and demonic voice, I looked up at him. My friends then no longer had short brown hair but their hair was long and a mixture of black and gray. It looked greasy and matted and I just gasped and slid back to get away from them. Suddenly my ankle was hurting again and I yelled out in pain. They both looked at each other, staring into one another's eyes for at least a full minute, and then they looked back at me. It was almost like they were telepathically communicating and also, moving in complete unison. They took a few steps to advance towards me when suddenly out of the surrounding woods I heard my father and both of my friends calling for me. My two "friends" who were standing in front of me stopped in their tracks, once again looked at one another and then they did something even more terrifying than almost anything else they had done up to that point. They got down on all fours and shot through the woods, vanishing from my sight and into the wilderness beyond within a matter of mere seconds. I heard the howling of the large cats we had all heard the night before and that's when I yelled for my dad.

He looked extremely concerned when he had found me and I was terrified of my friends at that point. I backed away from them when they asked me what was wrong and where I had been. I looked at my father in confusion and started to cry. He said that my one friend had asked if he could wait with us and he allowed him to because they were only a few minutes away from where they left us at that point. My other friend had jumped out and scared him but when they came back to where I had been sitting, I was gone. They ran back to the camp to get my dad and that's when they started looking for me. I was terrified and didn't want them anywhere near me and I was crying like a little child. My dad was really worried and I could tell my friends were too and so they kept their distance while my dad gently lifted me up and carried me back to the camp. I was sick for the rest of that trip and burning up with a very high fever. At the end of the weekend my dad dropped my friends off at home and then we went home. It took a few more days for me to feel completely better and that's when he asked me what happened to me when we were out in the woods and where I had gone. I told him and he freaked out. He wasn't mad at me or anything but he went to the phone immediately and called my friend's parents. I heard them all yelling and within an hour both of my friends were at my house with both of their parents, respectively.

The three of us kids piled into the bed of my dad's pick up truck and were told to lay down and not look up at all for the entire drive to where we were going. We tried to protest but our parents shut us down right away and reiterated that we were to simply lie there and not to look out of the truck, except at the sky, for the whole drive. My friend's parents drove behind us in a three vehicle caravan and we took off. It seemed like we had been driving for an hour or more when finally the vehicle stopped. We were scared to even sit up and when we finally did we were told to keep our eyes shut. Our parents led us by the hand into somewhere and we were finally told to open our eyes. A huge man, one that looked just like the "Indian Chieftains" you see in the really old, politically incorrect movies about them, was standing in the middle of the room. The man told us not to speak and then he waved some feathered thing all around and lit what I think was sage but I didn't know what it even could have been way back then. Then, he blew some sort of dust in our faces and he did all of that to each of us, one by one. Then he brought our parents into another room and after twenty more minutes we left. My friends and I didn't know what was going on and we didn't even talk to one another the whole time. I've since asked my dad and he said that we had somehow been the victims of skinwalkers and he brought us to one of his customer's homes on the reservation so that we could get a cleansing and a blessing from the chief. It took him almost fifteen years to be willing to tell me that story because he was always so afraid that by talking about it again it would bring them back to finish the job. I don't know if it was the blessing or something else but I'm still friends with those two boys to this day and none of us has ever experienced any other sort of paranormal activity since the day of the blessing.

CHAPTER NINETY-SEVEN

I BASICALLY SPENT the bulk of my childhood camping in Joshua Tree National Park. My family went there several times a year to camp, hike and spend time together. We all loved the great outdoors and once I graduated college and moved out on my own, that didn't change. I've had more experiences in Joshua Tree than I could ever write down but there are a few that stick out to me as totally unexplainable and completely bizarre. This one, the one I am writing about now, was downright terrifying. I was twenty two or twenty three years old at the time and I planned a solo camping trip to Joshua Tree before I moved to Las Vegas to start my "grown up job." Though there's no way for anyone, except maybe the people who work there, to know every single inch of a state park, I feel like I was pretty close to that. I had been going there for so long and I've always been one of those guys, even as a little kid, who likes to explore everything. I need to know everything about everything and it's actually served me very well while out in the wilderness. I was comfortable with Joshua Tree and I was really excited for the trip because I knew it would be a while before I was able to get back out there again. I planned on staying for four nights and packed as lightly as possible while still making sure I had everything I needed. I knew what kind of animals to be on the lookout for at that time of year and I was confident I wouldn't run into any trouble. This happened in the late seventies and things were a lot more lenient as far as areas where you could go and the things you could do and the park was a lot more deserted than how you would find it nowadays at any time of the year.

I was in my old Jeep and driving off road to some of the more hidden spots that my dad, brothers and I used to love to camp at, in the densest part of one of the wilderness areas. The area was supposed to be off limits but in all the years we had been going there no one ever said anything to us. We almost never saw other campers out there either and that's exactly what I was looking for at that time. It was late fall and the weather was getting a little more chilly than it normally was in that area of the country but it was no big deal and I was ecstatic to have been taking that trip. I made my way to the spot I was specifically looking for, it was near one of the water sources that are supposed to be reserved for wildlife. I didn't want to swim in it and I knew to stay a certain distance away from it lest I be dragged off in the middle of the night but I am trying to skip through the logistics and get straight to the encounter. When I was about a mile away from the water my Jeep suddenly started to feel like it was going out of control. I wasn't sure what was happening but it was scary. I heard an extremely loud hissing noise and didn't immediately recognize it as the sound of one of my tires basically exploding. However, after a couple of seconds I couldn't drive anymore so I stopped the Jeep and hopped out to see what the hell was going on. I looked and saw that my front right tire was slashed. I use that word very purposefully because it wasn't like I had run something over and it popped or slowly leaked. It looked like someone had taken a large knife or some similar object and jabbed it right into the tire and then pulled. There would have been nothing left of it if I hadn't pulled over when I did. I was so incredibly confused and like I said I had some strange experiences out there throughout my life but nothing that would give me a reason for why or how something like that could have happened to my tire. It was starting to get dark out and I knew I needed to set up my camp before the sun completely set. I left my Jeep right there where I stopped it and got out and figured I would deal with that the next day.

I wasn't planning on leaving right away anyway and I wasn't beat to let anything ruin my plans for those few days out there in the peacefulness of mother nature. I grabbed my gear out of the back and set up camp several feet away from where my Jeep was now stuck. I could still see it clearly from where I was going to be spending the night.

I had just finished setting everything up and getting a good fire going when night fell. The woods that had always been so peaceful and comfortable to me suddenly felt eerie and sinister. I knew with absolute certainty that I was being watched but I kept trying to convince myself that it was the animals in the trees that were making me feel that way. As I sat by the fire and ate some food, I went back to wondering what in the world could have possibly happened to my tire. I had a spare and I was so glad I had decided to bring it, it wasn't too hard to travel with spares when you had a Jeep, you know? But man, I was still just so incredibly confused and no matter what I did it's like my mind just kept right on going back to what could have happened to my tire. I was done eating and started going about cleaning everything up so that I could go to bed for the night and be well rested for all of the hiking I had planned for the next day. As I did that I noticed something else that seemed very strange at the moment and that was I couldn't hear any owls and I didn't hear any other animals scurrying around and running, as they always did at night when I was out there camping. It was a given I would be hearing and seeing those things but there was nothing but dead silence. I got the chills and looked around in the tops of the trees to see if I could spot anything. I was starting to think I was overtired because I was starting to become paranoid that another human being was lurking in the shadows to rob me or worse and that they were only waiting for once I put the fire out and got comfortable in my tent for the night in order to strike. Finally I just did what I always would do when my mind would start racing and I started to hum some of my favorite songs. After all, there was no one there to judge me and it did make me feel a lot better. By the time I was ready to put the fire out and retire for the evening, I was feeling a heck of a lot better but not completely. I still couldn't shake the feeling that I was being watched and possibly stalked. Just as I was about to put the fire out, as I turned to grab my bucket, I heard something hit the ground behind me with a loud thump. It sounded like it used to when I was a kid and me and my friends would all try to jump out of the trees and see who could land on their feet. It sounded exactly like that and before I turned around I thought for sure that someone had just jumped down from one of the trees and whoever it was had landed perfectly on their feet.

The realization gave me a chill and I was terrified to turn around and face whoever it was. I thought it was going to be some psycho or homeless person looking to rob me or take my money and my Jeep. However, when I turned around, there was no one there. I looked all around and even called out, asking if anyone was there. Of course I got no answer and finally I was more than ready to put the fire out and call it a night. As I leaned in to throw the water from the bucket onto my fire I saw something move. It looked like a human being ran past the fire but in a way it just looked like something. I had no idea what I had just seen but whatever it was it looked like it had left a trail because of how fast it had been running. I was so incredibly confused and at that point I started to become concerned that I might have been losing my mind. I said a prayer out loud just in case and finally went into my tent for the night. I was woken up a dozen times to what sounded like someone walking around my camp but every time I would peek outside of my tent I would see nothing and no one was there either. I was pretty spooked and also kept noticing the usual sounds of night-time in the woods; the insects, the animals and just the general sounds the woods made at night, were all very noticeably missing almost the entire night. I didn't know what was going on but fully intended to change my tire first thing in the morning and find somewhere else to camp for the following night.

I woke up at around eight in the morning and I immediately inspected my camp and some of the surrounding areas. I knew without a doubt that someone or something had visited it the night before while I was sleeping but there were no footprints and there was no other sign of anyone having been there either. The only thing I noticed that struck me as a little bit odd was the fact that there were what looked like drag marks all over the place. They were individual, short marks but they zigzagged and criss-crossed all over my campsite. I didn't know what was going on and I didn't want to know. I ate something and then went over to my Jeep and changed my tire. I was going to hike out further into the wilderness to find another campsite but I wanted to make sure that my Jeep was ready to go in case I had to get out of there in a hurry. I look back now and wonder what would have happened to me if I hadn't made that decision. Once the tire was fixed I packed up my gear and hiked to another spot about a mile away from the original place where I had chosen to camp. I had planned on staying in that one spot the entire time but I thought that maybe there was some sort of large, shy animal that was territorial and had been investigating me and why I was in its space or something. That was the only thing my mind could come up with and so I allowed myself to believe it, despite everything inside of me telling me I was wrong and that I should just pack up my things and get the hell out of there right then. I set up my tent and the rest of my camp right away and decided to get a little hiking done before lunch time. The forest was back to life that day and I finally felt like I could relax. Well, at least that's how I felt for a little while.

I decided to turn around and go back to my camp to grab my tackle box and fishing rod so I could go out and try to catch my lunch. I did that without any issues but once I made it to the water where I planned to catch my food, that eerie feeling of being watched overtook me all over again. I was really scared though and I just knew in my mind that something was about to creep up on me. I kept feeling like there was something or someone right behind me but every time I would turn around there would be nothing and no one there. It was incredibly nerve rattling. Finally, after so many times of feeling like that I guess I kind of just lost it and when I felt that way again I slammed my fishing rod backwards. I didn't ever expect I would hit anything and honestly, because of other things I had seen and experienced in Joshua Tree before, I thought maybe it was a ghost or something. It ended up being something way worse. When I slammed my rod back it did hit something and it felt like the stomach of a human being. I heard a noise that sounded like a cross between the hissing of a snake- very loud hissing, mind you, and the buzzing of an angry insect. I turned around so fast I almost fell down but again there was nothing there. Suddenly I heard a splash in the water in front of me and right before my eyes a fish came right up out of the water as if it were floating in mid air. It had been connected to my line because it was floating as well. I almost peed my pants and let out a loud scream. It sounded like a little girl screaming, that's how terrified I was.

I didn't immediately notice what was holding onto the fish and my line but I saw the fish hook be pulled out of the fish's mouth and then I saw the fish lose a chunk of itself. It looked like something invisible was eating the fish I had just caught, right in front of my face. I felt challenged to do something, in a way. Finally I saw something I will do my very best to describe here but it looked almost like when you watch those movies about invisible people and how they're only recognizable if the light hits them at the right angle or if they're wet. This thing was wet and shimmering in the sunlight. I looked beautiful but it was also the most frightening thing I had ever seen in my entire life, still to this day. That's saying something because, honestly, with everything I had seen and experienced in that park, I could have brushed it off had it been a ghost or something like that. I screamed again and then I dropped my pole, which I was still holding because I had been too shocked by everything else happening to drop it up until that point, and I turned to run. As soon as I turned I heard a loud sound that sounded almost like squawking and as whatever it was that was chasing after me did so, I heard rhythmic clicking sounds that I knew were coming from whatever the thing was that had just been messing with me in the water. I knew it was messing with me because why else would it have exposed itself like that to me?

Whatever that thing was moved very quickly and I didn't dare turn around the whole time until I made it back to my camp. By that time I didn't feel or hear it following me anymore. I saw more of those short drag marks in the dirt and through the foliage when I did finally turn around and there were a ton of them at my new campsite as well. I grabbed all of my stuff and as I quickly made my way back to my vehicle I started to hear the clicking sounds again. They sounded like they were coming from above me, like they were up in the trees, and it sounded like there were a lot of them up there. I didn't stick around to figure any of it out and once I got to my Jeep I got out of there as quickly as possible and never spoke about it again until one day I saw a movie that seemed to show a figure that was the exact same thing as what I had witnessed that day in Joshua Tree. It was the Predator movie and the entity in that movie is definitely and without a doubt what I had encountered that day. I believe it slashed my tire and also that it was what was lurking around outside of my original campsite all night long. The Predator Entity or as it's sometimes called nowadays, The Glimmer Man, is the most terrifying thing I have ever encountered in all my life. That incident at Joshua Tree was only the first of about a handful of times I've encountered this particular entity but all of the other times I've only sensed or heard it. I always get out of wherever I am when I feel there's one around me. I've tried researching the entity recently but all I can find are other people's encounters and no real information to tell me what they are, where they're from or what they want.

There are plenty of opinions on this entity and more theories than I could name if I listed them all day. However, I think that whoever wrote the movie The Predator knew something about this creature long before the general public did. I also think he or she got it right in that it's some sort of terrifying and deadly extraterrestrial. I don't know anything for an absolute fact, no one does, and all I can do- like everyone else- is speculate and theorize until someone who does actually know something comes forward with information. One more thing, I don't think it's a coincidence that so many people are going missing from our National Parks and other wilderness areas these days and honestly I would attribute a lot of that to this entity. I mean, it's pretty much and basically invisible and therefore impossible to fight. I got lucky and still have no idea why I was spared when so many others don't get another chance. I haven't taken that for granted and this experience has changed my life completely and for the better. I don't know what saved me or why but I'm sure glad it did.

CHAPTER NINETY-EIGHT

WHEN I WAS sixteen years old in 2004 I was exploring some woods near the house my parents had just moved us into when I had an encounter with something I still have a hard time believing is real. I was there, I saw it and witnessed it and therefore know that it happened but it leads me down this rabbit hole full of questions which all culminate to me wondering if there's something like what I saw that actually exists in this world and in this reality, then what the heck else is there out there that we human beings or at least most of the human race, are unaware of lurking around out there as we go about our everyday lives like everything is normal. I was the "fat kid" in school and didn't have many friends and so I was used to being by myself. That day was no different and after I unpacked all of my possessions and set my new bedroom up I went and had dinner. Then I asked my mom if I could go and explore the neighborhood. We had moved into that particular house after living in a tiny two bedroom apartment for most of my life. My parents bought the house and a bunch of land that was connected to it right along with it and I was really excited to see what was in the woods at the edge of the back-yard. The property my parents purchased was really desolate and the first house had been built in the seventeen hundreds or something. It had burned in a fire in the late eighteen hundreds and that's when the house we had just moved into was built in the same spot. I didn't have any siblings and therefore I was on my own. I hadn't ever had such a tremendous amount of space to explore all by myself before and I think my mom could see that I was really excited because, despite the fact that it was almost dark, she agreed to let me go out for a couple of hours.

I had always loved the woods and I've recently noticed that statement is one that shows up in so many people's encounter stories of terrifying things they've experienced while exploring or just hanging out in the great outdoors. I guess I'm no different. I was always going hiking, camping and/or hunting with my family; my dad, uncles and cousins, and for me it was a way to forget all the bullying at school and all of the terrible things I would feel because of how badly I was bullied, even if just for a little while. I had to start a new school for junior year in just a few weeks but we hadn't moved far enough away that I wouldn't know anyone at all from the new school and I was sure that my loser reputation would follow right with me there and that I had only a little time left of my reprieve. Alright, back to the night of my encounter. I left out the back door and cut through my backyard. I had a large flashlight with me and was dressed for the weather which was a little chilly and damp. I planned on only being gone a little while and then heading back home, figuring I would be able to do more exploring the next day, all day long while the sun was out. I'm not gonna lie I was a little apprehensive about being out there in the woods all alone at night. Even all the times I had gone out doing whatever in the woods with my family or my old best friend, someone had always been with me once the sun went down. However, I was determined to get to know the woods and let my imagination run wild. I was obsessed with horror stories and movies and the creepiness of it all kind of made me feel like I was starring in my own movie. I walked for about a half of a mile and then I saw something interesting that I had never seen before. It was a metal rod, almost like a ladder rung, sticking out from the ground right in the middle of the woods. I was literally in the middle of nowhere and excitement immediately took over any fear I may have been feeling at that moment.

I walked over to it and used my boots to move some of the old, wet leaves and dirt out of the way. I realized that it was some sort of door, leading directly underground. I pulled as hard as I could, thinking that it had to have been welded shut or otherwise impossible to open but it wasn't. In fact, I pulled so hard and it opened so easily, I ended up falling backwards onto my behind when it came flying open. It opened upwards, obviously and I quickly got up to see if I could see anything down there from up above where I was. I shined my flashlight down into the hole and saw ladder rungs made of some sort of metal going all the way down the side and leading far enough down into the ground that I couldn't see all of them or where they stopped. I was apprehensive and unsure whether or not I should proceed or wait until the following day when it would be light outside and I could ask my dad if he would go out there with me. However, I was excited and didn't want to wait. It didn't occur to me that anything supernatural or otherworldly would happen to me and I basically thought the very worst that would happen was I would run into some ornery and possibly vicious animals who had somehow burrowed in there. I took a deep breath and made my way down the rungs, very easily and one at a time. There were about twenty steps in that makeshift, built in ladder and I finally reached the bottom. I stepped off the bottom rung and onto a concrete floor. I wasn't expecting that.

I initially thought that there was going to be a dirt floor but I was pleasantly surprised from the beginning. I shined my flashlight down a small and very narrow corridor and kept on walking forward. I was a big kid but I wasn't claustrophobic and it's a good thing too because I never would have been able to walk all the way down there or be down there for as long as I had been if that weren't the case. I thought that I was being smart when I very stupidly left the bunker door open. I didn't really expect it to lead anywhere I guess but it seemed like I was walking down a cement corridor for a long time. There was cement all around me and then, very suddenly, everything opened up and there was a huge, circular room I had walked into. The only thing I could see besides cement though was what looked like one of those pressurized doors, I'm not sure what they're actually called, but they have them on ships and you close them if the ship ever starts going down and sinking. They completely seal shut and there's supposedly no way to open them again, or at least that was my understanding of those types of doors at the time. I was making my way over to the door to see what was inside when I heard what sounded like growling and panting coming from whatever was behind it. I thought, once again, it was some sort of known animal that maybe I just wasn't familiar with that I had disturbed or that had somehow trapped itself in there. I wasn't planning on letting it out but I still wanted to get a look at it, whatever it was. I saw there was a little rectangle of a window in the door. I stopped to listen first because I thought that I heard footsteps walking up on me from behind but when I shone my flashlight behind me, there was no one and nothing there. I chuckled at how foolish I was being. I took another step or two towards the door which was all the way on the other side of that circular room which was about twenty feet away from me at that point. This little room wasn't so little and it was amazing how big it really was considering where it was located underground like that.

I not only heard but actually felt someone breathing down my neck. I jumped and once again turned around as fast as I could and shone my flashlight all around. There still seemed to be nothing and no one there. I was starting to panic and sweating profusely. I suddenly realized how vulnerable I was and that any number of things could happen to me that would make me stuck down there and unable to ever get out. My mind was racing when all of a sudden whatever was in that room started slamming itself up against the door. It could have been slamming something up against the door for all I knew but I just had a feeling it knew I was there and it was trying to bust through that door and get to me. I heard incredibly loud growling and snarling and I was starting to think that maybe there was some type of larger animal behind the doors than I had initially thought. I couldn't breathe and suddenly didn't want to know what was behind the door anymore and I was starting to get the feeling that not only was I not alone in that bunker with whatever was behind the door, but that I wasn't going to make it out of there alive if I didn't turn around and run for my life immediately. I turned to run and I ran right into something horrible and terrifying.

I screamed and dropped my flashlight. I saw a quick glimpse of a face. It was hideously grotesque but otherwise looked like an old man. He was about as tall as me and that's probably why I saw him head on. I was on the ground searching for my flashlight and there was a sort of amused and very loud cackling echoing through the chamber at that point. I was frantic and wanted to get the hell out of there but I knew I wouldn't make it without the flashlight. Despite it only being one long corridor once I left the round room, I didn't know where the corridor was in relation to where I was inside of that room. I hadn't been paying that much attention. I couldn't breathe but luckily I found the flashlight fairly quickly. I raised it up and started looking all around when it landed again on the old man. He had rotten, green teeth and his face had all sorts of spots on it. He looked like he must have been a thousand years old and he just continued to gleefully cackle from the one corner of the room. He was standing next to the door where the person or creature was still trying its damndest to get out and get to me. The old man had regular clothes on for that part of the country at that time of year, even though they were a bit outdated. He wore a large straw hat, a pair of blue coveralls, a white t-shirt underneath and a heavy flannel over the top of it. He looked like he had something in his mouth and when he smiled again I recognized it as what we call "chew" around here. That's chewing tobacco.

I stood there unable to move due to the terror I was feeling. I was hyperventilating and close to passing out right there on the spot. The old man tapped his wristwatch that was on his left hand with his right pointer finger while I watched and then he reached his hand over like he was about to open that door. I couldn't even scream but I shook my head and sputtered out a lousy and weak "please don't" and then I started to cry hysterically. The old man shushed me, almost with affection, and when I looked back up at him his face looked demonic and distorted.

His whole face and head stretched out and snapped back together until finally he yelled "RUN!" It was extremely loud and seemed to make the whole underground bunker shake. I didn't have to be told twice and immediately took off running as fast as I could and I was holding on to my flashlight for dear life. Once I was about halfway back to where the opening to the bunker was I heard the door open and something come barreling out of it. Whatever it was it was chasing me and it was gaining on me quickly. I made it to the entrance and started climbing up the rungs of the ladder as fast as my chubby legs possibly could. I felt something grabbing at my legs and it was like little bursts of air every couple of seconds accompanied by what sounded like a dog yelping. I didn't look back until I was safely out of the bunker. Right before I closed the door behind me I saw what looked like a gigantic wolf, but it was slowly climbing up the rungs of the ladder towards me. It was snarling and stank to high heaven. It had bright red eyes and those eyes are something that stick out to me more than anything else because of how human they looked. The beast also had human hands, albeit they were covered in fur and most likely it had human feet as well because of how agile it seemed to be to be able to get up that ladder, though it was once again moving very slowly. It stared at me straight in the eyes and was determined to get to me. I slammed the door shut and took off running through the woods.

I made it back to my house and just as I crossed the threshold from the woods to my backyard, I heard an extremely loud howling coming from those same woods and in the direction where I had just come from. I ran inside and my mother was immediately concerned. I told her I had fallen, that I wasn't hurt and that I just wanted to take a shower and go to bed. She gave me my space and finally I calmed down enough to go to sleep. I spent a year terrified to even look out my bedroom window because it faced those woods and didn't want to be alone in them ever again. I never told anyone about what I had found because I was sure that no one would believe me but also I was fairly certain that whoever I told would want to go and see it for themselves. I recently went back to that spot in those woods for the first time since that night. That'll be the next encounter story I'll be writing about but for now, that's all I have.

CHAPTER NINETY-NINE

MY ENCOUNTER HAPPENED BACK in the early 1960s when I was eighteen years old. My best friend was getting married and I had to travel from California to Colorado in order to attend the ceremony. I was the best man and couldn't miss it but I was also just starting out in the real world and didn't have a lot of money. I barely had enough money to get them a gift and pay for gas. It was cheaper than flying, mainly too because our other best friend, Cody, also didn't have a lot of money or resources and needed to get to the wedding as well. Cody and I decided to go halfsies and we left without even knowing where we were going to sleep after the wedding happened. Our friend, the groom, said he was sure that between all of them, the bride's family would put us up for the night, even if it was separately. He didn't have much family and that's why the wedding was being held where the bride was from. We made it there with just enough gas to spare, attended the wedding and then went to the reception. The problem was, we didn't know anyone there except for the bride and groom and the guests weren't very friendly people to begin with. If I'm being honest, they were what we always called "mountain people" and if you weren't what they called "kin" or if they otherwise didn't know you, you were an outsider and suspicious. Needless to say, not a single one of them would give us a place to stay. The bride felt horrible but there was nothing she could do. She tried to convince her family to let us stay just until the morning when we could get some gas in my car and be back on our way home but they wouldn't budge. I guess I can't blame them, we were strangers and I don't think they ever really liked my friend who married into their family anyway. The marriage only lasted five years. The only thing we could think to do, and it was the groom's idea, was to camp for the night at a nearby wooded area where he and the bride had gone for hikes and had gone camping many times before. The weather seemed fairly mild and we knew we had enough alcohol to keep us warm should it have suddenly gotten too cold or something. While we weren't very excited or thrilled about the idea, there was no other option because the two of us wouldn't have fit in my little beat up vehicle. The groom and bride drove us out to the camping area after hooking us up with a few poles and some tarps. They gave us water and some snacks and promised they would be there early in the morning to pick us up. We were to walk to the access road at around eight o'clock and wait there for them. We trusted that they would be back when they said they would and somewhat begrudgingly made our way out to a clearing about fifteen minutes off the main access road in order to set up camp. It was around midnight by the time we got settled and our friends couldn't stay with us because it was their wedding night but also because they had left some of their guests in order to bring us there and they were trying to quickly get back.

Cody and I followed the instructions the groom had given us for how to set up the tarps so that we were fully covered and we took a few shots and went to bed. I don't know what happened to the weather but it was around three in the morning when we woke up freezing cold and with a heavy snowfall blanketing the woods. We were only in t-shirts and sweatpants to begin with and now that we had gotten just a few hours of sleep we were already feeling like crap because of all of the alcohol we had consumed the night before. Cody and I woke at almost the exact same time and it only took about fifteen minutes for us to realize that we were going to freeze to death if we didn't find somewhere to go inside for the night. We decided to leave everything there except our flashlights and try to find our way back to the main access road to see if we could hitch a ride somewhere or something. We were desperate and we were scared. I'm of course leaving a lot out in order to just focus on the encounter itself. We headed out and it didn't take long for us to realize we should have reached the road already and we were lost. Both of our watches had stopped at 3:15 in the morning and so we didn't even know what time it was. Looking back on it now I realize that the night had an ominous feel to it and something sinister was at play more than likely from the moment we set foot in that area of the woods or the woods altogether but back then it just seemed like a series of crappy coincidences. We were a bit panicked, freezing and feeling like absolute hell. We didn't know what to do and so we just kept walking. The whole time we were roaming the woods looking for a way out we kept hearing a wailing sound. It sounded like some sort of hurt animal and it was absolutely terrifying. We knew even then we were risking our lives wandering the woods at that time but we figured if our friends had thought it had been safe for us to camp there then it must have been safe for us to walk through as well. I know now after years of hunting and camping in the woods that that's ludicrous but it made sense at the time and we were both incredibly lucky we didn't get ripped apart by something wild out there that night.

Sparing the details I'll just say that at one point we saw a light in the distance that looked like an attic light on a house. We were excited for a second but then remembered how those "mountain people" were and thought that even if someone was home it didn't necessarily mean they would let us in or even answer the door in the first place. However, we walked in the direction of the light and before we knew it we came upon a very sinister looking, all dark and very small log cabin. It looked rugged and run down. The first thing we noticed was that we had only found it because we had been walking towards the light that was clearly on and visible to us in the attic but now that we were in front of the place there weren't any lights on at all. We were desperate and feared we would freeze to death if we didn't do something though and at least try to get someone to let us in and take pity on us. We marched up to the door, the snow was really coming down at that point too, and we knocked as though our lives depended on it. We stood there on the rickety old front porch waiting for some sign that someone was inside but none came and after knocking and waiting several more times but still hearing absolutely nothing at all on the other side of the door, we let ourselves in. It wasn't locked and we easily gained entry. We shined our flashlights all over the place looking for light switches or pull strings to turn on a light in the place but once we located them, they didn't work. The cabin didn't seem to have any electricity at all and we were still going to be in danger of freezing to death but thought that, at the very least, we could build a fire in the old fireplace. The place was ransacked and stunk to high heaven. It looked like no one had lived or even been in there for years. There were cobwebs everywhere and weird mason jars full of green and black muck with odd objects floating in them. It was straight out of a horror movie.

There seemed to be an incredible amount of firewood though because there was one entire room filled to the brim with it. It was almost like someone had incessantly chopped wood for days on end. We immediately set to work getting a fire started and within minutes of having done that we found some old, musty smelling blankets and clean enough pillows. Beggars couldn't be choosers at that point and we were just glad to be out of the snow. We hadn't thought anything through but then again, we never had, that's why we found ourselves in the predicament we were in in the first place. We eventually dozed off, meaning to be up in a couple of hours in order to go and trek back through the woods to meet our friends. We figured, even with the snow on the ground, we would easily be able to find the access road and get the hell out of there by the light of day. However, we ended up sleeping until late afternoon that day. I woke in a panic and the fire had gone out. It was freezing again so I woke Cody up and told him we messed up and we needed to get a fire going. He agreed and when I looked out the window I realized there was more than likely no way our friends were able to get to that road and were probably worried sick about us and sending out search parties while we were sleeping in this run down and abandoned cabin. I had never seen so much snow fall over such a short period of time. We were literally snowed in.

Cody and I built another fire but couldn't figure out what to do except wait for either help to show up or the snow to stop falling, whichever came first. Other than that we had to worry about food and also, we were worried whoever owned the place would be popping in and would shoot us for trespassing or something. As we sat there lost in thought with each one of us desperately trying to come up with a reasonable solution, we thought that the latter worry had begun to happen when the doorknob to the front of the cabin started jiggling violently. We both jumped and looked from each other to the door and back again. I whispered to Cody to be quiet and we hoped that maybe whoever it was would at least give us the chance to explain ourselves before blowing our brains all over the walls. We were scared but we had no idea that was only the beginning. The jiggling seemed to go on for a very long time and we wondered why whoever it was didn't just use a key. Then someone started pounding on the door from the outside. I went and looked to see who it was because I couldn't' take the noise anymore. I was starving and dehydrated and thought that maybe it was a search party or something. Of course, there was no one there. The snow on the porch right in front of the door where the person or people would have had to have been standing was fresh and undisturbed. Meaning, somehow, that there hadn't been anyone standing there at all. Our footprints were long since covered up and no others could be seen from where I was standing. I slammed the door shut and told Cody what I saw. He didn't believe me but after checking for himself he seemed shaken up. We didn't have time to process what was happening before we started hearing noises coming from the roof. It didn't sound like human footprints but like hooves or something. The reason I thought I knew what that sounded like was because of the old radio shows during Christmas time when they would do the story of Santa and the reindeer and they would land on the roof. It was terrifying. We both just stood there listening and staring wide eyed at one another.

It was like all of the activity started up all at once. The knocking on the door and then galloping on the roof; we didn't know what to think. After about five minutes the sounds stopped and we sat back down on the couch next to the fire and tried to think of a way out that wouldn't get us killed. We must have drifted off again while we were so deep in thought because the next thing I remember is waking up to the sound of tapping noises on the glass of one of the windows in the living room of the cabin. The room where Cody and I had been spending all of our time. I went to look to see what it was and that's when I saw a beast of a creature, unholy and unlike anything I had ever seen or imagined before. It was only a face and though it was dark I could clearly see that it was floating in mid air, level to the window. It was covered in black, thick fur and had bright green eyes. It had teeth that looked like a cross between fangs and tusks and they were yellow. The mouth was black and the nose was sort of piggish. It opened its mouth and the sound that came out sounded like the same one Cody and I had heard while traversing the forest the night before while we were en route to this place without even knowing it. That must be the creature that was making such terrible and inhuman sounds all night long out in the woods. I screamed and jumped back and when Cody jumped up too and asked me what the hell I thought I was doing, I turned back around and pointed to the window but the figure was already gone. I had looked away for no more than five seconds maximum and it had already disappeared.

Suddenly Cody grabbed my arm and pointed to the bottom of the front door. All of the lights in the house suddenly were blinking on and off which shocked us very much considering none of the electricity had worked up until that point. Then, I followed with my eyes to where he was pointing and there was thick, black fog coming in through the crack. We both kept backing up so that it wouldn't touch us but it started to take on a funnel shape, like a tornado but of black fog or mist and it smelled so bad we were both trying not to vomit. Finally we ran and we ended up going upstairs to the second floor of the cabin. Because we didn't belong there and were so worried about what would happen to us should the proper owners of the place show up and find us there, we had initially thought it best not to explore the place and only stay in the main room where there was a fire. We felt like we were being chased upstairs and all of the lights were off up there as well. There were two rooms up there, both looked like bedrooms. One of them had a big bed and a couple of dressers, nothing fancy but it did look a lot more lived in than downstairs. However, the light didn't work and there was no lock on the door. I don't know why we thought a lock would help keep fog out but we figured it would at least keep that creature out and so we went to check the other room. The light switched right on and we couldn't believe what we were confronted with in that room. There was a huge pentagram in the middle of the floor, drawn in what looked like either red paint or blood. There were rotting, dead cats and other small animals all over the place. Also, when we turned to check for a lock on the door we saw that there was one, but on the outside. We ran for our lives right out of the cabin. We didn't care about the snow anymore and just wanted to try and scream for help or find some neighbors. However, after about ten minutes of walking we knew we had no choice but to go back there, at least until the sun came up.

We went back and sat in the living room with the fire on full blast, the curtains drawn and the door barricaded with other furniture. We didn't sleep at all and stayed up until the sun rose talking to one another about what we could have possibly just witnessed. There was no further activity as far as what we knew or could see and we didn't care. Out of sight, out of mind. Finally, right after the sun came up there was a knock at the door. When we looked out the window there were emergency vehicles and so we opened the door immediately. We were starving and terrified and just wanted to be anywhere but that cabin. When we opened the door we were greeted by police officers and our two friends. They looked relieved and didn't stop apologizing the whole way back. They got us to a hotel room after we insisted we didn't need any treatment at a hospital and luckily the cops under-stood we weren't trying to trespass. They gave us a break and said that since we didn't actually "break in", we were free to go. No one knew who owned the cabin and it had been abandoned for years. The one officer did mention there were rumors a satanic cult spent time doing rituals there but he seemed like he thought it was obviously nonsense and so we laughed it off. Our friends noticed we were really quiet and like I said they apologized profusely but we just tried to also laugh that off and pass it off as us just being exhausted.

Like we had initially thought our friends also became snowed in because the snow had fallen at record rates and seemed to have come out of nowhere. Now, I'm not by any means trying to insinuate that the weather was supernatural but I do believe wholeheartedly that the cabin was under attack by demonic influences and that there were ritualistic animal kills performed there. I've kept this in the back of my mind for so long until one day I decided to do some research into that cabin but by the time the internet was available to me the place had long since burned to the ground. No one knows who started the fire but they know that it was an arson. That's really all I have to say about it. It was terrifying and I thought I was going to die several times and for several different reasons. I ended up going off to war and I saw things that scared me even more than that cabin and I even saw a lot of supernatural things out in the jungle I am probably going to write about someday soon. Cody never wanted to talk about it again and so we never did. I've brought it up throughout the years, especially in the last couple of decades where all of those shows about the paranormal or even regular horror movies became more popular but it wasn't influential in my life at all aside from some nightmares. I still have nightmares every once in a while, especially when it's on my mind so I'll probably have some tonight but I'm so old now that it doesn't even phase me. Most things don't. Maybe someone out there will get something out of this. You are all lucky that in this day and age you can research things and find at least some sort of answer almost as soon as it's all happening to you. I had to sit on this for more than forty years before I was able to even try and gather information. Cheers.

CHAPTER ONE HUNDRED

WHEN I WAS twenty-five years old I had finally moved out of my parent's home. It was a very exciting time in my life despite the fact that I had recently had a baby by someone who wanted nothing to do with me or the child. I had graduated college and gotten a degree and so I was able to find gainful employment fairly easily right out of school. I was confident I would be able to take care of both myself and my infant son and that we were on our way to our new lives together. My son's father had been abusive and the law wasn't really equipped to keep someone like him away for very long. So, I decided it would be best if I moved us halfway across the country to the midwestern United States and just start over again. My parents were sad to see me go but I knew that they were very proud of me for being the best mother that I could be and putting the needs of my child first. I have one brother who I have always been very close with and he managed to convince me to move to a town nearby where he had attended school. The idea was that he would move in with me and help me with looking for a place and then, while he worked on trying to find his own job, he would watch the baby for me. It seemed so perfect and for the first time in a very long time, I was hopeful for the future. I managed to convince the company I worked for that I was important enough an asset that they made exceptions for me when it came to who got what jobs and where and transferred me as per my request. That's something they never did and especially for the place where I would be working too. It was the top in the country for the work that I do and normally only the best of the best get placed there. I was ecstatic and everything seemed to be coming together.

Due to the fact of how much my company had invested in me because of the move, it was imperative I find a decent two bedroom for me, my son and my brother to live with enough time to get there and get everything set up before I had to be back to work and starting at the new place. My brother was having trouble finding rentals in that particular area but one day he called me and told me he couldn't believe his good luck when one of his college roommate's sisters was moving out of her rental suddenly and had to break her lease. Her landlord told her if she could find tenants so he didn't have to list the property then he wouldn't take the money needed to do so, or the fee for breaking the lease, out of her security deposit. I asked why she had to leave so suddenly that she couldn't finish out another few months but my brother didn't know and reminded me to never look a gift horse in the mouth, so to speak. I was on board and I got a U-Haul for the very next day. I loved the house! It had a gigantic backyard and the rooms were huge! There were actually two bedrooms and then one smaller room right off of the master bedroom that I planned on turning into my son's nursery. That way he would be right near me but didn't have to be in the same room. My brother hadn't told me that the house was extremely isolated and the nearest town was several miles away. There was also no public transportation and he didn't have a vehicle at the time. However, I told myself that it was as perfect an opportunity as I could ever hope to get and I was extremely optimistic. Within a week we were all moved in and set up and I had one more week to go before I had to start work in my new office.

My brother spent a lot of time bonding with my son and getting used to him in that week so that he wouldn't have to be like a stranger while he was with him all day. I sometimes had to work very long hours but the pay made it worth it so I tried not to complain. Before I knew it a month had passed and everything had been going perfectly.

It was better than I had ever hoped to imagine and I knew I was never going to have regrets or look back thinking "what if." This was home and would be for a long time. My brother and I had always gotten along and my son took to him immediately. I didn't work on the weekends and so normally my brother went out with his friends on Friday nights and then spent Sundays with me and the baby. We would normally order food and watch movies. Of course, no one delivered all the way out there and the drive to and from picking the food up took a little less than an hour but it was a fun time and that made it worth it. Plus, we loved horror movies and so I would have to go into town to the video rental store anyway. (Remember those?) The house had a large backyard and was surrounded by very dense woods. I didn't have a neighbor for miles and basically kept to myself anyway. I didn't want my ex getting wind of where I was and ruining it for me so I continued to just hang out at home on my days off with my family. There was something weird about the woods that I noticed right away. I had originally chalked it up to a pleasant surprise but it was a little strange when I thought about it after everything that had happened.

Once you left my yard and started walking into the woods, there was a swing set, a slide and one of those old merry go round things. It was just odd where it was located because there were no other houses there and it wasn't on my property. It was a very random and bizarre place for it but the equipment seemed to be in good shape and so I left it all there figuring one day I would have family visit and it would come in handy. That's exactly what happened when my parents came to visit us about a year after we had moved in. They had been to visit with us before but this time specifically they had brought my sister's daughter with them. My niece, Charla, was six years old at the time and she had no siblings. Her only cousin was my son who had only just turned a year old a few months before and so I was happy to have something there for her to do besides what she always did in hanging out with the grown ups. One night, just before dusk, my brother, my parents and I were hanging out on the back deck and barbecuing. We were having a few drinks, some beer and wine, and Charla asked if she could go and play in the playground. We would have been able to hear her but not see her while she was there and so my brother volunteered to go with her and my dad took over the grill. Within about ten minutes my brother came back alone in order to grab a beer. We asked him where Charla was and he said she was fine and he was only going to be a second. We didn't think anything of it. Until, that is, he went back and Charla was gone.

We called out for her and we were all in an extreme panic but she quickly turned up. She had walked about ten minutes into the woods and when we asked her why she had done that without asking anyone to go with her or telling anyone first, she said "The man" had told her to go with him. This immediately made all of the adults there, myself included, very worried. There seemed to be some strange man wandering the woods who lured my six year old niece to go with him. We thought she had almost been abducted, even though we didn't know that word at the time. We made her come back with us to the porch to tell us what happened and my brother and father grabbed some rifles and went off in search of the strange man. Charla told us right away that they wouldn't be able to find him because he was "made of smoke and fire" and we immediately thought that she had been making the whole thing up because she didn't want to get into trouble for wandering off the way she had without permission. I yelled for my dad and brother to come back and Charla was sent to bed right after dinner. We were upset and trying to teach her a lesson about honesty, even when faced with consequences. It should have been no big deal and honestly, it wasn't because none of us thought anything more about it and figured it would be fine the next day. We had no idea what we were in store for that night.

My brother let my parents have his bed and he slept on the couch. Charla slept on a cot in his room so she could be closer to my parents, who she was much more used to than me or my brother. We put my son to bed not long after Charla went and the adults went to bed at around midnight. It was summertime and I was taking my paid vacation in order to have my family there for a week. I had since gotten a promotion and had moved up in my company. I was saving to buy a house and everything was going better than I had ever expected it could have for me. It was around two o'clock in the morning when I woke to the sound of a woman screaming in the woods. It sounded like a woman was being attacked and hurt in some way and I immediately ran to get my brother. He jumped up and asked me what was happening and I told him I thought someone was being hurt in the woods. Now, I should explain here that some odd things were already happening at that point but nothing too crazy that we ever really thought too much about it all except that it was odd. We called the police a number of times for things that made no sense and they didn't seem to be the most helpful department and thought we made false calls. I wanted to make sure I wasn't hearing things or overreacting before we got them involved. I have thought about that moment so many times throughout the years and I honestly think I was being influenced to not call them right away. After all, why else would a woman be screaming the way she was if she weren't being attacked or, at least, severely hurt? I don't know and I can't give you any sort of rational answer when it comes to my frame of mind and thought process of waking up my brother and making him go out there.

He grabbed his gun and reluctantly went out to check and see what the problem was or at least if he could find the woman and get her side of the story before calling in the authorities. We had a general distrust of the police because of things I had been through with my son's father as well so that's also why it didn't seem so strange in the moment to be sending him out there. My brother came back about ten minutes later and he was pale white and shaking so badly he could hardly stay up on his feet. I asked him what was wrong and he told me to get inside and lock the doors. I asked him what was wrong and he told me what happened to him. I'm about to relay to you what he said. My brother said that he heard the woman screaming and tried to follow the sounds as best as he could. He said once he got right past the playground at the edge of our property where Charla had been playing and wandered off from earlier, the screams turned into mocking laughter. The mocking tone of the laughter was evident and the sound vibrated the trees and ground around him. He looked up and saw two glowing red eyes staring out at him from between two tall trees. The figure stepped forward and looked like something straight out of a horror movie. It was a shadow person but wearing a long cloak with a hood. Its arms were crossed over its chest and it looked like it was taking an aggressive stance. My brother just stood there, trying to wrap his head around what he was looking at but as he did the laughter just got louder and louder. Suddenly, the shadow person moved and he could somehow see a mouth moving on it, despite it still being featureless. It's hard to explain because he also had a hard time explaining that part to me.

He said the laughter all at once stopped and the being then opened its mouth and began screaming like the sounds of the screaming woman we had heard initially. He didn't know what to do so he started to pray out loud. As he did that the entity became angry and yelled for him to stop. It hissed and growled and then disappeared into nothing and my brother ran back home. We decided then and there not to talk about it with anyone and to just pretend like it didn't happen. I went back to my room and quickly checked on my son and when I went in his room I was immediately frozen in fear. I walked in just in time to see the same entity as the one my brother had just described to me standing next to my son's bed. It looked up at me and the mocking laughter started. I yelled for my brother and the thing floated through the wall and back outside into the darkness. I ran to my son and then to the window but I didn't see anything. My brother came running into the room and asked me what was wrong and I told him. I then told him to go into our parent's room and check on Charla.

He immediately did as I told him and said when he went in there she was sitting up in her bed and she told him the bad man had been there. When he asked her to elaborate she said the shadow man with the red eyes that had told her to come with him in the woods had just been there, trying to get her to go back out into the woods with him. She said something interesting and that was that "he looked much scarier this time." We never got anything else out of her about it and the next day she seemed to not remember anything about the incident at all. What I think happened is that the entity took on a different form in order to try and lure her somewhere with it during the day but that she somehow knew that the dark figure that visited her and her cousin that same night was the same evil entity. It was probably the eyes but that's just speculation. The rest of the visit went well, despite me and my brother being on edge the entire time and it was another six months before another incident happened in the house. Oddly enough it was around Christmas time and Charla was once again visiting. As she got older we realized she had some sort of supernatural abilities she has since learned to work and deal with but back then we didn't make the connection that it was linked to her mostly. After all, she wasn't doing anything on purpose and was attracting the entity completely by accident. That wasn't the only one we've dealt with throughout the years we were there either but that was the first one.

After her second visit it seemed like she might have opened something dark inside of the house because it no longer needed Charla in order to wreak havoc on the home and make us think we were losing our minds. That was the first encounter with the dark figure though and so that's why I started there. I'm writing the rest of them out and plan on having them all sent in soon.

CONTINUE WITH
THE MEGA MONSTER BOOK: VOLUME 3

ABOUT THE AUTHOR

Ethan Hayes grew up in Oklahoma and moved to Texas when he attended Texas A&M. Upon graduation he was hired by Texas Parks and Wildlife and remained there until he retired twenty-two years later. He currently lives in southeast Texas with his wife and two dogs. When he's not spending time enjoying the outdoors and writing, he sips a cold beer on his front porch while listening to Bluegrass music.

———

Send in your encounter story: encountersbigfoot@gmail.com

ALSO BY ETHAN HAYES

ALSO BY FREE REIGN PUBLISHING

ENCOUNTERS IN THE WOODS

WHAT LURKS BEYOND

FEAR IN THE FOREST

INTO THE DARKNESS

ENCOUNTERS BIGFOOT

TALES OF TERROR

I SAW BIGFOOT

STALKED: TERRIFYING TRUE CRIME STORIES

MYSTERIES IN THE DARK

13 PAST MIDNIGHT

THINGS IN THE WOODS

CONSPIRACY THEORIES THAT WERE TRUE

LOVE ENCOUNTERS

STAT: CRAZY MEDICAL STORIES

CRASH: STORIES FROM THE EMERGENCY ROOM

CODE BLUE: TALES FROM THE EMERGENCY ROOM

LEGENDS AND STORIES SERIES

10-33: TRUE TALES FROM THE THIN BLUE LINE

BEYOND THE PATH

FROM ABOVE: UFO ENCOUNTERS

WENDIGO CHRONICLES

MYSTERIES IN THE FOREST

STORIES FROM THE NICU

CRAZY MEDICAL STORIES

PAWSITIVE MOMENTS: LIFE IN A VETERINARY CLINIC

STORIES FROM THE NICU

VANISHED: STRANGE & MYSTERIOUS DISAPPEARANCES

DIAGNOSIS: RARE MEDICAL CASES

Made in the USA
Middletown, DE
10 September 2024

60756390R00361